STEPPING STONES

Dorothy Eaton Watts

STEPPING STONES

A Morning Watch book, prepared to assist in the daily devotions of junior youth.

REVIEW AND HERALD PUBLISHING ASSOCIATION
Washington, DC 20039-0555
Hagerstown, MD 21740

Edited by Raymond H. Woolsey
Designed by Richard Steadham
Cover art by Scott Roberts

Printed in U.S.A.

The author assumes full responsibility for the accuracy of all facts
and quotations as cited in this book.

Texts credited to NKJV are from The New King James Version.
Copyright © 1979, 1980, 1982, Thomas Nelson, Inc., Publishers.

Library of Congress Cataloging in Publication Data

Watts, Dorothy Eaton, 1937-
    Stepping Stones.

    Includes index.
    Summary: A collection of 365 readings drawn from the
lives of explorers, kings, athletes, missionaries, and others
who used the talents God gave them in positive or negative ways.
Each reading is accompanied by a related Bible verse.
    1. Youth—Prayer-books and devotions—English.
2. Devotional calendars—Seventh-day Adventists.
3. Seventh-day Adventists—Prayer-books and devotions—
English.   4. Adventists—Prayer-books and devotions—
English.   [1. Devotional calendars.   2. Prayer-books and
devotions]   I. Title.
ISBN 0-8280-0384-X

ABOUT THE AUTHOR

Bird-watching, hiking, and gardening are leisure-time activities of this year's author. A lover of animals, she has had a variety of pets, including a python and three monkeys.

Mrs. Watts grew up in the hills of southern Ohio and attended Mount Vernon Academy, Columbia Union College, and Andrews University. She and her pastor-evangelist husband worked in Saskatchewan before accepting a call to India, where they served 16 years.

While her husband traveled as president of South India Union and later as ministerial secretary of the Southern Asia Division, Mrs. Watts kept busy raising a family of three adopted children, two boys and a girl. She also has three grandchildren. At various times she worked as secretary, editor, teacher, principal, and home and family service director.

She was the first director of Sunshine Orphanage, a home for abandoned babies, which began in a bedroom of her home. She also directed the Adventist Child Care Agency, where she coordinated the sponsorship of 5,000 orphans and needy children.

More recently Mrs. Watts has worked as a church school teacher in Oregon and Michigan, where her husband has been a departmental director and editor of *Celebration.*

Mrs. Watts has written stories for *Primary Treasure, Guide, Insight,* and *Adventist Review.* She is the author of *This Is the Day,* the youth devotional for 1983.

STEPPING-STONES

One of the ways my academy girls' dean, Beth Bentley, influenced me was through selected quotations she placed on the inside of the toilet doors in the dorm bathrooms. One poem that I memorized in that manner was "A Bag of Tools," by R. L. Sharpe:

> "Isn't it strange
> That princes and kings,
> And clowns that caper
> In sawdust rings,
> And common people
> Like you and me
> Are builders for eternity?
>
> Each is given a bag of tools,
> A shapeless mass,
> And a book of rules;
> And each must make—
> Ere life is flown—
> A stumbling block
> Or a stepping-stone."

In this book, the story for each day comes from the life of a famous person and shows how that person used the "tools" God gave to fashion his or her life into either a "stumbling block" or a "stepping-stone." From the trials and triumphs of these well-known people we can learn how to hammer our own lives into stepping-stones.

CONTENTS

January / Explorers

February / Inventors

March / Kings and Queens

April / Musicians

May / Athletes

June / Preachers and Teachers

July / Scientists

August / Soldiers

September / Authors

October / Doctors and Nurses

November / Presidents and Prime Ministers

December / Missionaries

For my "other mother"
ELIZABETH BENTLEY LOWRY
who through four years at Mount Vernon Academy
and three years at Columbia Union College
helped mold my life into a
stepping-stone.

BJARNE HERJULFSON

All his commandments are sure. Psalm 111:7.

"Pull up the anchor!" the tall, blond Norseman shouted into the west wind that whipped his leather tunic about him and threatened to toss him overboard.

The young captain of the Viking ship gripped the sturdy oak steering oar and planted his feet firmly on the 90-foot deck. "Hoist the sail."

Captain Bjarne Herjulfson watched with pride as the sailors raised the single square, red-and-white-striped sail and secured it to the main mast with walrus-hide ropes. He breathed a sigh of relief as the wind caught in the cloth, bringing his ship out of the protection of the Norwegian fjord into the choppy waters of the North Sea.

"It's madness to begin a journey to Greenland in the middle of a winter storm," said the first mate, who stood next to Bjarne, holding on to the rigging for support. "Just look at those waves!"

"And look at the sail," Bjarne said. "See how full it is! At this rate we'll reach Greenland in half the time!"

"If we get there at all," the first mate shouted back.

After three days of gale-force winds, a heavy fog settled over the sea. The red-and-white sail hung limp as they drifted many days through fog so dense that they saw neither sun by day nor stars by night. Without the sun and stars to guide them they were lost, for in those days they had neither radar nor compass. When at last the fog lifted they were near Newfoundland, far south of their destination.

In a way, you and I are like Bjarne. This year stretches before us like a vast, unknown sea. Conditions in the world and the circumstances of our lives hang over us like a dense fog. Have we no choice but to drift aimlessly, taking what this year brings of good or ill?

No! Unlike Bjarne, we do have a compass to guide us: God's Word, the Bible. Just as the needle of the compass always points north, so God's Word always points us in the direction of heaven. This year, be sure to take a compass reading daily!

9

ERIC THE RED

But your iniquities have separated between you and your God. Isaiah 59:2.

Red-headed Eric was a bully. What he wanted he got. Those not scared into submission by his flaming red beard and fierce green eyes took one look at his bulging muscles and let him have his way. But one day he demanded a man's land.

"No!" the man cried. "Don't take my land! How will I live? Take anything else, but leave me my land!"

"How dare you defy Eric the Red?" the bully sneered. "I'll take your land and your life!"

When the king of Norway learned what Eric had done, he sentenced him to exile. Going to Iceland, again Eric began to quarrel and fight, demanding crops and land.

"We don't want bullies like you around," the people said after three years. "You must leave Iceland and live somewhere else."

"But where?" asked Eric. "I can't go back to Norway."

"Too bad," insisted the Icelanders. "But we don't want you here, either. We want to live in peace." So Eric traveled to uninhabited Greenland and there lived in exile.

Can you think of people in the Bible who were exiled, like Eric the Red, because of their sins? Greedy Jacob had to flee to a far country. Cain killed his brother and was forced to wander the earth as a vagabond. Adam and Eve disobeyed God and had to leave their beautiful Eden home. Satan was a bully in heaven and was cast out forever.

Sin does that to people. It causes quarreling between brothers and sisters. It stirs up fights on the playground. Because of sin we have war and destruction. Because of sin we have policemen and prisons. Because of sin we have separation and loneliness.

The awful thing about sin is that it leads not only to separation from friends and loved ones; it leads to separation from God, and that means to be lost forever. Nobody who is mean and quarrelsome will enter heaven. No one with a fighting spirit will ever see God. Can you imagine bullies in heaven?

LEIF ERICSON

Choose you this day whom ye will serve; . . . but as for me and my house, we will serve the Lord. Joshua 24:15.

"Look at that boy!" A neighbor pointed to a tall, red-headed youth. "He's the spitting image of his father, Eric!"

"He's already a good fighter," another agreed. "He'll be a great warrior like his dad."

"He will be greater than I," Eric the Red announced. "I have already made plans to send him to Norway to serve in the court of King Olaf. He will learn the ways of a nobleman and return to make us all proud."

Wicked Eric didn't know that while he had been gone from Norway King Olaf and his people had become Christians. They had stopped worshiping Woden, Thor, and Tiu, and now had faith in the one, true God.

After a few weeks in Norway, Leif Ericson declared, "I, too, want to become a Christian. Jesus Christ is more powerful than all those gods my father worships."

"I am pleased you have made that decision," King Olaf said. "When you return to Greenland you must tell the good news about Jesus to everyone. Ask Eric and all his people to become Christians like us."

"I'll do my best, Your Majesty," Leif said, bowing low before King Olaf. "My father is not a happy man. I know Jesus would make a difference in his life."

"I don't need a new god," Eric scowled as he listened to his son talk of the new religion. "Woden, Thor, and Tiu are good enough for me. I will not change."

Although almost all the inhabitants of Greenland accepted Jesus, Eric stubbornly refused and did all he could to dissuade his son. In spite of everything, Leif remained true to Jesus.

God asks you today to look at both sides and then choose for yourself. He hopes you will be like Leif Ericson, turning your back on the world and choosing Christ. Are you brave enough to do that today?

MARCO POLO

Moreover also I gave them my sabbaths, to be a sign between me and them. Ezekiel 20:12.

Seventeen-year-old Marco Polo sat entranced as his father, Nicolo Polo, and his uncle, Mafeo Polo, told of their adventures in the faraway land of Cathay.

"Could I go along on your next trip?" Marco asked.

"I don't see why not," his father replied. "You have grown to be a strong and clever lad. Yes, you may go."

In April of 1271 the three Polos set out on the long journey to Cathay (today called China). They went by boat from Venice to Palestine. From there they had to walk or ride camels. There were no roads, cars, or buses in those days. The country was wild, and treacherous men waited along the way to rob travelers.

"This will protect us on our journey," Nicolo said, taking out a round, golden tablet with strange inscriptions engraved on it.

"What is that?" Marco wanted to know.

"This is our safe conduct," Mr. Polo answered. "Kublai Khan gave it to us. It commands all the great Khan's servants to help us wherever we go. On it our lives depend."

With the protection of that golden tablet the Polos traveled through many countries of the East and returned home safely after 24 years.

God's people are going to face many dangers and hardships during the last days. There is going to be great trouble on the earth such as we have never seen. Those who despise God will want to kill those who love God and keep His commandments.

During that time of trouble we will have a golden tablet that will be our sign that God will keep us safe. It is the fourth commandment. When the decree goes forth that all those who keep the seventh-day Sabbath are to be killed, then all those who follow Jesus in keeping His law will be kept safe, just as Nicolo and Marco were kept safe on their journey. Because of their tablet of gold, no harm came to them. Because of God's law written in our hearts, we will also be kept safe.

Be true to God and His Sabbath. It is the golden tablet that will keep you safe. It is your sign.

CHRISTOPHER COLUMBUS

By this shall all men know that ye are my disciples, if ye have love one to another. John 13:35.

A soft wind stirred in the tops of the palm trees as Columbus and his men waded ashore on San Salvador on an October morning in 1492. After they had spent more than two months on ship, the land felt good under their feet.

"Thank You, God," Columbus prayed as he knelt on the sand. "Thank You for watching over our ships for the past two months, bringing us safely to this new land."

"Where are we?" one of the men asked as they stood on the shore.

"I don't know," Columbus answered, "but we should be in China or Japan."

"But, sir, look at those people coming out of the jungle," another sailor observed. "They don't have the color of skin and the shape of eyes that the Chinese have."

"They look more like the people of India," another noted.

"We must have sailed too far south for China and Japan and reached an island off the coast of India, instead." Columbus agreed. "Yes, these must be the Indies, and the people are Indians."

Of course, believing that he was in India did not make it so. India was still almost 12,000 miles away. Calling the natives Indians did not make them Indians at all.

Though we may think Columbus foolish, you and I do the same thing sometimes with people we meet. We misjudge them. Just because some folks go to church, we say they are Christians when they may not be at all. Just because some people look and act the way Christians act doesn't make them Christians.

To be a real Christian means to have Jesus as the ruler of our heart. Jesus never got in fights. He never called names. He didn't complain and tattle on other kids who were doing wrong. He was kind to everyone. He really loved people and tried to help them and make them happy. Are you really a Christian, or do you have a mistaken identity?

13

AMERIGO VESPUCCI

Lying lips are abomination to the Lord: but they that deal truly are his delight. Proverbs 12:22.

"I have discovered a new world," Amerigo Vespucci wrote in a book published at the beginning of the sixteenth century.

"Wherever I have gone I have kept careful records," Amerigo stated. "I have drawn maps and charts to prove it."

"What a smart man!" people who read his book said.

"The new world should be named after the great Amerigo Vespucci," scholars said. So the new world became known as "America."

The problem is that little of what Amerigo said was true. He never led any expeditions to explore the new world. He did go on some voyages with some men who had sailed with Columbus, but only as a pilot, or astronomer, as they were then called. It was his job to check the position of the ship by observing the sun and stars. The maps in his book were actually drawn by Christopher Columbus. From sailors he had gathered stories of previous explorations and then had told them as if they were his own.

What do you think about what Amerigo did? Do you think it was right to use Columbus' maps and charts and call them his own? Was it honest for him to claim to have discovered the new world? Amerigo got away with his fraud because in those days there was no way to copyright a book.

Look in the front of this book. On one page you will find the word "Copyright" followed by the letter "c" enclosed in a circle. This means that no one is allowed to copy anything out of this book without permission. And if you should need to copy a short part for a report, then it is necessary for you to put quotations around the words to show they are not your own. You also need to tell who really did write those words.

Let us be careful in our schoolwork that we do not make the mistake of Amerigo Vespucci. When we turn our work in to the teacher it should be our own, not a copy of someone else's work. To copy is to cheat. Cheating is lying, and lying is a sin. God says those who tell lies will not be allowed to walk the golden streets of the New Jerusalem.

14

BARTHOLOMEW DIAZ

Christ in you, the hope of glory. Colossians 1:27.

King John II of Portugal leaned forward on his throne, his eyes fixed on Bartholomew Diaz.

"Did you find a sea route to India?" the king asked.

"Yes, Your Majesty, I did," the nobleman Diaz said as he bowed before his ruler. "We sailed around the tip of Africa and several hundred miles up the eastern side. I wanted to sail on to India but the crew was unwilling, so we came home."

"Tell me about your journey," the king urged.

"After we passed the mouth of the Congo River we sailed south into unknown waters. Hot easterly winds covered our ships with red dust. Shortly after this we met a fierce gale, lasting 13 days and blowing us off course to the southwest."

"Yes," the king nodded. "Go on."

"When the storm was over we steered due east but sighted nothing but endless sea," Diaz said.

"Which means you must have passed the tip of Africa."

"Exactly my conclusion," Diaz continued. "We therefore headed the ships north and came to land. On the return voyage we stayed close to the shore and discovered a high cape jutting out into the ocean at the southern tip of Africa. I named it Cape of Storms in memory of our troubles in the great storm."

"Let us call it rather the Cape of Good Hope," replied the king, "because it gives us now the hope of reaching India."

Are you a pessimist, like Diaz, always looking on the dark side of life? Or are you an optimist like King John, preferring to look on the bright side? The pessimist has given up hope. The optimist is full of hope.

The pessimist looks at himself and says, "I don't see how I can ever be saved. I am so bad!"

The optimist is a sinner, too. But he turns his eyes away from himself and looks at Jesus. He says, "When I look to Jesus I don't see how I could possibly be lost."

Jesus Christ fills our hearts with singing. He makes us cheerful and optimistic. With Him in our hearts, we will reach our destination. He is our Cape of Good Hope.

VASCO DA GAMA

No man, having put his hand to the plough, and looking back, is fit for the kingdom of God. Luke 9:62.

Torrential rain beat upon the deck where Vasco da Gama stood. It plastered hair around his face and soaked his clothes. He peered into the grayness of the unknown sea. Ahead of him somewhere was India, and he was determined to find it.

One of the other ships in his fleet sailed nearer. Through the blur of rain da Gama recognized the captain of the ship, his hands cupped about his mouth.

"We must turn back or our men will kill us and sail the ships home themselves!" the captain shouted.

Da Gama knew he must act at once, or the crew would mutiny. "Calling all crew to my ship!" he shouted back at the captain.

With all the crew together, da Gama said, "If I agree to turn back to Portugal, you must sign a paper telling the king that you forced me to do this." The men agreed. Then da Gama chose all those sailors who knew how to sail the ships home and sent them to a cabin below deck to sign the paper. Once they were inside, with the help of some loyal men he locked them in chains. Then he gathered the compass and astrolabe, and threw them into the sea.

"Now," Vasco da Gama said, "we will sail with God as our pilot. With His help we will come safely to India." The fearless da Gama had left his crew no choice. They could not turn back. They would have to follow him to India.

Vasco da Gama had something we call determination. He was no quitter. With him there was no turning back.

God needs boys and girls who have the determination of Vasco da Gama. It's the people who see things through that succeed in life. It's the people who never give up who do really worthwhile things for God. It's the people who never turn back who will reach heaven at last.

Do you want to be a person with the determination of Vasco da Gama, not turning back but pressing on to the finish? Are you willing to follow Jesus for always, no matter what else happens in your life? Are there some things you need to throw overboard so you will not be tempted to turn back?

JOHN AND SEBASTIAN CABOT

Thou hast given a banner to them that fear thee, that it may be displayed because of the truth. Psalm 60:4.

Fourteen-year-old Sebastian Cabot jumped out of the rowboat and, rope in hand, splashed his way to shore. He stood on the narrow, rocky beach, looking for somewhere to fasten the boat securely until he and his companions were ready to return to the *Matthew.* At last he settled for a large boulder.

That job done, Sebastian turned his attention to the rugged rock walls that rose sharply from the shore. They seemed to be challenging him: "Climb us if you can!" Sebastian accepted the challenge and was soon on top. Looking down he watched his father, John Cabot, and the other sailors unfurl the flag of England on the beach. The sight of its colors snapping in the wind sent goose bumps of pride down his spine.

"We did it!" Sebastian shouted down at his father. "We reached Asia!"

Further exploration, however, brought doubts. The inhabitants were fierce-looking men painted red and wearing animal skins. The explorers found no large cities, no gold, and no spices. Nevertheless they claimed the land, whatever it was, for King Henry VII of England. Because of John and Sebastian Cabot the eastern coast of North America was opened to English settlers. The English claimed the new land, for their flag had been planted there first.

When you were born, there was a contest to see who could claim you. Would it be Jesus or Satan?

"He belongs to me," Satan insists. "I planted my flag on the human race in the Garden of Eden. Every child born since then has my flag stamped in his heart. He is mine."

"No," replied Jesus. "I gave him life. You took him away from Me, and I died to win him back. He is Mine, but I will not force him to follow Me. I will not make him fly My flag. He may have your flag if he wishes. I will let him choose."

What is your decision? Satan's flag flies in your heart until you make a different choice. Jesus wants to plant His flag in your heart. Will you let Him do it?

17

VASCO NUÑEZ DE BALBOA

Behold, how great a matter a little fire kindleth. James 3:5.

"Follow the sun," an old Indian told Balboa. "There you will find a great sea."

"It must be the sea that touches Asia!" Balboa exclaimed. "I must see it for myself." With a group of men, he set off across the Isthmus of Panama to find the great sea. By day they tramped through dense tropical jungle, and at night they felt they were being eaten alive by mosquitos. Shorty afterward many died of malaria fever.

The remaining men, including Balboa, struggled to the top of the last mountain ridge. There before them lay an ocean, blue and sparkling in the sun. Balboa drew his sword and claimed the great Pacific Ocean for his king.

When the Spanish government heard about his discovery, they wanted to cut a canal through the 45 miles of land that separated the Atlantic and Pacific oceans. However, it was more difficult than it seemed at first. There was no powerful earth-moving equipment in those days. The work had to be done by hand. The men sent to dig the big ditch got malaria and died. The project was abandoned for 400 years. Why?

It wasn't mountains, money, or any army that stood in the way. It was the tiny mosquito that spread malaria. The project was not completed until doctors discovered how to stop the little mosquito.

"I only took a piece of candy," Jan said. "It wasn't very big. Surely that wouldn't keep me out of heaven."

"I only told a little white lie," Eric said. "Surely that couldn't do any harm."

"That bad word I used was really small," Jay said. "It only had four letters."

Careful! Little thefts, little lies, and little bad words are still sin. Hanging on to one little sin shows your heart is not right with God.

Remember, it takes only a little mosquito to stop a whole country from building a canal. A little mosquito can kill a whole army.

Do you have any "little" sins in your life?

FERDINAND MAGELLAN

I can do all things through Christ which strengtheneth me. Philippians 4:13.

If anyone had an excuse to feel sorry for himself, it was Ferdinand Magellan. He was twice wounded in battle. A wounded knee caused him to limp the rest of his life.

In spite of his handicap, he was determined to continue his explorations. However, King Emanuel of Portugal took a dislike to young Magellan, and this dashed his hopes of further support from Portugal.

"Never mind," said Magellan. "I will go to King Charles V of Spain." King Charles outfitted Magellan with five ships.

Once on the high seas Magellan faced one trouble after another. One ship was wrecked in a storm. Another turned back to Spain. At the tip of South America Magellan and his remaining men were met by fierce storms that threatened to shipwreck them all. Food and water supplies were low.

"Let's give up," the sailors begged.

"Nothing doing!" brave Magellan declared. "We will go on even if we have to eat the leather riggings of the ship."

For three months their ships sailed on the calm waters of the Pacific Ocean without spotting an island. The ocean seemed devoid of fish. Their drinking water, stale and yellow, had to be doled out by the ounce. To satisfy their hunger the men gnawed on wood chips and pieces of leather rigging soaked in saltwater. They caught the rats on ship and roasted them.

Scurvy broke out, and many sailors died. After their leader was killed in battle in the Philippines, the remaining men sailed on to Spain, becoming the first men to circumnavigate the globe. Their courage had seen them through.

Jesus needs boys and girls who have courage. He needs strong youth who won't give up in face of ridicule or handicaps. He needs young people who are determined to succeed, no matter what people say or what circumstances may be. With Christ's help you can overcome any obstacle.

19

JACQUES CARTIER

Great peace have they which love thy law: and nothing shall offend them. Psalm 119:165.

With three ships Jacques Cartier sailed up the St. Lawrence River. As the river became narrower, the Frenchman anchored two of the ships, instructing some of his men to stay and build a fort. He continued upstream until he had to anchor the third ship as well. He proceeded then in the ship's longboat until he came to a large island in the middle of the river.

There more than a thousand Indians lined the shore in welcome. They led the explorers to their village, where the chief gave them corn and venison to eat. In exchange Cartier gave them hatchets, beads, and cloth.

It's a good thing the explorers and the Indians became friends, because that winter many of Cartier's men became ill with scurvy. Their mouths and gums became sore. Their teeth became loose and their joints painful. Wounds refused to heal. Death was imminent.

"We make medicine for great sickness," the Indians said when they visited the fort. "Come, follow us."

Cartier followed the men into the forest, where they gathered a basket of spruce needles. Back at the fort the Indians made a pot of steaming spruce-needle tea.

"Drink it," they ordered. "Good medicine."

The explorers drank and began to get better. Those not yet sick drank it and stayed well. Cartier and his men didn't know it, but scurvy is caused by not getting enough vitamin C. During the long expeditions the men had lived on salt beef and dry biscuits, without fresh fruits or vegetables. The spruce-needle tea gave them the vitamin C they needed.

Some people I know are suffering from spiritual scurvy. They are weak and listless in their spiritual life. They are very easily hurt. Their wounded pride is slow to heal.

People with spiritual scurvy need some good strong Scripture tea. There is something about the Bible that makes us more able to cope with life.

HERNANDO CORTES

The love of money is the root of all evil. 1 Timothy 6:10.

When Montezuma, king of the Aztecs, heard about Cortes and his fleet of flying ships, he suspected that the Spaniards were gods. Therefore, he sent his chieftans with gifts of gold, turquoise, and obsidian.

"Is this all you have to give?" Cortes sneered.

When Montezuma heard that Cortes was marching toward his city with an army and "iron dogs that spit fire," he sent messengers to Cortes with large gifts of gold, hoping to pacify him.

"Take these gifts and come no farther," Montezuma begged.

The gold only whetted the Spaniards' appetite for riches. Onward they marched, right into the Aztec capital. Montezuma was taken captive and persuaded to open up his treasure houses in exchange for his life. Still the Spaniards were not satisfied.

"Fill these three rooms with gold," Cortes demanded. Gold poured into the city from all over the empire. Still it was not enough. Cortes's men went into the temples and overturned their idols searching for gold. They ripped it off people's bodies. A bloody battle followed, in which Montezuma and thousands of Indians were slaughtered.

The love of gold caused Cortes and his men to behave as madmen, caring nothing for human life. Greed is a terrible thing. It makes people cruel today just as it did in the days of Cortes.

You might know some greedy people at school. They always want to be first in line. They must always be captain. They don't want to share the ball or the jump rope. Regardless of how others feel, they must have their own way.

It's possible to be just as greedy over Transformers and dirt bikes as over bigger things such as Lamborghinis and airplanes. We can know something is wrong whenever things become more important than people.

Let's ask Jesus to take away our selfishness, our love of things, and make us more like Him, willing to share, thinking of others instead of ourselves.

21

FRANCISCO PIZARRO

They that take the sword shall perish with the sword.
Matthew 26:52.

"It's impossible to take that city with 130 men!" Pizarro admitted as he looked down from his camp in the Andes Mountains to the rich valley where the Incas lived. "We are outnumbered two hundred to one!"

"I will meet you with my men fully armed," Atahualpa, the Inca king, warned Pizarro. Atahualpa had 40,000 soldiers with him, all armed with spears and lances.

"We come in peace," was the message Pizarro sent back. "Lay down your arms and come to us dancing and playing music."

Why did Atahualpa believe Pizarro? No one knows. At any rate he met Pizarro with dancing and music as requested.

Atahualpa listened politely while a priest told the story of Jesus and tried to persuade the Inca king to become a Christian. Angered, Atahualpa threw the Bible to the ground and, pointing to the sun, said, "There goes my god!"

At that Pizarro gave a signal to his men to open fire with their guns. Thousands of helpless Indians, including Atahualpa, were killed. Pizarro took charge of the kingdom in the name of King Charles V of Spain. However, Pizarro was a poor governor; he quarreled with his own captains. At a Sunday dinner he was killed by one of his own men whom he had angered.

Do you think Pizarro got what he deserved? Do you remember what Jesus said to Peter in the Garden of Gethsemane when the soldiers came to take Him captive? In an effort to defend Jesus Peter drew his sword and cut off the ear of the high priest's servant. "Put away your sword, Peter," Jesus said. "That's not the way I want you to act. If you are going to kill with the sword, then you will also die by a sword."

What does that mean to us today? It means that we get out of life just what we put into it. If we fight with others, then they will fight with us. If we call kids names, then we are going to get called names, too. All the meanness we give will come right back to us. That is one of the laws of life. We get what we give. We reap what we sow.

ABEL TASMAN

I say unto you, That ye resist not evil. Matthew 5:39.

"Well, Tasman, what did you find?" Van Dieman, governor of the Dutch possessions in the East Indies, asked.

"I sailed south and east around New Holland (Australia) as you suggested. On November 24 I sighted land off the southern coast of New Holland, which I named Van Dieman's Land."

"What was it like there? Did you land?"

"For a brief time, sir," Tasman answered. "It was a most frightening place. I heard loud trumpet-like noises coming from the trees, but could not see what caused them. On the ground I saw huge marks that I took to be the tracks of great, wild beasts. After putting up a marker, we sailed on."

"And then?"

"A month later we discovered a high, mountainous country, which I named New Zealand."

"Were there any people in this land?"

"Yes," Tasman replied. "Tall, strong, dark-skinned people with hoarse voices and long black hair, combed into a knot on top of their head. Their bodies were covered with tattoos. We found them very intelligent."

"Did you trade with them?" Governor Van Dieman asked.

"We did a little trading," Tasman responded. "However, one day the natives attacked a boatload of unarmed sailors and killed three of them. I named the spot Bay of Murderers and marked it on my map and sailed on."

"Didn't you take revenge?" The governor frowned.

"No, sir. We treated them only with kindness."

"You are too timid, Tasman," Governor Van Dieman replied.

Do you think it was cowardice on the part of Abel Tasman to leave New Zealand without taking revenge? Or was he showing a strength of character that few people have? It takes courage to follow the command of Jesus: "Resist not evil."

If you, like Tasman, are going to follow the advice of Jesus, how will you behave when someone hits you on the playground? How will you behave when a person calls you names? How will you behave when someone trips you and laughs?

23

CABEZA DE VACA

All ye are brethren. Matthew 23:8.

Four emaciated, barefoot men stumbled along the coast of Texas. Cabeza de Vaca, Andrés Dorantes, Alonso dol Castillo, and Estavan were the sole survivors of a 600-man expedition that had set out to explore the New World six months before.

"I can't go any further," Dorantes said as he slumped to the ground and laid his head on a rotting log.

Castillo sat down beside him and rubbed his swollen feet.

"We've got to keep moving or we'll die in the cold," Cabeza de Vaca warned. When no one made a move, he also sat down beside the log. With a sigh, Estavan joined them.

At dusk a group of Indians who were headed home after a hunt found the four ragged men huddled together for warmth. Their bony frames and sunken eyes made them look more dead than alive.

"Then the strangest thing happened," Cabeza de Vaca later wrote. "The Indians, seeing our misery, sat down beside us and cried. They howled in long lament for our suffering. Hearing them, I felt our calamity more. In my whole life I cannot remember anyone weeping for my suffering."

Not only did the Indians weep, but they covered the shivering men with their own bodies. They rushed the naked men from bonfire to bonfire until they reached their village, where they fed them fish and roots and sang to give them courage.

"I was surprised to find such kindness among these untaught people," Cabeza de Vaca said. "Their feelings were very deep."

Wouldn't it be nice if all of us could look on people who are different the way those Indians looked on the Spaniards? They looked beneath the color of their skin and saw their plight as other human beings. They really cared.

Underneath our skin and clothes we are all alike. If we could only understand that, we'd never be mean or unkind to a person of another race or culture again. We'd try very hard to help them and be their friends.

HERNANDO DE SOTO

For the prophecy came not in old time by the will of man: but holy men of God spake as they were moved by the Holy Ghost. 2 Peter 1:21.

Hernando de Soto stood on the deck of his Spanish galleon anchored near what is now Tampa Bay, Florida, and watched tall columns of black smoke drift toward the sky.

"Indians!" he said to his men. "They have seen us and are getting ready to fight. We have nothing to fear from them. They will not dare attack our armed men on horseback. We will not harm them as long as they supply us with guides."

De Soto was wrong. The Indians fought bitterly, refusing to help him with guides. Without guides and interpreters it would be impossible for the Spanish to find the gold they wanted.

One day the explorers met a group of Indian braves wearing war paint and armed with bows and arrows. All but one ran away when the Spaniards attacked.

"Wait!" he cried in Spanish. "Don't kill me! I am a Christian."

Astonished, the men lowered their spears. "Who are you?" they asked. "How is it you speak Spanish?"

"I am Juan Ortiz of Spain," the man in war paint said. "Twelve years ago I was captured by cruel Indians. I escaped and was taken in by a friendly tribe. They have been good to me, but how thankful I am to see my own countrymen again!"

"And we are thankful to find you!" De Soto exclaimed, shaking Juan's hand. "You can be our guide and translator."

Long ago God had a problem similar to De Soto's. Satan had control of this world. God needed to talk to the people here and tell them the truth about what He was really like. The problem was that the people couldn't understand Him. His voice sounded like thunder to them. So He called prophets such as Moses and Elisha. These men listened to God, then told God's words to the people. They were like Juan Ortiz. They were translators for God.

These men wrote down God's messages in a language the people could understand. The Old Testament was written mostly in Hebrew. The New Testament was written in Greek. Since then the Bible has been translated into about 2,000 different languages.

FRANCIS DRAKE

Be sober, be vigilant; because your adversary the devil, as a roaring lion, walketh about, seeking whom he may devour. 1 Peter 5:8.

The last rays of the setting sun turned the sea to gold as English pirate Francis Drake slid into the harbor at Callao, near Lima, Peru. The fleet of Spanish treasure ships paid no heed to the arrival of the *Golden Hind*, for she was flying a Spanish flag like all the rest.

As soon as darkness sent the Spanish sailors below deck, Drake and his armed men boarded the closest ship, *San Cristóbal*, taking its captain by surprise. In the scuffle that followed, someone ran above deck to sound the alarm.

"Pirates! Indians! Help!" In the darkness the Spanish weren't sure whom they were fighting. It took some time for the Spanish army to get to the harbor. By that time Drake had slipped out into the Pacific Ocean with his treasure ship in tow.

During the next few days Francis Drake raided two other Spanish ships in the same manner. He pretended to be a Spanish vessel, then, once alongside, he demanded their surrender. When he returned to England he had a treasure that included 20 tons of silver, more than 1,000 pounds of gold, and many pearls and diamonds. The value today would be somewhere around $15 million. For this theft he was knighted by Queen Elizabeth I and rewarded with $50,000.

We might look at Satan as a kind of pirate and buccaneer of the universe. He too tries to make us think he is on our side. Then suddenly he lets loose with his guns, and we are defeated. In this way he robs many young people through drugs, alcohol, movies, fashion, sports, and music.

When Satan pirates your life he's not after gold. He wants something far more valuable. He wants your mind, your heart, and your good character. He wants to rob you of your love for Jesus. He will take away all hope of eternal life.

Today that old buccaneer of the universe is going to try to board your ship. He will come posing as your friend. Then suddenly, when he thinks your guard is down, he'll try to steal your treasure. Are you going to let him get away with it?

VITUS BERING

I have set the Lord always before me: because he is at my right hand, I shall not be moved. Psalm 16:8.

Look on the globe and you will discover that North America and Asia are separated by a narrow body of water called the Bering Strait. Nearby is Bering Sea, which, like the strait, is named for Vitus Bering, the Danish explorer who discovered North America and laid claim to Alaska for Queen Anna of Russia.

One November day, after having drifted in a storm for three weeks, the lookout on Bering's ship spotted land. He ran to the captain's cabin, where Bering lay ill with scurvy. "Sir, wake up!" the sailor gently shook the old man's shoulder.

"Yes, what do you want?" Bering grimaced in pain as he turned to face the speaker.

"We have spotted land. It must be Kamchatka Peninsula. Please, sir, the men want to anchor."

"No," the weak man whispered. "We must sail on."

"That's impossible," the first mate said, entering the room just then. "The storm has ripped our sails and broken our ropes. The men are exhausted and ill. We cannot go further."

"Very well," Commander Bering reluctantly gave in. "Put down the anchor."

Unfortunately, they anchored too close to a reef. The tide drove the ship past the reef. The anchor cable snapped, and the ship was driven onto the rocky coast. The men were forced to winter on the barren island. They made dugouts for shelter and buried themselves in sand to keep warm. In his bed of sand Commander Vitus Bering died.

What a different story might have been told had the anchor held.

What about your anchor? Is your faith holding on firmly to Jesus? Only He can keep you safe in the storms of life "when the strong tides lift, and the cables strain." Faith is the anchor you need to keep you when a loved one dies. You must hold firmly to Jesus when doubts, fears, and temptations threaten to shipwreck your life. That is your only safety, your only hope.

JAMES COOK

Beloved, I wish above all things that thou mayest prosper and be in health. 3 John 2.

Lieutenant James Cook opened a small black box containing his instructions from the British Admiralty and read them in silence. "Hmm! Rather tall order, I'd say!" he said at last.

"You are to take three astronomers from the Royal Society to Tahiti in order to view the passage of Venus between the earth and the sun, which is to take place June 3, 1769. While there, you are to make friends of the natives and draw maps and descriptions of the islands."

"That part should be easy," commented Cook, who had recently surveyed the St. Lawrence and mapped Newfoundland.

"After the scientists are finished in Tahiti, you are to open the set of sealed instructions in the black box. All the time you are gone you are to look after your crew's health and keep your ship safe."

"That's going to be the hard part," Cook shook his head. Besides 11 passengers, he had been given a crew of 83, twice the number needed to sail a ship the size of the *Endeavour*. In those days it was expected that more than half the crew would die of scurvy or other perils of the voyage.

"There will be strict health rules on this ship!" Cook told the assembled crew. "The ship must be kept spotlessly clean and well aired. Everyone is to drink lots of water. You are to eat fresh fruit or vegetables every day. You will be issued daily doses of lemon juice to prevent scurvy. We have a goat on board to supply us with fresh milk daily."

As a result of Cook's health rules, 56 of the 95 returned home safely. Their three-year journey took them around the world; they explored Tahiti, New Zealand, and Australia. Compare that with Magellan's voyage. He started with five ships and 277 men. Only one ship, with 18 men, returned to Spain. The ratio of survival was six men out of a hundred. On Cook's voyage 60 out of a hundred survived, ten times as high a ratio.

God wants us all to be healthy and happy. That's why He gives us health rules. When we break those rules we will surely suffer. Can you name some of God's health rules?

MARTIN FROBISHER

And they shall be mine, saith the Lord of hosts, in that day when I make up my jewels. Malachi 3:17.

The year was 1576. Martin Frobisher stood on the shores of Baffin Island and gazed at the bleak, barren landscape. As far as the eye could see, there was nothing but snow, ice, and rocks. He stooped down to look more closely at the smooth, black stones that lay at his feet.

"I wonder if they could have any value," he mused. Picking one up, he stuffed it into his pocket. "Might as well take it back. At least I'll have something to show!"

The glistening black stone excited much talk in England. "It's a piece of gold ore!" the people declared. Soon a company was formed to mine the stones. Even Queen Elizabeth I bought shares in the company.

Frobisher was sent on a second expedition, from which he returned with 200 tons of black stones. Elated, the company sent him out with 15 more ships. Again he returned with a huge cargo of black stones. This time he was met with bad news. The rocks were useless. His cargo had to be dumped.

It was another 200 years before a German geologist, Abraham Werner, discovered that those black stones were graphite. Today graphite is a very valuable mineral with dozens of uses. From it is made many things, from pencils to the cores of atomic reactors. Graphite is also used to make synthetic diamonds. Imagine that! Those black stones Martin Frobisher found could have been used to make bright, sparkling jewels!

It seems to me that you and I are something like those worthless black stones. The world may look at you and say, "She isn't worth much. I wouldn't bother with her." Or "That boy is really worthless! He can't do anything!"

But God considers us not only in the way we are now. He also sees what we may become—not simply old worthless stones but sparkling jewels for His kingdom.

JOHN DAVIS

Looking unto Jesus the author and finisher of our faith.
Hebrews 12:2.

John Davis stood on the bridge of his English ship, quadrant in hand. Raising the instrument to his right eye, he squinted against the blinding brightness of the sun and took a reading. Going inside his cabin he consulted the charts and tables laid out on his desk.

"Ah! Here we are," Davis said, his finger stopping at 72 degrees north. "No one has ever been that far north before." He smiled with satisfaction.

He paused a moment then, closing his eyes to give them a rest before going outside again into the brightness of the Arctic day. "I sure wish we didn't have to look directly at the sun to get a quadrant reading," Davis said to himself.

Once outside, Davis realized he could go no further north, for before him rose an eight-foot wall of broken ice floes. As he watched, the ice moved. Ever so slowly it drifted south, taking his ship with it. It was several days before the ice floes broke up in warmer waters. Again he took a reading with the quadrant.

"Sixty degrees north latitude," Davis observed. Again he closed his eyes. He could still see the image of the sun through his closed eyelids. His eyeballs ached from the brightness.

Eventually John Davis invented a new kind of quadrant, and it was named after him. Using it, a navigator stands with his back to the sun, his instrument aimed at the horizon. The sun is reflected from a sight box to his eye, a lot less blinding than looking directly at the sun.

In our journey of life it seems we need something like the quadrant to help us. We need to be constantly checking our position to make sure we are on course.

The Christian's quadrant is the Bible. Each day we need to look into its pages to catch a glimpse of Jesus, the Sun of Righteousness. As we compare the image we get off Jesus with the position of our lives, we can get a reading of where we stand. With the quadrant of God's Word we can easily keep on a course that will take us to our heavenly home.

HENRY HUDSON

Though he fall, he shall not be utterly cast down: for the Lord upholdeth him with his hand. Psalm 37:24.

Gentle·summer winds blew across Hudson Bay, rocking the *Discovery* where she lay anchored in James Bay. The snow melted from around the log house where Henry Hudson and his men had spent the winter. Great flocks of birds, back from their journey south, were choosing nesting sites and laying eggs.

"Today we will gather birds' eggs," Henry Hudson announced to his ship's crew. "That will be our food supply as we continue our search for the Northwest Passage to China."

"Oh, no!" The words rose in a chorus of groans from the men.

"Sir, we cannot face another year of this wretched place living on birds, birds' eggs, and moss," said Henry Greene, stepping forward to address the captain. "We want to go home!"

"No way!" Hudson stubbornly insisted. "We came to find the Northwest Passage, and we will find it or die trying!"

"Let him die here if he wants to," the men said as they gathered birds' eggs. "We're going home!" A few days later on board ship they seized Henry Hudson at sunrise as he came out of his cabin. They forced him, his young son, and seven loyal crew members into a rowboat. With them they put one iron pot, some meal, a musket, powder, and shot.

"Go ahead and go to China!" the men laughed as they let go of the rope. "We're going home!"

Henry Hudson was never seen again. He must have died feeling very much a failure. However, his failures helped future explorers. They could use his charts and maps to learn what did not work. Learning from his mistakes, they went on to find a better route.

If you get a failing grade on an assignment, don't be discouraged. You can learn from your mistakes what is not right and then work to discover what is right.

We should have the same attitude when we fail in our spiritual life. Because we are human, we fall short of what God wants us to be. When we sin we must not give up. We must go on, learning from our mistakes. Jesus will help us not to do the same thing again.

31

WILLIAM BAFFIN

There is a way which seemeth right unto a man, but the end thereof are the ways of death. Proverbs 14:12.

A steady wind blew the *Discovery* northward along the western coast of Greenland until it reached the spot where John Davis had met the wall of ice. Again ice floes blocked the way.

"Haul down the sails," Commander William Baffin ordered. "We'll wait here until warmer weather breaks up the ice pack."

"But, sir," a young sailor protested. "Why not leave the sails up? The wind is strong. We could smash our way through!"

"That's where you're mistaken," Baffin explained. "Those icebergs are much bigger than the part we see. Only one eighth of the ice is above water. It's the seven eighths below water that we have to worry about. If we hit one of those mighty chunks of ice, our ship would be turned into kindling. There's no way our small boat could push that ice aside."

"Man! I had no idea they were so huge!" the young sailor said. "I'm willing to wait."

After several weeks the ice broke up, and the *Discovery* was able to thread its way between the icebergs for another 300 miles before having to turn back.

Sin is a lot like an iceberg. The devil lets us see only a little bit of it, the part that looks good. He keeps the bad effects hidden. Too late, unsuspecting young people find their lives shipwrecked and their happiness gone.

Alcohol is one of Satan's icebergs. He lets you see the happy parties where everyone drinks. He doesn't tell you how sick you'll feel afterwards. He doesn't show you the alcoholics, the broken homes, and the car accidents.

Drugs are another of his icebergs. He lets you see the "high" that others get from taking drugs. He shows you how great it is to forget your troubles. Only after you are hooked do you discover the seven eighths of the iceberg that can ruin your life.

Gambling, betting at the races, playing the slot machines, and lotteries are some other icebergs that look harmless.

Watch out for Satan's icebergs today. If you see one coming, remember how deceiving they are. Head the other way!

JOHN FRANKLIN

For the Son of man is come to seek and to save that which was lost. Luke 19:10.

"I wish to charter a ship to the Arctic," Lady Franklin said, coming right to the point. "Captain McClintock, you come to me with the highest recommendations. I request you to lead an expedition to find my husband."

"Thank you, madame, for your confidence," Captain Leopold McClintock replied. "What you request will be very hard to accomplish. Already more than a dozen search parties have scoured the Arctic for traces of your husband. The authorities believe there is no further hope in finding him, dead or alive."

"That's the very reason I'm financing this expedition," Lady Franklin said. "I cannot rest until I know what happened to John." Her voice broke then. "Please say that you'll go."

"How can I refuse? Yes, I will go. If the Lord wills, we shall find out what happened to your husband."

Thus Leopold McClintock joined what has been called "the greatest manhunt of all time." After several months he was able to retrace the steps of Sir John Franklin to the place where he and his men had starved to death in 1847 after enduring two years of hardship in the Arctic wasteland.

Although the search for Sir John Franklin stretched over 12 years and used hundreds of men, it was not the greatest manhunt ever organized. Nineteen hundred years ago God started a bigger manhunt than that.

He sent His Son, Jesus, into this world to seek and save boys and girls lost in the icy wilderness of sin. That search is still going on today, and thousands of Christians are helping in the search. They are looking in every continent and island of earth. They are scouring the remotest jungles and searching the wildest deserts.

Has Jesus found you? Are you His child? Then He expects you to be looking around the school for other boys and girls who are lost. He expects you to be searching your neighborhood for men and women who need Him. If you think really hard, I'm sure you can think of something you can do to help in the greatest manhunt this world has ever seen.

LOUIS JOLIET

How shall they hear without a preacher? Romans 10:14.

Two birchbark canoes sat poised on the edge of Lake Michigan.

A slim young man, dressed in coarse gray clothing and a beaver hat, stepped into the first canoe. In his hand was a leather pouch containing paper, pens, and charcoal for drawing maps and writing reports. He was Louis Joliet, commissioned by Governor Frontenac of Canada to find a great river the Indians told about, which we know as the Mississippi River.

Into the second canoe stepped another slender young man dressed in the long, black robe of a Jesuit missionary. On his head he wore a wide-brimmed, black felt hat. In his hand he held a small golden cross. He was Jacques Marquette, ordered to visit the Indians along the way and teach them about God.

Marquette and Joliet's journey took them beside the northern shores of Lake Michigan to Green Bay, where they entered the mouth of the Fox River. This took them to the village of the friendly Mascouten Indians.

"We have heard of a river called Wisconsin," Joliet told the chief. "We hope it might lead us to a wide, mighty river called Mississippi. Can you help us?"

"Yes," the Mascouten chief answered. "We will send guides to show you the way." With the help of the guides they followed the Wisconsin to a wide, swift-flowing river.

"We have found it!" Joliet shouted as he waved his beaver skin hat in the air. "We have found the great Mississippi!"

Imagine how the Mascouten guides must have felt at that moment. Without their help Marquette and Joliet could have wandered for years. They might have died in the wilderness.

There are thousands of people searching for another kind of river—the river of life. They, too, need a guide, for they don't know the way to God, who can give them life eternal. Without help they will surely perish.

You and I can be guides, leading them to Jesus. How thrilling it would be to hear someone say, "I have found it! I have found the river of life. I have found Jesus."

Are you willing to be that kind of guide?

34

SIEUR DE LA SALLE

The Lord is my rock, and my fortress. Psalm 18:2.

"Your Majesty!" The dark-haired young man removed his plumed hat and bowed before King Louis XIV of France. "I bring you news of your growing empire in the New World."

"I know of the colony of New France along the St. Lawrence River. Are there more?" King Louis asked eagerly.

"On April 9, 1682, I reached the mouth of the Mississippi River and claimed all lands drained by it for France. I have called the new land Louisiana in your honor."

The king smiled. "How large is this new possession?"

At this La Salle pulled out his maps showing French ownership of land stretching from the St. Lawrence Valley to Lake Erie and Lake Michigan, and from the Mississippi River Valley to the Gulf of Mexico.

"With your permission I will build a string of forts along the Mississippi," La Salle said. "These forts will open the way for French settlers to farm the rich soil of this vast land and for traders to deal with the Indians."

"Not only will I give you my permission," King Louis declared, "I will give you my blessing, with funds to outfit four ships to carry settlers to Louisiana."

Why was La Salle so anxious to build forts in the land he claimed for France? It was, of course, to protect them from hostile Indians, the Spanish, and the English. These forts became trading posts and safe centers for French settlers.

God is like a fort to those who trust in Him. He is our protection from the enemy, Satan. He is a safe place we can go to when tempted or in trouble.

After David's battle with Goliath he wrote a song in which he called God his fortress. You will find the song in 2 Samuel 22 and Psalm 18. Martin Luther used the same idea to write a hymn you will find at number 506 in the new *Seventh-day Adventist Hymnal.*

LEWIS AND CLARK

And God shall wipe away all tears from their eyes; and there shall be no more death. Revelation 21:4.

"My name is Charbonneau," the man in buckskins introduced himself to explorers Meriwether Lewis and William Clark. "I am a French-Canadian, a trapper. The Mandan Indians told me about your expedition for the United States government. I've trapped in these parts for many years. Perhaps I could help you. I can speak most of the Indian languages in the area."

"Say, that's great!" Lewis exclaimed as he reached out his hand in welcome. "We could use a translator!"

"That's my wife, Sacagawea." Charbonneau motioned to a young Indian girl who sat shyly to one side, rocking her baby. "She was stolen from the Shoshones by a hostile tribe. I purchased her from them to be my wife. She could help with cooking."

"She can help with more than cooking," Clark responded. Turning to Sacagawea, he said, "I hear the Shoshones have many horses."

"Yes, sir," she nodded, her eyes brightening. "They have beautiful horses!"

"We need to buy some horses," Lewis continued. "Could you lead us to the village of your people?"

"I will try," Sacagawea promised. When spring came she led them deep into the Rocky Mountain wilderness to the home of her tribe. Would her loved ones be alive or dead?

When Sacagawea saw a certain young Indian chief she ran forward weeping. "You are my brother!" she cried, throwing her arms around his neck. What a reunion! What joy! How good to see him after so many years!

There will be lots of reunions like that in heaven. Children whose mothers died will see them again. Wives who lost their husbands will rush into their arms. Brothers and sisters will meet once more. Grandmas and grandpas will be restored to their families. Oh, what a reunion that will be!

Loved ones will never have to part again. Jesus will wipe away all tears from our eyes. We will be with our family forever and nothing will ever make us sad again.

ROBERT EDWIN PEARY

God is faithful, who will not suffer you to be tempted above that ye are able. 1 Corinthians 10:13.

Robert E. Peary drew his coat tighter as protection against the biting wind that whipped across the Arctic Ocean. Icy spray clung to his walrus mustache and fur-rimmed parka hood. He stood for a moment, gripping the rail of the steamship *Roosevelt* and staring into the fog. After a few moments he climbed the steps leading to the bridge, where Bob Bartlett, a sturdy Newfoundland sealing skipper, was at the ship's controls.

"How's it going, Bob?" Peary asked.

"Making good time in spite of the fog," he answered. "I'm worried, though, what will happen when we hit ice."

"She'll plow right through!" Peary assured him. "I designed her myself. Her 30-foot sides will take a lot of beating. The iron-reinforced hull will cut through the ice like a knife."

"I hope you're right, Peary," Bartlett shook his head. "I'd prefer to avoid the ice, myself."

"Trust me," Peary replied, laying a hand on Bartlett's arm. "We've got to have a ship that plows through the ice floes if we ever make it to the North Pole."

Suddenly there was a jarring crash that threw the men off balance. "We've struck ice!" Bartlett shouted as he tried to hold the ship steady.

"Full steam ahead!" Peary ordered.

There was a splintering, grinding sound as the ship slowly broke through the ice and continued northward. Peary grinned. "I knew she could do it!" he said proudly. "I built this ship, and I know what she can take!"

Your life is your ship. Although the fog hides your future from view, you need not fear the ice floes of temptation and trial that may come your way. God knows the construction of your ship. He supervised its creation. Therefore, He knows very well how much pressure you can stand. He won't let you face more than you can handle.

"Trust me," God says. "You can take it. I'll see you through to your goal!"

37

ROALD AMUNDSEN

But God commendeth his love toward us, in that, while we were yet sinners, Christ died for us. Romans 5:8.

"An Italian airship has crashed near the North Pole," the newscaster announced. "There are survivors. They have radioed their position, and an experienced Arctic pilot is being sought to attempt their rescue."

"No one is more experienced in Arctic travel than I," 56-year-old Roald Amundsen said. "I will fly to their rescue."

"No!" his friends protested. "It does not mean rescue for them but death for you!"

"Was I not the first man to reach the South Pole?" Amundsen argued. "I took a ship through the Northwest Passage and survived plenty of ice and blizzards. Didn't I fly an airplane over the North Pole from Europe to America? Never fear. I know how to handle myself in the Arctic wilderness."

So the famous Norwegian explorer set out on his rescue attempt. He was never heard from again. Months later bits of the wreckage of his airplane were found. He had given his life trying to save the lives of the stranded Italians whom he had never seen.

Would you be willing to risk your life for someone you didn't know? Maybe you would do it for your mom or dad, your brother or sister, or maybe even a friend. But would you do it for someone you had never met?

Jesus did that for us. We were sinners, His enemies. He didn't have to leave the comforts of heaven to save us. He could have stayed in His Father's house, risking nothing. Yet He risked all to come to this cold, dark planet to save us.

Our Saviour not only gave His life on the cross of Calvary, He risked losing everything by living among us as a human being. Yes, Jesus could have sinned. He could have listened to Satan. But, praise God, He did not! Had Satan been able to get Jesus to sin, even once, then all would have been lost. We would be lost, and He would be shut out of heaven forever.

I'm glad He took the risk and succeeded. Aren't you?

DAVID LIVINGSTONE

I have finished the work which thou gavest me to do. John 17:4.

Doctor Livingstone sat alone in his little hut in Ujiji, a small village in the middle of the African jungle. Stranded, without food, medicine, or money, the old man felt ill and downhearted. It looked as though he and his two faithful servants, Susi and Chuma, would starve to death.

Suddenly, Susi ran in crying, "An Englishman, Master! An Englishman has come!"

Unable to imagine who it might be, the elderly, gray-haired man arose and walked out slowly into the village. A few minutes later the two men met in the marketplace amid a crowd of excited natives.

"Dr. Livingstone, I presume?" the stranger asked.

The old missionary explorer nodded and lifted his cap in greeting.

"I thank God, Doctor, that I have been permitted to find you!" the young man said, gripping the old man's hand.

"Oh?" Livingstone's eyebrows raised. "You were looking for me?"

"Yes, sir," the younger man said. "The whole world is concerned about your welfare. When we heard you had disappeared, the owner of a New York newspaper asked me to find you and write about your explorations. I am Henry Stanley. I have brought you food and medicine."

After Dr. Livingstone had recovered his health, the two men went exploring together for the source of the Nile River.

"Come to Zanzibar with me," Stanley urged when it was time for him to go. "I will send you to England for a much-deserved holiday. Then you will come back refreshed to do your work."

"No," Dr. Livingstone shook his head. "If I took a holiday, I should never come back. First I must finish my work here."

God needs young people today with the dedication of David Livingstone, young people who will not give up until the job is done. He needs boys and girls who can stick to a task until it is completed. He needs workers who, like Jesus, will be able to say, "I have finished the work Thou gavest me to do."

JOHANNES GUTENBERG

Blessed is he that readeth . . . the words of this prophecy.
Revelation 1:3.

"I wish I had a good book to read," Johannes Gutenberg sighed as he bent over his goldsmith's workbench in Strasbourg, Germany. He held up to the light the metal he was polishing and thought of better days when he could afford the extravagance of a book.

"If only it didn't take so long to copy a book by hand," Johannas mused, "then they wouldn't be so expensive. There must be an easier and faster way of getting books written so that everyone who wanted to could read and learn. Why should priests and nobles be the only ones with this privilege?"

As Johannes gazed at the signet ring in his hand an idea came to him. "Why couldn't I use something on the order of this ring to print words on paper?" Rising from his stool, he found some sealing wax and melted it. Pressing the hollowed-out ring into the warm wax, he formed a raised design.

"No, that's not quite it," he said at last. "The letters must stand forth, not be hollowed out." Grabbing a scrap of soft wood, he began to chisel. Then by putting paint on the raised parts he was able to print the design he had made in the wood. "It will work!" he said at last. "By this method I could print whole books!"

As he experimented he found that wooden blocks wore out too quickly. Soon he was making individual letters molded out of metal. These letters he clamped together to form words, sentences, and paragraphs.

Gutenberg began setting type in 1454 for the first printed edition of the Bible. There were 1,282 pages in Gutenberg's Bible, each one to be printed 300 times. In a couple of short years Gutenberg accomplished what it would have taken hundreds of years to do by hand.

Today there are only 47 copies of Gutenberg's Bible left. Each one is priceless! I doubt that you will ever own one of those rare books, but I guarantee that the blessing to be found in your own Bible is just as valuable. Have you found it?

LEONARDO DA VINCI

The entrance of thy words giveth light; it giveth understanding unto the simple. Psalm 119:130.

"These maps are worthless!" Cesare Borgia said, laying current maps of central Italy on the table before Leonardo da Vinci. "I have no way of knowing the exact distance between cities. Can you do better than this?"

"I can try," Leonardo promised.

During the next few weeks Leonardo da Vinci mapped all of Tuscany and Umbria, using an odometer he designed himself. It consisted of a wheelbarrowlike device that he pushed along the road. As the wheel turned, it drove gears that operated a dial that showed how many feet the wheelbarrow had moved. In this way da Vinci was able to give the exact distances between places on his map. His design was very similar to the odometer used in automobiles today, more than 500 years later.

Leonardo da Vinci's notebooks were soon full of scores of inventions such as machine guns, submarines, diving bells, and helicopters. He designed an anemometer to measure the speed of the wind, and he was the first person to design a clock that could indicate hours and minutes. He invented a jack for lifting weights, much like automobile jacks used today. He outlined a hydraulic pump and built a parachute that worked.

When he died Leonardo left behind nearly 7,000 pages of drawings with instructions about how to construct inventions of all kinds. The only problem was that no one could read what he had written because it appeared to be done in a kind of code. Then it was discovered that everything was written in mirror image. By holding it up to a looking glass, the message became perfectly clear!

God's plan for Planet Earth may sometimes seem as confusing as a page of da Vinci's sketchbook. Life seems a puzzle, and nothing makes any sense. Why does God allow divorce and racial violence? Why doesn't He do something about child abuse and earthquake victims? Why are there so many different churches? Why aren't our prayers always answered?

Try holding up life with all its puzzles to the mirror of God's Word. You'll be surprised at how much clearer things are!

GALILEO GALILEI

Now faith is the substance of things hoped for, the evidence of things not seen. Hebrews 11:1.

A portly merchant of Venice paused on the top step to catch his breath. Then he strode across the roof to a group of men gathered around a strange-looking tube mounted on a stand. "Well, what do you see?" the newcomer asked.

"Ships!" Galileo replied. "Two of them, coming from the southwest. They bear the flag of Venice."

"Nonsense!" The merchant frowned, shading his eyes to peer in the direction the others were looking. "I see nothing but water and sky. There are no ships!"

"Oh, but there are!" the others insisted. "Here, have a look for yourself."

Squinting one eye shut, the newcomer put his other to the small end of the tube, and two sailing ships appeared as if by magic. "Unbelievable!" he exclaimed.

"Come tonight and I'll show you mountains and craters on the moon," Galileo, the builder of the telescope, promised. "I can show you four moons around Jupiter and stars invisible to the naked eye."

"No!" the merchant declared. "This tube is an invention of the devil, for it makes you see things that are not there!"

"But didn't you see the ships on the sea?" asked Galileo.

"Yes, but there must be some trick, for we still cannot see them without the tube."

"Wait," advised Galileo, "and you will see them." Several hours later the two ships sailed into the harbor at Venice.

Galileo's telescope is an illustration of faith. Through faith we see angels walking beside us and God answering our prayers. Through faith we see Christ coming in the clouds, and the graves of our loved ones opened. Through faith we see the Holy City and the mansions that will be ours.

To those without the "telescope" we may appear to "see things that aren't there." But we know that in a little while what we now see by "faith" will appear in reality as surely as those two ships appeared in the Venetian harbor that day in 1611.

ANTON VAN LEEUWENHOEK

But God hath revealed them unto us by his Spirit: for the Spirit searcheth all things, yea, the deep things of God. 1 Corinthians 2:10.

Sixty-six-year-old Anton van Leeuwenhoek pushed his broom along the corridor of the city hall in Delft, Holland, as he had done for more than 40 years. He hummed to himself as he thought of his microscopes. Grinding lenses had been his hobby since his teen years. He had several hundred mounted carefully in oblongs of copper, silver, or gold. Fixed to them were all sorts of things: insects, seeds, hairs, bits of meat, an ox eye, fish scales, and skin fibers.

"Excuse me, sir"—a deep voice with foreign accent interrupted Anton's thoughts—"I'm looking for Anton van Leeuwenhoek, grinder of lenses."

"I am he," the old man said as he looked into the face of a tall Russian with wavy brown hair and a carefully waxed mustache.

"I am Peter, czar of Russia," the visitor explained. "I have heard of your microscope."

Leeuwenhoek fumbled nervously with the broom handle. "How do you know about my microscope?" he asked.

"My dear friend," the monarch replied, "your papers sent to the Royal Society in London and the French Academy of Sciences in Paris have made you world famous! Will you show me some of your work?"

"I should be honored," Leeuwenhoek said, leading the czar to the small room in his humble cottage where he kept his lenses. Putting a drop of rainwater under one lens, he let his guest see the tiny animals hatching, moving, feeding, and dying. Fascinated, the ruler of Russia examined the contents of one lense after another. "I never knew such things existed!" he exclaimed in awe.

That's just how I feel sometimes when I read the Bible. Somehow the Holy Spirit magnifies the Word and opens up to me new truths and ideas that I never knew existed. The more I study, the more fascinating the Bible becomes. There's a whole universe of exciting things hidden in God's Word that most people have never seen. Have a look today. You never know what you might find!

BENJAMIN FRANKLIN

Seest thou a man diligent in his business? He shall stand before kings. Proverbs 22:29.

Sweat poured from 10-year-old Ben's forehead as he bent over the hot tallow, dipping candles. The acrid smoke of soap fat stung his eyes and burned his throat. He coughed as his uncle entered the room. "How are things going?" the older man asked, placing a hand on Ben's drooping shoulders.

"OK," Ben shrugged, forcing a smile.

"It's not so much what you do in life as how you do it," his uncle said, giving Ben's arm a squeeze. Then, pulling a Bible out of his pocket, he read, "Seest thou a man diligent in his business? He shall stand before kings."

After his uncle left, Ben couldn't help thinking about what he had said. "Fat chance I have to stand before kings! I'm so tired I can hardly stand at all!"

At the end of two years his father told him, "Son, I can't bear to let you dip candles all your life. You deserve something better. What trade would you like to learn?"

"I should like to be a printer, sir," Ben replied. Within nine years Ben had completed his apprenticeship and was owner of the largest printing firm in America.

Diligent Ben always seemed to be working on some new project. He improved printing presses and type. He invented a smoke-free lamp and a stove that worked better than the fireplaces people were using then. He developed bifocal glasses and lightning rods. In spite of having only two years of schooling, he was granted the title of doctor of philosophy by the greatest universities in Europe and acclaimed as the greatest inventor of his time.

When entertained by Louis XVI in Paris, the kings of four nations came to see him. Returning to a hero's welcome in Philadelphia Benjamin Franklin perhaps thought of the Bible verse his uncle had read to him 60 years before.

What is your business today? Do it diligently. What chores do you have? Do them faithfully. Is there an assignment that needs attention? Do it to the best of your ability. Your future success depends on the habits you form now.

ALESSANDRO VOLTA

I will be with thee: I will not fail thee, nor forsake thee.
Joshua 1:5.

Do you know where there's a flashlight battery or transistor battery? Get it and have a look. Find the place where it says 1.5 volts (or possibly 9 volts). The number of volts tells you the "pressure" of the electricity. By comparison, there are either 120 or 240 volts in the electrical outlets in your home. Volts are a way of measuring power and were named after Alessandro Volta, the Italian professor of physics who invented the dry cell battery.

You could make a battery yourself. Volta took clean dry disks of silver, clean dry disks of zinc, and disks of cardboard soaked in a strong solution of salt water. He arranged them in a pile—silver, cardboard, zinc, silver, cardboard, zinc. From the ends of the pile, electricity flowed. He was the first person to produce a continuous source of electricity.

Another time, Volta covered the tip of his tongue with a strip of tin. He touched the bowl of a silver spoon to his tongue further back and touched the handle of the spoon to the tin. In this way he produced a small amount of electricity and illustrated the principle of the dry cell. He had used two different metals and a liquid conductor of electricity. The same idea works in your car battery.

If you were going to illustrate the power of God in your life, would you say it is more like an iron that you have to go to a certain place to plug in or like a portable radio that can go with you anywhere?

Is the power of God available to you only once or twice a week when you go to church? Or can you take God with you on the ski lift and in the shopping mall.

Can you make use of God's power to keep you from saying dirty words only as long as you are plugged in during morning worship? Or can you tune yourself to Him on the playground?

Will there ever be a situation when God's power won't work? Is there any spot on earth where it is unavailable?

JAMES WATT

Commit thy way unto the Lord; trust also in him; and he shall bring it to pass. Psalm 37:5.

"I declare, child, are you going to sit in that chair all day and gather wool?" James's aunt frowned and shook her head. "You ought to be outside playing games with the rest of the children."

"I'd rather do this!" James said, staring at the steaming teakettle that hung from an iron hook over the open fireplace.

"Do? Do what?" his aunt spoke with sarcasm.

"I'm studying!"

"Don't see any books," his aunt retorted.

"I'm learning about steam, Auntie," James replied. "Watch this. I'll do an experiment for you." Using metal tongs, James picked up a scrap of wood and held it tight against the spout of the teakettle. A sudden burst of steam raised the lid enough for the steam to escape.

"See how the steam lifts the copper lid?" James beamed in triumph. "Steam is strong. Imagine how much power there would be in a kettle this big." James stretched his arms wide.

"Hrmmph!" his aunt snorted. "I think you'd better go back to staring before you blow up the house!"

Young James settled back in the chair and dreamed of what might happen if someone found a way to catch the steam and make it work. Maybe it could turn the grindstone in the mill or push the boats when there was no wind.

A few years later James turned his dream into a reality when he built a model engine. Soon his engine was used in factories, coal mines, railroads, and ships. James Watt's steam engine began the Industrial Revolution.

Youth is the time to dream wild and wonderful dreams of what the world could be like. Nothing great was ever accomplished but first someone dared to dream that it could be done!

So this day I dare you to dream! I challenge you to find something that would make this world a better place and imagine how it might come about. Think big! Be creative! You might be surprised at what you can do.

MICHAEL FARADAY

We ought to obey God rather than men. Acts 5:29.

"Sarah!" Michael Faraday called as he burst into the house, envelope in hand. "I've an invitation to have lunch with Queen Victoria, and I don't know what to do!"

"Well, go, of course!" his wife laughed. "Why ever would you refuse?"

"Listen to this." Faraday opened the envelope and read: "Her Majesty, Queen Victoria, requests the honor of your presence for lunch at Windsor Castle this Sunday at noon."

"Oh, no!" Sarah's face fell. "You can't possibly go on Sunday. You'll miss church, and you are one of the elders!"

"That's the problem," Faraday agreed. "You know I never miss church unless I'm sick or out of town. I've attended faithfully since I was a child. I don't want to miss the meeting, but how can I say no to the queen? It would be most disrespectful! As a loyal Englishman, I cannot refuse my queen's invitation. I'm afraid I'll just have to miss church this once."

So Michael Faraday, the father of the electric motor and the electric generator, had lunch with Queen Victoria at Windsor Castle. The other elders did not agree with Faraday's decision. They said he should put respect for God before his respect for the queen. He was no longer allowed to be an elder. He couldn't preach in the church. In fact, for many years he was not counted as a member, though he attended services faithfully.

If you had been Michael Faraday, would you have turned down the queen's invitation?

Would it be all right to miss church so that you could watch a football game on TV? Would you stay away from church so you could attend the birthday party of a friend? Would you skip church for a chance to meet your favorite movie star?

What answer would you give the president of the United States if he invited you to the White House on Sabbath for a special reception in your honor?

How important is your appointment with God each Sabbath?

47

EDMUND CARTWRIGHT

And they have rewarded me evil for good, and hatred for my love. Psalm 109:5.

"Fire! Fire! The loom factory's on fire!" Within minutes half the town of Manchester, England, had gathered to watch Edmund Cartwright's life savings go up in smoke. No one made a move to put out the fire. No one tried to save the looms.

"Good riddance!" someone commented.

"That should put a stop to him!" another exulted.

Edmund Cartwright had no choice but to watch angry flames destroy the 400 looms that were all finished, waiting for delivery to a mill owner the next day.

"Rumors are that the millhands set fire to your factory," the mill owner told Cartwright. "They were afraid they'd lose their jobs if I used your new power looms."

"But don't they realize I was only trying to help them?" Cartwright asked. "I am their pastor. I love them and hate to see them work so hard weaving cloth by hand. I invented the power loom to make life better for them. They would work less hours and earn much more money if you installed the looms."

"Agreed!" the mill owner nodded. "But they don't understand. Build a new factory. Manufacture more looms. Eventually they'll see what you were trying to do for them."

"I wish I could," Cartwright sighed. "But all my money is gone. Someone else will have to build the looms. I have done all I can."

So someone else took Cartwright's idea and manufactured the power looms he had invented. He lost his family fortune trying to help others and got nothing in return. Yet to the end of his life he remained a happy, kind man. Not once did he try to get even with the weavers or those who stole his invention. Instead, he rejoiced that life for the poor people got better, just as he had hoped it would.

There may come a time when someone will reward your kindness with meanness. I hope you'll be able to keep on loving them just as Pastor Cartwright kept on loving his ignorant parishioners. In not retaliating, you will also be living like Jesus, who was killed by those He came to save.

ROBERT FULTON

Deliver me out of the mire, and let me not sink. Psalm 69:14.

Lightning flashed across the dark Parisian sky. Gale-force winds whipped the waters of the Seine River, creating waves that pounded the frail hull of a 70-foot boat tied to one of the wharfs. Thunderclouds poured buckets of water onto the newly constructed vessel.

Robert Fulton stood on the banks shivering, helpless against the fury of the storm. There was a sickening roar as the hull split in two, and he watched his work of several months sink below the waves.

"I've got to save the engine!" Fulton said as he tore off his coat and plunged into the icy waters. Down, down he went until his hands touched the oozy mud at the bottom of the river. Holding his breath as long as he could, he felt along the bottom for the missing engine. He found nothing!

Again and again he came up for air, then back he dived into the murky depths of the Seine, searching for his precious steam engine. Twelve exhausting hours later his hand touched the cold metal of the motor. Carefully he secured a rope and dragged it to shore.

It took him days to clean every trace of the mud out of the engine chambers. Painstakingly he rubbed and shined, greased and oiled, until the engine was as good as new. Then he set about to make another boat. A few weeks later, cheering crowds stood on the banks of the Seine as the steamboat performed for about an hour. Although Robert Fulton built many other steamboats, none was quite so precious to him as that one, because of the effort it had cost him.

Many a boy and girl is like Robert Fulton's first steamboat. Battered about by the storms of life, they sink deep into the mud and mire of sin. There is nothing they can do to save themselves. All seems lost.

Then, wonder of wonders, their Creator plunges into the waters and pulls them out of the mire. Lovingly He cleans and polishes until they're as good as new. Throughout eternity how precious they are because of the effort it cost to save them!

49

ELI WHITNEY

Do that which is honest. 2 Corinthians 13:7.

Long before Eli Whitney invented the cotton gin, he was a boy who liked to whittle boats, whistles, and wooden spoons. His tool was a homemade, single-bladed knife.

One night at a husking bee a new boy, Mose Hartley, pulled a jackknife from his pocket. "Want to see it?" he asked, tossing the knife to Eli.

Eli flipped it open. He ran his finger along the blade and whistled. "That blade's sharp!" At last he handed it back. How he wished he could have a knife so fine!

After the husking bee, as Eli started to climb into the carriage he noticed something shiny lying on the ground. He stooped to pick it up. "Why, it's a jackknife," Eli gasped. "How did it get here? It looks like Mose's knife!"

"Let's go, Eli," Mr. Whitney called.

"Just a minute, Father," Eli said. "I just found a jackknife that belongs to Mose. I'll be right back." Eli ran to the house, but Mose had gone.

All the way home Eli fingered the smooth knife in his pocket. That night he slept with it under his pillow to keep it safe. The next morning he woke excited. Pulling the knife from under the pillow, he stroked it lovingly. Oh, how he wished that it belonged to him!

"I could keep it, and Mose would never know," Eli told himself. "But I mustn't even think of such a thing. To keep it would be stealing. As soon as I can I must find out where Mose lives and return his knife."

The next day Mr. Whitney had business at the Hartley's, and Eli rode along for a chance to see Mose. "Is this yours?" he asked, holding out the shiny knife.

"It sure is! Where did you get it?" Mose asked.

"I found it at the husking bee," Eli answered.

"I never thought I'd see it again," Mose shook his head. "You could have kept it, and I'd never have known."

"I know," Eli grinned. "But I couldn't keep what wasn't mine. Besides, I'd rather be your friend than to have your knife."

CYRUS McCORMICK

Lo, I am with you alway, even unto the end of the world.
Matthew 28:20.

Twenty-two-year-old Cyrus watched as his father, Robert Mc-Cormick, checked the new reaping machine. The sickles, mounted on a wooden bar, glistened in the morning sunlight.

"She's ready to roll!" the elder McCormick said.

The horses strained, pulling the machine slowly through the field of golden grain. The spikes caught the straight, strong stalks of wheat and pushed them against the knife.

"Wow! Look at her go!" Cyrus yelled.

"The real test is just ahead," his father shouted back as they approached a windblown stretch.

Cyrus held his breath as the spikes passed over the broken stalks of grain, pressing them to the ground.

"The thing's a failure!" Angrily Robert McCormick jerked the reins of the horses, bringing the reaper to a halt. "For 20 years I've tried to make a reaper, and always it ends like this—a failure."

"But, Father," Cyrus objected. "It cut well at first!"

"And what of it?" his father retorted. "No reaper can be counted a success unless it will cut, rain or shine, straight-standing or knocked-down grain. You can't get a field made to order—you should know that, Cyrus."

"Yes, Father," Cyrus said respectfully, "but I still think there must be a way. I'd like to give it a try."

"Go ahead," the older man sighed, his shoulders sagging. "I'd be proud if my son succeeded where I failed."

Three years later, in 1834, Cyrus got his patent for a reaper that worked, rain or shine, with straight-standing or knocked-down grain, on smooth land or rough.

Life, like fields of grain, doesn't come made to order. There are rough times and rainy days. To succeed, we need more than a fair-weather God. We need a God for all seasons, one who can lift us up when we're bent and broken, one who can help us when we're down and out.

"I'm that kind of God," Jesus says.

ELIAS HOWE

Behold, he cometh with clouds; and every eye shall see him.
Revelation 1:7.

After inventing the sewing machine, Elias Howe became rich and famous. Although he was honored by important people on many occasions, none quite equaled the day in 1828 when he met John Quincy Adams, president of the United States.

It all happened when 9-year-old Elias went on a business trip with his father and stopped for the night at Red Brick Inn.

"You're lucky!" the innkeeper said. "There's just one room left. All the rooms are taken by President Adams and his men."

During supper Elias kept his eyes glued to the door. *I wouldn't want to miss the president!* he thought.

"I'm sorry, son," Mr. Howe said at last, rising. "I'm afraid the president has been delayed. We can't wait up any longer as we have many miles to travel tomorrow." Reluctantly, Elias followed his father up the stairs to their room. In minutes Mr. Howe was snoring while Elias lay awake, listening for the president's coach. Ah, there it was! Elias was out of bed in an instant and into the hall. Tiptoeing to the head of the stairs he peeked over the railing. He could hear them talking, but he couldn't see the president. He pushed himself farther over the rail until his feet were off the floor. How handsome the president was!

Just then the president said, "I think I'll go to bed now."

Oh, no! Elias thought. *He's coming up the stairs.* He tried to pull himself back over the rail, but couldn't. He was stuck! His nightshirt had caught on the railing post!

"Well! What have we here?" President Adams laughed.

"It . . . it's me, sir! Elias Howe."

"I'm pleased to meet you, Elias," the president said as he freed the boy and lifted him down. When Elias was an old man he still loved to tell about the night he met the president.

Have you ever wished you could meet a president, prime minister, king, or queen? Have you ever waited for hours to watch their motorcade pass by? Then you have a little idea of how excited we're going to be when we see Jesus, King of kings, coming in all His glory! I can hardly wait! What about you?

HENRY BESSEMER

For he is like a refiner's fire. Malachi 3:2.

"Your new type projectile is terrific!" Napoleon III, emperor of France, told young Henry Bessemer. "I like the way it rotates in flight, enabling a cannon to shoot farther and more accurately than ever before. There is only one problem."

"I know," Bessemer agreed. "My new projectile needs guns made out of steel instead of cast iron. The brittle cast iron blows up under the great explosive power needed to fire the projectile. What we need are steel cannons."

"Exactly," Napoleon agreed. "But steel is too expensive."

"Then I will find a way to make it cheaply," Henry Bessemer spoke with determination. He knew nothing about making iron and steel, but he set out to learn.

He soon discovered that cast iron was the easiest to make. This was made by heating iron ore with coke and limestone. The resulting product was cheap and hard, but brittle.

When more iron ore was added to the mixture, it caused the carbon from the coke to burn off. The product that remained was called wrought iron. It was tough, but soft and expensive.

To make steel, cast iron had to be turned into wrought iron, then some other ingredients added. It was the most expensive of all.

Henry Bessemer discovered he could force air, under pressure, into a huge blast furnace full of molten pig iron. This caused a mighty roar. Sparks and flame shot out the top of the furnace, leaving behind a pure liquid metal. It needed only the addition of ferromanganese alloy to become top-quality steel. Soon he was producing steel at $100 a ton less than anyone else.

The prophet Malachi must have had a similar process in mind when he said that God would come to us as a refiner's fire. God's people—you and I—are full of impurities that keep us from being really useful. In His love, God allows troubles and trials to come to us so that we might be purified of all the ugly parts of our character. He allows us to experience just the amount of heat we need to burn away our meanness and rebellion. Think how strong we'll be when He is finished!

53

SAMUEL FINLEY BREESE MORSE

*The race is not to the swift, nor the battle to the strong.
Ecclesiastes 9:11.*

Seven-year-old Finley Morse sighed as he looked up from his *New England Primer.* He was too excited to study spelling. Tomorrow would be his first day of school at Andover. How grown up he felt! He looked across the table at his 4-year-old brother, Sidney, who was learning his alphabet.

"Hurry up, Sidney," Finley urged. "Father says we can play as soon as we say our lessons." Sidney didn't look up.

Poor slowpoke Sidney! Finley thought. *When I finish my spelling I'll have to help him so we can play.* Finley's pen made circles on his paper. He smiled as he turned them into the faces of children.

"Finley, are your lessons finished?" Father asked.

"Why, yes, almost," Finley said. "But slow-poke Sidney will never get done. Could he be excused this once?"

"Sidney has already recited his lesson!"

"How did that happen?" Finley asked. "He's so slow!"

"Did you ever hear the story about the tortoise and the hare?" Mr. Morse replied, seating himself at the table.

"Of course," Finley answered. "But it's a silly story and couldn't happen. How could a turtle win against a rabbit?"

"By sticking to his task," Father's eyebrows lifted. "I saw a tortoise learn his alphabet today and win while a hare drew pictures and lost."

Finley Morse learned his lesson. When he got the idea for sending messages over an electric wire he kept at it until the telegraph was successful. It took him 12 years, but he persevered until he reached his goal.

We are all running in the race of life. It matters not whether you're a tortoise or a hare. The important thing is to keep running in the right direction. Many boys and girls will forfeit success, both now and eternally, because they haven't learned that the "race is not to the swift" but to the one who sticks to the task.

GOTTLIEB DAIMLER

For it is God which worketh in you both to will and to do of his good pleasure. Philippians 2:13.

Have you heard of the Mercedes car? The company that makes it was founded in 1890 by Gottlieb Daimler, the German engineer who developed the type of gasoline engine that most automobiles use today.

If you look up "gasoline engine" in the encyclopedia, you will learn what happens inside the engine of a car. First, a mixture of air and gasoline vapor is drawn into a cylinder. Next, the piston moves up, compressing, or squeezing, the fuel mixture. When it can't be squeezed anymore a spark from the spark plug sets the fuel on fire. As the fuel burns, it makes hot gases that expand rapidly, driving the piston downward. The downward stroke of the piston turns the crankshaft that transfers the energy to make your car go.

The piston moves up again, expelling exhaust gas. It moves down again, drawing in more fuel and air. Over and over, the cycle is repeated as you cruise down the highway: Fuel intake, fire, exhaust, fuel intake, fire, exhaust.

Eventually, of course, the fuel is all used up and the pistons stop working. The engine goes dead. The wheels refuse to turn. You are going nowhere fast!

The same sort of thing happens in our Christian experience. It's impossible to live the Christian life without Christ working from within. It is the spark of His love in your heart that gives you energy to do the works of a Christian. Without Him you are dead. Your spiritual wheels won't turn. Progress is not possible.

What is the problem when you find yourself stalled on the highway to heaven? Doesn't Jesus love you anymore? Of course He does. Has He given up on you? Of course not. It's a simple matter. You are out of gas. You need refueling.

So, go on, find a filling station or a gas pump: Sabbath School, church, or that quiet time alone with God's Word. As you learn Bible verses or meditate on Scripture you are being filled. With gas in the tank, going is easy.

CHARLES GOODYEAR

All things are possible to him that believeth. Mark 9:23.

If anybody ever tried to do the impossible, it was Charles Goodyear. One day after his hardware business failed and before he was put in jail for nonpayment of his debts, he happened into a rubber store.

"If you want to make a fortune," the clerk told him, "find a way to treat rubber so it won't melt in the heat and break in the cold. Everybody says it's impossible."

Challenged, Charles Goodyear made the improvement of rubber his life's goal. He had no money, but he had faith in his ability. He had no experience in chemistry, but he would learn. It didn't matter that they put him in jail; that gave him time to work on the rubber problem. He attempted the impossible.

Goodyear believed the secret lay in adding some substance to raw rubber, so he set out systematically to knead every known substance into rubber.

One day he mixed some magnesium salts with the raw rubber and boiled it in quicklime and water. It seemed to work until he spilled some vinegar on it, and the rubber dissolved into a sticky mess. "Never mind!" he said, setting to work again. "The difficult we do immediately; the impossible takes longer."

One day he attempted to clean a piece of rubber, using the nearest chemical at hand, which contained sulfur. That piece of rubber didn't melt as easily as the others. So he began kneading sulfur into his rubber. Then one day, quite by accident, a piece of the rubber he was tossing around fell onto the stove. That piece of heated rubber and sulphur was the strongest yet. Goodyear had discovered the principle of vulcanization. He had done the impossible.

Life is full of impossible situations. Children are born without limbs. Young people are paralyzed in auto accidents. An earthquake snatches away homes and loved ones. Poverty places an education beyond reach. Prejudice makes jobs difficult to find. Life is not fair!

You're right! But that is no reason to despair. With God you can succeed. You can do the impossible! Believe it!

CHRISTOPHER L. SHOLES

Esteeming the reproach of Christ greater riches than the treasures in Egypt. Hebrews 11:26.

Fourteen-year-old Christopher Sholes quit school and went to work in a newspaper office. From compositor he moved up the ladder to become pressroom boss, journalist, and eventually the editor of a large newspaper in Milwaukee, Wisconsin.

One day Sholes found the office unnaturally quiet when he walked in. Some of the employees were on strike. There was plenty of work to do but no one to do it. Sholes looked at the waiting machines and thought, *These machines are more dependable than men. If only I had a machine that could type!*

The idea of a machine that could type stayed with Sholes even after he became state senator, postmaster, and collector of customs. While serving in the latter post, he was successful in building a machine that could type. James Densmore, a businessman, joined him in the venture. Their typewriter was so successful that the Remington Company, where Sholes and Densmore went to have the machine manufactured, wanted to buy the patent rights.

Sholes couldn't resist the temptation of an instant reward for his years of hard work. He accepted $12,000 in cash. Densmore, on the other hand, chose to receive a small royalty on each machine sold. His reward was much longer in materializing, but over his lifetime he received $1.5 million. Who made the wiser choice?

Moses was faced with a similar decision. He could have enjoyed wealth and honor as a pharaoh in Egypt. With it would have come all the pleasure and possessions he could desire, but then in a few years he would die, and that would be the end. He chose rather to suffer affliction with God's people for the present, looking forward to an eternal reward.

When you think of it, what are a few years of pleasure in this life, if that's all there is? Satan offers you an instant reward, but be careful. It will soon be gone, and then what?

Compare that with the mansions of heaven, joys for eternity, and life forever. Consider well, and wait.

GEORGE WESTINGHOUSE, JR.

But the tongue can no man tame; it is an unruly evil. James 3:8.

If James were living in today's motorized society, he might write like this: "We can stop all manner of vehicles by simply pressing the brake. But there is no brake for the tongue. There's no stopping the damage it does!"

One April day in 1869, George Westinghouse witnessed a demonstration of the importance of good brakes. It was the day he decided to test his new air brakes on the *Steubenville Accommodation,* a train consisting of a locomotive and four passenger cars of the Panhandle Railroad in Pittsburgh, Pennsylvania.

On that morning George made a last-minute check of the newly installed air brakes he had invented. Everything was in perfect order. Superintendent Card arrived with his party. George climbed aboard the locomotive with engineer Daniel Tate.

"OK!" George said. "We're ready. Let's go!"

Tate clanged the bell, released the brakes, and opened the throttle. The train gained speed rapidly. Suddenly George caught his breath. Several hundred yards ahead of them a wagon pulled by two horses was parked on the tracks. A farmer was frantically trying to make the horses move. They lunged, throwing the driver in front of the oncoming train.

"Brakes!" George yelled. Tate reached for the lever, turning it all the way. There was a loud grating sound as the brake shoes went into place. The train ground to a halt within inches of the man.

"No doubt about it, your brakes are a success," Superintendent Card said as he slapped Westinghouse on the back.

It's easy to verbally knock down people who get in our way. It's easy to hurt others with our words. If only we had brakes in our mouths, how much heartache we could save!

Ask God just now to give you brakes for your tongue. With His power you can stop when you are about to say those cruel words. You can stop when you're about to put other people down or call them names. You can stop before you hurt a friend.

ALEXANDER GRAHAM BELL

A word spoken in due season, how good is it! Proverbs 15:23.

One cold, rainy day in March, 1875, a tall young Scot with bushy black hair, side whiskers, and a droopy mustache waited outside the office of Joseph Henry, secretary of the Smithsonian Institution. The grayness of his mood matched the grayness of the clouds over Washington, D.C.

"Mr. Bell, so good to see you!" Henry said. "Come in! I can see you have a heavy burden on your mind. Sit down and tell me about it."

Alexander Bell sighed and closed his eyes, searching for the right place to begin. At last he said, "I've been trying to send spoken words over wires. I see no reason why I should not be able to speak in Boston and you hear me in Washington."

"You have the germ of a great invention," Henry encouraged him. "What's your problem?"

"I know that I need to vary the intensity of an electrical impulse in the same way that sound waves vary," Bell continued. "The problem is that I don't have the electrical knowledge necessary to complete the experiment."

"Then get it!" Henry said, placing a hand on the young man's shoulder. "Morse conquered his electrical difficulties, although he was only a painter. You can do the same!"

"Thank you, sir." Alexander managed a smile. "I don't intend to give up. I'll find a way!"

By June he was sending musical notes over a wire, and nine months later he called to his assistant over the wires: "Mr. Watson, come here. I want you."

"I would have given up if it hadn't been for Joseph Henry," Bell confessed to his friends. "That day in his office he made me believe I could succeed. Without his encouragement I would never have invented the telephone."

Kind words, encouraging words, hopeful words, are very easy to say. They take just a moment and cost us nothing. Yet how often we fail to speak that word in due season.

Here's a project for you today: Find someone that looks unhappy. See if you can say a word to cheer them up!

THOMAS ALVA EDISON

Nevertheless not my will, but thine, be done. Luke 22:42.

Thomas Alva Edison has been called the greatest inventor of all time. He patented more than 1,400 inventions, among which were moving pictures, the record player, and the electric light bulb.

Tom's career as an inventor was launched at the age of 22 when he went to New York City to get a job. Arriving with 42 cents in his pocket, he slept on park benches for several nights. At last he decided to look up his friend, Frank Pope, who worked in the Gold Indicator Company.

Just as he got to the company office the stock indicator, or ticker, stopped. He watched as men rushed in and out of the offices. Managers tore their hair, and mechanics tried desperately to make the machine go.

"Can't anyone fix the indicator?" Dr. Laws, head of the company, asked.

"Yes, sir. I think I can!" Tom stepped forward.

"And who are you?" Dr. Laws glared at the newcomer. "Never mind. Fix it if you can." Within two hours Edison had the machine working smoothly.

"I'll pay you $300 a month to keep the machines running," Dr. Laws offered, and Edison accepted. Soon Marshall Lefferts of the Gold and Stock Telegraph Company heard of young Edison.

"Can you improve our stock tickers?" Lefferts wanted to know. Edison could and did.

"How much do you want for your invention?" Lefferts asked.

Edison thought of asking $5,000 but was afraid it would be too much. In his mind he settled for $3,000 but hesitated to name so large a figure. "Well, sir, suppose you make me an offer," Edison hedged.

"How would $40,000 do?" Lefferts inquired.

"It would do just fine!" Edison agreed. By letting Mr. Lefferts make the decision Tom made himself $37,000.

I wonder if we wouldn't be better off to deal that way with God. We have such small expectations! By accepting His will instead of our own we will never come out the losers.

WILBUR AND ORVILLE WRIGHT

Come unto me, all ye that labour and are heavy laden, and I will give you rest. Matthew 11:28.

A 25-mile-an-hour wind whipped sand into clouds around seven men and a flying machine on the beach at Kitty Hawk, North Carolina the morning of December 17, 1903. Above the whine of the wind could be heard the pounding of the surf and the cry of sea gulls.

"It's your turn, Wilbur," Orville nodded to his older brother. A gust of wind caught at Wilbur's cap, and he reached up to turn it around. Taking a deep breath, he climbed into the open plane. Lying on his stomach, he grasped the steering wires.

"I'm ready!" Wilbur called over his shoulder. "Start the motor." The four-cylinder gasoline engine coughed and sputtered. The plane shuddered, then began to move slowly down its track. Orville ran beside it, his coat flying in the breeze. The plane gathered speed and rose into the air.

"Look at her go!" one of the men shouted above the roar of the engine. "It's actually flying!"

"Most amazing thing I ever saw!" cried another. "First thing you know you men will be outflyin' the birds."

After 59 seconds aloft, the plane crashed into a sand dune. It had gone more than 800 feet. For the first time in history man had actually flown!

To be able to soar with the birds had been the dream of men for centuries. David once said, "Oh that I had wings like a dove! for then would I fly away, and be at rest" (Ps. 55:6). Have you ever wished you could fly far away from all the things that annoy and trouble you?

Because Wilbur and Orville Wright invented the airplane, we can fly almost anywhere we choose. However, flying away from home doesn't get rid of our problems. They go right with us on the airplane, for we cannot get away from ourselves.

Do you have troubles? Jesus says running away, or even flying away, isn't the answer; He is. He can give you the rest and peace you're seeking, right where you are.

HENRY FORD

Therefore all things whatsoever ye would that men should do to you, do ye even so to them. Matthew 7:12.

It was recess time at the little red schoolhouse near Dearborn, Michigan. Happy children burst through the doors into the sunshine, ready to play.

"Choose up for prisoner's base!" someone shouted.

"I'm tired of that game," Henry Ford complained. "Let's do something different."

"OK!" his friend agreed. "Let's play marbles instead."

"Or fox and geese," another suggested.

"We've played those games hundreds of times," Henry said. "I mean let's do something really different."

"Like what?"

"Like building a dam across the creek." Henry's eyes sparked. "I'll make a wooden waterwheel, something like the one at the old mill, to fit in the race. What do you say?"

"Sounds great!" his friends agreed.

And it was great! Before many days the dam was completed and the waterwheel was installed. The small lake formed by the dam made a wonderful place to sail boats. Then one day the fun stopped.

An angry farmer pulled his wagon into the schoolyard and confronted the teacher. "Your boys are ruining my potato crop with their dam! The whole field is covered with water! If you don't do something immediately, I'm calling the police!"

"I'm so sorry, sir," the teacher replied. "The boys will destroy their dam, and I will see that it is not rebuilt."

"I'll hold you to your word," the farmer muttered as he stomped to his wagon.

That day Henry Ford and his friends learned that fun stops being fun when it hurts someone else. Of course they hadn't meant to harm the farmer's potatoes. They just didn't stop to think of the consequences of the dam they had built.

As the boys tore out the mud, rocks, and sticks, they agreed that they wouldn't want someone to build a dam that made water overflow onto their farms. Henry spoke for all of them: "We'll think twice before we build another dam!"

GUGLIELMO MARCONI

While they are yet speaking, I will hear. Isaiah 65:24.

In the Marconi villa outside of Bologna, Italy, all was dark except for the dim light of a lamp on the third floor where 20-year-old Guglielmo sat studying his notes and equipment.

On one side of the room was what he called an exciter. It was a cylinder with wire coiled around it, attached to two spark balls and a battery. When he pressed a switch a blue spark leaped between the balls and crackled in the air.

Thirty feet away was the instrument he called a coherer. It was made of a glass tube and batteries and was wired to a bell. His goal was to send a signal from the "exciter" across 30 feet of air to the coherer, making the bell ring.

Marconi made a last-minute adjustment. His finger touched the switch. The blue spark jumped between the spark balls, the bell rang. Smiling to himself, he tiptoed down the stairs to his mother's room and tapped her gently on the shoulder.

"What is it?" Mrs. Marconi asked. "Is something wrong?"

"No, Mama," Guglielmo laughed. "Something is very right! Come and see." Without a word she followed him to the attic. "You stand right here, Mother, and listen," he said, then ran across the room to press the switch.

Mrs. Marconi's eyes grew wide in astonishment as she saw the spark leap and heard the bell ring.

"Isn't it wonderful, Mama?" Guglielmo exalted. "Don't you see, there were no wires, no wires at all! One day I'll be able to send messages around the world!" His invention was to form the basis for radio.

As wonderful as man's communication system now is, via satellite, it's nothing compared to heaven's communication network that allows you and me to send our voices across the vast stretches of space to the throne of God. Before we can so much as blink, God has received our prayer. In fact, while we are still speaking, He hears!

LOUIS BRAILLE

Children, obey your parents in the Lord: for this is right.
Ephesians 6:1.

People came from miles around to have Simon Braille make harnesses and saddles for their horses. His shop in Coupvray, France, with its scraps of leather, was a favorite play area for his 3-year-old son, Louis.

"I'm going to make a harness," Louis said one day. "Papa, may I use your awl? I need to make the holes."

"It's too sharp," Mr. Braille said, shaking his head. "You might hurt yourself."

"Please, Papa, I'll be careful," Louis begged.

"No," his father said. "These tools are too dangerous for little boys. Promise me you'll leave them alone!"

"I promise," Louis said, but in his heart he still wished he could make his harness. Then one day his chance came. Father was outside, waiting on a customer. Mother was in the kitchen. He could see the awl where his father had laid it on the workbench. Climbing onto a chair, he reached for the tool.

Clasping the awl in two chubby hands, he dug into the hard leather, barely making a dent. He leaned harder on the awl. It slipped. Louis fell forward, the sharp tool puncturing his eye.

"Papa! Papa!" Louis screamed as red blood flowed down his cheek onto his shirt.

Mr. Braille ran into the shop and saw at once what had happened. Gathering Louis into his arms, he ran out of the house to the nearest doctor. But the doctor could do nothing to save Louis's eyes. He became totally blind.

Later in life Louis became a teacher in a blind school, and he invented an alphabet of raised dots so that blind people could read books.

But that awful morning little Louis had only one thought. "Papa, I'm sorry I was a bad boy," he sobbed. "I won't ever touch your tools again!"

GEORGE EASTMAN

He that covereth his sins shall not prosper: but whoso confesseth and forsaketh them shall have mercy. Proverbs 28:13.

George Eastman made it possible for millions of people to become amateur photographers by inventing the inexpensive Kodak camera and flexible roll-type film. He grew up in Rochester, New York, where he loved to play ball.

One sweltering August day, George was playing with five friends in a vacant lot. Hobart crouched over home plate, looking fierce. Jimmy wound up and let go a fast ball. Hobart swung with all his might and hit the ball. Up, up, up it sailed through the air, over the heads of the fielders and over the tall wooden fence between the vacant lot and Widow Grant's house. The boys heard a crash and the tinkling of broken glass.

"Oh, no! Let's get out of here!" Ben yelled.

"Wait!" Jimmy shouted. "We've got to get that ball back. It's the only one we have!"

"Hobart should go, since he hit the ball," Jimmy decided.

"I'm scared." Hobart's chin started to quiver.

"Well, I think we were cowards to run away," George said. "I'll go with you, Hobart. Come on!"

George's legs felt weak as he and Hobart climbed the rickety steps to the porch. His heart beat wildly as he turned the rusty door bell. Suddenly the door swung open, and there stood Widow Grant—smiling at them.

"Is this yours?" she asked.

"Y-yes," George stuttered. "We're sorry, Mrs. Grant. We didn't mean to break your window. We'll pay for it."

"I know." There were friendly crinkles around Mrs. Grant's blue eyes. "I can't get out anymore, and I love to watch you play. Run along now and finish your game."

"She's nice!" Hobart said when they were on the street. "I'm glad we went back, aren't you?"

"Yeah," George agreed. He felt all warm and happy inside because he knew they had done the right thing.

WILHELM KONRAD ROENTGEN

For man looketh on the outward appearance, but the Lord looketh on the heart. 1 Samuel 16:7.

"School is dismissed," Charles Kettering, teacher of a one-room school in southern Ohio, announced one Friday after recess.

"Hurrah!" the children shouted.

"The younger children may go home," Mr. Kettering continued. "I'm taking the older ones to Loudonville to see the X-ray machine, invented by Wilhelm Roentgen, of Germany."

"We want to go, too," a third grader pouted.

"No," Mr. Kettering was firm. "Only the 10 oldest students may go. It's a five-mile walk there and another five miles home again."

Those who went considered the long walk worthwhile when they looked into the machine and saw the bones of their own hands and feet. "How does it work, Mr. Kettering?" the children asked.

"Inside, there's a glass container into which two electrodes are sealed and from which the air has been removed," the teacher said. He made a quick sketch for his students. "When an electric current passes through one of the electrodes, called the cathode, a ray is created. When this ray strikes the other electrodes, called the anode, or target, it gives off X-rays. This X-ray will pass through most substances."

"Like my shoes and socks!" observed one boy.

"Man! This is the best invention yet!" another exclaimed.

As wonderful as X-ray machines are, they have their limitations. They can show broken bones, but not broken hearts. Blood clots and tumors show up on film, but not what you know, think, and feel. Your thoughts are safe from the X-ray machine. It can't take a picture of your dreams and plans. It will never reveal how much you dislike someone or how you plan to get even.

On the other hand, God can see through to the real you. He sees the hurts, the heartaches, and the secret dreams. He sees the ugly as well as the beautiful, and loves you still.

ROBERT H. GODDARD

For as he thinketh in his heart, so is he. Proverbs 23:7.

"Bob, I've got a job for you," Mary Goddard told her teenage grandson one bright October day. "The old cherry tree in the orchard needs trimming."

"OK, Gram," Bob sighed as he laid down *The War of the Worlds,* by H. G. Wells. It was his favorite book, one he had read several times already. The book was an imaginary tale of Martians who traveled the solar system in big iron cylinders. Every time he read it, he got excited. What if such a thing were really possible?

Thoughts of space travel occupied Bob as he sauntered to the shed to get a saw. He was still thinking about it as he climbed to the lowest limb of the old cherry tree. He leaned his back against the tree trunk to rest. Warm autumn sunshine filtered through the leaves, warming his body. He closed his eyes. Then the strangest thing happened.

"It was almost like a dream," Bob said later. "I imagined a strange machine shaped like a long bar. It began to spin faster and faster until it lifted off the ground. Higher and higher it rose into the air and headed for the moon."

Excited, Bob jumped down from the tree, ran to his room, and sketched the machine he had imagined in the cherry tree.

Twenty some years and several hundred rockets later, Bob stood in a field in Massachusetts and watched his first liquid-fuel rocket lift into the air, brilliant orange and yellow flames streaking behind it. After climbing to 184 feet, it leveled off and landed. Before he died in 1945 he had launched a rocket that traveled two miles into the air. Today rocket probes, space stations, and space shuttles seem almost commonplace.

It all started that day in the cherry tree. Bob Goddard's imagination, fed by the books he read, helped make the space age possible. What he constantly thought about, he did. That seems to be one of the laws of life, that as we think, so we become.

What kind of person will you become? What do you think about? What occupies your attention? What kind of books do you read? What movies do you watch? What music do you listen to?

RENÉ ANTOINE FERCHAULT DE REAUMUR

But ask now the beasts, and they shall teach thee. Job 12:7.

René de Reaumur got up from the laboratory stool and stretched. Going to the window, he looked out on a lazy, sun-drenched world of midsummer. What a day to be stuck indoors in a stuffy old lab! Taking off his lab coat, he walked out into the sunshine.

Hurrying along the street, he was soon at the edge of town. Before him lay the woods he loved almost as much as his laboratory. In fact, it seemed to him but an extension of his lab. There was so much to see, so much to discover.

He could sit for hours watching a bullfinch build her nest, or lie on the ground all afternoon observing the ways of the ants.

On this particular day he came upon an old wasp's nest fastened to a bush. Curious, he broke off a sample of the paperlike substance and stuffed it in his pocket.

"I wonder what they use to make this," he said to himself. For weeks he worked on the problem in his laboratory. To his amazement he discovered the wasps made their paper nest out of wood. They bit off tiny bits of wood from trees and mixed it with their saliva until it was a pulp. Then they spread it out and let it dry. The result was paper.

"I have made a great discovery," Reaumur told the French Academy of Science in 1719. "I have learned how to make paper out of wood."

"Impossible!" the other scientists argued. "Everybody knows you have to make paper out of old rags, especially linen rags. That's how it's been done since the Chinese discovered it in A.D. 105."

"It *is* possible!" Reaumur insisted. "I have seen the wasps do it, and I have done it in my lab. Here are samples of what I have made out of wood pulp. Think what that will do for the paper industry. Wood is much easier to come by than linen rags. It will make paper cheap and plentiful."

It's amazing what secrets the beasts can teach us! I wonder what other inventions are waiting to be discovered.

HAMMURABI

But the word of the Lord endureth for ever. 1 Peter 1:25.

"Make a large pillar of stone," King Hammurabi ordered the chief stonecutter. "It must be big enough to write down all the laws of Babylon."

"How many laws are there, Your Excellency?" the artisan asked.

"Two hundred eighty-two," Hammurabi answered proudly. "I have searched the kingdom for all the old laws. I have rewritten them and made new ones where needed. I have made sure that strong people will not oppress the weak."

"I will do as you say," the stonecutter answered. After many weeks of hard labor chiseling out the hundreds of cuneiform letters, the stonecutter returned to the palace. "The pillar is finished. Where shall I put it?"

"Place it in the center of Babylon," Hammurabi declared. "I want no one to have any doubt as to the laws of our land."

For many years the magnificent eight-foot stone pillar stood in a prominent place in Babylon. Daily, visitors gathered around its base to gaze at the relief carving of Hammurabi receiving his authority from Shamash, the god of justice. Underneath the carving were inscribed laws dealing with lying, witchcraft, military service, land and business, family, tariffs, wages, trade, loans, and debts.

Then one day an invading Elamite king carried off the massive pillar as a war trophy. He got it as far as Susa, Iran, where it lay for nearly 4,000 years, buried in sand. In 1901 a tourist came along and wondered what lay beneath the strange mound.

Today you can see Hammurabi's stone pillar in the Louvre museum in Paris, a reminder of a great kingdom and a lawgiver that are no more. No one bothers to obey those laws chiseled in stone, for the lawgiver is dead and the kingdom vanished.

About the same time in history, another list of laws were chiseled onto two small tables of stone on Mount Sinai. Those laws, the Ten Commandments, are still in force today, for the Lawgiver, Jesus Christ, still lives, and His kingdom is forever.

IKHNATON

Thy word is true from the beginning. Psalm 119:160.

"The Hebrews have invaded our land," Abdu-Heba, king of Jerusalem, wrote on a clay tablet and sent it to Ikhnaton, pharaoh of Egypt. "They·came from across the Jordan River, and already many cities have fallen. We need your help!"

But Ikhnaton was not concerned about the plight of his Canaanite neighbors. The young ruler was too busy building palaces and sun temples in his new capital city, Akhetaton, on the banks of the Nile River. He had enough rebellion in Egypt to cope with, for the priests of Amon were angry with him.

As a teenager, Ikhnaton, then called Amenhotep, thought a lot about the gods his people worshiped. There were scores of them vying for the attention of the people. Many of the gods were cruel!

"I don't believe in these gods," Amenhotep declared when he was 15 years old. "I believe there is only one god who is the creator of the world. He is a loving, kind god, who makes the birds sing and the sheep dance on the hills."

Amenhotep called the name of his new god Aton, whom he said lived in the sun. He changed his own name to Ikhnaton, which meant that he was a worshiper of the god Aton. This angered the old priests.

As soon as Ikhnaton became king he moved his capital to get away from the priests of Amon. While hundreds of workmen built his temples and palaces, others were busy removing the names of other gods from all the monuments in Egypt. No wonder he had no time to worry what Joshua and the Hebrews were doing at Jericho and Ai.

Ikhnaton's servants filed away Abdu-Heba's letter, along with more than 350 others requesting help. There they lay gathering dust while the Hebrews established themselves in the Promised Land. There they stayed when his city was abandoned after his death. There they remained until 1887, when a local woman, digging in the ruins for waste to be used as fertilizer, discovered the ancient clay tablets.

These 3,000-year-old letters are important, for they give one more bit of proof that God's Word is true.

CROESUS

For what shall it profit a man, if he shall gain the whole world, and lose his own soul? Mark 8:36.

During the time of Daniel there lived in what is now the country of Turkey a king named Croesus. He claimed to be the richest man in the world. He used gold, silver, and precious stones to make a monument in Sardis that was one of the seven wonders of the ancient world.

According to legend, one day Solon, a Greek leader from Athens, visited Croesus and was given a tour of the treasures of Sardis. When he was finished, Croesus asked, "Tell me, Solon, who is the happiest man in the world?" The rich king leaned back on his couch, a grin on his face. He was sure Solon would name him.

"Tellus of Athens," Solon replied. "For he died gloriously on the field of battle."

"All right, who is happiest after him?"

"Two brothers I know who were devoted to their ailing mother before she died."

Disappointed, Croesus inquired, "But what about me?"

"Do not say a man is happy until you know the whole of his life," Solon answered. "There are things more important than gold and silver."

Croesus puzzled about Solon's answer for many years until one day Sardis was taken by the Persians. Croesus was captured, bound, and led to a pile of wood, where he was chained to a stake.

"Solon! Solon!" he cried as flames began to shoot up from the wood. "Now I know what is more important than gold and silver."

"Put out the fire!" Cyrus ordered, suddenly feeling sorry for the king he had condemned to death. The soldiers ran for buckets of water, which did little to quench the fire.

"O God, save me!" Croesus cried to the heavens. Just then a black cloud covered the sun. There was a clap of thunder and rain poured down, putting out the fire.

"Though I have nothing, I am indeed a happy man!" Croesus exclaimed, "for I have my life." The grateful king, now a wiser man, served in the court of Cyrus for the rest of his life.

ALEXANDER THE GREAT

The Lord is my light and my salvation; whom shall I fear? Psalm 27:1.

Alexander stood with his father, King Philip of Macedonia, as the royal horsemen inspected a new group of colts.

"Look at the black one go!" Alexander pointed to the liveliest colt in the bunch. "See? The one with the blaze of white on his forehead. The one that looks like an ox."

"He's no good. Too wild." His father shook his head. "No man will ever stay on his back!"

"I could!" Alexander's eyes sparkled. "Please, Father, let me try. Those men don't know how to handle him."

King Philip looked down at his young son and smiled. "So! You think you can do better than my handlers?"

"I know what's wrong. I'm sure I can manage him." Alexander spoke with confidence.

"OK!" his father said. "Give it a try. If you can ride him, he's yours!"

"Yippee!" Alexander shouted as he streaked across the field. As he came close to the black colt he slowed down. Taking the reins from the handler, he carefully began to turn the colt's head toward the sun as he stroked his neck and whispered softly in his ear. In no time the colt was calm. Alexander jumped on the colt's back and returned to his father, who waited under the cyprus trees.

"He's yours," King Philip said. "What's your secret?"

"I noticed that the sun casts very long shadows at this hour," Alexander replied. "He was scared of those dark, twisting shapes. I turned his face toward the sun, and there was nothing to frighten him."

And that's how Alexander won Bucephalus, the horse that he rode in battle to conquer the world.

What are some of the shadows in your life? Divorce? Disease? Drugs? Drink? Disabilities? Defeat? Disaster? Death?

Look away from the shadows to Jesus, your light and your salvation. He will calm your frightened heart. He will make you brave to face the future.

SHIH HUANG TI

For he is our peace, who hath made both one, and hath broken down the middle wall of partition between us. Ephesians 2:14.

When Paul wrote these words he was thinking about the wall that had separated Jews and Gentiles for centuries. Through Christ those barriers had come tumbling down.

That's not a wall you and I have to worry about, but we do face walls nevertheless. What about the wall of racial prejudice? Lots of people won't be friends simply because they were born a different color. That's a wall Jesus can help you tear down.

For some there's the wall of language and culture. People who are "different" are kept out of the circle of friendship, as though somehow they aren't quite to be trusted.

I've seen very definite walls dividing a classroom into two groups, those kids who have more money and those whose families are struggling to make ends meet. Nice clothes, cars, toys, and bikes can become a barrier, and oh, how hard it is to break down. Jesus wants to help do it in your school.

Shih Huang Ti, emperor of China from 246 B.C. to 210 B.C., went all out for building walls. He was determined to keep out the warlike Mongolian tribes who often swept down from the North. Thousands of workmen labored for many years to build the Great Wall of China, which stretches for 1,500 miles across that great country. It's the longest fortified line ever built.

Standing 25 feet high, the wall tapers from 25 feet thick at the base to 15 feet at the top. Constructed entirely by hand, the mammoth wall is incredibly strong. After 2,000 years it still stands as a monument to the determination of Shih Huang Ti to keep out his neighbors. Of course, it isn't terribly effective against airplanes, bombs, and missiles.

For Christians, walls are definitely out-of-date. Are there some walls in your life that need to come tumbling down? Remember how the walls of Jericho fell down by faith? Through faith your walls can crumble too.

ASOKA

If it be possible, as much as lieth in you, live peaceably with all men. Romans 12:18.

Two hundred fifty years before Christ, in the days of Shih Huang Ti of China, Asoka set out to conquer India. Marching south, he shut off the supply route of the Kalingas on the east coast. A bloody battle followed in which Asoka won.

Home from war, he stood in a balcony of his magnificent palace and watched the victory celebration. Musicians, dancing girls, bejeweled elephants, and brightly dressed soldiers paraded before him. The walls vibrated from the noise of the drums and the shouts of his subjects.

"Come, Your Majesty!" an attendant urged. "The people are happy! You must join them!"

The emperor sighed and shook his head. "Do you realize how many have died during the battle?" he asked.

"Certainly," the courtier answered. "Everyone is praising you for the 100,000 you have slain and the 150,000 more you have brought home as prisoners."

"To say nothing of the hundreds of thousands who died of disease and hardship! How terrible! How sad!"

"There is always killing in war, Your Majesty."

"Then we will have no more war!" Asoka decided. "We will live at peace with our neighbors, and I will do all I can to make up for this slaughter."

During the remaining years of Asoka's reign he was true to his word. He set up stone pillars over all his kingdom, admonishing his people to be kind to one another. He appointed special officials to travel throughout the land to see that the old and the poor were treated fairly. He even made killing animals a crime. Asoka became a follower of Buddhism, a religion of peace and nonviolence.

Two hundred years later Jesus came teaching a similar message of love, peace, and nonviolence. But He did more than teach and give an example. He died on the cross of Calvary to pay the penalty for all the cruel acts you and I or Asoka have ever done. And when we accept Him into our hearts He makes it possible for us to live peaceably with one another.

CLEOPATRA

The kingdom of heaven is like unto a merchant man, seeking goodly pearls. Matthew 13:45.

Mark Antony and his generals were astonished as they walked into the banqueting tent of Cleopatra, queen of Egypt. The magnificence dazzled their eyes. Guests sat on couches ornamented with purple and gold. The dinner service was made of pure gold, set with precious jewels. Servants fanned the guests with ostrich plumes while musicians played flutes and lyres. Silk curtains woven with gold shut out the desert heat.

"My dear Cleopatra," the Roman ruler said as he bowed to the lovely queen. "This is fantastic! I have never been to such a splendid banquet in my life! You really shouldn't have gone to such trouble!"

"Mere trifles," Cleopatra said with a shrug. "Take this golden dinner service as my gift, if you like it."

"Like it? It's gorgeous!" Mark Antony praised, "but really you are being too extravagant!"

"This is nothing to what you will see tomorrow night," the queen boasted. "The meal itself will cost 10,000 sestertia [equal to $300,000]."

"Impossible!"

At dinner the next night Cleopatra wore two pearl earrings, the largest in the world at that time. Each pearl was worth $222,000. Removing them, she motioned to a servant, who set before her a glass of vinegar. Dropping one pearl into the liquid, she watched it dissolve, then drank the contents. Before she could sacrifice the other pearl a general snatched it away.

It must have been such valuable pearls that Jesus had in mind when He talked about the merchant who found a "pearl of great price" and sold all he had to get that pearl.

If Jesus was the heavenly merchant man who came to this world in search of goodly pearls, then who do you think is the pearl of great price? It is the person inside your clothes. You are of infinite value. Jesus loved you so much that He died for you. If you were the only one who sinned, Jesus would have done it for you. You are more precious to Him than Cleopatra's pearls. You are the pearl of great price.

CAESAR AUGUSTUS

A time to build up. Ecclesiastes 3:3.

Caesar Augustus, emperor of Rome at the time of Christ's birth, definitely considered his reign a time to build. He set men to work building roads, bridges, and aqueducts. His workmen completed many beautiful buildings; among them were 82 temples. He commissioned sculptors to create decorations for his buildings. Once the great ruler boasted, "I found Rome brick and left it marble."

But more than buildings, Augustus built an empire. He brought peace after 100 years of civil war. He built free trade among the provinces, established a postal system, and founded colonies. The census that brought Joseph and Mary to Bethlehem for the birth of Jesus was part of the building program of Augustus. Building costs money, and money for government building comes from taxes. Whatever small tax the carpenter Joseph paid went to help Augustus's ambitious building program.

The month of August is named after this Caesar who built an empire so strong that it lasted for 200 years after his death, in spite of the weak rulers who followed him. Augustus takes his place as one of the great rulers of history because of his ability to build.

For you and me, 1988 is "a time to build." We can start by building roads and bridges of communication between ourselves and our parents. Take the time today to talk to your mom and dad. Share your disappointments and dreams. Tell them how you feel about them. Write them a note. There are many ways to build roads that bridge the generation gap.

We build people by appreciating the good things they do. Kind words and thoughtful actions build friendships. Explaining how to do a math problem, or helping someone learn how to bat, are good people-building activities.

Try building your school through enthusiastic participation in all its programs. Support your principal and teachers. Obey the rules. Tell everyone what a neat school you have. Stop complaining and think of positive things you can do to make it better.

Are there other ways you could be a builder today?

CONSTANTINE THE GREAT

*But the seventh day is the sabbath of the Lord thy God.
Exodus 20:10.*

All was silent in the Roman camp, save for the sighing of wind
in cyprus trees and the snoring of exhausted men. At the door of
Constantine's tent a guard struggled to stay awake. He yawned and
stared into the darkness, wondering who would win that day in the
battle between Maxentius and Constantine.

Inside, the emperor stirred, then coughed. "Guard!" he called.

"Yes, sir! I am awake. All is well!"

"Come here. There is something you must do."

Constantine's guard lifted the flap of his commander's tent and
went inside. "At your service, Your Majesty."

"Awake the men. We must prepare for battle. Instruct each one
to paint a cross on his shield. No exceptions!"

"Very well, sir, but why? The men will want to know."

"I have just had a vision in which I saw a great flaming cross.
Around it were written the words 'By this sign thou shalt conquer.'
The cross is a sign of our victory."

On that day in A.D. 312 Constantine's forces, with crosses on
their shields, defeated Maxentius at the Milvian Bridge on the Tiber
River. From that day forward Constantine became a strong supporter of Christianity. A year later he was baptized. During the
years that followed he made Christianity the official religion of the
Roman Empire.

In 321 Constantine made a law that commanded people to
observe Sunday as their day of rest. He reasoned that this would
make it easier for the pagans to become Christians, since that was
already the day on which they worshiped their heathen gods.

Some Christians obeyed the edict. They said that since Christ
arose from the dead on Sunday it would be all right to observe that
as their holy day. Others were greatly distressed, because the Bible
clearly states that the seventh day is the Sabbath of the Lord.
Saturday is therefore the day on which God's people should rest
and worship, not Sunday.

If you had been a Christian in 321, what would you have done?
How would you have solved the problem?

77

CHARLEMAGNE

Pride goeth before destruction, and an haughty spirit before a fall. Proverbs 16:18.

"This horn belonged to my grandfather, Charles Martel," Charlemagne declared as he placed an ivory horn in the hands of Roland, the finest knight in his army.

Roland turned the ancient horn in his hands and caressed it reverently. "May I blow it?" he asked.

"If you can. No one since my grandfather has had the strength to make it sound."

Carefully Roland raised the horn to his lips, took a deep breath, and blew a blast so loud that the king covered his ears.

"The ivory horn is yours," Charlemagne said. "If ever you're in trouble, blow that horn and I'll come to your rescue."

During the years that followed, the ivory horn went with Roland into scores of battles, but not once did he blow it. He took great pride in the fact that he could fight his own battles without the aid of the king.

Then one day a great test came. Roland was in command of the rear guard as Charlemagne's troops crossed the Pyrenees Mountains. Suddenly 1,000 Saracens surrounded him and his 100 knights.

"Blow your horn!" his friend Oliver urged.

"No way!" proud Roland said. "I can handle this on my own!" At his word the 100 knights rode forward to attack, their swords flashing. Although they fought bravely, they were no match for the Saracens. When half his men had fallen, Roland reluctantly blew a long blast on the ivory horn.

The sound of the horn carried over the mountains to Charlemagne as he rode at the head of the army. He whirled on his horse and ordered his army back to the pass. He was too late. He found Roland among the slain, the ivory horn still in his hand.

How often you and I are like Roland, too proud to admit that we need assistance. We struggle in the battle with sin and lose, when we might have won with Christ's help. The ivory horn of prayer is in your hands. Use it before it's too late!

ALFRED THE GREAT

Behold, I stand at the door, and knock. Revelation 3:20.

A cold north wind whistled around the humble cottage of a cowherder in southwestern England. He put another log on the fire and shivered. His wife checked the pot of stew bubbling on the hearth. "What was that noise?" she asked.

"Only the wind banging the shutters."

"No, there it is again. Someone's knocking." Wiping her hands on her skirt, she hurried to the door and lifted the latch. In the doorway stood a ragged stranger. "Come in. You must be half frozen," she said.

"I'm one of King Alfred's men," the stranger explained as he warmed his hands over the open fire. "I'm on my way home after fighting the Danes, but I am too weak to continue. Could I rest here for a day or two?"

"Certainly," the cowherder replied. "Stay as long as you like."

The cowherder's wife frowned because she knew it would mean more work for her. Later, after several days of caring for the stranger, she had had enough. He looked well enough to leave but still he stayed on, sitting all day staring into the fire.

"If all you're going to do is sit by the fire, you might as well watch these oatcakes while I go outside and do some chores," she spoke impatiently. The stranger nodded and continued staring at the fire.

An hour later she came back to find the stranger still staring at the fire; the oatcakes were black as cinders. "What a good-for-nothing you are!" the cowherder's wife stormed. "You're glad enough to eat the cakes, but you can't trouble yourself for a minute to keep them from burning! Who do you think you are? The king himself?"

How do you think she felt when she learned that indeed it was the king whom she had treated so rudely? King Alfred of Wessex had sat by her fire that winter of 877 and she had treated him like a beggar.

There's a stranger knocking at your heart's door today. He wants to sit by your fire. Will you let Him in? Will you give Him the honor He deserves?

CANUTE

Before honour is humility. Proverbs 15:33.

King Canute rode along the seashore with several advisers. He explained to them some of the problems facing England. "I need your advice," the king said. "What shall we do?"

"You are the ruler of the land and sea," one courtier answered. "Do anything you wish. All power is yours."

"You say I rule the seas?" the king questioned.

"Yes, of course."

"Come with me," Canute said, dismounting. His advisers followed him to the edge of the ocean where the tide was just beginning to come in. "Halt!" he shouted at the breakers. "Don't come any farther!"

The waves broke over his feet as before. "Halt! I am your ruler. Come no farther." A great wave rolled in and swirled around the king's knees, spraying water into his face.

"Your majesty!" cried his men. "Step back! You will be drenched!"

The king paid no heed. "Halt, waves! Do as I say!"

His puzzled courtiers grabbed him before the next wave broke, leading him to higher ground. "Why did you do such a foolish thing?" they asked. "You could have drowned!"

"Can't you see the lesson I was trying to teach you?" King Canute said. "I wanted to show you plainly that there is a limit to my power. Now, when I ask for your advice I expect to have reasonable answers that recognize that fact. Let there be no more talk about Canute being all-powerful!"

Some of us are not so wise as King Canute. We all dream of being supermen, superwomen, or superkids. Sometimes we almost convince ourselves that we are! Just listen to kids brag on the playground about how strong they are, how fast they can run, or how much they know. Humility is not a characteristic of most teenagers, yet it must be learned by all those who would be truly great.

The next time you get that superman feeling, stop a moment and remember King Canute. Don't be afraid to ask for advice. Maybe, just maybe, there is something you could still learn.

WILLIAM THE CONQUEROR

I am he that liveth, and was dead; and, behold, I am alive for evermore. Revelation 1:18.

On the morning of October 14, 1066, William, duke of Normandy, led his army to the foot of Senlac Hill near Hastings, England. At the top of the rise he could see Harold's flag snapping in the breeze, inviting him to attack.

At a signal from William the trumpets blared and the Norman knights charged up the hill. At the top they faced a solid wall of shields.

"Stand firm and let the Normans exhaust themselves," Harold ordered.

Three times the Normans charged the shield wall and three times they were turned back by a rain of arrows, javelins, hand axes, spears, and stones. By late afternoon there was time for one last charge before the sun set. Just as they reached the wall of shields an English arrow killed William's horse and he fell with it to the ground.

"The duke is dead!" someone cried. "Flee every man to the ships!" For a moment all was chaos on Senlac Hill. The Normans were retreating and the English broke rank to pursue.

William snatched off his helmet so all could see his face. Mounting another horse, he cried out, "See! I am alive! Back to the fight! Victory is ours!"

The Normans rallied around their commander, and by nightfall victory was indeed theirs.

The battle on Senlac Hill makes me think of another battle on another hill a thousand years before. On the hill called Calvary a group of disheartened men watched their Leader fall. For a few short hours they thought all was lost. Oh, what joy when they learned He was alive! Victory was certain!

You and I face our own Senlac Hills now and then. The battle is fierce and the outcome scary. Satan's arrows fly fast and furiously in our direction. We're exhausted from the uphill fight. It might even seem sometimes that God is dead and our cause hopeless. It's then we need to look into the face of Jesus and hear Him shout: "See! It's Me! I am alive! Fight on! Victory is ours!"

81

MARGARET

Therefore I love thy commandments above gold; yea, above fine gold. Psalm 119:127.

"Heaven have mercy on my soul!" the servant cried. "The queen's book has fallen into the river!" He dropped to his knees at Queen Margaret's feet.

"Oh, my precious book! My Gospel! We must find it, for it is more precious to me than all the gold in Scotland! Boatman, turn around," the queen commanded. "We must find my book."

"It's no use," the boatman said. "Already the current would have taken it far from here."

"Then follow the current and search for the book," Margaret insisted. "It has to be somewhere. We must find it before it is ruined!"

But though they searched for hours, they found no trace of the precious book. It would be difficult to replace, for in those days all books had to be copied by hand.

"Forgive me, your majesty," the servant begged. "I didn't mean to lose it."

"I know," Queen Margaret sighed. "Don't feel bad. It couldn't be helped."

Several days later one of the queen's servants was walking beside the river when he saw the precious book lying on the riverbed; waves were turning its beautiful pages. Diving into the water, he brought the book safely to shore. Marvel of marvels, it was unharmed except for a few water stains.

If you ever visit Oxford, England, go to the great library and ask to see Queen Margaret's Gospel that took a swim. As you look at the book that meant so much to that long-ago queen, ask yourself if God's Word means as much to you.

Could it be that we value our Bibles less today because they are so easy to buy? What if you lost your Bible? Would it make any difference? Would you feel sad?

What is your most precious possession? Is it a Cabbage Patch doll or a GI Joe transformer? Might it be a dirt bike or a computer? What could you possibly have that is of more value than your Bible?

RICHARD THE LIONHEARTED

Thy speech betrayeth thee. Matthew 26:73.

In 1190, King Richard of England set out on a crusade to the Holy Land to free Jerusalem from Moslem rule. Two years later he sailed for home, his mission a failure. To make matters worse, his ship wrecked and he had no choice but to walk the rest of the way home, a distance of several hundred miles.

Worse still, he was in the land of his enemy, Leopold, duke of Austria. Disguising himself as a merchant, Richard set out with one knight and a page. All went well until they came to a town near Vienna, where Richard sent his page to buy bread.

When the boy paid for the bread with gold the baker became suspicious. "Who are you, boy?" he asked.

"I'm just a poor scullion boy."

"Likely story! Scullions don't pay in gold!"

The page bit his lip and stared at the ground. What could he say to get himself out of this predicament?

"And what is this?" the baker cried, grabbing a pair of King Richard's gloves that the page had stuck in his belt. "Only the great ones in this world wear gloves."

"Yes, sir," the page brightened. "My master is a merchant."

"Bah!" the baker spat in the dust. "These are jeweled gloves fit for a king. I'm taking you to the mayor. You're under arrest!"

The young boy was taken first to the mayor and then to King Leopold, who tortured him until he told where Richard was hiding. Leopold's soldiers surrounded the inn where Richard was staying and took him captive, holding him for a large ransom.

That day the young page learned it's almost impossible to hide one's true identity. Sooner or later the truth comes out. In the case of the page, he was betrayed by the gold coin and the jeweled gloves. In the case of Peter at the trial of Jesus, he was betrayed by his Galilean accent.

If you were arrested for being a Christian, what evidence would there be to convict you? Would it be your kind, courteous speech, your simple, becoming clothes, your unadorned, peaceful face, or would it be the books you read and the music to which you listen?

EDWARD III

Thou art my beloved Son, in whom I am well pleased. Mark 1:11.

On August 26, 1346, King Edward stood on a little hill near Crécy, France, watching his son hold the battle line against the forces of King Philip. Time after time the French rode forward, only to be sent back by the fierce rain of English arrows. Edward watched a group of enemy soldiers break through and begin a hand-to-hand battle. He nodded as a second English battalion moved in to help his son.

"Sire! Come to the rescue of the prince," a messenger cried. "All seems lost! They request you to come at once with your reserve battalion!"

"Is my son dead or fallen?" the king asked.

"No, sire," the messenger admitted. "But the battle is hard and he needs your help."

"This battle belongs to my son. Send no more for me as long as my son shall live. If God wills, this day my son shall win his spurs."

Encouraged, the prince of Wales fought until darkness came. The French fled; victory belonged to the English.

King Edward and his company came down the hill to join the celebration. He embraced the prince of Wales, saying, "You are my good son and you have acquitted yourself nobly. Truly you are worthy to hold a kingdom."

The prince knelt before his father exclaiming, "My father, the king, all glory for the battle belongs to you!"

Another King watched His Son do battle with an enemy. In the Garden of Gethsemane Prince Jesus staggered and almost fell. In agony He cried out for help as Satan marshaled all his demons for the final attack on the Son of God.

Can you imagine Gabriel saying to the Father, "He needs You! Why don't You go to His rescue?"

"No," the King replies. "This battle belongs to My Son. Today He will win His kingdom."

Encouraged by Gabriel's message, Jesus faced Calvary. When darkness came that Friday night all heaven rejoiced. Satan was defeated; victory had been achieved.

PHILIPPA

Blessed are the merciful: for they shall obtain mercy. Matthew 5:7.

A few days after the battle of Crécy, King Edward led his army to the gates of Calais. He decided to starve its people into surrender. The siege lasted a year before the food supply ran out and the people were forced to eat dogs and rats.

At last the governor of Calais put up the white flag of surrender and sent a message requesting King Edward to take the town but to let the people go free.

"No!" thundered the angry king. "They have kept us waiting for a year. Every man, woman, and child shall die."

"How can you do such a cruel deed?" Sir Walter Manny, one of the bravest knights, questioned.

"Then let them send six of their chief townsmen, barefooted and bareheaded, with ropes around their necks. Let them bring the keys of Calais. I will kill them and let the rest go free."

"It is better for six to die than everyone," Eustace, the richest merchant in town said. "I will gladly go." Five others quickly joined him.

"Hang them!" King Edward ordered as the trembling men knelt before him. "Let the stubborn townsfolk see!"

"Wait!" Queen Philippa cried. "If you love me, grant this one wish. Be merciful to these six men of Calais!"

"I wish, good lady, you were somewhere else," the king said. "But for the love I have for you, I cannot refuse. Take the men and do as you please."

Queen Philippa led them to her tents, where she dressed them in new clothes, fed them, and sent them with gifts of food for the hungry people of Calais. And that day there was great joy and rejoicing, both in the city of Calais and in the camp of King Edward because of the mercy shown by the queen.

Sometimes people bring trouble onto themselves, but even then the merciful don't rub it in. They are like Queen Philippa, looking for ways to be kind to everyone. If you can find a chance to be merciful today, do it. You'll be surprised at how good it makes you feel.

ROBERT BRUCE

We are fools for Christ's sake. 1 Corinthians 4:10.

Hot, sweaty, and exhausted, Robert Bruce leaned against a tree at the river's edge to catch his breath. He heard the yelp of a bloodhound hot upon his trail. "Into the river!" he ordered his companion. "That's our only hope."

The two men jumped into the chilly waters and waded several yards downstream before climbing up on the other side.

That night in a skirmish with thieves his companion was killed. At dusk the following evening he came to a farmhouse at the edge of the forest. His knock was answered by an old woman who lived alone. "Who are you?" she asked.

"I am a lone traveler journeying through the country," the king replied. "I need a meal and a place to sleep."

"All travelers are welcome here, for the sake of one," the woman answered, opening the door wide.

"And who is that one for whose sake you make all travelers welcome?" Robert asked.

"It is for the rightful king of Scotland, Robert Bruce," she answered. "Now he is pursued with hounds and horns, but I hope to live to see the day he is king over all Scotland."

"Robert Bruce stands before you," the king said.

"Bless my soul!" the woman cried. "I will cherish this day as long as I live. Sit down, and I will fix your supper."

I wonder how many other travelers ate at the old woman's table because of Robert Bruce. She was kind to all and fed them willingly for the sake of her beloved king. Many a weary man had a cheery meal and a good night's rest because she wanted to be sure she didn't turn the king away should he come by her house. Others may have thought her foolish, but it didn't matter. She would do anything for the sake of her king.

What are you willing to do for the sake of your King, Jesus Christ? Will you share your lunch today for His sake? Will you befriend the new kid at school for His sake? For His sake will you do what is right? Are you willing to be called a fool for His sake?

86

HENRY V

And for an helmet, the hope of salvation. 1 Thessalonians 5:8.

The Battle of Agincourt in 1415 did not look good for the king of England. Most of Henry's soldiers were weak from wounds and sickness. He no longer had an army big enough to fight battles. Nevertheless, he marched on to Calais, determined to take at least one French city.

The French fled before the miserable army, burning or hiding all the food in their path. As a result, Henry's men were not only sick but hungry. They subsisted somehow on berries and walnuts that they gathered as they marched. Then rain began to fall heavily. The next day they would have to fight in mud.

They could go no farther in the darkness and rain; Henry knew they must either fight or surrender. Henry decided to fight, even though they were outnumbered more than three to one.

"Let every archer cut a six-foot stake from the woods, and sharpen both ends," Henry ordered. "Place one end in the mud. Slant the other toward the advancing army so that the point reaches the height of a horse's chest."

The next morning the archers took off their shoes so that they could get a good grip with their toes in the mud. They arranged themselves behind the pointed stakes and waited for the French to attack. The battle was fierce, but the English stakes did their work. The Frenchmen had to jump off their horses for hand-to-hand combat.

"King Henry is hit!" the cry went up. A French ax had crashed against his helmet, knocking him to the ground. In a moment he was up fighting again. When the French had retreated, everyone gathered around to see the dent in King Henry's helmet.

"This helmet saved my life!" King Henry said.

And a helmet can save your life just as surely as that one did King Henry's. Satan is ever ready to take a swing at you with his ax of doubt or his sword of temptation. Without your helmet you could lose your head and heaven, too. So in the rush to get going in the morning, don't leave without your helmet. In the thick of the battle you'll be glad you took the time to put on the helmet of salvation.

87

ISABELLA OF SPAIN

With God all things are possible. Matthew 19:26.

The setting sun cast long shadows as two weary travelers, a man and a little boy, approached the monastery. Seeing a monk walking in the garden, the small boy ran ahead. "Please, sir, may I have a drink?" the little boy asked. "My father and I have walked far, and we are tired and thirsty."

"Of course, my son," the old monk replied. "Who are you?"

"My name is Diego," the boy replied. "My father's name is Columbus. We are looking for ships to sail to India."

"This does sound interesting," the monk said, smiling at the eager child. "Call your father. Tonight you will stay with me, and I shall learn all about your great adventure!"

So it was that Columbus shared with the monk his dreams of reaching India by sailing west into the Sea of Darkness. "I tried to convince the queen of Spain, but it is impossible," Columbus said sadly. "I don't know where to turn next."

"Nothing is impossible with God," the monk replied. "I'm a friend of Queen Isabella. I'll write, urging her to listen to your proposal. Meanwhile, you will stay here at the monastery."

A few days later the queen wrote to the monk. "I am interested in what you have to say in this matter." He left at once to share with her his dream of sending missionaries with Columbus to make the Indians Christians. She agreed, and the monk wrote at once to Columbus:

"Our Lord has heard His servants' prayers. My heart swims in a sea of comfort, and my spirit leaps for joy. Start quickly, for the queen awaits you, and I yet more than she. Commend me to the prayers of my brethren and of the little Diego. The grace of God be with you."

This time Queen Isabella received Columbus with sympathy.

"What did I tell you?" the monk told Columbus when they were alone. "With God all things are indeed possible."

Are you praying for something? Don't give up. "With God all things are possible." If He sees it is best for you, it shall happen.

ELIZABETH I

But whoso looketh into the perfect law of liberty . . . shall be blessed. James 1:25.

There had been a shower, and the trees and grass around Greenwich Palace glistened in the sun. The large double doors of the palace opened, and Elizabeth I, queen of England, stepped into the sunshine. She was richly dressed in heavy silk brocade, with a collar of costly lace that stood up from her shoulders like an open fan behind her slender neck. Her light auburn hair was piled high on her head like a crown.

The earl of Leicester, Walter Raleigh, and others of her court followed the queen in a grand promenade through the park. When she came to a place in the path where the summer shower had left a shallow pool of water, she hesitated.

"Wait, your majesty," Walter Raleigh said as he took off his plush cloak and threw it on the ground before her. Taking her dainty hand in his own, he offered, "Let me help you across."

The middle-aged queen looked gratefully into the eyes of the handsome young man; he stood six feet tall and had curly brown hair and beard. She appreciated anyone who made her feel young and beautiful. For his courtesy that summer day, Raleigh received a gift of several suits. Queen Elizabeth also made him a knight, with the title "sir" before his name.

As Queen Elizabeth grew older she tried hard to hide the marks of her age. She wore elaborate wigs, huge ruffs, and lavishly jeweled costumes to draw attention away from the wrinkles on her face. At last she banned all mirrors from her palaces, for they, unlike the young men in her court, told the truth about her looks.

Do you know that some people refuse to read God's Word for the same reason? It tells the truth about them. The law of God, like a mirror, shows them exactly how they look. It reveals their sins and ugliness. So what do they do? They get rid of the mirror; they try to do away with God's law. Does that change anything? Of course not!

The next time you look in God's Word and it reflects something that is ugly in yourself, don't get rid of the mirror. Let God make you beautiful instead.

WILLIAM THE SILENT

Behold, the Lord's hand is not shortened, that it cannot save.
Isaiah 59:1.

"I know that the Protestant faith cannot be stamped out by any man," William, prince of Orange, told his mother, Juliana. He had come to Dillenburg, Germany, to flee Spanish persecution in the Netherlands.

"I plan to raise an army to make war against the Spanish," William declared. "I'll sell my jewels to finance it."

"Adolphus, Henry, and I will go with you," his brother Louis promised.

However, when they set out, many of the soldiers abandoned William, and Adolphus was killed in battle. William, left with a handful of men, retreated to the northern provinces of Holland. There he could hide among the canals and islands.

"Why don't you make an alliance with a foreign power?" one of his soldiers asked.

"My only alliance is with God," William replied. "I am firmly convinced that all who put their trust in Him shall be saved by His almighty hand."

In spite of his trust, things seemed to go from bad to worse. His remaining two brothers were killed, and the Spaniards laid siege to Leydon. William was helpless to free the city. His soldiers were gone, and he was sick with fever.

After two months, people began to die of hunger. Then William thought of a plan. With the help of some fishermen he cut the dikes and let the ocean flood the countryside. The dismayed Spaniards fled, allowing William and his fishermen to rescue the starving people of Leydon. Almost singlehandedly William had brought liberty to the Netherlands.

It's amazing what one man can do when he puts his trust in the Lord. There is no limit to what God could do through you if you gave Him permission. He can do mighty things today just as He did 300 years ago for William the Silent. What are your needs? Why not give God a chance?

IVAN THE TERRIBLE

If we confess our sins, he is faithful and just to forgive us our sins, and to cleanse us from all unrighteousness. 1 John 1:9.

"Your request to join our religious order is most unusual," the old hermit said as he shook his head. "Are you sure this is what you want to do? Life here will be very hard compared to the luxury of your palace. We could allow no exceptions to our strict rules of poverty and silence. You would have no contact with your family and others of the outside world."

"That's exactly what I want," Ivan said. "I am not worthy to rule Russia. My sins are greater than I can bear. Perhaps here I shall find solace for my tormented conscience."

"Indeed?" the hermit raised his eyebrows and waited.

"Surely you have heard how I ordered all the inhabitants of the city of Novgorod killed?"

"Yes," the old man nodded. "Go on."

"I have treated everyone with the utmost cruelty, even ordering the death of a high church official in Moscow. He did not deserve to die."

"I have heard. Is there anything else?"

Ivan was sobbing now, deep soul-wrenching sobs that shook his huge frame. "I—I struck my own son in a fit of rage, and he died. Oh, I am of all men most miserable. I have sought peace and forgiveness everywhere but have not found it. Has God forsaken me? Is there any hope?"

If you had been the old hermit talking to Ivan the Terrible that day in March, 1584, at the monastery in Russia, what would you have said?

Had God forsaken Ivan the Terrible? Had he done anything too awful for God to forgive? Can God forgive a man who would kill his own son? Is there any hope for people so mean and cruel as Ivan the Terrible? Think of the thief on the cross. Remember King David. Read his prayer in Psalm 51.

Now, think about yourself. Think back over your past life. Try to remember the worst thing you ever did. Did you lie, steal, hit someone, take drugs, or commit an immoral act? Is God willing to forgive you? 1 John 1:9 has the answer.

LOUIS XIV

In my Father's house are many mansions. John 14:2.

Can you imagine building a house worth more than $200 million? That's how much Louis XIV, king of France, spent in building his palace at Versailles, 12 miles out of Paris. The building is half a mile long and has hundreds of rooms decorated in the most ornate and lavish style. The palace is located in a royal park of 15,000 acres in a setting of lawns, ornamental lakes, flower gardens, and woodlands. It would take several days to see it all.

Thousands of servants looked after the palace and waited on King Louis and his family. In the evening, 10,000 candles were lit for dinner, which was attended by hundreds of people dressed in velvet, silk, gold, and precious jewels. On one occasion the king himself wore $50,000 worth of jewelry, as well as a black suit embroidered in gold.

Getting King Louis dressed in the morning was quite a ceremony. One servant pulled off the right sleeve of his nightshirt while another pulled off the left sleeve. One servant stood ready with the royal shirt while another held the royal pants. One servant put on the king's right shoe and fastened the buckle while another cared for the left.

From that day to this no one has equaled the pomp and ceremony, the glitter and extravagance, of Louis XIV. As beautiful as the palace of Versailles still is, it is nothing compared to the golden city, New Jerusalem, where our God dwells. The magnificence of the king's bedchamber will appear shabby beside the mansions Jesus has prepared for us. A banquet held in Versailles' hall of mirrors pales when compared to the heavenly banquet that Jesus is planning for us. The table will stretch for miles, as far as the eye can see.

The walls and foundations of Versailles, fashioned of stone and cement, are impressive. But just imagine the sight of a city's walls made of sparkling jasper, topaz, sapphires, and emeralds. Imagine gates of solid pearl opening onto streets of pure, transparent gold.

Picture yourself walking down those streets! All of that and more, Jesus is preparing for you!

MARIA THERESA

She looketh well to the ways of her household, and eateth not the bread of idleness. Proverbs 31:27.

When she was 23 years old, Maria Theresa's "household" included Austria, Hungary, Bohemia, and parts of Italy. When she died 40 years later she was called the most beneficent sovereign who ever wore a crown. To this day her memory is revered in the lands that she governed. Why? What made her so loved?

First, she really cared about her people. She built hospitals for sick and wounded soldiers and homes for army officers' widows and young women of poor families. She established a court system and public schools.

Like a true mother of her people, Maria Theresa was always ready to sacrifice herself for their good. She was never idle; indeed she regretted having to sleep. "I reproach myself," she once remarked, "that I have to spend time in sleep, for it is time robbed from my people."

On the night before she died, the queen busily signed papers and gave instructions to her son, Joseph. "Mother, you must be tired," Joseph said. "Why don't you get some sleep?"

"In a few hours I shall be gone," she replied. "Would you have me spend them in sleep?"

Another quality this wise woman had was fairness. It seemed to her that the nobles and clergymen, as well as the common people, ought to pay taxes. In fact, they were probably more able to do so.

Perhaps the quality that endeared her to her people more than any other was her trust in them. At one time she appeared before the Hungarian Assembly to ask for their help in war to save her kingdom from ruin. "I am helpless without you," she said. Then holding up her infant son she continued, "I commit myself and my children into your hands!"

The Hungarians responded with 100,000 soldiers. "We will die for our Queen Maria Theresa!" they shouted.

Believe it or not, trust, fairness, industry, and caring are in demand just as much today as they were 250 years ago in the kingdom of Maria Theresa.

MARIE ANTOINETTE

For we shall all stand before the judgment seat of Christ.
Romans 14:10.

A frail woman in a tattered black dress stood before the judges on October 14, 1793, and listened to 41 witnesses testify that she was an enemy of the French people.

"She feasted in the palace of Versailles while we starved," one declared.

"She lived in luxury, bankrupting the national treasury," another said.

Marie Antoinette endured the accusations for 20 hours. At last she heard the judge sentence her to die on the guillotine two days later. It didn't matter that most of the accusations were false. She knew that many of the men were hired to say what the people wanted to hear.

Death would be welcome after her long imprisonment. The last two months in the damp, cold dungeon had taken away all desire for life. The floor was covered with mud. A small pine table and a single chair were the only pieces of furniture. She slept on a bundle of filthy straw covered by a ragged blanket.

After the judge read her sentence, Marie Antoinette lifted her head proudly and answered: "I was a queen, and you took away my crown; a wife, and you killed my husband; a mother, and you deprived me of my children. My blood alone remains. Take it, but do not make me suffer long."

The next morning the one-time queen of France, clad in a white robe, climbed into an open one-horse cart and was driven through the streets of Paris. The crowds yelled and mocked her as 30,000 troops guarded her route.

At the scaffold she knelt for a moment to pray. Then the blade fell, and life for Marie Antoinette was over.

Sooner or later we must all stand before the judgment seat of Christ and face the record of our lives. We will all stand condemned, for all of us have sinned and come short of the glory of God. We all face the guillotine of eternal death.

But, praise the Lord, the blade need not fall! Jesus died that we might go free. He took our punishment! Eternal life is ours!

PETER THE GREAT

Be not unequally yoked together with unbelievers. 2 Corinthians 6:14.

Does it make any difference what kind of friends you have? Ask Peter, Czar of Russia from 1682 to 1725.

As a teenager, Peter spent his spare time with friends in the foreign quarter of Moscow. His best friends were Patrick Gordon, a wild Scot, and Francis Lefort, a wealthy Swiss exile. From them he learned of life in the West.

"I will make my country as strong and as modern as England, France, and Germany," Peter boasted when he became czar. "I want Russia to be like the powerful lands my friends have seen. I must go myself to see what makes them so strong."

For two years Peter visited Europe, learning Western dress and customs, Western architecture, shipbuilding, and science. He visited schools, museums, shipyards, and factories.

In the few years that Peter was czar, he turned Russia into a modern power. He built an army, a navy, factories, and a new capital. He founded schools, hospitals, museums, and a newspaper. He introduced a new kind of coin, and changed the alphabet and the calendar to make them more like the West. However, in his haste to transform Russia into a leading world power, he brutally suppressed all those who opposed him, and turned many against the government.

The teenage friends of Peter probably never knew how far-reaching was their influence. What a different ruler he might have been had he made friends of the Russian nobles.

Choose well your friends, for it is one of the facts of life that we become like those with whom we associate. Spend time with thieves and you will likely steal. Spend time with scholars and you will no doubt like books. Spend time with those who hate God and you will probably hate Him too. Spend time with those who swear and you will soon do the same.

Who are your friends? As someone so wisely said: "Show me your friends, and I will know your character."

NAPOLEON BONAPARTE

Two are better than one; because they have a good reward for their labour. Ecclesiastes 4:9.

"If you will do as I say, I will make those big country boys stop throwing stones at us," 8-year-old Napoleon promised. For some time there had been a feud between the town boys and the shepherd boys from the hills.

"OK," his friends agreed. "Tell us what to do and we will do it."

Napoleon led the boys to a place on the hillside where a large outcropping made a natural fortress. "Now gather stones and pile them in a row behind these rocks," Napoleon ordered.

When the boys had a good pile of stones lined up, Napoleon led the group up the hill to where the shepherd boys watched their sheep.

"Go away! Leave us alone!" the big boys taunted, pelting them with rocks. At this, Napoleon turned and ran down the hill, followed by his company. The shepherd boys gave chase just as Napoleon expected. When he reached the rock fortress, he shouted, "Halt!"

His "soldiers" obeyed.

"Stones!"

Each boy gathered up as many as he could hold.

"About-face! Fire!"

The astonished shepherd boys were met with a shower of rocks. The bigger boys scattered in all directions, surprised by the organized attack of the younger ones. That was the last time Napoleon and his friends had any trouble from the big country boys.

That day on the island of Corsica, Napoleon learned a valuable lesson that would serve him in good stead as a general in the years to come. A group, fighting together, can do much more than each man fighting alone. There is strength in unity.

Do you suppose that is why Jesus told His disciples to gather together in one place to wait for the Holy Spirit? As they united in prayer, they did have greater power than they would have had alone. Could this be the reason why we join together in churches today?

JOSEPHINE

Judge not, that ye be not judged. Matthew 7:1.

"Wait here," Josephine said to her fiancé, Napoleon Bonaparte, as they arrived at the office of her lawyer, Monsieur Raguideau. As the door accidentally was left ajar, Napoleon was able to hear all that was said.

"I plan to marry General Bonaparte," Josephine told her adviser. "I wanted you to be the first to know."

"My dear lady," he exclaimed, "think carefully before you take such a step. If you are rash enough to persist in this preposterous marriage, you will repent your folly all the days of your life. Who ever heard of a rational woman throwing herself away upon a man whose whole fortune consists of his sword and uniform?"

Although Napoleon was angered at the advice, he determined to say nothing. A month later Napoleon and Josephine were married. Eight years later the French Senate declared Napoleon emperor of France.

On the day of the coronation ceremony Napoleon remembered the comments of Monsieur Raguideau and sent for the lawyer to come at once to the palace. He arrived to find Josephine and Napoleon already dressed in their coronation robes.

"Ah, Monsieur Raguideau, I am most happy to see you," Napoleon said. "Do you remember the day in 1796 when I accompanied Josephine to your office? Do you remember the unfavorable advice you gave her? What do you have to say now?"

"Sire, did you really overhear?" the lawyer stammered as he felt his face grow hot with shame.

"Every word. And I have not forgotten!"

The lawyer turned pale. He could not imagine what awful thing would come next.

"I condemn you this day to go to Notre Dame and to witness my coronation ceremony in the seat I have reserved for you! After this, perhaps you will be a little less hasty to give judgment!"

"Indeed, sire!" Monsieur breathed a sigh of relief and hastened to take his place for the ceremony. You can be sure he thought twice before judging another's character again!

97

VICTORIA

But grow in grace, and in the knowledge of our Lord and Saviour Jesus Christ. 2 Peter 3:18.

"What is it, dear Lehzen?" 12-year-old Princess Victoria asked. "Open your history book," her teacher replied.

"I never saw this page before." Victoria studied her family tree carefully. When King George IV would die, Uncle William would be king. After Uncle William would be Victoria. Overwhelmed at the thought of being a queen, she burst into tears. Then, drying her eyes, she said, "I'll be good!"

Indeed, during the next few years the princess had no chance to be bad, for someone was with her at all times. She slept with her mother at night and was not allowed to even walk down the hall alone during the day.

Shortly before sunrise on the morning of June 20, 1837, two important men came to Kensington Palace to see Victoria. Bowing before the 18-year-old princess, they said, "Your uncle died a few hours ago. You are now queen of England."

As soon as they were gone she asked her mother, "Am I really the queen now?"

"Yes, my child."

"And may I have any wish of mine granted?"

"Yes, of course."

"Then, Mama, I should like to be alone for an hour!" For the first time in Victoria's 18 years she had the luxury of being alone. That night she requested a room of her own, and her mother had to move out.

It was quite a normal thing that young Queen Victoria wanted. What teenager doesn't want to be alone sometimes, to do one's own thing and think one's own thoughts? The teenage years are meant for testing your wings and finding out how to handle life on your own. It's a natural part of becoming an adult.

God meant that we should grow up spiritually, too. We cannot always stay children, depending on Mom and Dad for our Christian experience. We need to try our wings in prayer and meditation. Learning to approach God alone is part of growing up into Jesus Christ.

WILHELMINA

The trumpet shall sound, and the dead shall be raised.
1 Corinthians 15:52.

"Come, Wilhelmina," Queen Emma called. "It's time for your hour with Father."

"I picked these flowers from my garden," 7-year-old Wilhelmina said. "Do you think he'll like them?"

"I'm sure he will." Her mother smiled as she spoke.

Wilhelmina, dressed in her best, walked eagerly down the great staircase and across the drawing room to her father's study. Pushing open the heavy wooden door, she ran to her 70-year-old father and kissed his cheek. "I picked these for you myself," she said, laying the flowers on the desk.

"Thank you, my dear, they're lovely," King William of the Netherlands said. "Now, what would my little girl like to play today? Will it be dominoes or the bathtub?"

"The bathtub!" Wilhelmina's eyes sparkled. Father's new zinc bathtub was a wonderful toy. She had only to turn on a faucet and water came gushing out, ready for sailing paper boats.

One day the good times were over, for King William was dead. Wilhelmina had to stand beside her mother as a multitude of visitors, dressed in black, came to extend their sympathy to her, the 10-year-old new queen. The funeral with its mournful music and somber colors was depressing. By the time it was over, she had to go to bed with a stomachache.

Years later, when her husband, Hendrik, died, she refused to wear black. "Hendrik and I agreed to have white funerals," she explained. "I do not believe that death is the end. To me, white is the symbol of eternal life."

Death can be a pretty scary experience, especially to a child. It's awful to stand beside the graves of those you love and know they won't be there anymore when you need them. But somehow it makes things easier when you realize that for them the sleep of death will be just for a moment, a twinkling of an eye. The next sound they hear will be the trumpet, calling them to wake up. What a bright, happy, glorious day that will be! Dear Jesus, help it to be soon!

JOHANN SEBASTIAN BACH

I delight to do thy will, O my God: yea, thy law is within my heart. Psalm 40:8.

The house of Christoph Bach in Ohrdruf, Germany, was cold and silent a certain night in 1685. Ten-year-old Sebastian lay awake thinking of happier days before Mama and Papa died. His 24-year-old brother just didn't understand how much music meant to him. Why did Christoph insist he must play such simple pieces? They were so boring! He wanted to play music from the great masters that his brother kept locked in the high cupboard.

Sebastian threw back the covers and crept to the top of the stairs. Carefully he felt his way down the steps to the cupboard. Climbing on a chair, he squeezed his hand between the metal bars. He rolled the book tightly and eased it through the small opening.

Sebastian clutched the book to his chest as he tiptoed to his room. Laying the music on the window ledge, where moonlight streamed across its pages, the excited boy began to copy the notes. Working a little every night, then returning the book to the cupboard, Sebastian finished copying the book in six months.

The next day he waited until his brother had gone to church before sitting down at the clavier to play. On the third day of his secret practice, Christoph strode into the room.

"What's the meaning of this?" he stormed. "So you took the book and copied the music! Give it to me."

"No! You can't have my music!" Sebastian cried covering the copy book with his hands. His brother snatched the book and left.

The next day Sebastian sat on the clavier bench and looked at the empty music rack. He closed his eyes and tried to remember how the melodies went. His fingers found their places and began to play. A grin spread across his face. There was no need to be sad now. The melodies he had copied were safely locked in his mind where no one could take them away from him.

What would you do if someone took away your Bible? Would you be sad? Or would you be happy because of all the verses you had memorized? When God's Word is safely locked in your heart no one can take it away from you, ever.

GEORGE FRIDERIC HANDEL

Neglect not the gift that is in thee. 1 Timothy 4:14.

"No son of mine is going to be a good-for-nothing musician!" Dr. Handel declared. "You will be a lawyer."

"Yes, sir!" obedient George replied, but in his heart he yearned to play the organ.

When George was 8 years old his father took him to the court of the Duke of Saxe-Weissenfels, near Halle, Germany. While his father tended the ailments of the palace servants, George found his way to the chapel.

"Oh, ho! What have we here?" the organist smiled at the earnest face of the young boy who watched his every movement.

"I'm George Handel. I hope I'm not bothering you, sir. Someday I want to play the organ."

"Would you like to play it now?" the old man offered.

Half standing and half sitting, the 8-year-old delightedly explored the rows of keys. Pulling out first one stop and then another, he reproduced music he had heard in his church back home.

"You are marvelous!" the organist said.

When the duke saw the small lad at the huge pipe organ he was really impressed. "Whose boy is that?" he inquired.

"Handel's son, sir."

"Send Handel to me at once." When the doctor arrived the duke asked, "With whom has your son studied music?"

"No one, my lord."

"Remarkable!" exclaimed the duke. "You must place him under the best teacher in Halle. Will you promise?"

"Yes, my lord," Handel bowed. So George got a music teacher. By the time he was 17 he was assistant organist at the Halle cathedral. Because George did not neglect his gift, we have such beautiful music as *The Messiah.*

What is your gift? Is it singing, drawing, writing, talking, or playing the piano? Maybe you are really good at sports or arithmetic. You might have the gift of being friendly or of getting others to work with you on a team. Whatever your gifts and abilities, don't hide them. Use them to bless others as Handel did.

FRANZ JOSEPH HAYDN

Him that cometh to me I will in no wise cast out. John 6:37.

"One and two and three and . . ." Herr Reutter's baton kept time for St. Stephen's Boys' Choir one November day in 1749.

Seventeen-year-old Joseph Haydn fingered the scissors in his coat pocket. They were new, and he longed for the singing to stop so he could try them out. He opened and closed them to the rhythm of the choir master's baton.

His eyes fastened on the pigtail of the boy in front of him. A mischievous gleam sparkled in Joseph's eyes. Out came the scissors. One snip and the pigtail fell to the floor! The singing stopped, and all eyes stared at the severed pigtail.

Herr Reutter's eyes glared over his wire-rimmed spectacles at Joseph. His voice exploded like thunder. "Joseph Haydn, did you cut off that pigtail?"

"Yes, sir. I'm very sorry, sir."

"I've had all I can take from you, young man. You shall be caned and dismissed from the choir."

In a matter of minutes Joseph found himself alone, penniless, and hungry in the streets of Vienna. Like a gypsy, he wandered until he was chilled to the bone. Exhausted, he huddled under a streetlight and wondered what to do.

It was there his friend Spangler found him. "What are you doing here at this time of night?" he asked.

"I got kicked out of the choir," Joseph explained, telling the whole story of his disgrace. "I'm looking for a place to stay."

"It doesn't matter what you've done; you are still my friend," Spangler said. "You will stay with me as long as you like." Soon Joseph was eating steaming bowls of bread and milk beside Spangler's fireplace.

Some people think that God is like Herr Reutter, harshly punishing us when we do wrong, sending us out into the cold world to suffer the consequences of our sin. But God is really more like Spangler, a friend who comes to us in our misery and invites us home to His house, surrounding us with the warmth of His love.

WOLFGANG AMADEUS MOZART

Be ye kind one to another. Ephesians 4:32.

King Francis I and Queen Maria Theresa of Austria sat on high-backed chairs for three hours and listened to 6-year-old Wolfgang Mozart play first on the violin and then on the clavier.

"Bravo! Bravo!" the king cried. "You are a little magician."

"Amazing!" the queen said. "I can't believe anyone so young can play so beautifully."

Glad that the performance was over, Wolfgang ran to the queen, sprang into her lap, and kissed her.

"You did a good job!" the queen returned his hug. "Now run along and play with my daughters, Elizabeth and Marie Antoinette. They've lots of toys."

Wolfgang slid off the queen's lap and ran toward the two little princesses. Half way across the polished floor he tripped over the sword that was part of his court costume and fell flat on his face. He burst into tears as he heard all the people laughing.

"That's quite an exit, Mr. Mozart," Elizabeth said, joining in the fun at Wolfgang's expense.

Only 7-year-old Marie Antoinette refused to laugh. She helped Wolfgang up, then wiped away his tears. "Did you hurt yourself?" she asked kindly.

"You're nice," Wolfgang said with a smile. "When I get big I'm going to marry you."

"Why would you like to do that?" the queen asked.

"Because she was kind and helped me while her sister did nothing."

Wolfgang Mozart may have been a child prodigy, a genius who could write a concerto at the age of 5 and a symphony at the age of 7, but he was very much human. He felt hurt when others laughed at him, just as you would feel hurt. No matter who we are, we all appreciate it when someone is kind and caring.

If you see someone hurt or embarrassed today, I hope you will be as kind as Marie Antoinette was to Mozart. Don't laugh. Go to that person and do what you can to make him or her feel better.

LUDWIG VAN BEETHOVEN

Why art thou cast down, O my soul? . . . hope thou in God: for I shall yet praise him. Psalm 42:11.

It was a beautiful summer day in the Austrian Alps. Thirty-one-year-old Ludwig van Beethoven rambled through the countryside with his pupil, Fritz Ries.

"This, my lad, is the source of my music," Ludwig said, throwing out his arms to encompass forest and stream, mountain and sky.

"Is the shepherd boy also one of your sources?" Fritz asked. "It's a happy little tune he's playing."

"H'mmm? What did you say?"

"The tune the shepherd is playing on his pipe," Fritz spoke a little louder. "It's such a bright, lilting tune. It makes me want to dance. Don't you hear it?"

"A shepherd's pipe? Where?"

"There, to your left."

Not 30 feet away a shepherd lad sat on a rock, pipe in his mouth, his body swaying in time to the song. Ludwig stopped for a moment, straining to hear the music. He heard nothing but silence.

Oh, no! Ludwig thought. *I'm going deaf! How will I ever play music if I can't hear the sounds?*

Doctors gave him pills and potions, but nothing helped. He retreated into a life of solitude for a time, refusing to meet people or to perform. He wandered the hills and wanted to die. Life seemed hopeless.

Then one day he decided, "I will not let my infirmity get me down. I may not be able to hear music with my ears, but I can still hear it with my mind. This ugly thing that has happened to me will be transformed into beauty in my soul. I can still write music for the glory of God." He went back to work and produced much of the music for which he is now famous.

When something bad happens to you, don't let it get you down. Like Beethoven, you can transform your tragedy into beauty. You don't have to be discouraged. Your heart can still sing. You can still praise the Lord.

FRANZ SCHUBERT

Whoso mocketh the poor reproacheth his Maker. Proverbs 17:5.

Eleven-year-old Franz Schubert couldn't sleep the night before the choir school examinations. He was out of bed at the first streak of dawn, searching for something to wear. How he wished he had a new suit, but the meager salary of his schoolmaster father wouldn't stretch to cover such a luxury. The fourteenth child, he would have to make do with hand-me-downs.

"You look fine!" Frau Schubert beamed as she set a bowl of steaming mush before him. "I hope you do well!"

"Of course he'll do well," Herr Schubert declared. "Doesn't he know all of his scales?"

"And his voice is like that of an angel," his wife added.

Franz blushed at their praise, but he knew he was good. Even Herr Holzer, his music teacher, had said so. Warmed by the porridge and his parents' pride, Franz set off for the auditions, feeling good about his prospects.

His happiness was short-lived, for he was met by ridicule. Boys gathered in groups and pointed at his ill-fitting clothes.

"He looks dumb in that miller's suit," a fat boy sneered.

Franz hung his head in shame and bit his lip. He couldn't help what he wore. It was the best he had.

Seeing his discomfort, others joined in the cruel sport.

"Where'd you find that outfit?"

"From the charity box?"

"Or the rag man?"

Franz was relieved when the examinations began. In spite of his hurt, he sang the scales perfectly and sight-read without flaw the music presented to him. Imagine how his tormentors felt when Franz was the only one chosen to enter the choir training school.

Underneath the homespun clothes was a boy of exceptional talent and deep feelings. Before he died at the age of 31, Franz Schubert wrote more than 600 musical compositions.

Boys and girls haven't changed much in the past 200 years. There are still those who like to poke fun at poor kids. I hope you're not one of them.

FELIX MENDELSSOHN

It is accepted according to that a man hath, and not according to that he hath not. 2 Corinthians 8:12.

After a successful concert tour in England and Scotland, Felix Mendelssohn spent a number of days at the home of his friend, John Taylor, in Wales. One summer evening the whole family was in the woods helping to make a playhouse out of fir branches for one of the children.

At twilight someone suggested a bonfire. The group sat around the roaring blaze, laughing and telling stories until only the glowing embers remained.

"What we need now is some music," Mendelssohn said. "Could anyone get something to play?"

"We're near the gardener's cottage," one of the Taylor boys replied. "I think he has a fiddle."

"Off, then, and fetch it," Papa Taylor ordered.

Shortly they were back with the most wretched fiddle imaginable. It was battered and scarred, with only one string. When one of the boys tried to play it, everyone collapsed into fits of laughter over the weird, screechy sounds it made.

"No one can make music with such a fiddle," Mr. Taylor said when their sides were sore from laughing. "Take it back."

"No! Not yet!" Mendelssohn said, taking a deep breath to control his mirth. "Let me see what I can do with it."

Within minutes the most beautiful music imaginable was coming out of that miserable, beat-up fiddle with one string.

Is someone you know like that poor old fiddle? Maybe he has made a mess of his life with drugs or alcohol. There really doesn't seem much hope. But wait! Give the Master a chance to touch his life, and oh, what a difference it will make.

Are there people you know going through life with only one string? Maybe they don't have all the advantages you have. Maybe they don't have your mental capacity or abilities. They may seem worthless to you. But wait! You might be surprised at the music the Master can make with only one string!

FRÉDÉRIC CHOPIN

Walk in wisdom . . . , redeeming the time. Colossians 4:5.

What is time? Is it the striking of a clock or the numbers on a calendar? No, it is a talent lent to us by God. We are told that of no talent that God has given will He require a more strict account than of our time.

As we think of great men and women of the past, it is shocking to realize that actually they had no more time than we. Each of us is given 24 hours each day. It is how we invest this precious talent that makes the difference.

Paul says we need to redeem the time; but minutes wasted can never be recovered. The only way we can redeem the time is to make the most of today, especially those spare moments.

Frédéric Chopin understood the value of time. He made use of his spare moments to play the piano or compose music.

One day teenage Frédéric was on his way home to Warsaw, Poland, from a concert tour in Berlin, Germany, when his stage coach stopped at a small town to change horses. For some reason there was a delay, and the impatient passengers milled around the inn complaining.

Anxious to make wise use of his time, Frédéric looked around for a musical instrument and discovered an old piano in the corner of the room. He sat down and began to play, first softly, then with increasing depth of feeling. Soon the room was full of silent listeners.

"The horses are ready," called the coachman. "Let's go!"

"No! No!" begged the people.

"Play on, young man," the innkeeper said. "I will see that the fastest team in the village takes you to your destination."

When Chopin was ready to leave, the village people filled his carriage with fruits and homemade pastries to show their appreciation for his impromptu concert.

How did he get to be a great musician? It was by using his time wisely through the years to practice and improve.

What do you do with your spare moments? W. W. Taylor was right when he said, "It is in their leisure time that men are made or marred."

ROBERT SCHUMANN

The Lord will command his lovingkindness in the daytime, and in the night his song shall be with me. Psalm 42:8.

Frau Schumann sat up in bed with a start. "Father, wake up!" she whispered, shaking her husband's shoulder.

"What's the matter?" Herr Schumann asked as he rolled over.

"Listen! Someone is playing the piano, and it's after midnight!"

Mamma and Papa Schumann climbed out from the warm covers and tiptoed down the stairs. In the living room they found little Robert pounding away on the piano, producing somber, frightening chords that sent chills down their spines.

"Robert! You should be in bed. What are you doing here?" His father's voice sounded gruff.

"Papa! Mama!" Robert sobbed and ran to Frau Schumann, burying his face in her flannel nightgown.

"What happened?" Kneeling, Frau Schumann took the trembling boy in her arms.

"I had a bad dream. Those monsters were chasing me, and I was scared. I was all alone and they wouldn't go away, even when I woke up. So I came down here to chase them away with my music."

"My poor little Robert!" Mama Schumann stroked his blond hair. "Did the music make you feel better?"

Robert nodded his head.

"Then back to bed with you," Papa Schumann ordered. "And no more night concerts. Do you hear me?"

"Yes, Papa."

When Robert Schumann grew up he had many nights when he felt sad, lonely, or scared. Always he went to his beloved piano for comfort. There was something about music that soothed his troubled spirit and made life seem good again.

Robert Schumann makes me think of the shepherd boy David, who filled his lonely hours on the hillsides of Judea playing his harp. Many of the psalms are songs that God gave him in the nighttime experiences of his life.

Remember how Paul and Silas sang at midnight in the prison at Philippi? God gave them songs in the night to make them strong. He can do the same for you.

FRANZ LISZT

Christ also suffered for us, leaving us an example, that ye should follow his steps. 1 Peter 2:21.

Teenage Franz Liszt was a sensation. People crowded the halls to hear him play the piano. They called him a "boy marvel," and pupils came begging for lessons. Money, fame, and adoration were his. He was the talk of the town wherever he went. Then the bubble burst; his dream castle crumbled.

Seventeen-year-old Franz had just recovered from a long illness when his father became suddenly sick and died. Franz' concert tours gave way to the need of taking in pupils to support himself and his mother. Then on the same day he lost his job and the girl he loved.

Franz was devastated. Life held no meaning. He wandered about as one lost. He refused to play any music and thought about becoming a priest. His mother was worried.

"Franz, you've got to stop moping around like this," Mrs. Liszt said at last. "Here's a ticket for Paganini's concert. Go and enjoy yourself."

"Paganini?" Franz asked. "You mean the great Italian violinist?"

"That's right," Mamma Liszt smiled with satisfaction as she noted the excitement in his voice. "Will you go?"

"You bet I will. I wouldn't miss him for anything."

Watching the master violinist perform awakened in Liszt a desire to be like him. "I'm going to master the piano just as Paganini has mastered the violin," Franz told his mother.

With a picture of Paganini in his mind, Liszt set to work to make his dream come true. He spent five hours a day at exercises: scales, thirds, sixths, octaves, repeated notes, and cadenzas. Then he gave himself to several more hours playing from the works of Beethoven and Bach. For months he was seldom seen, and he never performed.

When he returned to the concert stage he electrified his audience. "Liszt is a master pianist," the people declared. "No one can equal his marvelous performance." By following the example of a master, Franz Liszt became a success.

Are you following in the footsteps of your Master?

GIUSEPPE VERDI

Be not hasty in thy spirit to be angry: for anger resteth in the bosom of fools. Ecclesiastes 7:9.

Have you ever been so mad that you broke a pencil or smashed a toy? If you have, then you know how 7-year-old Giuseppe felt the day he smashed his spinet.

When Papa Verdi brought home the spinet Giuseppe jumped up and down in excitement. He hit the keys with both hands. It sounded awful! After a while he discovered a chord that sounded good, and he played it again and again until his mom and dad made him go to bed.

Early the next morning Giuseppe was at the spinet again. He tried hard to make beautiful music he heard in church, but raucous, disonant sounds came out instead.

"You stupid old spinet!" Giuseppe yelled. "You're no good! You don't know how to make pretty music!" Grabbing a hammer, he began to smash the keys and pull at the strings.

Mamma and Papa Verdi came running. "Giuseppe! Give me that hammer!" Papa ordered sternly.

"What's wrong with you, child?" his mother asked.

"This spinet is no good," Giuseppe pouted. "It won't make nice music."

"Oh, honey," Mrs. Verdi said, holding him close. "It's not the spinet's fault. You have to play it right."

"But I don't know how," the boy whimpered.

"Never mind; you'll learn," his father said. "First we have to get this thing repaired. I'll send for Stefano."

When he was finished, Stefano pasted a note inside the spinet; it can be seen to this day in the museum in Milan. It says, "These hammers were repaired and recovered with leather by me, Stefano Cavaletti, and I fitted the pedals which I presented; I also repaired the said hammers gratuitously, seeing the good disposition the young Verdi has for learning to play this instrument, which is sufficient for my complete satisfaction. A.D. 1821."

After that Giuseppe learned both how to control his temper and how to play the spinet. He discovered how foolish anger is. Have you?

JENNY LIND

Whatsoever ye do, do all to the glory of God. 1 Corinthians 10:31.

Seven-year-old Jenny Lind stared at the small brown bird perched on a branch near her window ledge. "You're a lot like me, little brown bird," Jenny said sadly. "You're not very pretty, and neither am I. Just plain old Jenny. That's me. Do you ever wish you were beautiful like the swallows?"

As if in reply, the tiny bird lifted its head towards the sky, and began to sing.

"Oh, little bird, your song is pretty! Look over this way and sing for me."

But the little brown bird kept right on looking up at the sky as she warbled the sweetest melody Jenny had ever heard.

"I know why you won't look at me. You aren't singing for me at all. You are singing for Jesus, aren't you?"

After watching the plain little bird for some time, Jenny whispered, "I want to be like you, little bird. I'm not very pretty either, but maybe I could sing pretty songs. I want to sing for Jesus too. I'm going to ask Him to help me sing like you, little birdie. I know He will."

Jenny Lind, who talked to the little bird more than 150 years ago in Stockholm, Sweden, grew up to become a famous singer. She traveled throughout Europe and America, singing before large audiences. People said she had a voice like a bird. She was known as the Swedish Nightingale.

Royalty showered gifts upon her. Students pulled her carriage through the streets in happy processions. Flowers, jewels, clothes, and streets were named for her. Felix Mendelssohn wrote the *Elijah* oratorio especially for her, with many F sharps in the solos, because he considered that note the one she sang best.

When her admirers praised her singing she replied, "When I was a child I asked God to let me sing like the little brown bird beside my window. He answered my prayer, and I want to give Him all the glory."

What is your talent? Will you use it today for God's glory?

STEPHEN COLLINS FOSTER

Likewise the Spirit also helpeth our infirmities: for we know not what we should pray for as we ought. Romans 8:26.

Wind whistled around a house in Youngstown, Ohio, piling snow in high drifts. Ten-year-old Stephen Foster, who was visiting there with his mother and brother, felt bored.

"I wish Dad would send the comic songster he promised me," Stephen sighed. "Then maybe I could play a tune on it."

"What's a comic songster?" his big sister, Etty, asked.

"A squeaky tin whistle," Stephen answered. "No one else can play a tune on it, but I think I could if I had one."

"Then why don't you write Dad a letter and remind him?"

"Will you correct my spelling so it'll be perfect when Dad gets it?"

"Nothing doing!" Etty said firmly.

Stephen did his best, but it didn't turn out very well. There were ink blots all over the paper, and he was sure some words were not spelled correctly. Anyway, he sent it. There are at least 12 mistakes. See if you can find them all.

Youngstown Jany 14th 1837

My dear father,

I wish you to send me a comic songster for you promised to. if I had my pensyl I could rule my paper or if I had the money to buy Black ink But if I had my whistle I would be so taken with it I donot think I would write atall.

I remane your loving son
Stephen C. Foster

Stephen's dad found every mistake. He sent the letter back with the following note: "Your songster will be sent when you have made all the corrections in this letter."

Is God like that? Does He make us correct all our mistakes before He will answer our prayers? Do our petitions have to be perfect, without any flaws in grammar before He will grant our requests?

No. God understands our weaknesses. He knows how hard we try. The Holy Spirit corrects all our mistakes so that each prayer is a perfect one, saying just what we need to say. Isn't that neat?

JOHANNES BRAHMS

My voice shalt thou hear in the morning, O Lord; in the morning will I direct my prayer unto thee, and will look up. Psalm 5:3.

Johannes Brahms grew up in the slums, the poorest district of Hamburg, Germany. His father, a bass player in the local orchestra, made barely enough to feed the family. They lived in damp, poorly furnished rooms that were often cold in winter. The soup was thin. So they could afford to make it thicker, Johannes went to work at the age of 9, playing his violin in restaurants, sometimes until late at night.

In spite of having to work so hard, Johannes found time for lessons and several hours of piano practice daily, as well as time for writing music.

"The best songs come into my mind," he said, "while polishing my boots before daybreak."

Many great men have shared Brahms's habit of rising early. Christians of all ages have discovered that heavenly manna is best when gathered in the dew-laden hours before dawn. In the soft quietness before our busy life begins we can best hear the voice of Christ speaking to our souls.

John Wesley, a great preacher in England, rose at four o'clock to spend one or two hours in prayer. John Quincy Adams, president of the United States, studied his Bible first thing every morning. William Gladstone, prime minister of Great Britain, went every morning into the nearest church for prayer. J. Hudson Taylor, pioneer missionary to China, in his busiest times got up at three o'clock to pray. Ellen G. White would often rise in the wee hours of the morning to commune with God and write down His messages.

Jesus was an early riser. He got up long before dawn to spend time talking with His Father. Daniel would rather be thrown into the den of lions than to miss his morning appointment with God. David, too, found the morning hours special. Isaac Watts made a hymn out of today's text. You will find it as number 39 in *The Seventh-day Adventist Hymnal.*

Johannes Brahms discovered that there's a magic in the early morning hours. Have you experienced it?

113

SIR MICHAEL COSTA

Those members of the body, which seem to be more feeble, are necessary. 1 Corinthians 12:22.

Sir Michael Costa, a well-known musical conductor and composer who lived 150 years ago, had an experience that illustrates today's verse.

While conducting a rehearsal of the Covent Garden Theater orchestra in London, he became ill at ease. He frowned from time to time, and it was clear that something was wrong. Suddenly, he stopped the orchestra.

"I miss the piccolo," he said.

Can you imagine the embarrassment of the piccolo player as all eyes were fixed on him? Had he been dreaming? Had he lost his place? Or did he just want to rest?

No doubt he was surprised that one person's failure to do his job would matter. He was only one out of a host of players. The piccolo is, after all, a small instrument, and the sound is feeble compared to the horns. Most of us would never notice the difference, but Sir Michael did. The music could not be all it was meant to be without the piccolo's voice.

It's that way in God's church, too. Every member is important. Every person has a job to do.

Your voice may not be as loud as Deacon Brown's, but it is needed to help sing the hymns on Sabbath morning. I can imagine the angels frowning a bit as the songs of praise are sung. Ah, there is the problem. Brian is reading his *Guide.* And Stephanie is drawing a picture. Don't you think Jesus misses your voice when you are silent?

Your offering might not equal Dr. Smith's, but it is needed to help take the gospel into all the world. If you keep back your offering, small as it is, then some part of God's work will have to do without.

You don't have to wait until you are grown up to play in the church orchestra. You are a member of the team now. It's very important that you do your part.

PETER ILICH TCHAIKOVSKY

The soul that sinneth, it shall die. Ezekiel 18:4.

Cholera, a very infectious disease, was common a century ago. The bacteria settled in the intestines and poisoned the whole system. Severe diarrhea and vomiting weakened victims until they died within a few days. Thousands of people succumbed, and doctors could do little to help.

Today we can get a vaccination to help us keep from catching the disease, but in 1893 no one knew how to do this. The only way to keep from getting sick was to keep away from those who had the disease. This was hard when an epidemic hit a town, because people were ill in almost every household. It was absolutely necessary to boil all drinking water.

In the fall of 1893 a cholera epidemic raged in St. Petersburg, Russia. Ignoring the danger, Peter Tchaikovsky drank unboiled water. He was thirsty, and boiled water was not available. He didn't want to take the trouble to boil water and wait for it to cool. He wanted a drink right now.

Within a few days the man who wrote *The Nutcracker Suite* was dead, for cholera germs are no respecter of persons. The results are the same whether you are rich or poor, smart or dumb, famous or unknown. Cholera germs don't care if you're a brilliant scientist, a gifted musician, or an escaped convict.

Sin is a lot like a cholera germ. It is easily caught from brothers, sisters, friends, and neighbors. Just notice sometime how fast a filthy joke makes the rounds. One child brings it to school, and soon the whole class has heard it. Who teaches kids to swear? No one. Bad language seems to be in the air. One person infects another until we have a real problem on our hands.

Television, radio, cassette players, books, and magazines, as well as our playmates, carry the germs of sin. Some of us are like Tchaikovsky, taking no precautions against infection. We think that somehow, because we are Christians, we are immune. We aren't. Sin is no respecter of persons.

Although there was no cure for Tchaikovsky's cholera, there is a remedy for sin. "The blood of Jesus Christ . . . cleanseth us from all sin" (1 John 1:7). Thank God, we don't have to die.

115

ANTONIN DVORAK

My soul longeth, yea, even fainteth for the courts of the Lord: my heart and my flesh crieth out for the living God. Psalm 84:2.

Antonin Dvorak's shoulders sagged as he climbed the steps to his home near the National Conservatory of Music in New York City. As he opened the door the smell of simmering cabbage rolls made him think for a moment that he was back home in Nelahozeves, Bohemia.

He closed his eyes and could see again the village green where his jolly young father, the innkeeper, plucked a zither as boys and girls danced. He could see his mother, red-cheeked and sweaty, stirring a kettle of steaming beet soup.

"Antonin, are you all right?" his wife cried as she ran to his side, concern in her eyes and voice. "Did something go wrong at the conservatory?"

"No," Antonin sighed. "Things are going well there. It's going to be a splendid school when we are finished."

"Then what is it? Have you been for another of your long walks?"

Antonin nodded. "I went to the docks and watched the ships leave for Europe. Made me wish we were on one, headed home."

"I know," his wife agreed, a tear stealing down her cheek. "I long for the quietness of our country home. Life is so fast here. I went to the market today and longed for our little village market back in Nelahozeves."

"It won't be long now," Antonin spoke more bravely. "Soon my work will be done here, and we can go home."

Dvorak's homesickness found expression in a symphony he wrote at this time. Entitled *From the New World*, its theme was based on the Negro spiritual "Goin' Home."

Sometimes I feel like Antonin Dvorak. I want to go home . . . to my heavenly home. I miss my mom and dad so much. They're dead, and I can't see them again until Jesus comes. I miss my grandma's stories and my grandpa's hearty laugh. I want to talk with my guardian angel, and I've many questions to ask Jesus. I want to live in my mansion and pick fruit from the tree of life. I'm homesick for heaven. What about you?

EDVARD GRIEG

In all thy ways acknowledge him, and he shall direct thy paths. Proverbs 3:6.

Fifteen-year-old Edvard Grieg whistled as he made his way home from a hike. Suddenly the staccato beat of a horse's hoofs echoed down the valley. Edvard looked up to see a stranger on a gray Arabian horse gallop into view. Slowly as he approached the teenager, the man called, "Can you tell me where Landaas lies? It belongs to a family called Grieg."

"Sure do! I'm going there now. My name is Edvard Grieg."

"And my name is Ole Bull."

"The violinist?"

"That's the one," the big man grinned. "I knew your parents long ago. Now that I'm living nearby, we must get acquainted again."

Edvard thought his heart was going to stop beating. All his life he had heard stories about Ole Bull and his wonderful concert tours throughout Europe and America. To have his hero there in person was almost more than Edvard could believe.

After an hour of talk and music Mrs. Grieg said, "Edvard has made some little compositions of his own."

"Let's hear one," said Ole Bull.

Embarrassed, Edvard played *Variations on a German Melody for Piano.*

"Very good!" Ole applauded. "You have originality. Do you want to be a musician?"

"Yes, I do."

"Pay no attention," his father apologized. "Boys think they can do anything at this age. Only yesterday he was going to be a bishop!"

The family laughed, but Edvard was sure in his heart that he would be a musician, and that's what he became.

Do you know what you will be when you are grown? God has a plan for your life, a special work for you to do that no one else can accomplish. Are you praying that He will guide you to it?

JOHN PHILIP SOUSA

To every thing there is a season, and a time to every purpose under the heaven. Ecclesiastes 3:1.

John Philip Sousa had a problem. The 11-year-old was scheduled to play a violin solo at a school concert. On the same day he had to play ball. The Navy Yard boys, for whom he was pitcher, were playing the Capitol Hill team.

"You can't let us down," Edward said. "You're the best pitcher we've got."

"But I have to get ready for the concert!"

"The game won't be long," Edward insisted. "You'll have lots of time to get ready."

However, the teams were evenly matched, and the game lasted until six o'clock, just 30 minutes before the concert was to begin. Philip rushed home to change. To his dismay, his mother was sick and had not ironed his shirt.

If only I had time to iron it myself, Philip thought, but that was out of the question now. Grabbing one of his father's shirts, he pinned up the sleeves and tails with straight pins. The collar was three sizes too big, but it would have to do. He raced to the school and took his place just as the concert started.

All went well until John's solo. It was a fast number, and he had to move his arm back and forth with quick, short strokes. This was hard on the shirt. Pins came loose. The shirt tails came out and hung to his knees. The sleeves worked down until they covered his hands and got in the way of his bow. He stopped playing and dashed off the stage.

The audience laughed. The other members of the orchestra tried not to laugh, but they couldn't help themselves. His teacher was so angry that he forbade Philip to eat any cake at the reception that followed.

"I learned one thing today," Philip told himself as he crawled into bed that night. "From now on when it's time to work I'll work. And when it's time to play I'll play. Never again will I try to mix the two."

EDWARD MACDOWELL

The stone which the builders rejected, the same is become the head of the corner. Matthew 21:42.

Are you a collector or a throw-away person? Did you ever throw something away and then wish you had kept it? The builders of Solomon's Temple were throw-away people.

When the stones came from the quarry, one seemed worthless, so they tossed it. However, when the time came to put the cornerstone in place, they couldn't find a stone that fit. Then someone remembered that strange stone and retrieved it from the rubbish heap.

Edward MacDowell, an American composer, was another throw-away person. When a piece of music didn't seem right, he wadded it up and threw it in the fire.

One night, after MacDowell had left his study, his wife entered to put things in order. Noticing a crumpled piece of music paper on the hearth, she picked it up and smoothed out the wrinkles. Softly she hummed the melody he had written. It was beautiful!

After breakfast the next morning Mrs. MacDowell handed her husband the salvaged piece of manuscript. "Edward, this is really lovely. I think it's too good to throw away."

"Really? Let me see what it sounds like." MacDowell went at once to the piano and played the short melody. "Not bad! In fact, I think it has distinct possibilities."

The finished work is called "To a Wild Rose," one of his best-loved works.

Karen is also a throw-away person, only what she is throwing away is more important than a manuscript or a stone. She is throwing away her religion. She said, "I don't need the church anymore." I asked her to take another look at what she was discarding. I hope she does.

Eric threw away his belief in Jesus Christ as the divine Son of God. He joined a commune centered around an Indian guru. Now his guru is gone, and he has a big empty hole in his life. The Stone he discarded is still waiting. I hope Eric finds Him before his life crumbles.

Be careful what you throw away today.

119

SIR EDWARD ELGAR

Ye should do that which is honest. 2 Corinthians 13:7.

Have you ever attended a graduation? More than likely you watched the graduates march in to the thrilling beat of Edward Elgar's *Pomp and Circumstance March.*

Chemistry was Sir Edward's hobby. He had a little laboratory fitted up in a backyard shed. One of his favorite experiments was to make a concoction out of phosphorus that, when dried out, would go off by spontaneous combustion. He loved to smear it on a piece of blotting paper and then wait for the big bang.

One day in the middle of his experiment he got an idea for a musical composition and wanted to go and write it down. He stuck the phosphorus paste into a pot with a lid and put it in the water barrel, thinking it would be safe.

Suddenly Sir Edward heard a loud crash followed by the sound of rushing water. He ran to his shed to find bent hoops and pieces of the barrel all over his laboratory.

Outside dogs barked, windows flew open, and heads popped out. A moment later Sir Edward strolled down the street as unconcerned as if nothing at all had happened.

"Did you hear that noise, sir?" a neighbor called from his gate. "It sounded like an explosion."

"Yes," admitted Sir Edward, "I did. What was it?"

Sir Edward kept a straight face and walked on.

Was Sir Edward being honest? Should he have told his neighbor that the explosion had been his phosphorus experiment? By misleading his neighbor into thinking nothing was wrong in his house, was he in reality telling a lie?

When someone asks you, "How are you?" and you reply, "Great!" when actually you feel rotten, are you being honest?

When Sherri says, "Do you like my new dress?" and you reply, "It is really neat!" when you're thinking, *What a bad color combination!* are you being honest?

Is it necessary to tell everything you know? Must you always say exactly what you think?

CLAUDE DEBUSSY

Ye were not redeemed with corruptible things, as silver and gold, . . . but with the precious blood of Christ. 1 Peter 1:18, 19.

"My watch! It's gone!" Claude cried out. "I've been robbed!"

The 22-year-old composer stood in front of the cupboard and stared at the empty box in his hand. He had tucked the gold watch away in a corner of the cupboard after returning from his visit in Moscow with the von Mecks. Mrs. von Meck had presented it to him in appreciation for his work with her children.

"Oh, no! What am I going to do? It was one of a kind. I can never replace it! I wonder who the thief is."

Father Debussy coughed and shifted in his seat at the dining room table.

"Father, who could have taken it?" Claude approached the older man, his hands clenched. "Who has been in here?"

His dad's face was red as he stammered, "I—I—I'm the one who t-t-took it."

Claude stared in disbelief. "But why? Didn't you know how precious it was to me?"

The older man stood and placed a trembling hand on his son's arm. "I'm sorry, Claude. I should have asked you, but I didn't want you to know how bad our finances were. I pawned your watch to pay the bills."

"Oh, Father! I had no idea we were that bad off. I have my prize money from the cantata I wrote. I can help."

"Then use it to redeem your watch," Mr. Debussy sighed.

Claude rushed down to the pawnshop and paid the redemption price. Once again the watch was his.

You are like that watch, one of a kind, a precious possession of Jesus. He wanted to keep you forever because He loved you so much. A thief named Lucifer claims possession, and the redemption price must be paid.

On Calvary's cruel cross Jesus paid your redemption price, His own blood. He died for you. Once again you belong to Him.

Can you begin to comprehend how much Jesus loves you?

IGNACE JAN PADEREWSKI

Reverence my sanctuary: I am the Lord. Leviticus 19:30.

An American tourist girl sauntered into Beethoven's house, which is now a museum in Bonn, Germany. She ran her hand along the shiny grand piano used by the master to compose many of his famous works and plopped down on the antique chair before the keys. Nearby a frowning custodian watched her as she indifferently played a light, popular tune.

"Do you get many visitors here?" she inquired.

"Ah, yes, a great many."

"Do any famous people come?"

"Yes. Paderewski, the great pianist and composer, was here not long ago."

Her fingers ran a scale on the keys. "And what piece did the great Paderewski play on this piano?"

The custodian straightened his shoulders, and with a hint of rebuke in his voice, replied, "Paderewski did not consider himself worthy to play on Beethoven's piano."

It is right that we honor great men and women. No one likes to see a child race around inside a museum. Respect for the famous people who made the museum possible demands that we walk quietly and do not touch the exhibits unless invited to do so.

How much more important is it, then, to show respect for the living, all-powerful God when we go into His house on the Sabbath to worship. If we could somehow catch a sense of the presence and glory of God, we would fear to run up and down the aisles, disturbing the service.

Is someone reverent when he chews gum in a meeting? Do you think God is pleased with scuffling and whispering when the Scripture is being read? Do young people honor the Creator when they rustle papers and draw pictures in the hymnbooks? How do you think the angels feel when someone keeps her eyes open during prayer?

JEAN SIBELIUS

They received the word with all readiness of mind, and searched the scriptures daily, whether those things were so. Acts 17:11.

To please his grandmother, Jean Sibelius entered the University of Helsinki to study law. He had good intentions of reading his law books, but they were boring compared to violin and music theory.

One day, when he tired of reading law, he laid the book on the windowsill, open at the place where he had stopped. He really meant to get back to it soon, but music beckoned. The book lay there open but untouched for months. Sunny days yellowed its pages and faded its print.

Who knows how long the law book would have lain there untouched had not Jean's uncle come on a surprise visit. Picking up the neglected book, he realized that his nephew had his mind on something else besides law.

"It would be best for you to devote yourself entirely to music," his uncle advised, "seeing that study does not interest you any more than this."

"You're right, Uncle," Jean agreed. "What I want more than anything else is to be a musician."

Anyone who watched Jean Sibelius knew that this was true. While the law book was lying untouched on the windowsill, his violin was never neglected. Daily he took it with him on walks into the Finnish countryside. He could sit on a rock by hours and put the sights and smells of nature into sound. He even carried his beloved violin with him on an ocean voyage and played to the waves.

If you have a musical instrument, try playing "Finlandia," found in *The Seventh-day Adventist Hymnal* (No. 461). If Sibelius had become a lawyer, we probably wouldn't have this lovely hymn.

What interests you? A visitor to your home would soon be able to figure out what gets the most attention. Which is used more in your house, the *TV Guide* or your Sabbath school lesson quarterly? Which has the more tattered edges, your Bible or a comic book?

Are you, like the Bereans, one who searches the Scriptures daily? Does today's verse apply to you?

SERGEI VASSILIEVITCH RACHMANINOFF

Whatsoever thy hand findeth to do, do it with thy might.
Ecclesiastes 9:10.

Thirteen-year-old Sergei Rachmaninoff wiped his sweaty hands on his trousers and took a deep breath to quiet his pounding heart. Today was the culmination of his year's study under Zvierev, the famous music teacher in Moscow. Sergei felt his future as a composer depended on how well he did in his harmony examination that day.

At nine o'clock Zvierev handed out the examination papers. Sergei noted that he had two problems to solve: He had to harmonize a melody by Haydn in four parts and write a prelude to include certain stated elements. There was no time limit, and he was not allowed to use a piano.

One by one the other boys finished their papers and went out to play. Only Sergei remained. Oblivious to time and his surroundings, the teenager worked until five o'clock. He smiled with satisfaction as he handed in his paper. He knew he had done his best.

The next day he had to play his compositions before a board of examiners, which included his hero, Tchaikovsky. Two weeks later Sergei learned that he had been given a score of 5 with four plus signs grouped around it. No one had ever received higher than a 5^+ before. His mark was unique.

In the years that followed, Sergei continued to be a 5^+ student. Everything he did with his whole heart and soul. When he graduated from the Moscow Conservatory he was given the gold medal and his name was entered in the roll of honor.

What brought young Sergei these awards? Was it because he was a talented boy, especially gifted by God with great musical ability? Then why do not all talented and gifted children receive such honors? Was it because he was handsome and likable? Lots of good-looking, friendly boys end up doing nothing with their lives.

Could it be that Sergei followed the advice of Solomon and did everything with his might?

Would you like to succeed in life? Then do every task you receive to the best of your ability. Strive to be a 5^+ worker.

PHILIP BLISS

And thine ears shall hear a word behind thee, saying, This is the way, walk ye in it. Isaiah 30:21.

Philip Bliss was in Chicago for a musical convention when he heard some people singing hymns on the courthouse lawn. He stood at the edge of the crowd for a few minutes listening to their halfhearted efforts.

"They need some life in their singing," Philip said to himself. "They sound half asleep! Guess I'd better wake them up!"

Philip opened his mouth and began to sing. Heads turned to see who had arrived. Inspired by the enthusiasm in his strong voice, the whole congregation sounded better. The very sound of his singing breathed life and joy into everyone.

When the music stopped, Philip turned to go, but he was stopped by a man who had been sitting on the courthouse steps. "Do you have a minute?"

"Yes, sir," Philip said. "What can I do for you?"

"My name is Dwight L. Moody. As I watched the transformation you brought to our singing band, I felt impressed to tell you that God needs you to sing full time for Him. He can use your voice to help save souls. I want you to join me as a singing evangelist."

"I'll pray about it and let you know," Philip promised. Later he shared his burden with a friend, D. W. Whittle, a lay preacher. The two of them decided to hold a three-night series of meetings in Waukegan, Illinois. If God could use them to achieve unusual results, they would know they should go into full-time Christian service.

On the first night, 30 people came to the altar, and the next two nights brought similar results. Philip was convinced that God wanted him to be a singing evangelist.

While working with Mr. Moody he composed many hymns. Two of them are in the new Adventist hymnal. Look them up and see if you know them: numbers 286 and 530.

Philip Bliss did not actually hear God's voice audibly speaking to him. Instead, God addressed Philip through Dwight L. Moody, answered prayer, and the circumstances of life.

God might speak to you today. Will you be listening?

AARON COPLAND

Men ought always to pray, and not to faint. Luke 18:1.

This verse is from the parable of the widow who would not give up. Day after day she visited the judge, begging him to help her win a court case. Day after day he refused. At last, because she kept troubling him, the judge gave in and helped.

Jesus said, "Now, if that judge who didn't love God or man would do that much for a poor widow, don't you think your heavenly Father will be willing to help you? So don't give up. Keep on asking."

Aaron Copland, an American composer, is an example of someone who understood the meaning of perseverance in asking.

"Please, Mama, I want music lessons," he begged day after day. "I want to learn to play the piano."

"We've already wasted enough money on music lessons for your brothers and sisters," his mother replied, shaking her head.

"Never mind," his sister Laurine said, "I'll teach you how to play the piano."

Aaron was delighted. After six months Laurine said, "You know more than I learned in eight years of lessons. There's nothing else I can teach you."

"Then I'll practice by myself," Aaron said. For a year and a half he practiced faithfully every day. Time and again he tried to convince his mother that he must have lessons.

"I'm trying really hard, Mama," Aaron pleaded. "Please, I do so want to learn more, and there's no one to help me."

"Well, all right," she agreed, after Aaron's thirteenth birthday. "You can have a teacher, but you must find the teacher yourself and make the arrangements."

Aaron Copland knows that it pays to keep on asking.

Is there something you've been praying about for a long time? Maybe you need to get a Christian education but there's no money to pay for it. Perhaps someone you love dearly is very sick. It could be that you are having trouble overcoming a bad habit. Don't give up. Keep on asking. God will help you.

MARIAN ANDERSON

I will even make a way in the wilderness, and rivers in the desert. Isaiah 43:19.

The sun burned down on the brick sidewalks of Philadelphia one summer day in 1919, but teenaged Marian Anderson, standing in front of a big gray building, hardly noticed. She checked the address. No doubt about it, this was the School of Music. She entered the reception room filled with chattering girls who were waiting to register. Quietly Marian took her place in line.

"Good morning," Marian said as she smiled at the receptionist.

The woman looked right past her as if she weren't there. "Would you like an application blank?" she said to the girl behind Marian.

Marian stepped aside and waited patiently. When all were gone, she again approached the window.

"What do *you* want?" the receptionist snarled.

"I'd like an application blank, please."

"We don't take ____" The receptionist used a racial slur and banged the window shut.

Marian stood there a moment in disbelief, tears filling her eyes. Her face felt hot; her knees shook. Why? What had she done to deserve this? She couldn't help the color of her skin. Would she have to give up her dream simply because her skin was black? The lump in her throat stayed there all the way home.

Her mother's arms were deep in a tub of laundry when Marian entered the kitchen. "Well, when do you start?"

"Never." Swallowing hard to keep back the tears, Marian told what had happened. "Mama, can't I be a singer because I'm Black?"

Mother Anderson crossed the room and put an arm around Marian's drooping shoulders. "Of course you can be a singer, Marian. God will make a way for you. There will be some other way to learn what you need to know."

And God did make a way for Marian through the wilderness of prejudice and hatred. She got her lessons and became an internationally loved soloist.

Are you having a tough time in life? Don't despair. God will make a way for you just as He did for Marian. Trust Him.

MAHALIA JACKSON

Better is it that thou shouldest not vow, than that thou shouldest vow and not pay. Ecclesiastes 5:5.

A vow is a solemn promise. To make a vow to God is a very serious thing, and we should never make one unless we fully intend to keep it. Mahalia Jackson, a famous gospel singer, understood that the night she made her vow.

It all started when Grandfather Paul came to visit. He and she laughed and talked and had a wonderful time together.

"Grandfather," she said. "Please have your picture taken while you're here. I'll pay for it."

"Nobody wants a picture of an old man," Grandfather replied.

"Well, I do," insisted Mahalia, so Grandfather Paul went the next day for his photograph. While there he had a stroke and was rushed to the hospital.

"He's seriously ill," the doctor told Mahalia. "He may not live through the night."

Tears blinded the girl's eyes as she stumbled down the hospital corridor to an empty room. Going in and closing the door, she fell on her knees. "O God, forgive me for my selfishness," she cried. "Please let Grandfather live."

Somehow she felt his illness was her fault, for she had asked him to go to the photographer. She was eager to make any sacrifice necessary if only Grandfather could live. Was there anything she was doing that God might not approve? She thought about the theater. She did enjoy movies and vaudeville shows. She remembered the fiery sermons against worldliness she had heard her father preach in the little Baptist church in New Orleans.

"If you will let Grandfather live," she prayed, "I'll never go to the theater again."

After several days Grandfather rallied, and Mahalia thanked God for saving him.

True to her promise, Mahalia Jackson never went to a movie or vaudeville theater again. God had answered her prayers, and she intended to keep her part of the bargain.

DEL DELKER

What doth the Lord require of thee, but to do justly, and to love mercy, and to walk humbly with thy God? Micah 6:8.

Teenaged Del Delker didn't exactly feel humble that night in Lodi, California. It was during the first camp meeting she had attended after her conversion and she had been asked to sing before the large crowd of people. Her dark eyes sparkled as she stood before the audience and sang "The Love of God" in her rich, contralto voice.

After the meeting a crowd gathered around, smothering her with kisses and compliments.

"You were marvelous!"

"I have never heard anyone sing so beautifully!"

"Tremendous! You must sing more often!"

Eventually, of course, the crowd drifted away, and Del was left alone. That warm, good feeling she had felt when surrounded by her admirers was gone. Her room that night seemed cold and dark. In her heart there was an emptiness and the same feeling of despair she had known before conversion.

She left her room and walked to a nearby grape vineyard, where she knelt down and told Jesus all about how she felt.

"Dear Lord, if singing for You is going to do this to me, take it away. I don't want to be proud. I want You with me. I want Your blessing."

As she knelt on the cool earth, God surrounded Del with the warmth of His love. He assured her that as long as she let Him control her life He would keep her humble. Her joy returned and still radiates from her face each time she sings.

Were the people wrong in praising Del that night long ago? Is it wrong to give love and appreciation to those who do well? Is it a sin to tell the preacher that we liked his story and it really helped us? Shouldn't we tell others when they do a good job? What is the difference between flattery and sincere appreciation? How should we handle praise directed our way?

If you have ever performed in public, you probably know how Del felt. Have you ever had trouble with a "big head"? Have you tried asking God to keep you humble?

BABE RUTH

God sent forth his Son . . . that we might receive the adoption of sons. Galatians 4:4, 5.

"Hey, Skinny George! What are you doing here?"

"Yeah! What makes you think you can play ball, Beanpole?"

"Look at the way he runs!" an old-timer laughed. "Did you ever see a pigeon-toed baseball player before?"

"And he's left-handed, besides!" another added.

"Dunn must have been scraping the barrel when he found you!"

The taunts were directed at a tall, awkward teenager with a big body and thin legs who had just joined the Baltimore Orioles. He was George Herman Ruth, who had grown up in the slums of Baltimore. He had scratched for food wherever he could find it until he was sent to St. Mary's Industrial School, a home for orphans and juvenile delinquents. This was his first job, and he didn't know how to handle the razzing of the older men.

"OK, you guys!" the coach warned. "That's enough! Lay off the kid. Don't forget, he's Dunn's babe."

Jack Dunn, owner-manager of the Baltimore Orioles, had adopted George Herman Ruth in order to get him released from St. Mary's Orphanage to play for the Orioles. From then on George was called "The Babe" or just plain "Babe." The razzing stopped, and Babe Ruth went on to become one of the greatest baseball players of all time. Fifty-six of his records still stand. He made 60 home runs in a single season and 714 home runs in his entire career.

It seems to me that you and I are in the position of teenaged George. We are rookies in the game of life. The devil knows it and starts his accusations. "You're no good, kid! What makes you think you can succeed in this game? You're a sinner, and sinners can't make it!"

Then Christ Jesus, our "coach," steps in and says, "Lay off, Satan! That kid has possibilities! He's a winner! Don't forget, he's God's babe."

Praise the Lord! You are a child of the living God! You are adopted into His family. He will stand up for you. He has faith in you. He will make you a champion!

TY COBB

But seek ye first the kingdom of God, and his righteousness;
and all these things shall be added unto you. Matthew 6:33.

Are you putting first things first? Are your priorities in order? What is the most important thing in your life? If you waste your time on unessentials, you'll come out the loser. Ty Cobb learned that in the opening game of the 1905 baseball season in Augusta, Georgia.

Nineteen-year-old Cobb was playing outfield. Smug about his acceptance on the team, he sauntered into outfield with a bag of popcorn in his hand. His glove under his left arm, the bag of popcorn in his right, he munched on the salty kernels as one by one members of the opposing team struck out.

Suddenly, Ty looked up to see a ball coming his direction. What could he do? He didn't want to drop the popcorn. After all, he'd paid good money for it! The ball whizzed by him.

"What's the big idea, Cobb?" The manager glared at the sheepish player after the game. "Are we paying you to play ball or eat popcorn?"

"Play ball, sir."

"It didn't look like it this afternoon! You could be a good ballplayer, Ty. You might even be famous someday. But you'll never amount to anything if you don't keep your mind on the game."

That was the last time Ty Cobb ate popcorn when he was supposed to be playing ball. He got his priorities straight. Because he learned to put first things first, he became a baseball star, holding the highest lifetime batting average, a mark of .367.

Are you putting first things first in the game of life? Do you have your priorities straight?

Which is more important, making money or serving God? Are you in school to goof off, or are you there to prepare yourself for a place in God's work? Who comes first in your plans, friends or Jesus? Is a good time more important than your eternal salvation?

LOU GEHRIG

Thou shalt not kill. Exodus 20:13.

The sky was turning from green to gold the morning 7-year-old Lou Gehrig raced up Amsterdam Avenue on New York's Eastside. The vacant lot where he stopped was empty at that hour. Taking his new beanshooter out of his pocket, he gathered a handful of small pebbles and tried shooting them at home plate. He hit it every time.

This was too easy! Lou looked around for a more difficult target and saw a sparrow hopping along the fence. "I wonder if I could hit him," the small boy said to himself.

Lou put the tin beanshooter to his lips and sucked up a pebble. He carefully aimed the metal cylinder at the fluttering, twittering brown bird and blew with all his might. The sparrow hopped away as the stone hit the wooden fence. He tried again, and the bird flew to a low bush farther away.

Intent on hitting his moving target, Lou crept closer, worming his way along the ground. He put in a smooth pebble and gave a tremendous puff. The stone hit the sparrow on the head, and it fell to the ground.

"I did it!" Lou yelled as he ran to the bush and picked up the fallen bird. Its body lay still in his hand. Had he killed it? He shook it a little and spoke to it in a soft voice. It didn't move. He knew then it was dead.

A lump came to his throat, and he fought back the tears. He was only playing a game. He hadn't meant to hurt the bird. With a sigh, he laid it gently on the ground while he took the beanshooter in both hands and broke it over his knee. Then he threw the pieces as far as he could throw.

Picking up the still form of the little sparrow, Lou went over to the fence and scooped out a grave, where he laid the bird that would never sing again. Sobbing, he ran all the way back home, threw himself on his bed, and buried his face in the pillow.

"Whatever is the matter?" his mother wanted to know.

"Oh, Mama," Lou cried. "I killed a pretty bird. I didn't mean to. I won't ever do that again."

"You've learned a valuable lesson today," she said.

JACKIE ROBINSON

Thou shalt not follow a multitude to do evil. Exodus 23:2.

Life for teenager Jackie Robinson was rough. His dad had died while he was a baby, and his mother had to work hard to support five children. When he came home from school there was no one to meet him and nothing in the house to eat. With time on his hands, he did what lots of inner-city youth do: he joined a gang. They called themselves the Pepper Street Gang.

The boys amused themselves by throwing rotten fruit at passing cars or swimming in the city water reservoir, where No Swimming signs were posted. They got a thrill out of trying to outrun the police, but on more than one occasion Jackie ended up in the police station.

After one run-in with the authorities, one of Jackie's teachers called him aside after class. Laying a hand on the youth's shoulder, he said, "Jack, you know in your heart that you don't belong in the gang. Most kids end up in gangs because they're afraid to be different, afraid not to follow the crowd. Right?"

"Yeah, I guess so." Jackie looked down at his scuffed shoes, unable to meet his teacher's eyes.

"Well, let me tell you something, Jack. Only first-class suckers allow others to lead them into doing what they don't want to do. It takes guts to be different, to stand on your own two feet."

"And be called a chicken?"

"What's wrong with that? You'll not only be a much better kid, but much better off, too, if you resist doing wrong and don't worry about being called chicken."

Jackie thought a lot about what his teacher had said. It made sense. He decided he didn't want to follow the gang; he wanted to do something worthwhile with his life. He set his goal to be a good athlete and refused to follow the crowd in drinking and smoking. It was this same willingness to be different that enabled Jackie Robinson to become the first Black to play in major league baseball.

Do you have the courage to be different?

JOE DiMAGGIO

And he said unto him, Follow me. Luke 5:27.

Seventeen-year-old Joe DiMaggio wanted to see his brother Vince play baseball for the San Francisco Seals, but he couldn't afford the price of a ticket. However, near the players' entrance there was a knothole at just the height of Joe's eye.

One afternoon he was watching the game through this knothole when he felt a hand on his shoulder. Shivers ran down his spine, and his heart skipped a beat. Was it the park policeman?

Slowly Joe turned to face a smiling man in a business suit. "Are you Vince DiMaggio's brother?"

"Yes, sir," Joe gulped. "How'd you know?"

"I'm Spike Hennessy, scout for the Seals. I've seen you play a few games on the sandlots. You're good!"

"Thanks," Joe beamed. "I hope you don't mind my watching the game through the hole."

"Not at all," Mr. Hennessy laughed. "But why stand on the outside looking in? Follow me."

"But . . . why?" Joe was still apprehensive.

"I want you to meet Mr. Graham, who owns the Seals. Come on! Nobody's going to eat you!"

So it was that a rather frightened Joe DiMaggio followed Hennessy through the gate, down the dark hallways under the stands, and into Graham's office.

"No need to go around peeking through knotholes," Mr. Graham said when he heard the story. "Here are some passes. By the way, I hear you're a pretty good ballplayer yourself. Are you interested in trying for a job on our team?"

And that's how Joe DiMaggio became a professional baseball player. During the next 20 years he didn't have to worry about finding knotholes, for he was on the inside. He was part of the team.

Are you on the outside of God's church looking in through your little knothole? Today Jesus says to you as He did to Levi Matthew long ago, "Follow Me. Why stand on the outside looking in? It's much more fun to be part of the team."

ROY CAMPANELLA

I will strengthen thee; yea, I will help thee; yea, I will uphold thee with the right hand of my righteousness. Isaiah 41:10.

It was 2:30 a.m., January 28, 1958. Roy Campanella, catcher for the Los Angeles Dodgers, was on his way home to Glen Cove, Long Island, when his car skidded on an S curve. The lurching automobile crashed into a telephone pole, caving in like an accordion, with Roy trapped inside.

In a nearby house Dr. W. Spencer Gurnee heard the crash, jumped out of bed, and looked through his window. Grabbing bathrobe, slippers, and his black bag, he ran into the street while his wife called the police and an ambulance. Dr. Gurnee found Roy Campanella bent over like a pretzel, moaning, "My back hurts—oh, how it hurts."

As Dr. Gurnee gave Roy an injection of morphine he noticed that Roy didn't even flinch. Already paralysis had set in. Later, in the hospital, X-rays showed that Roy's neck was broken. He would never walk again. Indeed, he was lucky to be alive.

The news of Roy's shattering accident was soon on everyone's lips. Millions of people whom Roy had never met prayed for his recovery. Of course, his wife and three children prayed for his healing, too. In spite of all these prayers, Roy was not healed. Did Roy feel as though God had forsaken him?

"No," Roy smiled. "God has not forsaken me. He has been with me through all my long months in the hospital. He has strengthened me and helped me in my struggle to live. It was God that gave me my success in baseball, and I know He'll continue to be with me and give me success in the new life I have to live."

And God did continue to be with Roy. He gave him courage to become independent again, able to operate a store from his wheelchair, and to bring up and educate his children. Through his testimony he was able to help countless people with handicaps. He inspired them with hope and courage to live useful lives. Because they could see that God was with Roy, they knew He would be with them, too.

TED WILLIAMS

Wherefore come out from among them, and be ye separate, saith the Lord. 2 Corinthians 6:17.

Twice Ted Williams, a .400 hitter, had to quit baseball to go to war. The first time was during World War II, when he served as flight instructor for the Marine Corps. He was called up again in 1952 to go to Korea as a jet bomber pilot. He flew 39 missions against the enemy, miraculously escaping death several times.

Once Ted's plane was badly shot up in action. His radio was dead, his brakes wouldn't work, and he had no way of lowering the landing gear.

"Jump!" his commanding officer signaled.

Ted Williams shook his head and prepared for a crash landing. The other planes scattered as he brought the bomber in on its belly. It skidded, swerved, and lurched to a stop. Only then did Ted realize he was surrounded by smoke and flames.

"Oh, no! It's on fire!" Ted cried. At any mment the flames would reach the fuel. He leaped out and ran faster than he'd ever run on the ballfield! Seconds later his plane exploded.

"If I'd known it was on fire," Ted later admitted, "I'd have listened to my commanding officer. I came mighty near to losing my life!"

Like Ted William's bomber, Planet Earth is headed for destruction. Like angry flames headed for the fuel tank, the wickedness of this world spells her doom. The day is coming soon—none of us know how soon—when this planet will burn as an oven. Peter says that it's going to be so hot that the elements will melt. Sin, Satan, and all the evil in this world will be consumed.

Jesus, our heavenly commanding officer, signals, "Jump! Come out of the world and its evil ways. Separate yourself from sin and Satan, or you will be destroyed with them."

According to the Bible, time is running out. The only way we can escape is to take the leap of faith onto solid ground. Will you obey your Commanding Officer today? He loves you and wants you to live with Him forever.

DON DRYSDALE

For whom the Lord loveth he correcteth; even as a father the son in whom he delighteth. Proverbs 3:12.

"How'm I doing, Dad?" Don Drysdale asked in the spring of his senior year at Van Nuys High.

"Not bad," Scott Drysdale responded. "There are a couple of things you're still doing wrong, but generally you're doing OK."

"What do you mean, OK?" Don frowned. "I thought I was doing great. Tell me, have I lost a game yet this season?"

"No," the older man agreed, "but then you're pitching against amateurs. This summer you might find yourself in the minor leagues and then what? One flaw, and you're in trouble!"

"Right," Don sighed. "What am I doing wrong?"

"It's your delivery. You throw sidearm, and that works well for you. But sometimes you drop your arm and throw with an underhand flip. It kills your control and takes some of the zip out of your fastball."

"Really? I never noticed."

"Most players can't spot their own mistakes. That's why they have coaches and managers."

"I'll have to work on that," Don agreed.

"I've got an idea that might help," his father suggested. "Every time I see you drop your arm, I'll whistle—like this." Drawing his lips tight, Mr. Drysdale gave a shrill, piercing whistle.

"Great idea, Dad! When I hear it I'll know what I did wrong and correct it on the next pitch."

With the coaching of his father, Don Drysdale overcame his weaknesses and made the Los Angeles Dodgers. In 1962 he won the Cy Young Award for being the most valuable pitcher.

You and I are players in the game of life. None of us is perfect. Our eternal success depends on our willingness to take correction from our Coach. Like a loving father, He will show us our faults, then help us to correct them.

Listen today for His whistle. It may come in the form of a Bible verse, a letter from a friend, a word from a teacher, or plans that don't work out. God has a thousand ways to communicate His corrections. Are you listening?

FRANK SELVY

For all have sinned, and come short of the glory of God.
Romans 3:23.

Something happened in the 1962 National Basketball Association playoffs that illustrates today's verse. On April 18 the Los Angeles Lakers faced the Boston Celtics in the final game of the season. Both teams had three games to their credit. The seventh game would determine the championship.

Excitement mounted as the final game progressed. Eighteen seconds remained, and the score was tied. The Celtics got the ball, tried for a basket, and missed. There were seven seconds left.

Frank Selvy took the ball. Could he win the game for the Lakers? He dribbled quickly up the left side of the court. Fifteen feet from the basket he stopped and threw the ball. Nearly 14,000 fans held their breath as the ball hit the rim of the basket, then rolled off. The buzzer sounded; the Lakers and the Celtics were still tied. In the overtime Boston scored, winning the playoffs.

Inside the Lakers' locker room Selvy sat alone on a bench staring at his bare toes. "I missed the big one," he moaned, and shook his head. "I missed it! I missed it! It was there for me, and I missed it! All that work wasted!"

Have you ever tried to do something really well, only to blow it, just as Frank Selvy did? Losing makes you sad when you have tried so hard to win. Maybe you've tried to be a good Christian and have ended up feeling as dejected as Frank Selvy because of your failures.

The only one who has lived a sinless, spotless life is Jesus Christ. The rest of us can try, but we always fall short. We miss the basket; there is no score. Coming close is not enough when you're aiming at eternal life.

"I'm winning!" Satan shouts as you fail again and again to overcome temptation. "You might as well give up. You are a sinner, and there is no way you can make a basket in life."

Ah, yes, but there is. Jesus is on your side. He never misses. Pass the ball to Him. Don't try to do it yourself. Trust Him with the ball, and you will win!

DON MEINEKE

Wisdom is the principal thing; therefore get wisdom: and with all thy getting get understanding. Proverbs 4:7.

"This school stuff is for the birds!" 16-year-old Don Meineke told himself. He dropped out of school and took a job at General Motors in Dayton, Ohio.

His assignment was to remove excess pieces of rubber from shock absorbers. Night after night it was the same routine. Even school hadn't been this bad. Bored with the repetitious, monotonous job, Don decided to try for something better.

"What are you standing around for, Slim?" the foreman asked when he found Don daydreaming about a better job. "There's work to be done. Let's get with it!"

"I'm sick of this job!" Don threw down a piece of rubber. "How about giving me a promotion? I don't want to spend the rest of my life doing this."

"Well, Slim," the foreman shrugged his shoulders. "What else do you know?"

As the older man walked away Don nodded his head. The foreman was right. He didn't know anything else. Unskilled, boring jobs were all that he could hope to get without further education. He signed off the job that morning for the last time. When Wilbur Wright High School opened a few days later, Don was there, determined to finish his education.

After his high school graduation Don became a professional basketball player, first for the Fort Wayne Pistons and later for the Cincinnati Royals. After five years in basketball, Don became a successful businessman. None of this would have been possible had he not made the decision to follow Solomon's advice to seek knowledge, wisdom, and understanding. Without his education Don might have spent his whole life working at a job that he found boring, monotonous, and unsatisfying.

God has a place for you in His work that will be rewarding to you and a blessing to others. For it you will need knowledge, wisdom, and understanding. That's why it's important that you get all the education possible. Work hard this week in school. Do your best. You are building your future.

RAY FELIX

The righteous shall flourish like the palm tree: he shall grow like a cedar in Lebanon. Psalm 92:12.

Ray Felix, like most basketball players, grew like a tree. At 12 years of age, he was six feet one inch, towering above all his classmates.

"My, child, but you are tall!" his teacher commented in front of the class. "Come here; I want to measure you."

Ray tried to make himself look smaller as he shuffled to the wall where his teacher waited with a measuring tape. His face felt hot. He hung his head as the other children giggled. He felt like crying, but he knew they would only laugh more.

"Why can't I be like other kids?" Ray wondered. "I don't like being this big. Everybody makes fun of me, and nobody wants to be my friend. I wish I would stop growing."

But he didn't stop. By the time he was 18 Ray was six feet eleven inches tall, but he no longer resented his height. He had learned it was an advantage on the basketball court. He made the best use of the assets he had, going on to a career in professional basketball with the Bullets, Knicks, and Lakers. After retiring from basketball he managed a community center for boys in Harlem, helping disadvantaged youngsters learn to walk tall, holding their heads up in pride.

How tall are you? I don't mean physically, but spiritually. Are you growing up tall and straight like a tree? Righteous, godly young people really do stand out in a crowd, just as a tree stands out in a grassy meadow. This isn't always fun. Ungodly children often ridicule those who are tall spiritually.

If that has happened to you, take heart. Jesus had the same experience when He was growing up. His righteous character made Him stand like a cedar of Lebanon among the grass of His ungodly companions. They often laughed because He refused to take part in their wrong actions. It must have hurt, but Jesus did not give in to their taunts. He kept doing what was right and standing tall. He will help you do the same.

TERRY DISCHINGER

I waited patiently for the Lord; and he inclined unto me, and heard my cry. Psalm 40:1.

"I'm very sorry, Mrs. Dischinger, but your son will have to stop playing ball. He has a heart murmur."

"Very well," Mrs. Dischinger spoke calmly. "We'll see that he obeys your orders."

"No! No! No!" 14-year-old Terry cried out. "I don't want to be an invalid all my life. First I had that problem with my knee, and now it's my heart. It's just not fair! Why did God do this to me?"

"God didn't do this to you," his mother explained. "He's simply letting it happen for a purpose. In His wisdom He sees that there is something you need to learn."

"Like what?"

"Like, maybe, patience . . . and faith. Think how upset you get with yourself when you do anything less than perfect. It takes time to grow and learn. Have faith in God, and everything will come out all right."

"How can I have faith in God when everything is going wrong?" Terry groaned. "I'll never be happy again. It's like the end of the world for me."

"I know." Mrs. Dischinger consoled him the best she could. "But you must try to believe God loves you. Don't waste your time complaining; just get on with learning the lessons He wants you to learn."

In the dark days that followed, Terry did learn patience. Day by day he followed the doctor's orders and struggled towards a complete faith and trust in God. After 12 long months the heart murmur disappeared, and Terry was able to resume his active sports life. He won state championships in football, baseball, basketball, and hurdles. In addition he was offered scholarships to more than 50 colleges. He went on to become a star in professional basketball.

Is God trying to teach you a lesson through some setback you're experiencing? Hang in there! Have faith in God. Believe that He loves you. When the time is right He will answer your prayers.

MAURICE RICHARD

Owe no man any thing. Romans 13:8.

Jacques Fontaine not only believed in paying his debts, but he found a unique way to do so.

The 14-year-old manager of a kids' hockey team in the outskirts of Montreal wrote to the Canadiens of the National Hockey League: "Please, could you send us some money to help outfit our club with hockey equipment?"

"We've lots of worn and surplus equipment lying around here," the pro club's manager said after reading the letter. "We might as well send it to those kids."

"Thanks a million," Jacques Fontaine replied. "We won't ever forget what you've done for us. In five years I promise to pay you back by sending you a real good hockey player."

The Canadiens manager chuckled as he shared the letter with others in the office. Fontaine's promise was filed away and soon forgotten.

Five years later, in 1941, a tall, skinny young man of 20 knocked on the door of the Montreal Canadiens office. "I'm Maurice Richard [pronounced ree-SHAR]," he said. "Jacques Fontaine sent me."

"What for?" asked the puzzled Canadiens manager.

"To play hockey, of course."

"But I don't know any Jacques Fontaine," the manager insisted.

"Do you remember the kids' hockey team you outfitted five years ago? Jacques promised you then that he'd pay you back by sending you a real good hockey player. Well, . . . here I am!"

"I can't believe this!" the manager replied. "We never really expected him to do it. Anyway, now that you're here, let's see what you can do."

Maurice Richard turned out to be not just a good hockey player but one of the all-time greats in the game.

Whom are the people you owe? Has anyone done something nice for you? What can you do to repay their kindness? You may not have money, but there are other ways you can say thank you. Why not sit down right now and make a list of the bills you need to pay.

STAN MIKITA

Whosoever he be of you that forsaketh not all that he hath, he cannot be my disciple. Luke 14:33.

"No! No! I don't want to go to Canada. I don't want to leave you!" Eight-year-old Stanislas Gvoth wrapped his arms around a pole in the Prague railway station and wouldn't let go. Tears streamed down his cheeks as he looked hopefully at his mother and father.

"Uncle Joe and Aunt Anne love you. They will give you a good life in Canada. Here there is no future for you—for any of us—since enemy soldiers have taken over our government. Be a brave boy now. Give Mom and Dad a hug. It's time to get on the train." Mrs. Gvoth smiled as she held out her arms.

Just then the conductor, smartly dressed in a black uniform and red-braided cap, walked by and blew his whistle. Stanislas kissed his mother and father goodbye and reluctantly climbed the steps of the train, followed by Joe and Anne Mikita, of Saint Catharines, Ontario, his new "parents."

Stanislas took a window seat and pressed his face against the glass. The shrill train whistle cut through the confusion on the platform. The conductor waved his signal flag, and the cars lurched forward, slowly clicking out of Prague. The frightened 8-year-old was no longer Stanislas Gvoth, the Czechoslavakian, but Stan Mikita, the Canadian.

In those sad moments there was no way Stan could know he would play for the Chicago Black Hawks and become one of hockey's greatest centers. The red-eyed boy who plotted how he could jump off that train and run back to his mother and father had never heard of hockey, the sport that made him famous.

At some time in our lives all of us find ourselves in the position of little Stanislas at the Prague railway station, torn between our past and the new way of life that Jesus offers. An enemy has taken over our planet, and there is no hope, no future, under his regime. Jesus offers to adopt us and give us everlasting life in a new country, a heavenly land. Why is it we so often hang back, hugging the familiar poles of our past? Today, let's forsake our sins and climb onto the train that is bound for glory.

GORDIE HOWE

Let us therefore come boldly unto the throne of grace, that we may obtain mercy, and find grace to help in time of need. Hebrews 4:16.

Are you shy? Do you find it hard to make friends? Do you find it difficult to tell your teacher that you don't understand something? Is it hard for you to ask for help?

If you answered yes to any of these questions, you understand how 10-year-old Gordie Howe felt. Because he was big and clumsy, he was teased continually, but he suffered the cruel remarks in silence because he was too shy to let anyone know how he felt.

"Stupid!" his classmates taunted.

"Doughhead!" they laughed. "You don't know anything. You failed third grade twice!"

On the last day of school after his second year in third grade, he came home crying and handed his report card to his mother. "Gordie will have to spend another year in third grade," it said.

"Sit down, Gordie," his mother sighed. "Tell me what's wrong. Is the work too difficult? Don't you understand the teacher? Do you ask her questions about what you don't understand?"

"No, Ma. I don't want to bother her." Gordie was just too shy to get the help he needed.

Although all his life Gordie Howe had problems with his shyness, there was one place he wasn't shy, and that was on the hockey rink. There he boldly chased the puck, becoming one of the National League's superstars.

Are you, like Gordie Howe, too shy to get the help you need in school? Do you find it difficult to ask your Pathfinder counselor for help on a project? Is it hard for you to go boldly to God in prayer?

Would it make it easier if you knew that God wants you to come to Him with your problems? He is interested in the smallest detail of your life. He wants you to talk to Him about the kids at school, your math problems, or that broken bicycle. Don't be shy with God. Talk boldly to Him. He will listen.

KYLE ROTE, JR.

Abstain from all appearance of evil. 1 Thessalonians 5:22.

Nineteen-year-old Kyle Rote was a star football player for Oklahoma State University the night he and his friend Henry Davis were arrested by Stillwater police.

"Oh, no!" Kyle groaned as he saw the flashing blue and red lights in his rearview mirror. He pulled over to the side of the road and dug in his pocket for his driver's license.

"OK, guys! Out of the car! You're under arrest," the policeman ordered.

"What's all this about?" Kyle questioned.

"We haven't done anything," Henry declared.

"There'll be plenty of time to talk at the police station," one of the officers said.

At the station they were told, "We have evidence that the car you're driving has been used in several robberies. You're driving the car; therefore we suspect that you're involved."

"This isn't even our car," Kyle explained. "We just borrowed it to come downtown for a hamburger. I promise you, I've never stolen anything in my life! We're not thieves!"

"So you say," the officer grinned. "Who is your friend that owns the car?"

Eventually three of the real thieves were rounded up and brought into the station. "Kyle Rote is our ringleader," they lied, thinking that by their naming a star athlete, the whole thing would be hushed up.

Kyle was in deep trouble, and it took a lot of time and effort to put the record straight. Even after the newspapers printed the truth, some people wondered if Kyle and Henry were really involved. The next year Kyle and Henry changed schools so they could have a clean slate. You can be sure that after that they were very careful about the friends with whom they associated.

Kyle and Henry learned that it isn't enough to not do evil. You've also got to avoid the appearance of evil. Whether we like it or not, people are going to judge us by the friends we keep and the evidence they see, wrong as it may be.

KNUTE ROCKNE

Whatsoever he saith unto you, do it. John 2:5.

Everybody who watches football has heard of Notre Dame. About 75 years ago, when Knute Rockne joined the team, hardly anyone had heard of the little university in South Bend, Indiana. After Rockne was graduated from Notre Dame, he stayed on as coach and put Notre Dame on the map as a great football power. In the 13 years he was coach his team lost only 12 games. For five straight years they won every game they played.

Their strength lay in speed, strategy, and skill rather than in physical size and brute force. It also lay in their willingness to obey their coach.

One day Coach Rockne explained his theories on blocking. "Two-man blocking is not necessary," he insisted. "One-man blocking is more effective because of the element of surprise. You can come at your man from a different angle each time."

"One man doesn't have enough strength to block a runner," one of the players objected.

"He does if he does it right," Rockne continued. "Come at your opponent from a low crouch, your legs spread wide apart like this." The coach demonstrated what he meant. "Now let's see what you can do."

All of the players except Joe Bachman, a veteran first-string player, tried the one-man blocking position. "Come, here, Bachman," Rockne called. "I don't think you understood what I want you to do. Here, I'll show you again. Watch carefully, then get out there and try it!"

I don't have to do what he says, Bachman thought. *My way worked fine before Rockne showed up. I'm not changing.* He went back to practice, but refused to try the new method.

"Turn in your uniform, Bachman!" Rockne yelled. "You're through! We can't have a team without teamwork. You've got to obey my orders!" Stunned, Bachman apologized for his behavior and promised to obey in the future. He was immediately reinstated.

Jesus is your coach in the game of life. You are pitted against Satan and all the forces of evil. If you want to win, you must obey your coach. Whatever He tells you to do, do it.

JIM MARSHALL

Strait is the gate, and narrow is the way, which leadeth unto life, and few there be that find it. Matthew 7:14.

On October 25, 1964, the Minnesota Vikings, of the National Football League, were playing the San Francisco 49ers in San Francisco. The ball was in the hands of Bill Kilmer, 49er halfback. He was hit and fumbled the ball. Jim Marshall, of the Vikings, jumped a player in front of him and scooped up the loose ball on the run. Without hesitation he sprinted toward his own goal line, 66 yards away.

The crowd went wild with excitement, drowning out the shouts of Jim's teammates. No one blocked his progress to the end zone. He was elated, thinking the crowd was cheering his touchdown.

San Francisco's Bruce Bosely threw his arms around Marshall and cried, "Thanks, man, for the safety!" Jim knew then that something was wrong.

"Jim, you went the wrong way, the wrong way!" exclaimed Viking quarterback Fran Tarkenton. Only then did Jim realize he had run in the wrong direction. Mortified, he buried his face in his hands and wished the earth would open up a way of escape from his embarrassment. When it didn't, he jogged back to the bench to face his coach.

"Forget it, Jim," Coach Van Brocklin said, slapping him on the back. "Go back in there and make the fans forget."

You can be sure that for the rest of the game Jim Marshall ran in the right direction! Minnesota won, 27-22.

Are you running in the right direction in the game of life? There are only two ways to run. There's the narrow way, which leads to heaven, and the broad way, which leads to destruction.

You probably won't be blocked as you race pell-mell toward destruction. You will no doubt enjoy your run with the ball in that direction. The crowds will cheer and your heart will race as you look forward to success. How awful to reach the end and discover it was all for nothing! You were running the wrong way, away from Jesus and His cross . . . away from heaven and the victor's crown.

You have the ball. Which way are you running?

RED FRIESELL

Confess your faults one to another. James 5:16.

Confessing your faults is not easy. It takes an honest man, a brave man, to say "I was wrong." Referee Red Friesell was that kind of man.

It happened on November 16, 1940, on the Dartmouth football field. Dartmouth was playing Cornell, which had not lost a game in three seasons. Nine seconds remained. Referee Red Friesell blew his whistle to announce a penalty and called for the ball, then gave it to Cornell.

A Cornell player aimed a pass at a receiver in the end zone, but Ray Hall, the Dartmouth fullback, leaped high and knocked the ball down at the goal line. Dartmouth moved to take over the ball.

At that point, with three seconds remaining, Red Friesell became confused. He was not sure which team should have possession of the ball. He started to give it to Dartmouth, then stopped and threw it to Cornell again. They made a touchdown and apparently won, 7-3.

"You're wrong!" Howie Odell told Friesell. "Cornell had five downs. That last touchdown play was illegal."

"If that's true, we'll try to reverse the score," Friesell said. As soon as Red Friesell saw a film of the game he knew that he had made a mistake.

"I was wrong," the referee admitted. "I gave Cornell an illegal extra down. It was totally my fault."

After Friesell's confession the president of Cornell sent a wire to the president of Dartmouth: "We congratulate you on the victory of your fine team. The Cornell touchdown was scored on a fifth down, and we relinquish claim to the victory and extend contratulations to Dartmouth."

Because of Red Friesell's truthfulness, the score was changed to show that Dartmouth won that day, 3-0. But somehow I think that in the books of heaven Cornell and Red Friesell were also written down as winners. They lost the football game, but they certainly came out champions in the game of life. Honesty is more important than winning. A good character is the greatest trophy you can have.

JIM THORPE

Behold, I come quickly: hold that fast which thou hast, that no man take thy crown. Revelation 3:11.

The 1912 Olympics were over, and it was time for King Gustav V of Sweden to present the awards. He stood on the victory stand in the center of the vast stadium and called the winners one by one.

"Pentathlon, first place to James Thorpe, U.S.A.," the king declared.

Proudly Jim stepped forward to receive his prize, a bronze bust of King Gustav V and a gold medal. The applause of the crowd was deafening.

"Decathlon, first place to James Thorpe, U.S.A." The king of Sweden smiled again at the youth standing arrow-straight, scarcely breathing in his excitement.

Jim took from the king's hand a magnificent gold and jewel-encrusted chalice molded in the shape of a Viking ship, as well as the gold medal for first place. The audience roared its approval.

"You are the first person who has ever won the gold medal for both the pentathlon and the decathlon," the king said, draping a large laurel wreath over Jim's shoulders. "You are the greatest athlete in the world."

However, Jim Thorpe's glory was short-lived. About a month later he was called into his coach's office. "Did you get paid for playing baseball in Rocky Mount and Fayetteville?"

"Sure," Jim admitted. "Everyone did."

"But you're an amateur, and amateurs aren't supposed to get paid. You will have to give back your Olympic medals. The bust of King Gustav V and the golden chalice will have to be sent back to Sweden."

"But I didn't know I was doing wrong," Jim protested. It didn't matter. His name was struck from the Olympic records.

When you accepted Jesus He promised you the crown of everlasting life. He's coming back soon to hold the victory celebration. Don't let anyone cheat you of that glorious golden moment. Hold on to the promises of God's Word. Hold on to your faith. Don't let anyone take your crown.

BOB MATHIAS

Take therefore no thought for the morrow: for the morrow shall take thought for the things of itself. Matthew 6:34.

Have you ever met a worrywart? He is a person who worries a lot, especially over things that are not important. He is a fretful sort of person who is anxious about things he cannot change. He wrinkles his forehead, wrings his hands, and looks at you with troubled eyes as he moans, "Whatever am I going to do about tomorrow?"

Bob Mathias, who won the decathlon gold medal twice, was definitely not a worrywart, even when he might have had an excuse to be one. His first Olympic decathlon contest was held at London's Wembley Stadium in the rain. The 17-year-old had to perform in the worst possible conditions of mud and fog against older, more experienced men.

Bob's first-day showing was poor. In fact, he knocked down the crossbar twice during the high jump. He lost points on the shot put because he stepped out of the box on the wrong side. At the end of the day he was third, behind contestants from Argentina and France.

In spite of his setbacks, Bob came bounding out of the locker room to greet his parents with a smile of victory. "I'll be up on that winner's stand to get a medal. You just wait and see!"

"It looks bad," his father said, shaking his head. "Aren't you worried?"

"Nope," Bob replied. "They don't give points for worrying!"

That night Bob went to bed early and got a good night's rest. The next day he put all his energy into throwing the javelin, jumping the broad jump, and running in the 1,500-meter race. At the end of the day his tired muscles ached. He was cold and wet. But he had won the gold medal.

Gold medals are won by work, not by worry. All the fretting in the world wouldn't have given Bob a single point. Likewise, all the stewing and complaining you might do will not move you one inch closer to your goal. So forget about being a worrywart. Put all your energy into being a winner.

RAFER JOHNSON

A good name is rather to be chosen than great riches, and loving favour than silver and gold. Proverbs 22:1.

Opening day for the 1960 Olympics in Rome, Italy, dawned bright and beautiful. Visitors from around the world watched the grand opening parade of more than 4,000 athletes. The team from each country was led by a flagbearer.

"The honor of carrying the American flag," the announcer said, "goes to Rafer Johnson, an athlete of world renown. He is also a young man of the highest character."

Proudly Rafer led his countrymen into the great stadium as spectators cheered. In the games that followed, Rafer won the decathlon gold medal in spite of a back injury suffered in a car accident.

It was a long road from the Black ghetto of Dallas, Texas, to the winner's stand in Rome, Italy. Somehow, in traveling that rough highway, Rafer developed a shining character that was of greater value than the gold medal he so proudly claimed.

Hard work was one of the ingredients in Rafer's character that was apparent from his childhood. His family was very poor, and he often was up at dawn, urging his sleepy brothers, "Come on, get up! We've got to get out there and pick fruit. Mom and Dad need all the help we can give!"

During high school days in Tulare, California, Rafer became a star in basketball, football, and baseball, in spite of racial prejudice and poverty. When the tide turned and people began to respect him for his abilities, he held no grudges.

During college Rafer belonged to a fraternity and three honor groups. He took part in six different committees and two choirs and still had time to be president of the student body and practice five or six hours a day for the decathlon.

Another plus in Rafer's character was his honesty. "I trust Rafer," one of his professors said. "I'd leave him alone with the answers for tomorrow's test and know he'd never peek."

Rafer Johnson had earned a character gold medal long before he received the Olympics gold medal. In your opinion, which was more valuable?

JESSE OWENS

Inasmuch as ye have done it unto one of the least of these my brethren, ye have done it unto me. Matthew 25:40.

"The Olympic Games will prove that fair-skinned athletes of the Aryan race are the supermen of the world," Adolf Hitler, dictator of Nazi Germany, boasted in 1936.

When Jesse Owens, a 20-year-old Black youth from Alabama, proved Hitler's theory wrong, the dictator was furious. "I will not shake hands with him," the dictator frowned when the winner was announced. "He is not to be allowed in my box."

When it came to the broad jump, the first two of Jesse's jumps were declared invalid. He had only one try left. Before going back to make his jump, he knelt down and drew a starting line of his own one foot behind the official one. He was determined that there would be no excuse for calling a foul. When he set an Olympic record with a jump of 26 feet, 5 5/16 inches, the embarrassed Adolf Hitler still refused to shake his hand and acknowledge his feat.

When Owens won the 200-meter dash on the following day, a flustered Hitler ducked out of his box and fled the stadium to avoid congratulating Jesse Owens.

Ignoring the slights of the German ruler, Jesse Owens went on to win a fourth gold medal as a member of the United States 400-meter relay team.

When Jesse Owens returned to Germany in 1951, he was warmly welcomed by the mayor of Berlin. "Fifteen years ago Hitler would not shake your hand," the mayor said before a crowd of 75,000 people. "Here, I give you both of mine." Then he threw his arms around Jesse's neck and hugged him.

Can you imagine how hurt Jesse must have been when Hitler refused to shake his hand simply because he was of the wrong color? It feels terrible to be rejected. It's terrible to be left out.The pain goes deep when you are not accepted.

I wonder if Hitler would have acted differently had he understood that the way he treated Jesse Owens was recorded in the books of heaven as being done to Jesus.

Would you reject Jesus? Would you refuse to play with Him? Would you try to keep Him off your team?

PHEIDIPPIDES

But thanks be to God, which giveth us the victory through our Lord Jesus Christ. 1 Corinthians 15:57.

The year is 490 B.C. The place is the plain of Marathon, 25 miles from Athens, Greece. Six thousand four hundred Persians lie dead upon the battlefield. Weary Greek soldiers are already gathering the 192 of their own dead into a pile for burial to protect them from the vultures that are circling the field.

Running through the battlefield, leaping over the sprawled bodies, comes a messenger. It is Pheidippides, returning from his 150-mile race to Sparta to bring reinforcements. Exhausted, he drops at the feet of Miltiades, the Athenian general.

"Did you give my message to the Spartans?" Miltiades asks.

"Yes, sir, I did. They will come but only after the moon is full and they have completed their religious ceremonies."

"It doesn't matter," Miltiades answers. "We have won the battle without them. The Persians have fled by sea. I fear they are headed for Athens, and the city may surrender. You must run to Athens and tell them of our victory."

"Is there no one else? I am still weary from the journey to Sparta."

"The others are just as tired from the battle. I have no one else. You must go."

Gathering every bit of his remaining energy, Pheidippides begins the 25-mile trip at top speed. He forces his tired muscles to respond, and he covers the distance in record time. Arriving at the gate of the city, he cries out, "Rejoice, we conquer!" and drops dead.

Like Pheidippides, you and I also have a message to carry for our general—a message of victory. What a wonderful message it is! Jesus Christ has won the victory over Satan in the battle for this world. The enemies of sin and death have been defeated.

Will you be a runner for Jesus, taking the news of victory to those who have not yet heard?

SPIRIDON LOUES

Know ye not that they which run in a race run all, but one receiveth the prize? So run, that ye may obtain. 1 Corinthians 9:24.

In 1896, almost 2,400 years after Pheidippides made his legendary run from Marathon to Athens, the first modern Olympic Games were held in Greece. The last event was to be a marathon race retracing the route of Pheidippides. One hundred fifty thousand spectators lined the road from Marathon to Athens while another 70,000 waited in the stadium.

No Greek athlete had yet won a gold medal, and the Greek spectators were anxious for a victory. They were pinning their hopes on Spiridon Loues, a slender 25-year-old shepherd who had trained by running in the hills where he tended his flocks.

When the starting gun sounded at 2:00 p.m., 25 runners started the rugged 26-mile course. A Frenchman took the lead, followed by an Australian, an American, and a Hungarian, with Spiridon Loues in fifth place.

"Run faster!" shouted the spectators. "You are far behind."

"Don't worry," answered Loues as he ran by. "I will overtake them and beat them all."

The test came when, six miles from Athens, the course went uphill. The American had already quit. The Frenchman slowed to a walk, then dropped out. The Australian faltered, stumbled, and collapsed. As Spiridon Loues nimbly raced uphill he put more than a mile between him and the Hungarian. Spectators went wild with excitement as he neared the finish. Spiridon Loues, a Greek, won the gold medal.

Like Spiridon Loues, you and I are also in a race, a kind of spiritual marathon from Planet Earth to the New Jerusalem. We too must travel a rough road that leads upward to the Holy City. Often we may be tempted to slow our pace to a walk or even to quit, but we must keep on to the finish. We may stumble and fall but we must get up and keep running toward our goal. The gold medal of eternal life will be worth the effort. In this race everyone who makes it to the finish will receive a victor's crown. Will you be one of them?

GARRY BJORKLAND

Wherefore seeing we also are compassed about with so great a cloud of witnesses, . . . let us run with patience the race that is set before us. Hebrews 12:1.

Garry Bjorkland was sure he would make the 1976 Olympics team until the moment he lost his shoe on the track at Eugene, Oregon. It was an accident. Someone stepped on his heel, and the tab tucked underneath his foot. Frantically Gary pulled at the heel tab, but there was no way he could get the shoe back on unless he stopped, so he kicked it off.

"At first I had a wild dash of hope that everything was going to be all right," Gary said. "But when you lose a shoe on the track, you realize in a hurry that your whole rhythm and flow is dependent on having that spike there. It helps you with your landing and your pull-through and your power-off on the next stride."

Garry's bare foot skidded as it came down. After 200 yards of shuffling around the track Garry was ready to drop out. As he rounded the corner where he had lost the shoe someone from the crowd shouted, "Don't give up. Hang in there!"

With a spurt of energy Garry set off on the next lap. When he came around the curve this time 25 people were shouting, "Come on, man! You can make it!" He came around again and 75 people were pulling for him. The next lap 150 shouted encouragement. The next time there were 300. Then 500. Everytime he came around, the group rooting for him grew bigger and yelled a little louder. Finally, with two laps to go, 7,000 fans were urging him on to the finish.

"I lost all feeling," said Garry. "I forgot about my bare foot. All I knew was the rah-rah-rah of the crowd. It was as though all their energy was funneled right into me."

The crowd roared its approval as Garry's bare foot crossed the finish line. He had made the Olympic team!

Are you, like Garry, running your life's race with a handicap? Does it seem that other kids have a lot easier time of it than you? Do you sometimes feel like quitting? Listen to the crowd of heavenly spectators cheering you on: "Don't give up! Hang in there! You can make it!"

BABE DIDRIKSON

So he built the house, and finished it. 1 Kings 6:9.

Starting a project is easy; finishing it is more difficult. It takes real strength of character to complete what you begin, in spite of the obstacles that may come your way. There are lots of starters in the game of life but very few finishers. Babe Didrikson was one of those rare individuals with determination enough to finish whatever she started. Like the time when she was 8 and decided to mow Mr. McClain's yard.

"We've been away for quite a while," Mr. McClain answered in response to her plea for a job. "See how tall the grass is. It's too big a task for a little girl like you!"

"Oh, no, sir!" Babe shook her curls. "Please let me try it! I know I can do it! I want so much to earn money for my harmonica."

"Well, all right," Mr. McClain conceded. "You can try. If you finish, I'll give you enough money for your harmonica." He was quite sure she'd give up when she found out how hard it was to cut overgrown grass.

It was a lot harder to cut than Babe had thought. She pushed and shoved the mower in the tall grass, but it would move only a few inches at a time before the long weeds wrapped around the cutting blades, making it impossible to move. Discouraged, she sat down in the tall grass and moaned, "I'll never finish it at this rate!" Then she thought of her dad's sickle. That would take care of those pesky weeds! It took her all morning and half of the afternoon before she had cut down the tall weeds and was ready to make another try with the hand mower. It was almost dark when she finished, and in the process she had said no to an inviting ball game in the park.

"I must admit I wasn't sure you could do it," Mr. McClain said as he gave her the money for her harmonica.

"I guess I usually pretty well finish what I start," Babe said, smiling broadly.

That same determination made Babe Didrikson successful in everything she tried. It was that quality that made her an Olympic gold medal winner when she grew up. It's the magic quality that will make you a winner, too.

WILMA RUDOLPH

Exercise thyself rather unto godliness. 1 Timothy 4:7.

"When can I take these braces off?" 11-year-old Wilma Rudolph asked her doctor.

"We'll see."

"But I don't want to be a cripple all my life!" Wilma insisted. "Isn't there something we can do?"

"I guess it wouldn't hurt to exercise your legs a little each day," the doctor replied cautiously. "I'll teach your mom and dad how to exercise your legs with massage."

"A lot of exercise is better than a little exercise," Wilma reasoned. When her parents left the house, Wilma took off the braces and painfully walked around the house for hours.

Then one day she told her doctor, "I have something to show you." Carefully she removed her braces and walked across the office to where he sat.

"How long have you been doing this?" he asked.

"For more than a year," she admitted. "I sometimes take the braces off and walk around the house."

"Since you have been honest with me," the doctor replied, "sometimes I'll let you take them off and walk around the house." Wilma never put them on again.

At 12 Wilma decided to conquer all phases of women's sports. By the time she was 14 she was a member of the University of Tennessee women's track team. At 16 she was training for the Olympics. At 20 she breezed to easy victories in the 100-meter and 200-meter dashes and helped the U.S. women's team to first place in the 400-meter relay. In 1960 Wilma Rudolph became the first woman ever to win three gold medals in track and field!

Are you a spiritual cripple, depending on your mom, dad, pastor, or teacher to keep you hobbling along your way to heaven? Isn't it time you took off your braces and exercised the muscles of your spiritual legs every day? Couldn't you spend more time with God on your own? Aren't you old enough to study your Sabbath school lesson without help? Couldn't you begin to do the right things without urging from those who are older? Do you want to go through life always leaning on the spiritual arm of someone else?

FELIX CARVAJAL

And lead us not into temptation, but deliver us from evil.
Matthew 6:13.

By far the most colorful participant in the 1904 Olympic Games was Felix Carvajal, a postman from Havana, Cuba, who had trained by running his mail route every day. He paid his own way to the United States, only to have all his money stolen in New Orleans. Without money for bus fare, he ran the 600 miles to St. Louis to compete.

When he arrived at the stadium his fellow athletes welcomed him with cheers and a collection to pay for his board and room. When it was time to begin the marathon race he showed up in the clothes he had worn from Havana, for that's all he had. Quickly someone found a pair of scissors and cut off his sleeves and trouser legs.

Felix looked very much out of place as he took his position with the other runners to wait for the starting signal. Even so, he was fast enough to have won had it not been for some apples. While runner after runner dropped out of the race because of the heat, Felix had no trouble keeping up with the leaders until the course passed an apple orchard. How good it would feel to sink his teeth into a cool, juicy apple! He stopped to pick some, stuffing one into his mouth and the rest into his pockets to eat as he ran.

In spite of the delay to pick apples, Felix still kept up with the leaders. Then suddenly he clutched his stomach and staggered off the course. "It's the apples I ate," he groaned. "They have given me a stomachache."

In a moment the cramp had passed, and he was up and running again. But by this time the other marathoners were far ahead. He placed fourth. Yielding to temptation had lost him the race.

On our journey to heaven all of us are tempted to stop and pick forbidden fruit. For David and Samson the "apple" was a woman. For Ananias and Sapphira it was money. For you the "apple" might be rock music, movies, clothes, drugs, or dirty jokes. The devil has a thousand ways to keep you from winning the race. Is your "apple" really worth losing eternity?

GLENN CUNNINGHAM

*Wherein thou judgest another, thou condemnest thyself.
Romans 2:1.*

"Daddy, look at that funny man down there!" a small girl high up in the stadium pointed at one of the competitors beside the starting line. While others stood around waiting for the signal to line up, he pranced and contorted his body in all sorts of weird positions.

"That's Glenn Cunningham, the showoff!" her father answered. "Who does he think he is, anyhow?"

"They call him the Kansas Flyer," another spectator commented, "but Kansas Clown is more like it!"

"All right, Cunningham, we see you," others yelled. "Boo! Boo!"

What the jeering spectators couldn't see were the horrible scars on the runner's legs. Because the scar tissue went so deep, Glenn couldn't limber up as other runners did. He had to go through these painful exercises just to make it possible for his legs to work in the race.

When Glenn Cunningham was a boy he had been trapped in a schoolhouse fire. Before he could be rescued, he was badly burned. For many days his family and friends didn't think he would live. He was in bed almost a year. When at last the burns healed, the doctors felt sure he would never walk.

But Glenn Cunningham was a boy with courage. He got out of bed and limped painfully around his father's farm. He forced himself to walk and then run. He was called the Kansas Flyer because he could run a mile in four minutes and four seconds. What most people didn't know was that every race was a test of his courage because of the tremendous pain he had to go through to get the blood flowing through the scar tissue of his legs.

In reality the spectators were condemning themselves when they jeered Glenn. They were labeling themselves as ignorant, rude people. Those who knew Glenn Cunningham cheered him for his wonderful courage.

Did you ever notice that when you point a finger at someone else, three fingers are pointing back at yourself? I can't imagine Jesus pointing and making fun of someone, can you?

PAAVO NURMI

I keep under my body, and bring it into subjection. 1 Corinthians 9:27.

A trolley car rattled down the street of Turku, Finland, with teenager Paavo Nurmi behind it. As the trolley gathered speed Paavo quickened his pace to match. His wiry legs beat a steady rhythm on the pavement.

"Hurry, Paavo," a friend called from the sidewalk. "You can catch it!"

"Faster, Paavo, faster," another called.

"Why doesn't the conductor stop?" a stranger to town asked. "You'd think he'd see how badly the man needs to get on!"

"Paavo doesn't really want to catch the trolley," his friend laughed. "Chasing the trolley is his way of training for the Olympics. He does this every day during lunch."

"He must really want to win!" the visitor said. "The day you'd find me chasing a trolley car down Main Street!"

The visitor was right. Winning was the passion of Paavo Nurmi. Although he had had to go to work as a laborer when he was 12, he never gave up his dream. He used every spare moment to run, strengthening his muscles, bringing his body under the subjection of his will, making it do what he commanded it to do. When he was called into the Finnish Army, Paavo only intensified his daily workouts. Stopwatch in hand, he practiced endlessly, trying to beat his record time.

When the day came for Paavo to run in the Olympics, his body was ready. He set a world record on the mile run, and he created a sensation by winning the 1,500-meter and 5,000-meter races in the same day. Two days later he won a gold medal in the 10,000-meter steeplechase under a broiling sun that forced two thirds of the competitors to quit the race.

Paavo Nurmi brought his body under subjection so that he could win a laurel wreath that would soon fade. How much greater should be our desire to be healthy, so that we might win in the race of life.

AUGUSTINE

But put ye on the Lord Jesus Christ, and make not provision for the flesh, to fulfil the lusts thereof. Romans 13:14.

On a sultry day in Milan, Italy, in A.D. 387, a faint hint of a breeze stirred the leaves of a fig tree. Its branches cast a cooling shadow on the prostrate form of Augustine. His face to the ground, he clutched at the grass to steady his trembling body. The wall of his pride had crumbled, allowing the tears of remorse to flow freely down his sun-tanned cheeks.

"O God, save me," Augustine cried out in anguish. "My sin is greater than I can bear."

A picture of a great lake of fire formed in Augustine's mind. It was the place prepared for Satan and his followers. He imagined himself writhing in the flames, tormented for all the wrong, hateful things he had done.

"I'm an evil, wicked man," Augustine continued in his prayer. "Unless You save me I'm a lost man, for I cannot break my sinful habits. How long, Lord, how long must I remain in this wretched state? Tomorrow? Why not now? Why can't this be the hour to end my uncleanness?"

At that moment Augustine heard the voice of a child in a nearby house chanting, "Take up and read; take up and read." Sensing that this was God's answer to him, Augustine picked up the Scripture he had been reading when the feeling of his wickedness had overwhelmed him. Grasping the book with trembling fingers, he let it fall open to Romans 13. His eyes focused on verses 13 and 14: "Not in rioting and drunkenness, not in chambering and wantonness, not in strife and envying; but put ye on the Lord Jesus Christ, and make not provision for the flesh, to fulfil the lusts thereof."

"The moment I read those words all the gloom of doubt vanished away," Augustine later wrote. "A wonderful peace and security came into my heart, and I knew that I was forgiven. I had no more fear of death, for Jesus Christ was with me."

Are you, like Augustine, struggling with the power of sin in your life? Let this be the day when Jesus comes into your heart, taking away the burden of guilt and shame, and giving you in its place joy, peace, and power to live a godly life.

SAINT FRANCIS OF ASSISI

Blessed are the poor in spirit: for their's is the kingdom of heaven. Matthew 5:3.

Inside the cave of Monte Subasio it was cool, dark, and damp. Bats clung to the rough ceiling, observing the strange creature that knelt among their droppings on the cave floor. The praying figure was Francis Bernardone, son of a wealthy merchant in Assisi, Italy. He came often to this isolated spot to seek God's will for his life.

"Lord, what would You have me do?" he cried out.

At first there was no sound save the dripping of water and the rustling of bat wings. Then, somewhere deep within his mind, he heard God's voice speaking, "Blessed are the poor in spirit: for their's is the kingdom of heaven."

Francis thought of the poor: homeless, maimed, blind, diseased. "How can those miserable wretches be blessed?" he replied. "Do You expect me to become like the beggars? I was hoping to be a knight, doing glorious deeds in Your name."

"Blessed are the poor," the inner voice repeated.

Still uncertain, Francis decided to go to church. Maybe there God's voice would be clearer. As he passed among the outstretched arms of the poor riffraff who cluttered the steps of the cathedral, he heard again the voice of God to his soul, "Blessed are the poor."

Grabbing the shoulder of a filthy beggar of about his own height, Francis blurted out, "I'll trade clothes with you."

"Are you crazy or something?" the disheveled man said, stepping back. "You would trade your fine suit of velvet and silk for my dirty rags?"

"That's exactly what I mean," Francis said, beginning to remove his jacket.

Dressed in the beggar's tattered clothes, Francis pleaded in French for alms. Side by side with beggars, he felt he was walking with Jesus. After that experience he gave away all his possessions and spent the rest of his life as a poor man, preaching God's message of love and humility wherever he went.

What lesson do you think Francis Bernardone learned that might help you in your walk with God today?

JOHN WYCLIFFE

For we can do nothing against the truth. 2 Corinthians 13:8.

Five hundred years ago Bibles were rare, for they had to be copied by hand. The few copies available were written in Latin or Greek, languages understood by only a few scholars in monasteries and universities. One of those who read and understood was John Wycliffe, professor of theology at Oxford University.

"These words of truth are too good to keep to myself," Professor Wycliffe declared. "I am going to translate the Bible, so that every man in England might read the wonderful works of God. Then the common people will no longer be deceived by the friars."

"The friars are making themselves rich on the money they collect from poor men's pockets," Wycliffe taught. "They are selling pardons and granting absolution to the worst of criminals. If people had the Bible in their own language, they could readily see that salvation is a free gift of God."

"We must put a stop to Wycliffe's teaching," the friars decided. Although they tried, it seemed impossible to silence Wycliffe until he became sick with a deadly disease. Eight representatives of the church gathered around his bed.

"You are going to die," they gloated. "Now's your chance to take back what you have written about the pope and his friars."

"Help me up," Wycliffe said to his attendant. After he was propped up in bed, . . . he looked his accusers straight in the eye and replied in a firm, strong voice, "I shall not die, but live; and again declare the evil deeds of the friars."

The astonished monks hurried from the room to plan another way to stop him.

Wycliffe did get well and continued to translate and teach. Three times he was brought to trial for his beliefs. At his third trial he said, "With whom do you think you are contending? With an old man on the brink of the grave? No! You are fighting with truth—truth that is stronger than you."

John Wycliffe was right. Truth did triumph, and because it did, you and I can read the Bible in our own language.

JOHN HUSS

I will give him unto the Lord all the days of his life. 1 Samuel 1:11.

These words spoken by Hannah about Samuel have been repeated by godly mothers through the centuries as they have dedicated their children to God. Mrs. Huss, from a village in southwestern Bohemia, was no exception.

It was not easy for Mrs. Huss to raise her boy. While John was still a baby, his dad died, leaving her to struggle alone to provide food, shelter, and clothing.

"I'll quit school and get a job," John must have offered many times. "I hate to see you so worn and tired."

"No!" she replied as she straightened her tired shoulders, "you are going to get a good education and make something of yourself. I believe God has a special work for you to do."

When John finished the provincial school, he was given a scholarship to attend the university at Prague.

"I'm proud of you, John," Mrs. Huss said.

When it was time to go to Prague, John packed his few belongings and set out by foot, with his mother for a companion. As they approached the city Mrs. Huss turned to her only son and said, "My boy, I have nothing to give you but my love and my prayers." Kneeling there beside the road, she prayed, "O God, bless my boy! Use him in a mighty way and keep him faithful to You! Amen."

Little did Widow Huss realize how God would answer that prayer for her son. He completed his course with honors and was made a priest and a professor. He went on to become the rector of that great university and one of the leading Protestant Reformers. Finally, he gave the ultimate sacrifice when he was burned at the stake because of his faith in Jesus. His persecutors threw his ashes into the Rhine River, expecting that to be the end of Huss and his message. But even as those ashes washed out to sea and around the world, so the work he began took root in many other countries of earth, yielding an abundant harvest for Christ's kingdom.

MARTIN LUTHER

The just shall live by faith. Romans 1:17.

One day in 1505, 22-year-old Martin Luther was walking from his home in Mansfeld, Germany, to the law school in Erfurt when a storm struck.

Lightning flashed, thunder roared, and rain came down in sheets that drove him to seek shelter under the nearest tree. The wind tore at his clothing and broke off tree limbs as he crouched in the darkness. Suddenly a jagged bolt of lightning hit the earth nearby, knocking Martin to the ground.

In a moment there flashed before him all the sins he had ever committed. He saw again the stained-glass window in the Mansfeld church that had terrified him as a boy. It portrayed Jesus with a frowning face, sitting on a rainbow. On one side was a lily representing Jesus' blessing on the good. A flaming sword on the other side symbolized His anger against the wicked. There was no doubt in Martin's mind as he lay on the wet ground. God was angry with him.

He remembered, too, the altarpiece, which depicted a ship sailing toward heaven with only priests and monks on board. The common people were drowning in the sea except for a few who grasped ropes thrown out by the holy men. Becoming a monk seemed the surest way to salvation.

"O Lord, save me!" Martin cried out in his anguish. "Save me from this storm and I will become a monk!"

And there was no better monk than Martin Luther. He spent hours in fasting and prayer. He beat himself in penance for his sins. He refused blankets in winter to show remorse for his wicked ways. He climbed the sacred staircase in Rome on his knees, saying the Lord's Prayer on each step. Once he confessed his sins to another priest for six hours straight, but felt no forgiveness.

Nothing brought Martin peace until the day he read Paul's words in Romans, "The just shall live by faith," and understood for the first time the love and grace of God. He spent the rest of his life telling others that forgiveness was theirs through faith. The penalty for their sins had already been paid on Calvary. Heaven was theirs for the asking.

ULRICH ZWINGLI

All things work together for good to them that love God, to them who are the called according to his purpose. Romans 8:28.

In August of 1519 the highways leading out of Zurich, Switzerland, were crowded with oxcarts, pushcarts, donkeys, cows, goats, and people running from death. Thousands of feet beating a retreat on the dry roads filled the air with dust.

"This dust is choking me!" one traveler complained.

"Let's go back home!" a child whimpered. "I'm tired."

His mother replied, "Hush! Heat, dust, and sore feet are nothing compared to the plague."

The boy hushed, for he had seen a neighbor, an uncle, and a cousin die of the dreaded bubonic plague. He had seen them suffer from chills and fever, headache, and body pains. In nearly every household he had heard the wailing for dead loved ones. He knew his family was lucky to have enough money to leave the city. Almost everyone who stayed got the fever, and one in three died.

One of those who chose to stay in Zurich that August was Ulrich Zwingli, the priest. He worked day and night burying the dead, comforting the bereaved, and pointing the dying to Jesus Christ, their only hope. In September he caught the fever. In those days when death was near, he found God very real and close. At that low point in his life he wrote: "Thy purpose fulfill. Nothing can be too severe for me. I am but Thy vessel to be made whole or broken in pieces."

Zwingli came out of his sickness a different man. He believed God had raised him up for a purpose, to spread the message of God's love and forgiveness. He vowed to preach the Bible and the Bible only as the rule of faith and practice.

Another blessing to come out of the Zurich plague of 1519 was the interest people now had in hearing the gospel. Their long weeks of dealing with sickness and death had taught them the hopelessness of relying on money or good works to gain salvation. Although the plague was a terrible experience, God worked through it to bring about something good.

COTTON MATHER

It is appointed unto men once to die, but after this the judgment. Hebrews 9:27.

On April 16, 1669, 6-year-old Cotton Mather stood unnoticed in a corner of his grandfather's sick room to watch him die. Servants hurried back and forth with basins and blankets, trying to make the old man comfortable. Cotton stared through misty eyes at his own father, who bent over the bed of the dying man, listening to his final words.

"Ah, to be in England in the springtime!" The old man's voice, usually loud and full, was now so feeble that Cotton had to hold his breath so he could hear. "Me thinks I can smell the hedgerows . . ."

"Father, Father!" his daddy's voice seemed harsh as he shook the old man to bring him back to reality. "You are on the verge of meeting your Maker. You must think more serious thoughts!"

"I am ready," the old man's voice croaked. "I have given the best years of my life to God and five sons to the service of the church."

"Yes, Father, but now you are going to face the judgment bar of God."

"I have tried my best," the old man replied. "I have preached the truth and kept the faith. I'm ready to go."

Cotton blinked hard to keep back the tears. He crept closer to the big bed, wondering about death and the judgment. It all sounded so scary. What would it be like to stand before God? Even kids died sometimes. What would God do to a boy who didn't like to sit still in church and sometimes forgot to say his prayers?

Fifty-nine years later Cotton knew what it was like. He faced his own death unafraid, just as his grandfather had done. More than fifty years of getting acquainted with the Judge made him feel he was going to meet a well-loved friend.

Do you feel that way about the coming of Jesus? Whether you die and are buried, or whether you live to see Jesus come, it is the same. At His return we all will face our Judge. If you have made Him your friend, there is nothing to fear.

GEORGE WHITEFIELD

Ye must be born again. John 3:7.

"Mr. Whitefield! Mr. Whitefield!"

George Whitefield looked up to see a distraught woman stumbling along the bank of the Thames River, waving her arms. As she came closer he recognized her as the wife of an inmate of the jail where he visited regularly.

"I have done a terrible thing," she sobbed, collapsing at his feet. "I couldn't stand the cries of my starving children any longer, so I jumped off the bridge. A gentleman swam out and rescued me. I see now how wicked I am. Is there any hope for me?"

"Here, take this money and buy some food for yourself and the children," George said, placing a few coins in her hand. "I'll visit you, and your husband in jail, this afternoon."

He arrived at the jail as promised, bringing with him his Bible. He opened it to John 3 and began to read about the new birth. The couple listened quietly until he reached verses 15 and 16:

" 'That whosoever believeth in him should not perish, but have eternal life. For God so loved the world, that—' "

"I believe! I believe!" shouted the woman in ecstasy. "I shall not perish because I believe in Jesus! I am born again!"

"Help me!" her husband cried, grasping George's hand. "I'm a sinner bound for hell!"

" 'For God so loved the world, that he gave his only begotten Son, that whosoever believeth—' "

"I believe too," her husband exclaimed. "I'm born again. Oh, joy, joy, joy!"

George was astonished. He had been struggling for nearly a year to achieve what these two experienced in a moment. It was not until several months later that he was willing to accept salvation as God's free gift as the couple had done. When he ceased struggling and simply believed, he had what he sought—the new birth, the joy of knowing his sins were forgiven. From that day forward George Whitefield joyfully proclaimed the message of "the new birth." Together with John and Charles Wesley he helped start a revival in England and America during the eighteenth century.

JOHN WESLEY

Let us draw near with a true heart in full assurance of faith.
Hebrews 10:22.

"Mr. Wesley! Guten Morgen! So nice to see you!" The speaker was a German of the Moravian religious group that had sailed on the same ship with John and Charles Wesley from England to Savannah, Georgia. They had arrived a day or two before, on February 5, 1736, after a journey of more than three months.

"Good morning, Mr. Spangenberg!" John answered. "It's great to be on land after such a perilous journey. There were times I didn't think we'd make it."

"What if we hadn't? Wouldn't you have been ready to die?"

"Well . . . er . . . uh . . ." John hesitated, remembering how frightened he had been of death. "I don't think anyone is ever ready to die. After all, I'm still a young man at 33."

"That's not what I mean," the German continued. "Are you saved? Are you a child of God?"

"I've been a Christian ever since I can remember," John replied. "My father was a minister in the Church of England. The church has been my life."

"That's not what I asked," his friend insisted. "Do you personally know Jesus Christ?"

"I do," John answered. However, that night he wrote in his diary, "I fear they were vain words." It was not until two years later that he understood that one is saved, not by what one does, but by what Christ has done. With the acceptance of what Jesus offered as a free gift, John felt the assurance that he was indeed a child of God.

If you were in a fatal car accident today, would you be ready to die? Do you have the assurance that your sins are forgiven? Do you know that there is a mansion in heaven prepared for you? Is Jesus your friend? Have you accepted His offer of salvation? Do you know you are a child of God?

If not, bow your head right now and ask Jesus to come into your heart. Say, "Dear Lord, I know I am a sinner. I cannot save myself. I trust in You for my salvation. Take away my sins, forgive me, and make me Your child. Amen."

HORACE MANN

What man is he that liveth, and shall not see death? Psalm 89:48.

Sooner or later we all experience the pain of losing someone precious to us. It is never easy to say goodbye. In his teenage years Horace Mann found that out when his older brother drowned while swimming alone at Uncas Pond.

The feelings Horace had during the weeks following the death of his brother are those that all of us share when we face loss. Understanding Horace may help you understand a friend.

Denial: "No! Stephen can't be dead. He's a good swimmer! I know this is not true. I must be dreaming!"

Neighbors came to the house and sat with the family. They brought food and did chores. They cried with them at the funeral. During this stage Horace needed a friend.

Anger: "Why did God let this happen to me? It's not fair! God could have saved my brother!"

During this stage Horace needed someone to listen to him without judging him to be a bad boy because of his anger.

Depression: Horace hoed the weeds in the garden that Stephen had planted, and thought, *I don't care about anything anymore. For sure, I'm not going to academy without Stephen. I can't sleep and I don't want to eat. Life isn't any fun without my brother.*

During this stage Horace needed someone to talk to, to share memories of Stephen with. He needed a chance to share his hurt and know that it was all right to cry.

Acceptance: One warm night in August when Horace felt he couldn't stand the loneliness anymore, he went to a little hill back of the house where he and Stephen had made so many plans. He lay down on the grass and cried. After a while he sat up and decided he would get an education and make the dream he and Stephen had shared come true.

As a result of that decision, Horace Mann became a teacher who did a lot to establish public elementary schools in the United States.

THOMAS GALLAUDET

He maketh both the deaf to hear, and the dumb to speak.
Mark 7:37.

On a warm day in early summer of 1815 Pastor Thomas Gallaudet sat on the front steps of his home in Hartford, Connecticut, and watched a group of children play tag. Apart from the group stood a little girl in a pink pinafore.

"Teddy," Mr. Gallaudet called, beckoning to a small boy. "Who is that girl in the pink dress?"

"Oh, her," Teddy replied, wrinkling his nose in disgust. "That's Alice Cogswell from down the street. She's deaf and dumb. She doesn't know anything, not even her name."

Teddy ran back to the game, and Mr. Gaullaudet walked slowly across the lawn toward Alice. She let him take her hand and lead her back to the wooden steps.

"How can I get through to her?" he wondered. On a sudden inspiration he took off his gray top hat and placed it on her head. Picking up a stick, he wrote the letters H, A, and T in the sandy dirt. Retrieving his hat, he placed it directly above the letters. He pointed first to the hat and then to the word. He retraced the letters and pointed to the hat again. For more than an hour the two played the game. Suddenly Alice grabbed the hat and plopped it down on her head. She pointed to the word in the sand, tapped the hat, and jumped up in excitement.

In a flash Mr. Gallaudet was beside her, lifting her into his arms. Alice giggled and the hat fell to the ground. She rescued the hat, again pointing to the word. Pastor Gallaudet wanted to shout. He had found a way to help her communicate.

That afternoon was the beginning of Mr. Gallaudet's interest in education for the deaf and dumb. He went to Europe to learn sign language and came back to open the first school for the deaf in America. Through his school he helped hundreds of children hear with their eyes and speak with their hands.

Do you know any people who are deaf and dumb? Wouldn't it be exciting to learn sign language so you could talk with them? In this small way you could be like Jesus and Thomas Gallaudet, helping the deaf to hear and the dumb to speak.

MARY LYON

Trust in the Lord with all thine heart. Proverbs 3:5.

One hundred fifty years ago when most girls didn't dare to dream of going to college, Mary Lyon dreamed of opening a college for women. In America at that time there was no woman doctor, no woman lawyer, no woman minister, no woman college president. All professions were closed to women. In fact, women couldn't vote or own property.

"A woman's place is in the home," most men of her day argued. "She doesn't need book learning. Besides, girls don't have the intelligence for Latin, chemistry, and mathematics."

"Girls are every bit as smart as boys," Mary insisted, and proved it when she enrolled at Sanderson Academy. She learned her lessons so quickly that the principal had to give her extra assignments constantly so that she could be busy.

One Friday afternoon he handed her a copy of Adam's *Latin Grammar,* sure that at last he had found a task that would occupy her for weeks. On Monday he called on her to recite the first chapter. She answered all questions perfectly. Amazed, he continued quizzing her through to the end of the book. She had mastered the complete course in one weekend!

Shortly after she started to raise money for Mount Holyoke College for Women, the economy took a turn downward. Times were hard and donations dwindled to a trickle.

"We advise that you give up your dream," the school's trustees told Mary. "There's no way it can happen!"

"What do you think Mary will decide?" neighbors asked her mother.

"Mary will not give up," she replied. "She just walks the floor and says over and over again, when all is so dark, ' "Commit thy way unto the Lord, trust also in him; and he shall bring it to pass." Women must be educated—they must!' "

And Mary didn't give up. Her trust in God paid off. Mount Holyoke College stands today in South Hadley, Massachusetts, as a memorial to her faith.

What is your dream? Faith can bring it to pass.

ANTOINETTE BROWN BLACKWELL

I will pour out my spirit upon all flesh; and your sons and your daughters shall prophesy. Joel 2:28.

Twenty-one-year-old Antoinette Brown stood at the rail of an Erie Canal boat one night in August 1846 listening to an elderly minister tell of his missionary work along the canal. "There is so much wickedness along the canal," he said. "And so few to preach the message of God's love."

"I, too, believe in that sort of God," Nettie said. "Ever since I was a little girl I've wanted to talk to people about a loving God. I want to help them so they won't be afraid to live and afraid to die."

"God bless you," the old man said, nodding his approval.

Encouraged, she went on, "I have never told anyone before, not even my mother or father. You see, sir, I hope one day to become a minister of the gospel."

The missionary stepped back and frowned. "You speak blasphemy, my child. Have you not read what Paul wrote, 'Let your women keep silence in the churches: for it is not permitted unto them to speak'?"

"Just because I'm a woman can I not do the Lord's work?" Nettie asked. "Surely we have misunderstood that verse."

Impatiently the minister continued, "Haven't you read in Timothy where it says, 'I suffer not a woman to teach, nor to usurp authority over the man, but to be in silence'?"

Nettie was silent. She would finish theological training, and then she would better know how to answer such objections. But getting into Oberlin College Theological School was not easy. Finally she was allowed to attend classes but not to register. They refused to let her graduate and to receive a ministerial license.

But Nettie knew God had called her to be a minister. She kept studying and praying until the way opened for her to be a pastor in a small church in South Butler, New York. She became the first ordained woman pastor in the United States.

In these final hours of earth's history God needs girls as well as boys to preach and teach His message. He will pour out His Spirit on females as well as males. Are you ready to receive His power and give His message?

WILLIAM MILLER

If I go, . . . I will come again, and receive you unto myself.
John 14:3.

If anyone believed in the coming of the Lord, it was William Miller, of Low Hampton, New York. In fact, he had it all figured out that Jesus would return about the year 1843. The idea excited him, and he talked about it to everyone he met.

"Esquire Miller is a fine man, but a monomaniac on the subject of the Second Coming," a certain physician remarked.

Not long after that, one of Miller's children became sick, and he sent for the physician who had ridiculed him. During the doctor's visit Miller sat quietly in a corner.

"What's wrong with you, Miller?" the doctor asked.

"I don't know, Doc," Miller replied. "You'd better check me over."

"Can't find a thing wrong with you," the physician said after a thorough examination.

"You must have missed something." Miller shook his head. "I think I'm a monomaniac. Doctor, how can you tell?"

"That's easy," the physician answered, his face reddening. "A monomaniac is reasonable on all subjects but one; and when he is touched on that particular subject, he goes crazy."

"Well, let's see if I am one or not," Miller said with a sober face. "If I am, you must cure me. Sit down while I give you the reasons why I believe Jesus is coming soon. By the time I'm finished, you should know for sure whether I'm one or not."

The doctor tried to escape, but finally accepted the challenge and was soon looking up Bible texts that Miller gave him in proof that the end of the world was near.

"Mr. Miller," the doctor said at last. "Jesus is coming soon and I'm not ready to meet Him. Please help me." He came back to Miller's home every day for a week until he was sure he was prepared for the coming of the Lord.

Christ's coming is much closer now than it was when William Miller talked to his physician. Are you ready?

ELLEN G. WHITE

The Lord . . . is not willing that any should perish, but that all should come to repentance. 2 Peter 3:9.

Twelve-year-old Ellen Harmon sat with her friends on a hard bench in the Casco Street Christian Church in Portland, Maine, and listened wide-eyed as William Miller explained why he believed Jesus was coming in three more years.

I'll be sixteen then, Ellen thought. *I do hope I'm ready. How awful to be left behind, to be lost forever!*

"Now is the time for sinners to repent," William Miller was saying. Ellen was on her feet in an instant, pressing forward with hundreds of others to pray at the altar. But somehow she didn't feel that she was really forgiven.

That summer, at a Methodist camp meeting in Buxton, Maine, Ellen resolved to find pardon for her sins. One day while bowed at the altar, she prayed: "Help, Jesus; save me, or I perish! I will never cease to entreat till my prayer is heard and my sins are forgiven." Suddenly her heart felt light and she knew Jesus had forgiven her.

But during the next two years the light of joy seemed to go out and she was tortured with doubts. One day she confided in her mother: "For weeks I have not been able to sleep. I get out of bed and seek God with tears, but I have no assurance that I will be saved. I am afraid the Holy Spirit has left me and I shall be lost forever."

"I think you should talk to Elder Stockman," Mother said.

After Elder Stockman had heard Ellen's story, he placed his hand affectionately on her head, saying with tears in his eyes: "Ellen, yours is a most singular experience. I believe that God is preparing you for some special work. Yes, I know there is hope for you through the love of Jesus. The very agony of your mind is evidence that the Holy Spirit is striving with you. God loves you. He is not willing that any should perish. Trust in Jesus, for He will not withhold His love from you."

"I left his presence comforted and encouraged," Ellen later wrote. She spent the next 73 years sharing that comfort and encouragement with others as a teacher, preacher, writer, and prophet of God.

JAMES WHITE

For he shall give his angels charge over thee, to keep thee in all thy ways. Psalm 91:11.

Snow covered the ground as 21-year-old James White approached a country schoolhouse near Augusta, Maine, in January of 1843. As he tied his horse to the hitching post, he noticed that the windows were open and a large crowd waited outside. He knew that among them were a number of ruffians sent there by his enemies to break up the meeting.

The eyes of the malicious mob were on him as he strode into the building with his Bible under his arm. As he began to preach, it seemed that all hell let loose. Snowballs pelted the building. His voice was drowned by catcalls and howls.

"Get out of here, White. We don't want you!"

"Go back where you came from, you devil!"

James White closed his Bible and shouted: "Repent, and call on God for mercy and pardon. Turn to Christ and get ready for His coming, or someday you will call for the rocks and mountains to fall on you. Now you scoff; then you will pray."

Reaching into his pocket, James took out an iron spike. "Some poor sinner cast this at me last evening. God pity him! Why should I resent this insult when my Master had them driven through His hands?" At those words he stepped back against the wall and raised his arms as though he were hanging on the cross. The mob became silent and the audience inside the church began to weep.

"God loves you. He died for you," James cried out. "How many of you feel your unworthiness and want me to pray for you tonight?" Nearly a hundred stood.

When he had finished the prayer, he put his Bible under his arm and made his way to the schoolhouse door to face the mob. As the sullen men glared at him, a tall, distinguished-looking man stepped from the group and locked arms with the young preacher. The crowd parted to let them pass. When James was safely on his horse, he turned to thank his benefactor. No one was there. Who do you think that tall man was?

FREDERICK WHEELER

If ye love me, keep my commandments. John 14:15.

It was quieter than usual in the little white church in Washington, New Hampshire. Today was Communion Sunday and Frederick Wheeler, a Methodist preacher, was having the sermon.

Mrs. Rachel Oakes, recently arrived from New York State, sat with her daughter Delight, the local schoolteacher. She must have felt a bit out of place because she was worshiping among strangers, and on Sunday at that. She was a Seventh Day Baptist who believed in keeping the Sabbath, Saturday.

"Examine yourselves," Pastor Wheeler was saying. "All who take Communion today should be ready to obey all the commandments of God."

Mrs. Oakes had a hard time keeping her mouth shut. She wanted to stand up and say "You had better set that Communion table back and put the cloth over it, until you begin to keep the commandments yourself." She was glad when he came to visit her later that week. It gave her a chance to speak.

"Do you remember, Elder Wheeler, what you preached last Sunday at Communion?"

"Certainly. It was about the Ten Commandments."

"I agreed with everything you said, but wondered how you could preach like that when you are continually breaking one of them yourself. I almost got up in meeting and told you so."

"Well! I'm glad you didn't, Sister Oakes," Elder Wheeler replied with a smile. "Now tell me what you mean."

Mrs. Oakes came right to the point. "The fourth commandment says to keep the seventh day holy, yet you keep Sunday, the first day of the week, instead of the Sabbath."

"Thank you, Mrs. Oakes. You've given me something to think about. I'll study into it." He kept his word and found that Mrs. Oakes was right. A few weeks later he kept his first Sabbath and became the first Sabbathkeeping Adventist.

Do you think Jesus still expects us to keep the seventh-day Sabbath? Why?

JOSEPH BATES

But my God shall supply all your need. Philippians 4:19.

"Joseph, will you please go to the store and get me some flour? I'm baking bread today, and there's not enough to finish." Mrs. Bates stood at the door of her husband's study, wiping her hands on her apron.

"Of course, dear." Joseph Bates closed his Bible and stood. He was writing a tract on the Sabbath, but it would have to wait until he got his wife's flour. He put one hand into his coat pocket and felt the lone York shilling, twelve and a half cents. "How much do you need?"

"About four pounds, I guess. And here are some other things I need." She handed him a list.

Soon he was back from the store with the four pounds of flour and other items. He set them on the table and went back to his writing.

In a few minutes his wife was at his study door again, the four pounds of flour in her hands. "I can't believe this!"

"Isn't that what you requested?"

"Yes, but you always buy it by the barrel. Why is the great Captain Bates coming home with only four pounds?"

"Prudence," he said, taking a deep breath. "For that flour I spent the last money I have on earth."

"What happened?" she cried.

"I've spent it all to tell others of Christ's return."

"Whatever are we going to do?" she wailed.

"The Lord will provide."

"Oh, that's what you always say!" she sobbed.

A few minutes later Mr. Bates felt impressed that he should go to the post office where he would find a letter waiting for him. There was a letter all right, but postage was due on it.

"Open it," he told the postmaster. "I think there's money inside."

Sure enough. There was a ten-dollar bill. He paid the postage and then went to the store to order a barrel of flour and some other provisions for his wife. With the rest of the money he printed the tract he was writing. The Lord had provided.

JOHN McNEILL

Yea, though I walk through the valley of the shadow of death, I will fear no evil: for thou art with me. Psalm 23:4.

At half past 12 on a Saturday night, 12-year-old John was walking the four miles from the railway station to his farm home on the highlands of Scotland. He made the lonesome journey every Saturday night, but this particular night was darker than usual. There was no moon to light his pathway through the wild moorland. Clouds hid the stars, making it blacker still.

"There is nothing to be afraid of," John told himself as he pushed through the darkness. "Those are not men with guns standing there. They're only trees, and you know it. And that was just an old cow walking through the bushes. Why is your heart pounding so hard? Get hold of yourself, John."

A bird fluttered in its sleep, and John thought for a moment his heart would stop beating. When he was almost halfway home, he thought he heard footsteps as he approached a deep ravine. He stopped to listen. Yes, there they were. Where could he hide? His knees trembled; he tried to whistle to make himself brave.

"Is that you, John?" came a familiar voice out of the blackness.

"Dad!" John shouted, starting to run toward the shadowy form that he now knew was his father.

"I noticed how dark it was and thought you might be afraid, lad," Mr. McNeill said, taking his son's hand in his.

"Not anymore," John replied.

John McNeill grew up to become a great preacher. Once when he was preaching on the twenty-third psalm, he told the story of the night on the moors when he was so much afraid, and how comforted he was by his father's presence.

It seems to me that's the way it is in our walk on this earth. We must all pass through the dark, lonesome valley. Things happen to us that are hard to understand. A loved one dies. A dream is shattered. It seems we cannot go on. And then it is we hear our heavenly Father's voice. We walk on in the darkness unafraid, for He is there.

DWIGHT L. MOODY

Whither shall I go from thy spirit? or whither shall I flee from thy presence? Psalm 139:7.

"Hello, little girl; what's your name?" asked Dwight L. Moody, a famous evangelist who lived 100 years ago.

"Mary," answered the ragged child from the Chicago slums.

"Well, Mary, we are having a special class for children next Sunday morning in North Market Hall. If you come, you'll have a good time singing. Will you promise me you'll come?"

Mary shook her head.

"I'll tell you lots of nice stories. We'll have fun."

"No," Mary insisted. "I ain't comin'."

"Oh, but you must come, Mary. I won't take no for an answer." The big man with the beard smiled at her.

"OK, I'll come," she said at last, just to get rid of him. She had no intention of going to Sunday school.

Pastor Moody missed her on Sunday morning, so when the service was finished, he went looking for her. She spied him at the same time he saw her. Off she flew like a deer running from dogs, with Mr. Moody right behind.

She dashed into a saloon, past the tables, and out the back door with Moody in hot pursuit. She raced up some rickety steps to her tenement flat and into her bedroom, where she rolled under the bed. Moody found her there, panting. His long arms reached under the bed and pulled her out.

Just then Mary's mother appeared. "Leave my girl alone!" she demanded. "What are you doing in my house? Get out!"

"Excuse me for intruding like this," he apologized. "I am Dwight L. Moody. Mary promised to come to Sunday school today, and she didn't show up. I wanted to find out why. I'm sure you would want her to learn about Jesus."

"Indeed, I do," Mary's mother said. "She'll be there next Sunday, along with all her brothers and sisters."

"There's no use trying to run from Mr. Moody," Mary decided. "He'll catch you sooner or later!"

"So will God," said Mr. Moody.

BOOKER T. WASHINGTON

The folly of fools is deceit. Proverbs 14:8.

"How was your first day of school, Booker?" Mama asked.

"It was all right, I reckon," Booker said as he shrugged his shoulders and sighed.

"What's wrong, child?" His mother continued scrubbing pots as she spoke. "You don't sound very excited for a boy who's been begging to go to school."

"I need a hat," Booker blurted out. "All the other boys wear hats. I felt stupid without one."

"OK," Mama agreed. "I'll make you a hat."

"Can't I please have a store hat?"

"No, son. I can't buy you a store hat," his mother said firmly. "We don't have the money and I won't go into debt."

"Mama, please!" Booker begged. "All the other boys have store hats, and they're just as poor as we are."

"A homemade cap will have to do," she spoke with finality. "There's no use pretending to be what we are not, just to impress somebody."

The next day Booker wore a cap made of two pieces of jeans material sewed together.

"Since that time I have owned many kinds of caps and hats, but never one of which I have felt so proud as the cap made of two pieces of cloth sewed together by my mother," Booker wrote when he was a grown man.

"When I think of the incident, I have always felt proud that my mother had strength of character enough not to be led into the temptation of seeming to be that which she was not. I have always felt proud that she refused to go into debt for that which she did not have money to pay for."

The lesson Booker T. Washington learned from his mother on his first day of school was one he tried to teach the boys who attended Tuskegee Institute, a school in Alabama he founded for Blacks.

ANNE SULLIVAN

Love never fails. 1 Corinthians 13:8 (NKJV).

A gray-haired nurse sat on the cold stone floor outside of Annie's cell and opened a brown paper sack. She removed a brownie and held it out to the teenage girl huddled in a corner of the tiny room. "Come, Annie, see what nurse has brought you."

Annie made no move to take the food. Her sightless eyes stared straight ahead.

"I wish you'd talk to me," the nurse sighed. "I know life has been hard on you. First your dear mama died when you were 8 and then two years later your father deserted you. Then you and Jimmie had to come to this poorhouse. That was tough, wasn't it?"

Annie gave no sign that she heard.

"Then to top it off your brother died and you went blind. No wonder you kicked and screamed so much that they put you here. I'd have been mad, too. I know you're not crazy, like they think. You're just hurting real bad. I love you, Annie, and I'll come back tomorrow to talk."

Although Annie refused to talk, she ate the brownie after the nurse left. The old woman's love for Annie kept her coming back day after day. And every Thursday she brought brownies. Little by little Annie began to respond to the nurse's kindness. She started to smile and talk. She stopped kicking and screaming.

The doctors noticed the change in Annie and decided she didn't need to be isolated anymore. She was sent to a school for the blind in Boston, where she learned sign language and found kind teachers who loved her and believed in her as much as the old nurse. They helped her get an operation that gave her back her sight.

When she was 20 years old, Anne Sullivan was asked to go to Tuscumbia, Alabama, to teach 6-year-old Helen Keller, who was blind, deaf, dumb, and as uncontrollable as a wild animal.

The fact that she succeeded in helping Helen Keller become a lovable, educated young woman is one more proof that love never fails.

VIRGINIA RANDOLPH

A soft answer turneth away wrath: but grievous words stir up anger. Proverbs 15:1.

"Miss Randolph, a lady's comin' up the road with a big stick in her hand," a child warned.

The 18-year-old beginning teacher at Mountain Road School recognized the woman as the mother of one of the children she had disciplined the day before.

"I'm going to whip that teacher just like I whipped all the others," the mother had boasted the night before. Now she was on her way to fulfill her promise.

"O God, help me," Miss Randolph prayed silently, hoping the children couldn't see her trembling knees.

"I gotta speak to you!" the angry woman said, thumping the schoolhouse floor with her stick.

"I'm so glad you've come," Miss Randolph said. "I'll talk with you right after we finish morning devotions."

The woman frowned, but nodded her consent. The Scripture reading that morning was from 1 Corinthians 13, about love. When it was time for prayer, Miss Randolph said, "Children, this morning we are going to say a prayer for this dear mother who has come to visit us, and ask Jesus to bless her."

After prayer the children sang "I Need Thee Every Hour." Then Miss Randolph said, "Now, children, I know you all feel very proud that this is our first visitor at school. She is a mother with two lovely children. You have all heard it said that 'the hand that rocks the cradle is the one that rules the world.' I'm going to ask her to say a few words to us now."

There were tears in the mother's eyes as she spoke. "I came for one thing, but found another. I'll never come to disturb the school again."

Because she was willing to give a "soft answer" to an angry parent, Virginia Randolph gained a friend and a willing supporter of the school. Miss Randolph became an outstanding Black educator who traveled widely, helping promote better schools for her people. The school she started with 14 pupils eventually became the Virginia Randolph School, with more than 200 students enrolled.

MARY McLEOD BETHUNE

And whatsoever ye shall ask in my name, that will I do. John 14:13.

"You can't stop now! We're not half finished plowing this cotton field!" Fifteen-year-old Mary Jane McLeod spoke reprovingly to the family mule, which had just fallen down in front of the plow. "Poor Old Bush. I'm hot and tired, too, but we have to keep going." She gave his rump a gentle slap.

"Dad, come here!" she called. "I can't get Old Bush to budge."

Sam McLeod knelt in the dirt beside his faithful mule and ran his hand over its neck. "Mule's dead," he said. "I guess you children will have to plow without Old Bush's help."

Mary Jane wanted to cry. Instead she strapped the harness around her waist and started to pull the plow. Her grandma used to say she was strong as a mule; now she would see if it were true. When she got tired, her brothers and sisters relieved her. Eventually they finished the cotton field.

"All the extra money will have to go for a new mule," Mary Jane told herself. "There's not much chance I'll get any more schooling."

But Mary Jane wanted very much to go to school. The three years she had in the elementary school five miles away had only whetted her appetite for more learning. She dreamed of being a teacher, and for that she'd need to know lots more.

"Please, Lord, let me go to school some more," Mary Jane prayed as she worked in her father's cotton field that summer. "If it is Your will, I want to be a teacher and help others as Miss Wilson has helped me."

One day as she bent over the cotton plants she saw Miss Wilson walking fast down the dusty road toward their farm. She was waving something white. Mary Jane ran to meet her.

"Mary, God has heard your prayers," her teacher said, giving her a big hug. "Here, read this letter."

The letter was from Scotia Seminary in Concord, North Carolina, asking Miss Wilson to choose a worthy Black girl to receive a scholarship.

"I chose you," Miss Wilson smiled, hugging her again.

MOHANDAS GANDHI

Blessed is he whose transgression is forgiven, whose sin is covered. Psalm 32:1.

"We've got to be careful," 15-year-old Mohandas whispered to his cousin after school. "My uncle suspects us of taking his cigarettes."

"We'll just have to find another way to get them," his cousin replied, frowning. "What can we do?"

"I know where my mother keeps the servants' pocket money," Mohandas suggested. "She'll never miss a few coppers."

"Great idea!" his cousin agreed. "Let's go do it now."

It was just as easy as they had expected. No one was in the room where the money was kept. They helped themselves and ran off to the market to buy some cigarettes. They hid behind a bush to smoke them, but it wasn't as much fun as they had anticipated.

"I feel so bad, I just want to die," his cousin said.

"Me too," Mohandas agreed. "How can we kill ourselves?"

"I know where some poison berries grow," his cousin said.

In a moment both boys were on their feet, running through the forest to find the poison berries. They had eaten only one or two when Mohandas said, "I'm scared. Let's not do it."

"I agree," his cousin said. Then they both promised each other never to smoke or steal again.

Still the guilt of what he had done weighed heavily on Mohandas' conscience. At last he wrote out a confession of all his sins and signed a vow not to do them anymore. Summoning all his willpower, he took the confession to his father.

Tears ran down Mr. Gandhi's face as he read the letter.

"I'm sorry, Father," Mohandas cried. "I'll never smoke or steal again. I promise!"

Without a word, his father tore up the confession. Mohandas saw that he had been forgiven, and a great feeling of love and happiness welled up in his heart. When Mohandas Gandhi grew up, he became a great teacher for the Indian people and tried to help them learn to love and forgive each other.

Is there a confession you need to make today?

PETER MARSHALL

The angel of the Lord encampeth round about them that fear him, and delivereth them. Psalm 34:7.

It was a long way to Bamburgh by the regular road, and Peter Marshall was tired. *I'll take a short cut,* he thought.

The night was inky black. The wind in the heather and the occasional far-off bleating of a sheep was all he heard as he tromped through the fields. He had no light to guide him, but he felt confident he was going in the right direction.

Suddenly an urgent call broke the eerie stillness, "Peter!"

"Yes, who is it?" he asked as he stopped. He hoped he would hear the voice again and determine where the person was. "What do you want?"

His only answer was the sighing of the wind. "Who's there?" Still no answer. The moors seemed deserted.

Guess I imagined it, Peter thought, and he went on a few more paces. Then the voice came again, only louder and more urgent this time: "Peter!"

Startled, he stumbled and fell to his knees. Putting out a hand to get his balance, he found nothing there. Cautiously he felt the ground around him and discovered that he was on the edge of an abandoned stone quarry. Had he taken one more step he would have fallen hundreds of feet to certain death.

"There was no doubt in my mind about the source of that voice," Peter said whenever he told the story. "I felt that God must have some great purpose for my life, to have intervened so dramatically."

A few months after this incident Peter stood in the church and testified, "I have determined to give my life to God for Him to use me wherever He wants me."

God led Peter Marshall to the United States to be a preacher. He became famous as chaplain of the United States Senate, where he had many opportunities to share how God had protected and blessed him through the years.

Maybe you haven't heard your angel speak to you as Peter Marshall did, but he is beside you just the same. He has saved you from harm and danger more times than you can imagine.

MARTIN LUTHER KING, JR.

*God hath shewed me that I should not call any man common
or unclean. Acts 10:28.*

Martin Luther King, Jr., grew up at a time when he was
considered to be inferior in some way simply because his color was
black. When he was a small boy, there were many places Blacks
were not allowed to go.

One day Martin's dad took him to town for a new pair of shoes.
They stopped for a moment to admire the shiny black and brown
leather shoes in the window. Martin's eyes grew bright with
anticipation. At last his father took his hand, drawing him away
from the window. They walked together through the big glass doors
and sat down.

"I'd be glad to serve you if you'd sit in those seats at the back of
the store," the White clerk spoke firmly but courteously.

"We like these seats just fine," Mr. King smiled. "I think we'll
stay right here."

"But we don't serve colored folk in the front of the store," the
clerk repeated. "You must go to the back."

"If we can't be served in the front of the store, then we won't be
served at all." Mr. King took Martin by the hand and walked out.

"But, Dad, I wanted those shoes I saw in the window," Martin
complained once they were outside.

"There's nothing wrong with us," Mr. King explained. "We are
decent people. I'm tired of being treated like dirt!"

When Martin grew up, he became a preacher like his father. He
did everything he could to make it so Black boys and girls would
not have to experience the humiliation he had gone through. For
his wonderful work he won the Nobel Peace Prize. But he was
assassinated by someone who didn't want Blacks to be equal with
Whites. He gave his life in the fight for equality.

Still there are kids in every school whom others look on as
inferior because of the way they dress, how they talk, or where they
live. God needs boys and girls with the courage of Martin Luther
King, Jr., who will help put a stop to the way such kids are treated.

BILLY GRAHAM

Therefore if any man be in Christ, he is a new creature: old things are passed away; behold, all things are become new. 2 Corinthians 5:17.

Dr. Mordecai Ham, a balding, red-faced evangelist from Kentucky, had come to town. Setting up a rough, wooden tabernacle on a vacant lot, he began to preach about the sins of Charlotte, North Carolina, and large crowds lined the planks to hear him. Among them was 16-year-old Billy Graham.

One night Dr. Ham pointed a long, bony finger at Billy and shouted, "You're a sinner!" Billy immediately ducked behind the large, billowy hat of the lady in front of him.

After that, Billy thought it would be safer to join the choir. But even there he trembled as the evangelist thundered, "There's a grea-a-a-at sinner here tonight!"

At the close of one service, as the choir had begun to sing "Just as I Am," J. D. Prevatt, owner of the local men's store, tapped Billy on the shoulder. "Billy, wouldn't you like to become a Christian?" he whispered.

Billy nodded.

"I'll go down with you," Mr. Prevatt offered. Billy shuffled along in the sawdust behind him to join those weeping at the altar.

"I can't say I felt anything spectacular," he said later. "In fact, I felt a bit like a hypocrite because I didn't."

"Son, I'm so glad for what you did tonight!" his mother said, sniffling. His dad gave him a hug.

"I can't believe that Jesus, the Son of God, would go through all that on the cross for me!" Billy said. He lay awake a long time that night in the moonlight that flooded his room, and thought about the momentous thing that had happened.

"The next morning the world looked different—even the trees, the grass," Billy remembers. "Suddenly life had a purpose and meaning."

Are you tired of the weak, sinful person you are? Jesus is just as willing to make you anew as He was Billy Graham. You don't have to wait for an altar call. He can do it today as you kneel by your bed and invite Him to take charge of your life.

RALPH BUNCHE

Let all bitterness . . . be put away from you. Ephesians 4:31.

Fourteen-year-old Ralph Bunche delivered newspapers for the Los Angeles *Times*. During the summer he, along with the other carriers, was invited for an outing at Venice, California. The biggest attraction was the "Venice Plunge," a swimming pool.

"Sorry, no Blacks allowed in this pool," the gatekeeper said, shaking his head. "You two will have to stay outside." He was looking at Ralph and his friend, Charlie Matthews.

"We went on all the rides together," a White boy said. "Why can't they come in here with us, too?"

"That's the rule," the guard insisted. The White boys hesitated a moment, embarrassed. Then they raced for the pool and left Ralph and Charlie standing outside the gate.

The two Black boys sat on a bench in the hot sun outside the wire fence and watched their friends splashing and dunking each other in the cool water.

"It's not fair!" Ralph said when he told his grandma about it that night. "That guard made me so mad! I've as much right as anyone else to swim in that pool."

"I know how you feel," Nana sympathized. "But that won't change anything. If you get bitter, you're not going to hurt those White folks who kept you out of the pool. You're just going to hurt yourself."

With Nana's encouragement Ralph tried hard to let insults roll off his back so they couldn't get inside to make him bitter. He remembered her words when the seniors were called together to hear the roll call of new members elected to the city-wide honor society. Ralph's grades were the highest in the class, and he was certain he would hear his name called. It wasn't. Of course it hurt, but he refused to let it make him angry and bitter.

As a result of Ralph's courageous attitude, he became the first Black American to receive a Ph.D. He was the first Black to hold a high position in the U.S. State Department, and the first Black to win the Nobel Peace Prize.

WALTER RAYMOND BEACH

Son, go work to day in my vineyard. Matthew 21:28.

"Mother, I'm having a hard time deciding where to attend college," Walter admitted. "I don't know whether to go to Willamette Law School and then back to Yale, or whether to go to Walla Walla College and prepare for God's work."

"Let me tell you a story," Mrs. Beach began.

"I think I know what you're going to say," Walter interrupted. "When I was born you dedicated me to God."

"That's right," his mother continued. "We had just become Adventists, so we were too old to train for denominational service. You were God's gift to us, intended for that purpose before you were born."

"But I could serve God as a lawyer," Walter argued.

"Let me tell you the whole story. The night you were born was at the end of a week-long blizzard. The nearest doctor was many miles away. Your father sent a farmhand to bring one, but we didn't know if he would come. I was worried."

"Did you pray?" Walter asked, anticipating the outcome.

"Yes, we had sundown worship as usual. Your father placed me in God's hands and pleaded that the baby we had dedicated to Him would somehow arrive safely. While we were kneeling, and just as your father said 'Amen,' we all heard a few strains of music."

"Where did it come from?" Walter wanted to know.

"We thought some sleigh with its tinkling silver bells had pulled up. Your father went to the door to welcome our visitors, but no one was there."

"Do you think it was angels?" Walter puzzled. "Or was it music from far away? I understand that in cold air, music travels far."

"It doesn't matter. I believe God sent a special message by some means to ease my anxiety. The doctor did show up, and you were born just after midnight," Mother concluded, tears in her eyes.

In his mother's story Walter heard God's call to work in His vineyard. He went to Walla Walla College. God used him for many years as a minister, as president of the Southern European Division, and as secretary of the General Conference.

ARCHIMEDES

Rejoice with me; for I have found my sheep which was lost.
Luke 15:6.

"There's a problem I can't solve," Hiero, king of Sicily, confided in Archimedes. "But I'm sure you can come up with the answer. After watching you pull a ship, single-handedly, into the sea with your pulley device I believe you can do anything!"

Archimedes bowed to acknowledge the compliment. "What is the problem, King Hiero?"

"I ordered a crown made by the goldsmith, for which I gave him a quantity of gold. The finished crown is of the same weight as the gold I gave him. However, I suspect he has cheated me by mixing silver with the gold. How can I prove that is true without destroying the crown?"

"Give me some time, and I will find the answer," Archimedes promised. However, he went away puzzled. Silver was lighter than gold, he knew. If it were added to the crown, it would take up more space than an equal weight of gold would. The problem was to find the space, or volume, taken up by the crown without melting it.

The answer wouldn't come, so he went to the public baths instead. As he lowered himself into a tub he noticed the water overflowed. It suddenly occurred to him that his body was pushing water out of the tub. The volume of water pushed out must be equal to the volume of his body pushing in.

"All I have to do is suspend the crown in water." Archimedes began talking to himself in his excitement. "I'll catch the water that spills out and measure it. Then I must obtain a volume of gold equal to the volume of water and check its weight against the weight of the crown. That's it!"

Archimedes jumped out of the bath and ran home through the streets of Syracuse dripping wet, shouting, "Eureka! Eureka! I've found it! I've found it!"

Eureka is also the word the shepherd shouted when he had found his sheep. Can you see *eureka* in today's verse? Read all of Luke 15 and see how many times you can find the word *eureka.* The word is still used today to announce a glad discovery.

NICOLAS COPERNICUS

But of that day and hour knoweth no man, no, not the angels of heaven, but my Father only. Matthew 24:36.

Thousands of people streamed into the churches of Poland on February 11, 1524, to await the end of the world. Outside, a storm raged, the wind whipping snow into large drifts.

"Today, God will send a deluge more terrible than Noah's flood. This time none will survive," predicted Professor Stoeffler, of Tübingen. "For on this day is the conjunction of two planets under the constellation of Pisces the Fishes."

Most people believed that doomsday had arrived. A few had built arks for themselves and stocked them with food, hoping to ride out the flood as Noah had done. The rest huddled in churches.

"Don't you think you ought to be praying instead of studying the stars?" a priest at Frauenburg Cathedral asked Copernicus. "Don't you know the world is coming to an end?"

"Let it end," Copernicus said. "I don't believe in astrology. God, not stars, is in control of this planet."

"But people are saying it is all your fault because you are teaching that the earth is not the center of the universe."

"I believe my calculations are correct," Copernicus replied. "The sun and planets don't revolve around the earth as people have believed for the past 1,500 years. The earth and all the planets revolve around the sun."

"But even some of the bishops say God is angry because you have tried to upset the order of the universe," his colleague continued.

"Nonsense! The day will close and the people will go home. It's not the end of the world," Copernicus retorted.

Copernicus was right on both counts. The sun is the center of the solar system, and the world did not come to an end on February 11, 1524. The Bible clearly says that nobody has information about the time of Christ's coming and the end of the world. But people in 1988 are still setting dates for that event. You'd think we'd learn to believe what the Bible says.

TYCHO BRAHE

But he that shall endure unto the end, the same shall be saved. Mark 13:13.

I had heard of people with artificial legs, arms, eyes, teeth, hair, and hearts, but I had never heard of anyone with a spare nose until I read about Tycho Brahe, an astronomer who lived more than 350 years ago in Denmark.

At the age of 19 Tycho Brahe got into an argument with a young man named Manderupius about mathematics. So heated was the exchange that they decided to fight a duel with swords. In one wild sweep Manderupius cut off Tycho's nose.

"No problem!" said plucky Tycho. "I'll just get me a new one!" And that's what he did. He made a nose for himself out of gold and silver, using a special cement to keep it in place. He always carried his little box of cement with him because he never knew when he might sneeze and send his nose flying!

He was a colorful figure with red hair, blue eyes, reddish mustache and beard, and a golden nose. He was also the greatest observational astronomer who ever lived, and he worked before the telescope was invented. In 1592 he published a book listing the hundreds of stars he had studied. Look at a map of the moon, and you will find a large crater named in his honor.

On November 11, 1572, Tycho discovered a new star in the constellation of Cassiopeia. It was a marvelous sight, so brilliant it could be seen in the daytime. It was called Tycho's Star. It was actually a supernova, an exploding star. It remained visible for more than a year, then gradually faded from sight.

Did you know there are Christians who are like Tycho's Star? They shine brightly for a while, then their light goes out. They turn their back on Christ and His church and go back to walk in the ways of the world. Sometimes even a pastor's or teacher's light goes out. Listen to these prophetic words: "The time is not far distant when the test will come to every soul. . . . Many a star that we have admired for its brilliance will then go out in darkness" (*Prophets and Kings*, p. 188).

I pray that will not be you!

JOHANNES KEPLER

When they persecute you in this city, flee ye into another.
Matthew 10:23.

The early-morning sun sparkled on the spears of the soldiers guarding the church door in Graz, Austria, one July morning in 1598. Johannes Kepler, astronomer, was one of several hundred men milling about the churchyard before six o'clock that morning. He noticed that all the men were Protestants; they had come at the command of the archduke.

"There he comes!" someone shouted. The Catholic prelate entered the church, followed by his dignitaries and the sullen men who had been summoned. The soldiers then closed the church doors, their swords barring exit.

The church official read in Latin from a large scroll: "All Protestant citizens in Graz shall declare their intention of accepting the Catholic faith. A period of grace of 10 days shall be granted for this conversion. Those who refuse shall suffer the penalty of banishment from the territory of Styria province forever."

One by one the men were called before the officials to state their intention. Most agreed to convert. Persecution and fleeing were not for them. Their homes and farms were here. Their families and their heritage centered around the village. It wouldn't really matter which church they attended. God would understand.

Johannes Kepler was not one of those. When his name was called, he stepped forward, his head held high.

"I am Kepler."

"Will you convert?"

"I cannot give up my belief in the Protestant faith. I will not give up my heritage so lightly. I will not convert."

"Johannes Kepler, you are to leave the land of Styria forever in banishment. You have six weeks to close your affairs."

Obedient to the words of Jesus, Kepler did not stay to be an unnecessary martyr. He packed his belongings and fled to another city, Prague. It was after this experience that he made his calculations that proved that the orbits of the planets were in the shape of ellipses, not circles.

WILLIAM HARVEY

Thou shalt not bear false witness against thy neighbor. Exodus 20:16.

Have you ever noticed that often when you tell one falsehood, it calls for another? If you're not careful, you'll end up telling a lie so big that sensible people will not believe it. That's what happened to 10-year-old Edward Robinson of Lancashire, England, in 1634.

"You played hooky from school yesterday," Edward's schoolmaster accused.

"Oh, no, sir," Edward shook his head innocently. "I really wanted to come, but I couldn't."

"And why couldn't you?" the stern schoolmaster questioned. "Don't give me the excuse that you were sick, because I have already asked your mother."

Edward looked at the stick in the schoolmaster's hand and knew he must avoid it. "I was walking through the woods on my way to school when I saw two greyhounds. A hare approached at the same instant, so I tried to get the greyhounds to chase the hare, but they refused. I took a switch and was about to beat them, when one of the dogs became transformed into a woman and the other into a little boy."

"Did you recognize them?"

"Yes, the woman was our neighbor, Mrs. Dickenson. She offered me money to sell my soul to the devil, but I refused," Edward said. Noticing that he had the schoolmaster's goodwill, he decided to make his story better yet. "A host of other witches soon appeared. I'm sure I could recognize them should I ever see them again."

Edward was led from church to church to identify the witches; many good people were arrested. Seven of the women were condemned and about to be executed when it occurred to the king to ask his physician, William Harvey, what he thought. The king knew that Dr. Harvey had dissected many animals in his efforts to learn about the circulation of the blood.

"It's utter nonsense!" Dr. Harvey said. "The boy has told a lie. It is impossible for animals to change into people." As a result of his testimony the women were pardoned and released.

EVANGELISTA TORRICELLI

My son, if sinners entice thee, consent thou not. Proverbs 1:10.

Here's an experiment for you to try. Fill a glass half full of water. Hold a thin piece of cardboard, such as an index card, firmly on top of the glass. With your hand still on the cardboard, turn the glass upside down, over the sink. Now remove your hand. The cardboard should stay in place, keeping the water inside the glass.

What kept the cardboard and water in place? It was the pressure of air pushing up on the cardboard. Evangelista Torricelli was the first person to understand air pressure. He lived in Italy during the seventeenth century.

For one of his experiments he had a glass tube four feet (48 inches) long; one end of the tube was closed. He filled the tube to the brim with mercury. Carefully holding his thumb over the open end of the glass, he inverted the tube and placed it in a bowl that was partially filled with mercury. The mercury came out—but not all of it. The top edge of the mercury stood about 30 inches above the level of mercury in the bowl. Why didn't all of the mercury run out?

Torricelli explained it this way: "We live submerged at the bottom of an ocean of air, which, by experiment, I have proved has weight. On the surface of the liquid in the bowl a 50-mile column of air presses down, making the mercury rise in the tube. The mercury goes up until it equals the weight of the air pressing down."

Weather reporters sometimes say the barometer is rising. They are referring to the level of mercury in the barometer tube. When it rises it means the air is warm and is pressing harder. Good weather is on the way. The weight of cold air is less, and causes the column of mercury to fall. That means that bad weather is coming.

There are other pressures in your life besides air pressure. One is peer pressure. Your friends put on a lot of pressure for you to do what they do. That's OK if it's something good. When it's something evil, you need to resist the pressure. With the power of Jesus in your life you can do it.

ROBERT BOYLE

I have chosen the way of truth. Psalm 119:30.

"Robert, you are to stay away from the plum tree I have marked," his sister warned. "Father wants to save the plums on that tree for our sister-in-law."

"OK," Robert said and wondered what could be so wonderful about the plums on that particular tree. Why wouldn't plums from any of the trees in the orchard do? The more he thought about it, the more he wanted to find out what they tasted like. His sister discovered him at the tree a little while later, stuffing plums into his mouth.

"Robert!" she spoke sternly. "What are you doing?"

"Eating plums."

"Didn't I tell you not to go near that tree? I told you we were saving those plums for our sister-in-law."

"Yes, you did warn me," Robert admitted.

"You're a naughty boy for disobeying. You must have eaten six of them."

"No," the boy answered. "I didn't eat six plums."

"You little liar!" his sister yelled. "I saw you eating plums and now you deny it."

"I don't deny eating the plums," Robert answered, his chin quivering. "But I deny eating six. I remember eating 20!"

"What an extraordinary boy I have," Mr. Boyle said when he heard the story. "I have never seen a child who disliked lying so much."

The facts were that Robert told the truth because he had a very real sense of God's eyes upon him. He knew that lying was wrong. He was determined to always tell the truth.

Robert Boyle, sometimes called the "founder of modern chemistry," was born into an age of superstition and lies, but he was determined to experiment until he discovered what was true. He was never willing to accept a lie simply because others believed it. When he died, his colleagues payed tribute to him by saying, "Robert Boyle could smell the truth!"

Have you chosen the way of Robert Boyle, "the way of truth"? Can people count on your honesty?

CHRISTIAN HUYGENS

The heavens declare the glory of God; and the firmament sheweth his handywork. Psalm 19:1.

When Christian Huygens was born in 1629 in the Netherlands, there was no accurate way to tell time. There were hourglasses, candle clocks, and cumbersome water clocks. Christian became the first person to make a successful pendulum clock. He was disappointed, however, when it didn't work on a ship. He kept at the puzzle until he invented a clock that ran by a spring.

Next, Christian turned his attention to the stars, but couldn't see much more than Galileo had seen. He improved the telescope by finding a new way to grind and polish the lenses. His telescope was 210 feet long. You can imagine how excited he was when he tried it out for the first time.

"I'll have a look at Saturn," Christian said. "I wonder if I can see those mysterious moons." Galileo had seen two moons. The next time he looked, they were gone. Where had they disappeared?

What Christian saw caused him to rub his eyes. Saturn was no longer a little speck in the sky, but a brilliant ball, girdled with a huge ring, with moons riding around the outside of the ring. It looked like a magnificent toy of the gods.

One winter night Christian pointed his telescope at a constellation called Orion, or the Great Hunter. Ancient astronomers imagined that the bright stars outlined the form of a hunter and his dog. Around the hunter's waist was a belt of stars from which hung a sword of stars. Focusing the telescope at the sword, he saw what no one had ever before seen.

It looks like a great wreath of shiny smoke, Christian thought. *It must be another nebula.*

Two hundred years later the Lord gave Ellen White a vision of the second coming of Christ. In the book *Early Writings,* on page 41, she writes: "Dark, heavy clouds came up and clashed against each other. The atmosphere parted and rolled back; then we could look up through the open space in Orion, whence came the voice of God. The Holy City will come down through that open space."

ISAAC NEWTON

Wisdom strengtheneth the wise more than ten mighty men.
Ecclesiastes 7:19.

"You're a sissy!" an older boy at Kings School taunted young Isaac Newton. "I'll bet you're afraid to fight."

The truth was Isaac didn't want to fight. He didn't like the rough games most boys played. He'd much rather spend his time reading, drawing, or doing experiments.

"Fraidy cat! Sissy!" the bully continued. When Isaac didn't respond, the bully gave him a savage kick in the stomach.

That was more than Isaac could take. He flew into a rage, pounding the other boy with his fists. Caught off guard, the bully tumbled to the ground. A crowd gathered around cheering Isaac on.

"Let him have it!" his friends yelled. "He deserves it. Rub his face in the dirt!"

When Isaac was finished with him, the bully slunk away. Although he had won, Isaac didn't feel happy about it. There must be some better way to get the best of his enemy. He thought about it overnight and came up with a plan.

The other boy was far above him in his schoolwork. In fact, although Isaac was smart, he was interested in other things and had not bothered to try at school.

"I'll work hard and beat that bully at his lessons. He'll think twice before he teases me again!" Isaac decided.

The headmaster was surprised and delighted. Soon Isaac was the top student at Kings School. He went on to become the greatest scientist of his time. He discovered the laws of motion and gravity, the reflecting telescope, and calculus, among other things. Because of his scholarship Isaac won the respect of not only the bully in his school but of all men who knew him.

Isaac tried two ways to conquer the bully. Which way do you think was better? How does the experience of Isaac Newton illustrate today's verse? Can you think of any other ways you can get the better of someone who is giving you a difficult time? Romans 12:20 might give you a clue about one way to do it.

ANTOINE-LAURENT LAVOISIER

Blessed is the man that walketh not in the counsel of the ungodly. Psalm 1:1.

"Birds of a feather flock together."

"Show me a man's friends, and I will show you his character."

"A man is known by the company he keeps."

These common sayings bear the same message as our verse for today. Be careful about the company you keep. People will judge you to be cut from the same cloth. If you don't want to be classified as a thief, don't hang around with thieves. If you don't want to be hauled in for selling dope, then stay away from dope peddlers.

Antoine Lavoisier, who did much to advance the science of chemistry, learned this lesson too late.

His trouble started when he didn't have enough money for his experiments. To meet his needs he joined the General Farmers, a private organization that collected taxes on salt, tobacco, and other items for the government. The tax collectors had to pay the government a fixed sum. All they collected over that amount they kept for themselves. Most tax collectors gouged every cent they could from the poor. Naturally, the common people hated them.

Lavoisier was honest in all his dealings. He tried to lower the taxes of the poor rather than raise them for his benefit. He even donated much of his wealth to public projects to help the poor. In spite of his good works, people who didn't know him classified him as a tax collector, and despised him along with the others.

During the Reign of Terror of the French Revolution the common people took revenge against those who had participated in the injustices of the past. In November 1792 the order was given to arrest all former members of the General Farmers. Antoine Lavoisier was arrested along with the others. On May 8, 1794, he lost his head like the other tax collectors did. Afterward the people were sorry they had killed such a brilliant man, but it was too late. He had been judged by the company he kept.

CAROLUS LINNAEUS

But every man hath his proper gift of God. 1 Corinthians 7:7.

"I want to be a doctor and a botanist," 20-year-old Carolus Linnaeus announced after his graduation from high school in Växjö, Sweden, more than 200 years ago.

"The training is long and very expensive," his father frowned. "Also, a doctor doesn't have the honor a minister has."

"Surely Sweden needs good doctors," Carl argued.

"I had hoped you would follow in my footsteps. That's been your mother's dream, too."

"You know I'm terrible at Latin and Greek."

"You could do better in them if you put your mind to it. I should have put a stop long ago to your roaming the fields."

"But that's the whole point. That's the only work I enjoy. I would hate being a pastor."

"You know I don't have much money. I don't see how I can put you through the university at Uppsala."

"If it's God's will, won't He provide the way?"

Just then a thrush sang its melody from a nearby apple tree. The bird was a favorite of both father and son. They stood there quietly listening until it stopped. There were tears in the old man's eyes when the magic moment had passed.

"It's a sign," Carolus whispered.

"All right, Carolus," his father sighed. "I won't try to force you into my mold any longer. God has given you the gift of understanding nature. We'll manage somehow. May God bless you and give you success."

God did bless Carolus. His extensive observations laid the foundation for the botany classes taught all over the world today.

You, too, will be successful as you develop the interests and talents God has given you. Don't try to fit yourself into someone else's mold. It's impossible for you to fill anyone else's shoes. You are a unique individual with special gifts that God has given you. He does not expect you to be what you would be unhappy being. Use the gifts He has given you, follow His leading, and you will be happy and successful.

EDWARD JENNER

Trust in him at all times. Psalm 62:8.

"Is it going to hurt?" asked 8-year-old James Phipps, eyeing the knife in Dr. Jenner's hand.

"No, I promise," the doctor said, smiling. "Watch if you like."

Dr. Jenner made two small scratches on James's left arm. Taking a small bottle out of his black bag, the doctor took some yellow sticky stuff and rubbed it into the scratches.

"What's that?" James asked.

"Pus that I got from a cowpox sore on Sarah Nelmes. In a few days you should have cowpox yourself."

The boy's face clouded. "I don't want cowpox! It'll make me sick. I'll have fever."

"Correct!" Dr. Jenner agreed. "That's exactly what we want to happen."

"But why?"

"If I can make you sick with cowpox, then you won't ever get smallpox. You wouldn't want to get smallpox, would you?"

"No way! I would look gross with all those pockmarks."

"Exactly. Besides, people don't die of cowpox, but millions die of smallpox. I'm giving you cowpox to protect you against something much worse. Do you understand now?"

James's smile was his answer.

Seven days later James felt pain in the armpit of his left arm. Two days later he had a headache and refused to eat. That night he tossed with fever, but the next day he was OK. A month later Dr. Jenner inoculated him with smallpox germs. James didn't get sick.

Was Dr. Jenner being cruel when he let James get sick with cowpox? In allowing the boy to experience something bad, was the doctor being mean and unfair?

Try to look at God's work in your life in the same way. Sometimes He allows bad things to happen because in His wisdom He knows He is keeping you from something far worse. You may not understand, but God's way is best. Trust in God at *all* times—the bad as well as the good.

LAZZARO SPALLANZANI

God is not a man, that he should lie. Numbers 23:19.

"Beetles don't have mothers and fathers," an English naturalist, Ross, declared 200 years ago. "They grow spontaneously out of cow manure."

"Horse hair turns into worms," everyone agreed. "Rats spring out of mud and maggots out of meat."

"How could these things be so?" puzzled Spallanzani. "Everything has to have parents, even flies and the tiny animalcules I see under my microscope."

Then he read about an experiment by a scientist named Redi. Redi took two jars and put meat in each one. He covered one jar and left the other open. He watched while flies came in and out of the open jar and landed on the meat. After a few days there were lots of flies in the open jar. They had hatched from eggs laid by the mother flies. There were no flies in the closed jar. "Flies must have parents," scientists had to agree.

"I will prove now that microscopic animals also must have parents," Spallanzani decided.

He put bean soup in a sealed glass bottle and boiled it for an hour. He put more soup in a lightly corked bottle and boiled it an hour. After several days he looked through a microscope at the soup from both bottles. There was no life in the sealed bottle. In the other bottle were many tiny microbes. Through many similar experiments he was able to prove that microbes come from other microbes, just as cats come from other cats.

I don't know if Spallanzani knew it or not, but his experiments proved that God was not a liar when He said that all creatures of the earth were to reproduce "after their kind." That's easy for us to accept now that it has been proved, but it was hard for the superstitious people of 200 years ago to accept. To them it seemed that God didn't know what He was talking about.

There are still some parts of the Bible and the Spirit of Prophecy that are hard to correlate with our present understanding of things. This is where we need faith to believe God. Someday the proof will come, for God does not lie.

JOHN DALTON

And knowest not that thou art wretched, and miserable, and poor, and blind, and naked. Revelation 3:17.

In 1826 John Dalton was awarded the Medal of the Royal Society of England for his atomic theory. In the early 1830s John received several honorary degrees, including one from Oxford. Shortly, thereafter, he was invited to London, but there was one problem. His visit would include meeting the king.

"Court etiquette requires that you come dressed in knee breeches, buckled shoes, and a sword," the invitation stated.

"What can I do?" John inquired of the palace officials. "I wish to meet the king, but I am a Quaker. The articles of dress you mention are forbidden to Quakers."

"You may wear your university robes," came back the reply. What the palace officials didn't know was that the collar of the robe was scarlet and Quakers were forbidden to wear scarlet!

No problem! John Dalton inspected his new robe and found the collar to be green. He wore the black robe with its scarlet border with no twinge of conscience. John Dalton was color-blind!

To this day Daltonism is another name given color blindness. People who have this problem cannot tell all colors apart. Some, like John Dalton, can distinguish yellow and blue but confuse red with green. Others see only white, gray, and black. One in 12 boys is color blind, but only one in 200 girls has this problem.

I don't know if you are one of the few color-blind persons in the world, but I do know that you suffer from another kind of blindness. You were born "sin-blind" along with all other humans.

"Sin blindness" makes it difficult for us to tell right from wrong. Most of us can distinguish the really dark, gross shades of sin, such as murder, stealing, and committing adultery. We are not going to murder our mothers nor rob a bank. Where we get into difficulty is in the pleasing pastel sins, the gray areas of life.

Dear God, open our eyes that we may see the enormity of sin! Anoint our eyes with eyesalve that we may distinguish between right and wrong!

LORD KELVIN

Thou wilt cast all their sins into the depths of the sea. Micah 7:19.

How deep is the sea? William Thomson, a great British physicist of the past century, needed to know so that he could lay the first transatlantic cable in 1866. When he had successfully accomplished that feat he was knighted by Queen Victoria, taking the name Lord Kelvin.

At that time sailors had a very inaccurate and time-consuming process for deep-sea sounding. The ship had to be stopped, and they would let down a rope with a sinker on the end of it. When it touched bottom, they hauled it up and measured the length of wet rope. It was impossible to carry a rope long enough to reach the deepest parts of the ocean.

"There has got to be a better way," Lord Kelvin said. He invented a sounding device that could be wound automatically. Instead of rope he used first piano wire and later steel cable. It worked much more accurately but still it could not penetrate to the deepest valleys of the ocean bottom.

Today scientists use sonar devices, which bounce sound waves off the ocean floor. The distance to the bottom is found by measuring the time it takes a sound wave to return.

The deepest known spot in all the oceans is Challenger Deep, in the Mariana Trench of the Pacific, southwest of the island of Guam. The bottom is 36,198 feet below the surface. That is almost seven miles deep!

Imagine having your sins buried in the mud of Challenger Deep with seven miles of water above them. Do you think you'd ever be able to find them again?

Of course, the sea bottom is not strewn with the actual sins of thousands of people. What God is trying to help us see is that He doesn't remember them anymore. He doesn't keep them to be held against us in the future. When God forgives He wipes the slate clean. He puts our sins behind His back; He buries them in the sea. In other words, He not only forgives, He forgets.

"Buried in the deepest sea; yes, that's good enough for me. Praise God! My sins are gone!"

ROBERT KOCH

By one man sin entered into the world, and death by sin;
and so death passed upon all men. Romans 5:12.

"My boys, drop everything and go see Dr. Koch—this man has made a great discovery!" Professor Cohnheim shouted to the students in his laboratory. He was gasping for breath, for he had just run across the campus of Breslau University.

"Who is Koch? We've never heard of him."

"He's nothing but a country doctor, but no matter—it is a great discovery!"

"Tell us about it, Herr Professor."

"Go, I tell you! See for yourselves," he ordered.

In the botanical laboratory they found Dr. Robert Koch explaining about his discovery of the anthrax germ. He took a drop of infected sheep's blood and placed it under the microscope. Taking their turns at the eyepiece, the students saw tiny rod-shaped creatures. As they gazed, the microbes began to divide, making more rod-shaped creatures like themselves.

"How rapidly they grow!" a student remarked.

"Suppose one of these microbes were to divide in two in 20 minutes," Dr. Koch proposed. "Then in 20 minutes each microbe would have grown to full size and divided again. At the end of one hour we would have eight. At the end of two hours there would be 64. At the end of eight hours we would have 16 million germs! All a cow needs is to eat one of these tiny microbes. Within a matter of hours its blood will be black with anthrax germs and it will die."

Dr. Koch had discovered the first of the deadly microbes. Before his death he had found and photographed the germs of 11 other diseases, including tuberculosis, cholera, typhoid, diphtheria, pneumonia, and bubonic plague.

It seems to me that sin is a kind of deadly microbe that has infected our planet. It all started deep within the heart of Lucifer. Before he was cast out of heaven, one third of the angels had been infected. Then through Adam the whole human race has been made sick. From one generation to another the disease has been transmitted. Until Christ comes, death is certain. We all need the healing touch of the Master Physician. He alone has the remedy.

LOUIS PASTEUR

Neither is there salvation in any other: for there is none other name under heaven given among men, whereby we must be saved. Acts 4:12.

On July 4, 1885, on his way home from school 9-year-old Joseph Meister was attacked by a mad dog. He was knocked to the ground and bitten in 14 places before a bricklayer came to his rescue, chasing off the rabid dog.

"There is only one man in the world who can help your son," the doctor said as he cleaned Joseph's wounds. "That is Louis Pasteur in Paris."

Two days later Joseph and his mother arrived in Pasteur's laboratory. "Please help my son!" Mrs. Meister begged. "My doctor says you can cure rabies."

"Madame, I have treated only dogs with my vaccine," Pasteur replied. "What if I should make him worse? It is a terrible risk. Are you willing for me to try?"

"You're our only hope!" the mother burst into tears. "There's nowhere else to go!"

"Come back at five this evening," Pasteur said. He needed time to decide. Going to Dr. Vulpian, who was familiar with his experiments, he asked, "Do I dare go ahead and treat the boy? What if he dies?"

"He will definitely die if you do not treat him," Dr. Vulpian advised. "It is your duty to try to save his life."

That evening Joseph received his first injection. Over the next ten days he got eleven more. What a relief for Louis Pasteur when Joseph recovered!

Soon patients from all over Europe were coming to Pasteur's door. On one occasion 19 men from Russia who had been bitten by a rabid wolf came for treatment. Louis Pasteur was their only hope. To have gone elsewhere would have been foolish, don't you agree?

Jesus Christ is this world's only hope of salvation. He has the only known cure for sin. Yet thousands seek it through other names: Buddha, Muhammad, Krishna, Sai Baba, Rajneesh, and scores of other so-called holy men. They seek in vain. Christ is the one and only Saviour. Have you tried Him?

GREGOR JOHANN MENDEL

Render therefore to all their dues: tribute to whom tribute is due, . . . honour to whom honour. Romans 13:7.

"I wonder why some people have red hair and others black?" Hugo de Vries pondered the question of heredity in his study in Holland in 1900. Before announcing his conclusions, he decided to see if anybody had ever researched heredity before. To his surprise he found an amazing paper in a 34-year-old scientific magazine written by a monk named Gregor Mendel.

"Why is it that all puppies in the same litter are not the same color?" wondered Karl Correns in his laboratory in Germany in 1900. He decided to see if anybody had ever done a study on it before. Guess what? He found a paper in a 34-year-old scientific journal written by a monk named Gregor Mendel.

"Why do children in the same family have different colored eyes?" In 1900 Erich Tschermak of Austria-Hungary puzzled over the question of heredity. He decided to check to see if anyone had ever written on the subject before. He was amazed to discover a treatise in a 34-year-old scientific magazine written by a monk named Gregor Mendel.

After eight years of growing peas in his monastery garden in Brünn, Austria, Gregor Mendel had discovered the laws that govern the passing on of physical characteristics from parents to children. His study stated the same principles that the three scientists discovered 34 years later. He had laid the foundation for a science that we now call genetics.

If you had been Hugo, Karl, or Erich, what would you have done? Would you have ignored the work of a monk who was long ago dead, suspecting that no one else would ever know you had not been the first to discover the laws of heredity? Would you have announced the laws as your own great discovery?

The three scientists, by the way, had no communication with one another. They had no idea what the others had found. Yet each came to the same conclusion. They would give honor to whom honor was due. Each abandoned his own claims and called attention to Mendel's discovery. That's what I call honesty.

JOSEPH LISTER

Wherewithal shall a young man cleanse his way? by taking heed thereto according to thy word. Psalm 119:9.

Is there anything cleaner than a hospital? Workers there wash, scrub, disinfect, and sterilize 24 hours a day. It was not so in 1860 when Dr. Lister became chief surgeon at Glasgow Royal Infirmary.

Dr. Lister felt sick at his stomach as he toured the wards. Filth and stench were everywhere. Feverish people lay on dirty cots, their wounded limbs oozing pus. Nine out of 10 patients died of blood poisoning and gangrene.

"Take the patient out of the hospital if you would have him recover," stated one surgeon. "Take him to the church, school, or stable. Take him anywhere but to the hospital, for that will be his grave!"

"But why?" Dr. Lister wondered. "There must be a reason why wounds putrefy. The man who solves this problem will gain the world's undying blessing."

"Perhaps you'll be that man," his friend Tom Anderson said. "By the way, have you read the papers of Louis Pasteur?"

"No," he replied, "but I will." As Lister read about microbes that ferment grape juice and sour milk, the idea came to him that it must be these same microbes that cause flesh to rot. He must find a way to kill the microbes. By chance, he read a newspaper article that told about the use of carbolic acid to kill the odor of sewage.

"The stinking odor of sewage is like the stinking odor of a putrefied wound. It must be microbes that cause both. I will use carbolic acid on my patients," the doctor reasoned. "I will saturate a cloth with it and cover their wounds. I will scrub the floors with it. I will cleanse my surgical instruments and my hands with it. We will kill those microbes."

His plan worked. Within a year he had stamped out blood poisoning and gangrene. He had eliminated the sickening smell of rotting flesh and death. Sunshine, cleanliness, and joy had replaced darkness, filth, and sorrow.

Our hearts are like the surgical ward of Glasgow hospital before Joseph Lister and carbolic acid. What do you think is the Christian's antiseptic?

209

SIR HUMPHRY DAVY

We . . . are changed . . . by the Spirit of the Lord.
2 Corinthians 3:18.

Sir Humphry Davy, fashionably dressed in a canary-yellow waistcoat, gleaming satin breeches, and a blue velvet coat with long tails, stood before an audience of London's elite to explain the marvels of electrochemistry.

"I have here two ordinary glasses of water," Sir Humphry said with a flourish. "I will use this wire to connect them to this box, which is a battery. This will cause a current of electricity to flow through the two glasses. Notice what happens."

The audience sat on the edges of their seats, not wanting to miss a thing. Immediately bubbles of two different gases began to form, and the water disappeared as if by magic.

"Water is a compound of two gases, hydrogen and oxygen," Sir Humphry continued. "The electric current has broken the liquid up into its two parts."

"Sir Humphry is a scientific wizard!" people exclaimed. "What will he do next?"

What he did next was to use an electric current to change lye into sodium. He extracted potassium from potash. In this way he discovered seven new elements. Besides sodium and potassium, he isolated magnesium, strontium, calcium, chlorine, and barium. In every case the change was brought about through electricity.

Do you need a change in your life? Don't try electricity; you might electrocute yourself. What you need is the magnetic power of the Holy Spirit. Marvelous things happen when you let Him work in your life.

As His power sweeps through your soul, bad habits, impure thoughts, and evil desires evaporate. His daily action in your life produces love, joy, peace, patience, goodness, temperance, gentleness, and faith.

"Whatever has happened to you?" your friends will say. "You are surely different from what you used to be. You don't do the same things nor act the same way. You even look different. What is your secret?"

WALTER REED

The words of a talebearer are as wounds, and they go down into the innermost parts of the belly. Proverbs 18:8.

"Yellow fever is caused by a mosquito!" Carlos Finlay insisted. Nobody believed the eccentric old doctor from Havana. Hadn't Pasteur, Lister, and a host of other microbe hunters proved that disease came from germs?

Although Dr. Walter Reed and his Yellow Fever Commission scalded, disinfected, and scrubbed with a passion, it made no difference. The yellow killer raged through Cuba in the summer of 1900. During the previous two years the fever had killed more soldiers than had Spanish bullets.

The hospitals were full of delirious people with pale yellow skins and bloodshot eyes. The stink of their black vomit hung in the sultry air. Dr. Reed had tried every means to track down the microbe, to no avail. "It wouldn't hurt to try old Doc Finlay's idea," he sighed at last. "He just might be on the right track."

There was something strange about the way yellow fever spread. Nurses who worked in the yellow fever wards did not come down with the disease, though they had every opportunity to contact the germs. Why? A man in a house on one street would come down with the disease. Then it hopped around the corner or across the street to take someone else. The people had not even known each other. There had been no contact. Something must be carrying the microbe from person to person. What? Could it be the tiny mosquito?

Dr. Reed's experiments proved that old Doc Finlay was right. The culprit was the female mosquito of a certain species. He got rid of the mosquitoes and there was no more yellow fever.

In every school and community, there are people just as destructive as the mosquito. They run from person to person, bearing bad news and bits of juicy gossip. They are the talebearers, the gossipers. Their "bite" has caused the death of a multitude of friendships and untold heartache.

Do you know what I'm talking about? Have you felt the deep-down hurt a "gossip mosquito" can bring? Let's stamp out talebearing. Let's put an end to the "gossip epidemic."

WILLIAM CRAWFORD GORGAS

I am crucified with Christ: nevertheless I live; yet not I, but Christ liveth in me. Galatians 2:20.

"What is the weak spot of the enemy?" Lieutenant William Gorgas asked. "There we should strike. The more we know about her habits, the easier will it be for us to win."

The enemy of whom he spoke was guilty of human slaughter worse than that of Genghis Khan. It had once wiped out an army of 10,000 men on the island of Santa Lucia. In 1878 it mowed down 13,000 people, military and civilians alike, in the Mississippi Valley. During the Spanish-American War it killed more people than all the guns on both sides. The enemy was the female mosquito of a particular species, carrier of the deadly yellow fever.

"Get rid of the mosquito!" ordered Dr. Gorgas.

"What?" people jeered. "Are you crazy? We can't kill all the mosquitoes in the world!"

"I'm going to try," decided the determined sanitation expert. "I will start by studying the mosquito, learning its habits and searching for its weak point."

He discovered that the mosquito egg hatches into a wormlike wriggler, which lives in water. When the wriggler is about a quarter of an inch long, it changes into a mosquito. One day as he watched the wrigglers he found the weak spot of the enemy. The wrigglers had to come to the surface of the water for air.

"All we have to do is to prevent them from getting air," Dr. Gorgas reasoned. "I will pour oil on top of the water. The wrigglers will be imprisoned and unable to breathe. Then there will be no mosquitoes and no more yellow fever."

Within a few months there were no more mosquitoes in Cuba. Yellow fever had been wiped out there. In 1904 Dr. Gorgas went to Panama and did the same thing there.

You and I are fighting a life-and-death battle with sin. Like any good soldier, we need to learn where the weak spot of our enemy lies. I think I have discovered it right in the middle of the word *sin*—the word *I*. Putting self first, selfishness, is the heart of all sin. Like the female mosquito, self needs to die so that Christ might live out His life in us.

ALEXANDER FLEMING

Seek, and ye shall find. Luke 11:9.

For 19 years Alexander Fleming, a middle-aged Scotsman, had been looking for a "magic bullet" that would kill disease germs. In the fall of 1928 his laboratory shelves were lined with petri dishes. Each contained agar, on which colonies of various germs flourished. Each colony had its own distinctive shape and color. He examined the dishes now, occasionally removing a cover so that he could look more closely at the colonies.

"Mold again!" Dr. Fleming complained. "As soon as you uncover a dish, something is bound to fall in."

He stopped talking and looked more closely at the dish. "This is odd," he spoke to his assistant, Merlin Pryce. "Please hand me a scalpel." Pryce obeyed.

The older doctor picked up a piece of the blue-green mold and studied it. "Look here," he motioned to Pryce. "The colonies of germs close to the mold have lost their color. There's a clear ring around each patch of mold."

"Did the mold kill the germ colonies?"

"Looks like it," Fleming nodded. "I'll grow more of this stuff and see what happens." His hunch was right. Out of that mold Fleming was able to extract a yellow substance that became known as penicillin, the wonder drug of the twentieth century.

I've wondered a lot about what happened that September day at St. Mary's Hospital in London. Why was Alexander Fleming the lucky one to discover penicillin?

Mold spores had been in the air for thousands of years. Solomon was a wise man and a great naturalist. Why didn't he come up with the magic medicine? Luke was a physician who must have seen his share of mold. Why didn't he discover the wonder drug? The answer is None of these were looking for it. Alexander Fleming had one goal for his life, to find the magic bullet. Because he sought, he found.

What wonderful things might yet be discovered if someone would only look for them. Close your eyes and dream a daring dream of something you would like to find for the good of humanity. Then start looking! Only those who seek will find!

MARIE AND PIERRE CURIE

Can a man take fire in his bosom, and his clothes not be burned? Proverbs 6:27.

A frail young woman in dusty, acid-stained overalls stood in a small courtyard and shoveled brown dirt, called pitchblende, into a boiling vat atop a cast-iron stove. Then she stood for hours stirring the smelly liquid, finally pouring it into great jars to be stored in the laboratory. Later the coffee-colored syrup would be strained, treated, and analyzed.

The woman was Marie Curie. Together with her husband, Pierre, she was trying to isolate the element that caused the dirt to be radioactive. In 1898 they had only a pinch of grayish-white powder to show for tons of pitchblende and four years of grueling labor.

One night after they had put their two girls to sleep, Marie said, "Pierre, could we go down to the laboratory for a moment?"

"Sure," he said. "Why not?"

They walked arm in arm through the crowded streets of Paris to their laboratory on Rue Lhomond. Pierre fumbled for his key in the darkness, then opened the squeaky door of the little shed where they worked.

"Don't light the lamps," Marie said in a hoarse whisper. "Look, Pierre, look! Isn't it beautiful?"

A row of test tubes glimmered like bluish glowworms. The phosphorescent radium lit the inky darkness of the shack. This was the Curies' gift to the world, an element a million times more radioactive than uranium. It can make a clock dial glow, kill seeds, and destroy bacteria and cancer cells. In the end this powerful element destroyed its discoverer. Marie Curie died of leukemia. The radiation with which she had worked for more than 30 years had destroyed the cells in the marrow of her spine. She had taken radium, a kind of fire, into her bosom, and she paid with her life.

Those who experiment with sin will also suffer the consequences. Like a hidden fire, it kills from within. Spiritual leukemia follows, and eternal death is certain. Don't be fooled by its glitter and glow!

GEORGE WASHINGTON CARVER

Honour all men. 1 Peter 2:17.

A tall, slightly stooped Black man withdrew from the crowd of passengers that had just alighted from the train at Washington, D.C. With a sigh he set his battered wooden case on the pavement. His eyes brightened as he saw a redcap coming his way. He lifted his hand, but the porter didn't see him. The elderly man called out then in a quivering voice, "Porter . . . could you help me with my case?"

The smartly uniformed porter stopped a moment to see who had spoken. It was nothing but a poor working-class Negro with ill-fitting trousers and muddy shoes.

"Sorry, Pops, I can't. I've been sent to meet a big shot from Tuskegee, Alabama. He's a world-famous scientist. Gotta run or I might miss him!"

"But—I—I—" It was too late. The porter was lost in the crowd. The old man's mustache wiggled as he chuckled.

"I hope he won't waste too much time looking for that big shot from Tuskegee!" He chuckled again at his joke. Picking up his case, he hurried outside to hail a taxi. He was soon on his way to the Capitol where he was to speak that very day before Congress.

You've guessed it! The old man with the muddy shoes and battered wooden box was Dr. George Washington Carver, the world-famous scientist from Tuskegee, Alabama. He had come to show the lawmakers what could be done with peanuts and sweet potatoes. In his box he had samples of the hundreds of products he had made from them, everything from milk to paint.

What an opportunity one redcap missed that morning in 1921! It would have been something he could have bragged about to his grandchildren! He could have told how he carried the box of the famous Dr. Carver from Tuskegee, who did more for the economic development of the South than any other man. He missed all this because he wasn't in the habit of honoring all men—only the rich ones.

Do you honor all men and women? Rich or poor, old or young, neat or scruffy, Black or White, educated or uneducated, Christian or Muslim, famous or forgotten, citizen or foreigner?

ALBERT EINSTEIN

For thou hast made him a little lower than the angels, and hast crowned him with glory and honour. Psalm 8:5.

"Everybody back! Come on, move it!" the burly policeman walked along the front edge of the crowd.

As the policeman came his way, one small boy reluctantly gave up the spot he had been saving and stepped backward with his father. He craned his neck to see the great man who was arriving on the afternoon train.

"There he is!" someone down the line shouted.

The boy saw him then, a big man with an impressive head of white hair. He wore a turtleneck sweater and a rumpled tweed suit. He walked briskly, his shoulders slightly stooped, a warm smile emerging under his bushy moustache. He waved and nodded to his admirers.

When the great man had passed, the boy's father gripped his shoulder and said, "Never forget this, my boy. You have just seen Albert Einstein, the man with the greatest mind in all history."

Everyone agreed he was a genius, although most couldn't understand his theory of relativity. They were fascinated by his discussion of such things as the fourth dimension, time. He said that a traveling clock runs slower than one that is at rest. He proposed that if a man could travel fast enough, he could go for a month's vacation into space (as calculated by the spaceship clock) and come back to a son who was 20 years older than his father!

His theories pushed us into the age of space and nuclear power. His famous formula looks like this: $E = mc^2$. In simple language it means that energy can be made out of matter, and matter can be made out of energy. He saw his prophecy fulfilled in the atomic bomb.

However, I think the boy's father was wrong. Adam, not Einstein, had the greatest mind in history. Wouldn't it be fun to see the two together and hear them discuss the universe? If you want to learn something exciting, read the last two paragraphs of chapter 2 in *Patriarchs and Prophets*. Try to imagine what the two great minds would say to each other.

216

ENRICO FERMI

Freely ye have received, freely give. Matthew 10:8.

On December 2, 1942, a stocky, short-legged man wearing overalls blackened with graphite dust stood in an old squash court under the University of Chicago stadium and looked at one of the greatest secrets of World War II, the first atomic pile.

It was simply a pile of black rocks that looked like coal, but was actually graphite. The pile, weighing six tons, nearly filled the room. Embedded in some of the rocks were chunks of uranium. Three sets of cadmium control rods stuck out at strategic places in the pile of rocks.

From a balcony at one end of the squash court Enrico Fermi supervised the removal of the rods. His helpers took out the last rod very slowly as the scientist carefully watched the dials of the Geiger counter and other instruments.

"When the rod is all the way out, the chain reaction will begin," Fermi said, slide rule in hand, his eyes glued to the instruments, his muscles tense. Finally he gave the word, "Pull it out!"

One minute. Three minutes. Four minutes Fermi stood there motionless watching the dials of his instruments. "We've done it!" he shouted, his face breaking into a grin.

For 28 minutes he let the chain reaction continue. Every second neutrons were splitting atoms, releasing more neutrons, which were splitting other atoms, which released still more neutrons. At last Fermi ordered, "Put in the rods," and the experiment was over. Three years later his team had developed the atomic bomb. The result of the chain reaction from that bomb on August 6, 1945, was the annihilation of more than 60,000 people and the devastation of 600 city blocks. What tremendous power a chain reaction can unleash!

Would you like to start a different kind of chain reaction that would end in a powerful explosion? You could start one with a smile for your mom. She passes it on to Dad who gives it to his secretary at work. She smiles at a customer who takes it home to his wife who gives it to a neighbor. The neighbor gives it to her kids, and there is really no end. By a simple smile you can cause an explosion of love and happiness.

LISE MEITNER

Master, I will follow thee. Matthew 8:19.

"Papa, may I talk to you?" 22-year-old Lise Meitner asked as she approached her dad one evening.

"Of course." Dr. Meitner laid aside his legal briefs. "What's going on in that pretty head of yours?"

Lise's hands were sweating and her throat felt dry. She was afraid to bring up the subject, but she knew the time had come. "Papa, I want to enroll in the University of Vienna."

"Whatever for?"

"I want to go into one of the professions."

"There are no women in the professions. Not a one! No lawyer, doctor, or professor. What good would a university education do you?"

"But, Papa, you don't understand." Lise tried to explain what she had been thinking about for months. "I want to do something really important with my life, something that will benefit humanity."

"I see," her father's eyebrows raised. He moved forward on his chair. "And just what did you have in mind?"

"I—I—I'd been thinking of something in science. You know, like Marie Curie."

"Marie Curie! That's not any profession. She is something called a radioactive physicist, whatever that is."

"My mind is made up. That's what I want to do," Lise insisted. "All my life I have admired Madame Curie. I love mathematics, physics, and chemistry. You know I'm good at them."

"Well, it certainly isn't my choice for you," her father sighed. "I don't consider it much of a life, but if that is what you want, I won't stand in your way."

So it was that Lise Meitner began studies that earned for her a Ph.D. in physics. Her experiments led to the first splitting of the atom and the release of nuclear energy. It had started with a dream of being like Marie Curie.

What are your dreams? Whom do you idolize? Who is your hero? Whom do you want to be like? Choose wisely, for you will travel in the direction of the one you follow.

JONAS E. SALK

Perfect love casteth out fear. 1 John 4:18.

Fear makes your heart beat faster and your knees tremble. It can make your mind go blank and your tongue stop working. People speak of being "petrified" with fear. It's as though they are paralyzed by their fears, unable to do anything.

It's something like polio, the crippling disease that hit Franklin Delano Roosevelt on August 9, 1921. On that day, while he was sailing, he fell into the ocean and inevitably swallowed some of the water. The next day he was tired, and the day after, his left leg refused to work; then the other. There was no vaccine, no medicine that could help him. He remained a cripple as long as he lived.

When Roosevelt became president of the United States, he declared war on polio. He set up the National Foundation for Infantile Paralysis. That group campaigned for money and paid scientists to look for a way to prevent this crippling disease.

One researcher who responded was Jonas Salk. In his Pittsburgh laboratory he bred polio viruses, then killed them with formaldehyde and boiled them for many days. His experiments showed that an injection of the dead viruses induced the body to make its own antibodies to fight polio germs.

One day in May 1953 he, his wife, and their three sons took the first shots of polio vaccine. It proved safe for them, so he would allow it to be used on others. Since then scientists have developed a vaccine that can be drunk.

Jonas Salk received a Presidential Award and a Congressional Gold Medal for his discovery of a polio vaccine. He refused all financial awards. It was enough for him to know he had kept thousands of children from being crippled.

Now, what about our fears, which can also cripple? Is there any vaccine for fear? You bet there is! It's called love. A friend's love pushes you on. Your parents' concern and care help you overcome fears. God's love chases away the last remnants of your dread. So the next time you're afraid, try to think about how much someone loves you.

JOHN MUIR

Resist the devil, and he will flee from you. James 4:7.

Carlo, the Saint Bernard who was John Muir's constant companion in the High Sierras, came to a standstill. His tail and ears went down and his nose thrust forward.

"What do you see, old boy?" Muir whispered. He crept to a low ridge of moraine boulders on the edge of a meadow. There he hid himself behind a large tree and cautiously peeked around its trunk to see what Carlo was nervous about.

A stone's throw away he saw a huge cinnamon bear standing upright, his back to Muir. His hips were covered by tall grass and his front feet rested on the trunk of a fallen fir. He seemed to be listening intently, his sharp muzzle sniffing the air.

Magnificent! Muir thought. The shaggy hair of the 500-pound creature harmonized perfectly with the trunks of the trees and the lush vegetation. *I wonder what he would look like running? I've heard this kind of bear always runs from man unless cornered. I think I'll give him reason to run!*

Muir jumped from his hiding place, screaming, his arms waving. Slowly the giant bruin turned to face his attacker. He lowered his head, his beady eyes looking fiercely at Muir. He stood his ground, swaying on his hind feet, large claws outstretched, ready to fight.

"Suddenly I began to fear that upon me would fall the work of running," Muir wrote afterward. "But I was afraid to run, and therefore, like the bear, held my ground. We stood staring at each other in solemn silence within a dozen yards separating us, while I fervently hoped that the power of the human eye over wild beasts would prove as great as it is said to be."

After what seemed an eternity, the bear put his huge paws down, turned, and walked leisurely up the meadow. Frequently he stopped, turned to see if Muir was following him, then disappeared into the forest.

I wouldn't advise you to go chasing bears or the devil. However, should you come face-to-face with your enemy today, stand your ground. Stare him right in the eye and say, "You're not going to get me, for Christ is with me!" As you resist him in Christ's name, he will have no choice but to flee.

CHARLES HENRY TURNER

Go to the ant, thou sluggard; consider her ways, and be wise.
Proverbs 6:6.

Charles Turner lay flat on the ground, his stomach pressed against the bare, brown earth. His eyes were just a few inches from a tiny hole in the ground, no bigger than a period. Ants came and went from the hole, fanning out into various directions in search of food.

How do they find their way home without getting lost? Charles wondered. *Perhaps they smell their own footprints and thus find their way back to their nest. I'll have to find out.*

For his experiment, Dr. Turner set up an artificial ant nest on his laboratory table. He then constructed a cardboard stage from which an inclined cardboard bridge led down to the ant nest. He transferred some ants and pupae from the nest to the stage above the nest. Immediately the ants began to carry the pupae back down to the nest, using his bridge. They came back up the same bridge to take more pupae.

Next he made a second bridge and placed it on the opposite side of the stage. No ants used that bridge. Then he switched the bridges around so that the one with the smell of their footprints would be on the side they had not been using. They ignored it and used the new bridge on the same side of the stage they had used before.

Through a series of other experiments he proved that they followed light, not smell, in finding their way back home.

Further studies revealed that ants clean themselves often, combing and brushing one another. They also have a dump pile where they carry refuse matter. They even have a graveyard where they bury their dead. They go in funeral processions, two carrying a fallen ant, and two going behind to dig the grave.

He learned that some ants grow gardens, and others keep aphids and milk them. The more he studied them, the more he was amazed at their industry and wisdom.

When you have time, find some ants to study. From them you can learn industry, wisdom, cleanliness, caring, and how to find the way to your heavenly home.

GENGHIS KHAN

And [they] shall know that I am the Lord, when I have broken the bands of their yoke. Ezekiel 34:27.

After the death of their khan the few Mongol warriors left alive were scattered, their herds lost. Thirteen-year-old Temujin, son of the khan, eluded his pursuers for days. At last, weakened by hunger, he tried to slip through the bands of Taidjut warriors but he was caught. The Taidjuts fastened a kang on his shoulders. This was a heavy wooden yoke, with holes for his neck and wrists.

"I will find a way to escape!" the young khan promised himself.

One evening the Taidjuts held a feast. The soldiers, who were drunk, danced around a blazing campfire, leaving Temujin alone with a single guard. With the end of his kang he knocked out the guard and fled. A full moon lit his pathway but the wooden yoke hindered him, and he could hear the warriors who chased him coming up close behind. His heart pounding, he raced toward the river. There he hid himself among the rushes, with only his head showing above the murky waters.

As the warriors searched the bank, one man saw him but he did not betray his hideout. Encouraged, Temujin took a desperate chance. He followed the men back to their camp and crept into the tent of the one who had seen him in the rushes.

"Please, help me," the dripping boy whispered as he crawled toward the embers of the fire.

The stranger split the kang and burned the pieces. "I will be killed if they find you here," the man said. "Go away quickly to your people."

The boy who escaped that night became the great Genghis Khan, the fearless chieftain who led the Mongols in their conquest of Asia during the thirteenth century.

Are you, like Temujin, held captive in the enemy camp? Has Satan fastened the heavy yoke of sin about your neck? Are you burdened by your heavy load of sin and guilt? Do bad habits keep you captive? Do you feel helpless to free yourself? Jesus can break the yoke. Fall on your knees and whisper, "Lord, help me!" He will set you free!

CHEPE NOYON

Set a watch, O Lord, before my mouth; keep the door of my lips. Psalm 141:3.

The mighty Mongol hordes of Genghis Khan had swept down off the Gobi Desert to capture the kingdom of Cathay. General Chepe Noyon was given the task of taking the seaport of Liao-yang. However, his bows and arrows were powerless against the fortified city. His soldiers tried to climb the walls but were beaten back by men on top. He had no way to knock down the walls, and the enemy garrison refused to come out to fight.

"If we can't take them with our arrows, we will take them with our brains," Chepe Noyon said, his dark eyes blazing. "We will trick them into thinking we have retreated."

The Mongolians chuckled to themselves as they rode off one morning, leaving their tents, carts, and baggage behind. They took only their herds with them as they slowly retreated. For two days they marched slowly away from Liao-yang. Then in the darkness of the second night they mounted their fastest horses and sped back to the city, arriving there shortly after dawn.

The gates of the city were wide open. No guards stood on the walls. All the people from the city were busy in plundering the abandoned camp. Even the children had been enlisted to help carry the loot back to their homes. The soldiers had laid down their weapons and were working alongside the townspeople.

Chepe Noyon and his soldiers rode straight through the open gates and took the city.

Your mind is like the walled city of Liao-yang. As long as you keep the gates locked and your guards on duty, there is no way Satan can take control.

But the devil is every bit as smart as Chepe Noyon. If he can't take your mind by force, then he'll try to do it with trickery. He will make you think he has retreated. He's counting on you to open your gates so he can ride in.

There are five gates in the city of your mind. They are the five senses. The only way Satan can reach your mind is through your eyes, ears, mouth, nose, or sense of touch. Can you name some ways he lures you to open each of these mind gates?

SIR AYMERY DE PAVIE

But as for me, I will walk in mine integrity. Psalm 26:11.

In the summer of 1347 King Edward III of England captured the walled city of Calais and put it under the charge of Sir Aymery de Pavie, his most trusted knight.

"Is Sir Aymery a man of integrity?" the king of France asked Sir Geoffry. "Could we bribe him to open the gates?"

"I suspect he's a greedy man," Sir Geoffry answered. "He's a Lombardy knight, and quite poor."

"Then a little gold should do the trick!" The king winked at Sir Geoffry. "See what you can do."

After a good deal of bargaining, Sir Aymery agreed to accept the sum of 20,000 crowns to deliver Calais into French hands. Word of the plot somehow reached King Edward, who sent for Sir Aymery.

"You have betrayed me by selling Calais to the French," King Edward accused. "The penalty for your crime is death."

Sir Aymery fell on his knees and pleaded, "Noble king, I implore your mercy. I have not yet received a penny, and the bargain can still be broken. All is not yet lost!"

"No, nothing is lost but honor." The king looked at his knight with contempt. "You will go forward with your bargain. As soon as you have fixed a day and time to deliver the town up to him, you will let me know. On that condition, I will spare your life."

"I will do as you say." The grateful knight bowed before his king. He returned to Calais and made arrangements with Sir Geoffry for the yielding up of the city to take place on the first day of the new year. When Sir Geoffry arrived, he discovered more than 1,000 English troops waiting for him.

On that night Sir Geoffry lost 20,000 crowns without winning the castle of Calais. Sir Aymery lost something more valuable than silver and gold—his integrity. From that day on no one would trust his word. People knew that here was a man who could be bought with gold. He had no sense of honor.

In what ways might you be tempted to throw away your integrity?

JOAN OF ARC

Forgive, if ye have ought against any. Mark 11:25.

She was only 19, the dark-haired girl who sat in the executioner's cart. In her long white dress she looked more the part of an angel than a criminal. Surrounded by English soldiers, the cart creaked its slow journey through narrow cobblestoned streets to the market square in Rouen, France. Thousands of people had gathered to watch her die.

Across from the church three platforms had been built. Two were for the churchmen and civil judges. The third was for Joan. In the center was a post to which were attached chains. Underneath it a bonfire had already been laid. At the top of the stake a placard read: "Heretic! Witch! Blasphemer!"

"It's not true!" Joan cried out. "I was only doing what God asked me to do!"

Because she believed God spoke to her in visions, Joan had gone to war, dressed as a boy, to lead the French troops to victory in five different battles. When the sixth battle failed, the Burgundians sold her to the British for about $3,000. On May 30, 1431, she was led to the stake.

"Forgive the judges and the English, Lord!" She prayed so fervently that all who listened began to weep. "Please, Lord, forgive the king of France and all the princes of the kingdom. They don't know what they are doing!"

The judge waved his hand to the executioner. "Do your duty," he said.

The executioner hesitated in face of all the weeping. Surely they wouldn't go through with the burning.

"Go on—go on!" the judge called out. Then two soldiers led her to the stake and fastened the chains about her. The fire was lit.

"Jesus . . . Jesus . . ." she cried out, her eyes looking upward. "Jesus . . . Jesus . . . Jesus . . . Jesus!" Her head fell forward.

If you had been Joan, would you have forgiven your enemies? Would you have prayed for your executioner? Do you do it now? Can you forgive those who are mean to you? Do you pray for those who hurt you? Do you ask God to bless those who call you names?

GEORGE WASHINGTON

Honour thy father and thy mother. Exodus 20:12.

Fourteen-year-old George Washington sprawled on the grassy banks of the Potomac River. A dreamy, faraway look came to his eyes as he watched its brown waters flow to the sea. He knew the Atlantic Ocean led to all sorts of exciting places such as England, Spain, Africa, and the islands of the Caribbean.

Beside him on the grass was his 28-year-old half brother, Lawrence. Oh, how George admired his big brother, who had been to England and back on that wide ocean. He had also fought the Spanish in the Caribbean. What stories he told of those far-off lands!

"Lawrence." George sat up as he spoke. "I wish I could be the captain of a handsome sailing vessel and travel to distant lands. I'm tired of the farm and the woods."

"The best way to get started is to join the British Royal Navy," his brother said. "I have friends in England who could get you a post. It would give you good experience."

"I'm going home right now and pack my trunk!" George exclaimed.

"Hold your horses!" his brother laughed. "I need to write some letters to my friends in London, and of course I must talk over our plans with your mother."

"Nothing doing!" Mary Washington responded to the proposition.

"Come on! It would be good for the boy," Lawrence said, trying to convince her. "He needs to get away and see the world."

Mrs. Washington shook her head. "I will not allow him to throw his life away. He's my oldest son and I'm counting on him to take care of me and manage the farm. He cannot go."

And that was that. George obeyed his mother. He took up surveying instead of sailing, and became a gentleman farmer.

I wonder what would have happened if he had disobeyed his mother and run off to sea. Would he have become the commander in chief of the Colonial army in the War of Independence? If he had been a reckless, headstrong youth, do you think there would be a Washington Monument in his honor?

PAUL REVERE

Prepare to meet thy God. Amos 4:12.

His heart pounding with fear, Paul Revere leaned low on the horse's neck. Could he outdistance the redcoat that was chasing him? He sped through the salt marshes and clay pits to the road. He thundered down the narrow highway to the small wooden bridge that led into the town of Medford.

All was dark. In the moonlight it seemed like a ghost town. He reined his horse at the steps of the first house. Leaning over in his saddle, he beat on the wooden door with the handle of his whip.

"The British are coming!" he yelled. "To arms! To arms!" He pounded the door again, and a light came on.

He galloped to the next house and roared, "The British are coming! The regulars are out! To arms! To arms!"

Candles had been lit in many houses now. Windows flew open. "It's Paul Revere!" someone shouted.

"The British are coming!" the panting rider boomed in reply. "To arms! To arms! We have no time to waste!"

Men with muskets in their hands were streaming from all the houses now. One of them ran to the church and rang the bell. Children huddled with their mothers in the open windows, searching the shadows for the hated redcoats.

Paul Revere spurred his horse and rode on into open country, stopping at farmhouses along the way to give his message of alarm. "The British are coming! To arms! To arms!"

Thanks to Paul Revere, the minutemen were prepared to meet the British soldiers at Lexington and Concord that early morning of April 19, 1775.

There's another breed of minutemen riding the highways of earth today. In Fords, Fiats, Toyotas, and Saabs they roar down the highways of our world giving the news of Christ's soon return. "Jesus is coming! Get ready!" In dugout canoes, sampans, kayaks, and yachts they are racing over earth's waters declaring, "Jesus is coming!" They go walking, flying, cycling, and sledding into the remotest corners of our planet to give the message: "Jesus is coming! Prepare to meet thy God!"

Will you be one of His "minutemen" today?

ETHAN ALLEN

Lest coming suddenly he find you sleeping. Mark 13:36.

A waning moon looked down on the shadowy forms of about 80 men emerging from the wilderness. They milled around the dying embers of a campfire on the shores of Lake Champlain. They were the Green Mountain Boys, come to join their leader, Ethan Allen, in the capture of Fort Ticonderoga.

Ethan Allen stood at the water's edge, peering into the heavy mist that hung over the lake. He could see neither the fort nor the boats that had been promised him. If they didn't arrive soon, it would be too late to cross under cover of darkness and take the British by surprise. Then out of the gray mist two boats slipped into the cove.

The men piled in, talking softly. As they neared the western shore the gray walls of the fort pierced the mists. The first glimmering of morning showed in the eastern sky as they nudged their boats ashore. The lonesome cry of a waking loon drifted across the lake.

Stealthily the men climbed the rocky hill toward the fort, their muskets and swords gleaming in the half light of the pearly dawn. Would they succeed in their surprise attack?

Ethan was the first to reach the wicket gate at the top of the hill. The sentry lay sprawled on a bench, snoring, an hourglass running low beside him. A twig snapped under Ethan's foot. The guard was on his feet in an instant, his musket aimed at the intruder. He pulled the trigger. There was a flash, but no sound. His gun had misfired. He dropped it and ran inside the fort, yelling "Enemy attack! Enemy attack!"

Ethan Allen and his Green Mountain Boys followed him inside. The commandant of the fort appeared with a sword in one hand and his red breeches in the other. He surrendered without a fight.

Satan would like to find all of us sleeping on duty. He is pleased when videos and storybooks put us to sleep. He is delighted when we are too tired to study our Sabbath school lesson. He is joyful when we can't hold our eyes open long enough to meditate on God's Word and pray. He knows that sleeping Christians will surrender without a fight.

NATHANAEL GREENE

Bear ye one another's burdens. Galatians 6:2.

If anyone needed someone to help bear his burdens, it was Nathanael Greene on the night of February 1, 1781. General Davidson had been killed in a battle with Cornwallis, the British commander. His soldiers had then panicked and fled. At that moment it appeared to Greene that the patriots' cause was lost.

He saddled his horse in a bone-chilling rain and set out to meet his good friend, Dr. Read, at Steele's Tavern.

"What's this? You're all alone, General?"

"Yes, Doctor, tired, hungry, alone, and penniless." He threw a weary leg off the horse and slid to the ground. "Davidson is gone. My men have all vanished."

"That's awful!" Dr. Read sympathized. "Let's go inside out of the cold. We can talk better there."

Inside, a cheerful fire warmed the room. General Greene sank into a chair near the fire and took off his dripping tricornered hat. He dropped his head into his hands and sighed.

"This should make you feel better!" Mrs. Steele said, placing a plate of steaming hot food under his nose.

"I can't remember when I ate last. This is wonderful!"

"Thank you, General." Mrs. Steele was back at his table, this time with a small leather bag of money in each hand. "I overheard what you said to Dr. Read," she continued. "Take these, for you need them. I can do without them."

"God bless you, Mrs. Steele. You have done your country an honor tonight."

At that moment Greene noticed a picture of King George III on the wall. He went to a nearby writing desk and dipped a quill pen in the inkhorn. He strode to the picture and turned it over so that King George faced the wall. He wrote, "Hide thy face, George, and blush."

General Greene was ready then to saddle his horse and go back to fighting the war. He had renewed energy because two people had lifted his burden. Read the story again and see if you can find five ways Dr. Read and Mrs. Steele did it.

THADDEUS KOSCIUSZKO

Thy word have I hid in mine heart, that I might not sin against thee. Psalm 119:11.

The Polish countryside was ablaze with autumn color as General Thaddeus Kosciuszko marched his army across war-blackened fields toward the Vistula River. They passed several villages that lay in ruins, ravished by the invading Russian forces. At Maciejowice they stopped. Ahead of them they could see the enemy encamped along the banks of the river.

"Brothers! Defend your country!" General Kosciuszko shouted. "Defend her boldly! You will conquer!"

And they almost did. For three hours they held the Russians back.

"We are going to win! We will be free!"

Then the cannons were silent. The guns ceased to fire. The Polish Army was out of ammunition.

"Fight on!" Kosciuszko urged. "Reinforcements are on the way. Don't give up! Victory is ours!"

The brave soldiers fought on, with no weapons save their hands and the butts of their rifles. They fought until they were struck down by enemy bullets or bayonets. Their general was carried on a stretcher from the battlefield, a prisoner of the enemy. The Polish rising of 1794 was over.

Why didn't Kosciuszko conquer as he had hoped?

Was it because he was a poor general, untrained in the ways of war? No. He had fought for eight years in the American Revolution beside George Washington and Nathanael Greene.

Was it because their cause was evil? No, they were fighting for the freedom of their nation.

Was it because the soldiers didn't want to win? No, they gave the battle everything they had, even their lives.

The Polish rising failed because they ran out of ammunition. With nothing to use against the enemy, they were soon overcome.

You and I are facing an enemy stronger than the one those Polish soldiers fought. If we hope to win, we must have ammunition. Where do you think we get it? (Read the verse again.)

SIMÓN BOLÍVAR

Thou art worthy, O Lord, to receive glory and honour and power. Revelation 4:11.

"*Vive el Libertador!*"

In early August 1813, Simón Bolívar entered Caracas in triumph. In his first campaign as general he had fought six battles in six weeks and defeated five armies. He had freed all of western Venezuela.

"*Vive el Libertador!*"

For the first time Bolívar was greeted with "Hail the Liberator!" The crowds roared their admiration. Everyone, from the plantation owner to the slave, sang his praises. Church bells rang out. Cannon boomed. Flowers fell on him, tossed from balconies and rooftops.

"*Vive el Libertador!*"

The 30-year-old liberator rode in a chariot. Behind him marched the dirty, sweaty troops who had fought with him from the Colombian border to the capital city of Caracas.

"*Vive el Libertador!*"

The celebration continued all night. In the plaza people danced and bands played. Fireworks lit the tropical sky. Food and wine were in abundance.

Picture now another triumphant celebration of victory. The place is heaven, the time is soon.

"Hail to the Liberator!"

A mighty throng that no man can number has gathered from every nation, kindred, tribe, and people. Leading the procession is Jesus. Together they have come through a campaign lasting 6,000 years. Satan has been destroyed.

"Hail to the Liberator!"

Again and again the crowd roars its admiration for the One who died that they might live. Harps strike up a chord. The mighty choir begins to sing, "Worthy, worthy is the Lamb!"

"Hail to the Liberator!"

The procession moves to the sea of glass, where the jubilant people take off their golden crowns and cast them at the feet of their Saviour. That is only the beginning of a celebration that continues throughout eternity.

DAVY CROCKETT

For this my son was dead, and is alive again; he was lost, and is found. Luke 15:24.

The heart of 15-year-old Davy Crockett beat faster as he walked the familiar trails near the Nolichucky River in what is now Tennessee. The very air smelled like home. He paused a moment in the dusk before a large weather-beaten log cabin. Several wagons were already parked in the large yard. A hand-carved wooden sign above the door read, "Crockett's Tavern, Room and Board."

"I can't do it," Davy shook his head. "What if they don't remember me. After all, it's been two years!"

He remembered his leaving as if it were yesterday. He was only 13 and attending school for the first time. On the fourth day he had beaten up a boy. Fearing a beating from the stern schoolmaster, Davy had hid out in the woods. When his father found out about his truancy he promised a whipping the next day if Davy didn't go to school. Caught between two whippings, he had hired himself to a man who was about to drive a herd of cattle to Virginia. Now he was back. What reception would he have?

"I'll go in just like any other traveler," Davy decided. "Maybe they won't even recognize me." And they didn't. After all, they had long ago given him up as dead. It was not until they were seated around the supper table that his oldest sister recognized him.

"Davy!" she screamed, running around the table and giving him a big hug. "Davy, my lost brother! Where have you been?"

"I can't believe it!" his mother cried through her tears. "All this time we thought you were dead! Oh, but I'm glad you've come home!"

"The joy of my family at my return was such that it humbled me," Davy wrote later. "It made me sorry that I hadn't submitted to a hundred whippings, sooner than cause so much affliction as they had suffered on my account."

Davy had experienced what it was like for the prodigal son to come home to his father. The love and acceptance he knew that night is the same every sinner feels when he returns to his Father's house.

WILLIAM BARRET TRAVIS

Wherefore take unto you the whole armour of God, that ye may be able to withstand in the evil day, and having done all, to stand. Ephesians 6:13.

"Santa Anna is on the way here with 5,000 Mexicans," Lieutenant Colonel William Travis told his band of 150 Texans. "There is no way we can defend the whole city of San Antonio. We'll have to retreat to the Alamo and hold them off until reinforcements come."

"Good plan," agreed Davy Crockett.

"How long do you think we can hold out?" James Bowie asked.

"Ten days . . . maybe two weeks," Travis said. "Surely help will come before then. At any rate, we have no other choice but to quit San Antonio and leave it to Santa Anna. Defending the city is out of the question. We must stand our ground."

Five days after the siege began, a mud-soaked courier rode into the small frontier town of Washington-on-the-Brazos with the following message from Travis:

"To the People of Texas and All Americans in the World: . . . The enemy has demanded a surrender. . . . I have answered the demand with a cannon shot and our flag still waves proudly from the wall. I shall never surrender or retreat. . . . Come to our aid with all dispatch."

By March 5 the guns of the Alamo were silent. Ammunition was low. Santa Anna and his men scaled the walls and killed all the remaining defenders of the fort. The Texans had fought bravely to the end, using their muskets as clubs. They had been true to the call of the commander, "Never surrender or retreat."

Are you ready to fight for your faith in Jesus to the end? You may have to, someday. Then you will need the courage of William Travis to stand firm. Will you be that strong? If you retreat now, ashamed to witness for Jesus, you will retreat then. If you surrender now to the small temptations of Satan, it will be ever so easy to surrender when the big one comes. Now is the time to put on the whole armor of God. Now is the time to decide, "I will never surrender or retreat."

SAM HOUSTON

As often as ye eat this bread, and drink this cup, ye do shew the Lord's death til he come. 1 Corinthians 11:26.

Promptly at 3:30 p.m., on April 21, 1836, Sam Houston barked his orders to the 900 men of the Texan army, "Line up. Form into your fighting ranks! The time has come to give Santa Anna a lesson!"

"Remember the Alamo!" someone shouted.

"Remember the Alamo!" The excited men took up the cry. Already some were loading their guns, anxious to get even with the Mexican general for slaughtering Texans at the Alamo.

"Hold your fire, men!" Houston roared. "Wait until I give the signal. No use firing until it'll do some good!"

Within 20 yards of the Mexican barricade Houston wheeled his white stallion, grabbed his beaver hat, and threw it into the air. "Now!" he yelled.

The men broke into a run toward the barricade, shouting all the way, "Death to Santa Anna! Remember the Alamo!"

The Mexicans, aroused from their siesta, were confused. Within 18 minutes the battle was over. One of the most decisive battles of history had been fought. Because of it the United States later stretched across the continent to the Pacific. A million square miles had been added to the nation's territory.

Not far from Houston, Texas, is a historical monument built in remembrance of the Battle of San Jacinto. All who visit that memorial are reminded of the battle cry of Houston's men: "Remember the Alamo!"

Two thousand years ago the most decisive battle of history was fought on Mount Calvary. There, single-handedly, Jesus overcame Lucifer and the powers of darkness. Because of the battle won that day, all who accept His victory will be saved. Because of what He did, we can all face our individual battles, crying, "Remember Mount Calvary!"

In every Christian church, we have a memorial of the Battle of Mount Calvary. It is called the Lord's Supper. Each time we drink the grape juice and eat the bread, we are shouting to the world, "Remember how Jesus died for us! Remember Mount Calvary!"

JAMES BOWIE

Thou ... hast redeemed us to God by thy blood out of every kindred, and tongue, and people, and nation. Revelation 5:9.

What James Bowie saw made his blood boil. A brawny White man had tied a Black man to a tree and was beating him unmercifully. The slave appeared to be unconscious. Blood streamed down his back.

"Anyone who would treat a slave like that ought to be shot!" Jim shouted. Leaping from his horse, he grabbed the whip, giving the man some of his own medicine.

The slaveowner seized the other end of the whip, and the two White men stood glaring at each other.

"It's none of your business what I do with my slave!"

"I make it my business when I see such cruelty!"

"This slave won't work! He deserved a flogging."

"Nobody deserves what you were giving," Jim said, letting go of the whip. "Lucky I came along or he would be dead by now. How much do you want for him?"

"He's not for sale."

"But you said he won't work. You ought to be glad to get rid of him, if he's no good."

"You can have him for $1,200," the owner challenged.

Without another word Jim took out his wallet and wrote a check for the amount. "That's a pretty stiff price to pay for a slave who's no account!" he said, unloosing the bonds of his new property.

"God bless you, Massa!" Great tears were running down the Black man's face. "I'll make you a good slave, as God is my witness."

Jim helped the slave onto his horse and took him home.

In the years that followed, Big Sam was more than a good slave; he was a friend who was willing to do anything for the man who had saved his life.

Read the story again, putting your name in place of the Black man. Satan is your first owner and Jesus is the one who rescued you. Can you say "Thank You, Jesus. I'll love You and praise You forever"?

BENJAMIN BONNEVILLE

This poor man cried, and the Lord heard him, and saved him out of all his troubles. Psalm 34:6.

"Oh, God of the wilderness, save us!"

Captain Benjamin Bonneville shivered inside his warm plaid greatcoat, but he kept stumbling on through the blizzard. He scarcely knew where he was going, but he knew he must keep his men moving if they were to survive.

"We can't go on much longer, God," he continued his prayer. "We're out of food, and our strength is almost gone. If You are going to do anything, it's got to be soon."

For two months Bonneville and three other men had been struggling through the Snake River Canyon, searching for the Hudson's Bay Company trading post. First, the mule carrying their food supply had slipped into the river and was dashed to pieces on the rocks. Then blinding snowstorms had forced them to kill another mule for food. Now there was nothing left to eat.

"We ain't going to make it, Cap'n," Old Matt prophesied. "I see Death a-followin' us!"

"Hurry up, then!" Captain Bonneville joked. "We'll outrun him!" But nobody laughed. The men could barely put one foot in front of the other. It was plain that the other men believed the old trapper.

"We're going to make it with God's help!" Bonneville said with more confidence than he felt.

By noon the next day every step was an agony of effort. The men fell into the snowdrifts and used precious energy digging themselves out. Wind whipped the loose snow into their faces, stinging their skin and blinding their eyes. Just ahead of them was a rocky ridge blown clear of snow. Bonneville staggered to the rocks for shelter, but he found himself looking down on a wide, greening valley. For 53 days they had battled ice and snow in the mountains. He could hardly believe that down there in the valley it was spring.

"God has saved us," Captain Bonneville said. Within a few hours they were eating dried salmon and berries in the tents of friendly Indians.

STONEWALL JACKSON

My covenant will I not break, now alter the thing that is gone out of my lips. Psalm 89:34.

Eleven-year-old Tom Jackson walked along the road from the Monongahela River carrying a three-foot pike over his shoulder. He smiled in anticipation as he thought of the 50-cent piece Conrad Kester would pay him for this fish. Tom had struck a bargain with the local gunsmith that he would sell him all the fish he caught of a certain size for 50 cents each.

"Mighty fine fish you got there, Tom," Colonel John Talbott called from his front porch.

"Thanks, Colonel!"

"What'll you take for it?"

"Sorry, this fish is sold."

"I'll give you a dollar for it."

"No, sir, I can't take it. I have promised this fish to Mr. Kester."

"I'll give you a dollar and a quarter," Colonel Talbott argued. "Will Mr. Kester give you that much?"

"Colonel Talbott, I have given Mr. Kester my word. I mean to never go back on my word. When I say something, I plan to do it. I want people to be able to count on me."

When Mr. Kester saw his fish he offered to pay Tom a dollar. "No, sir, a bargain is a bargain," Tom replied. "Sometimes you have paid me for fish that were a little short. It's only fair that you sometimes get ones that are bigger."

When Tom Jackson grew up he became a famous general called Stonewall Jackson. People knew they could always count on the word of General Jackson.

Do you know anyone, besides God, of course, who is as honest as Tom Jackson? When you promise to clean your room, can your mom count on you to carry through? When you promise your teacher to do a project by a certain date; can she count on you to get it done? Would you keep a bargain even if it meant a loss to you?

ROBERT E. LEE

Be gentle unto all men. 2 Timothy 2:24.

Gentleness is one of the fruits of the Spirit that all Christians should possess. Yes, even strong, macho men should be soft and tender at times. There's nothing wrong with a boy gently soothing away the tears of a small child. It is Christlike to cry with those who are suffering. A true Christian always takes time to help the weak.

No one presents a more macho image than General Robert E. Lee sitting astride his fine gray horse, leading brave men into battle. Yet his eyes were often softened by tears. He sympathized with the wounded, no matter which side they were on. He was never so great as when he took time to soothe a small child's fears.

Once on a battlefield in Mexico he came upon an enemy drummer boy pinned under a dying soldier. Beside them knelt a little Mexican girl. She was a poor girl, without stockings or shoes. Her ragged dress was sprinkled with blood. Her hair hung in a long black braid down her back, nearly touching her hips. She had clasped her hands over her breast as if to keep her heart from breaking. Her large black eyes were streaming with tears.

"What's wrong, little one?" the great man asked.

"My brother's arm is broken," she sobbed. "He's hurting and the man is dying."

"Does it hurt bad?" Lee asked the boy kindly, thinking of his own son back home. "I'll get help, and we'll send you to the hospital. Soon you'll be all right."

The little girl's sorrowful eyes followed him as he walked away. Soon he was back with four medics who carefully lifted the dying enemy soldier and the drummer boy onto stretchers and carried them off to the hospital.

"Mille gracias, señor," the little black-eyed girl said, smiling through her tears.

Somehow I would like to think that when the rewards are passed out on the sea of glass, a special medallion called the "Medal of Gentleness" will be given to men like Robert E. Lee.

SARAH EMMA EDMONDS

Thou shalt not be afraid for the terror by night; nor for the arrow that flieth by day. Psalm 91:5.

A fierce battle raged at Malvern Hill between the Confederate Army and the Union forces. Above the thunder of the guns Franklin Thompson could hear the piteous groans of the mangled, helpless ones who had fallen. Hunger gnawed at his stomach. His buddies were near collapse. Someone must go foraging for food.

"I'll go," Franklin volunteered. During a lull in the firing he crept to a farmhouse just beyond the Union lines. It was deserted but the cupboards were stocked with a good supply of food.

"Wait till the guys sink their teeth into this meat!" he said, throwing a large side of beef onto a bed quilt. To this he added flour, tea, coffee, an iron skillet, and a teapot. Then, twisting the four corners of the quilt, he made it into a rough bundle. To this he tied a long piece of cord.

Just then a shell crashed through the wall of the house, forcing him to hide in the basement. A few minutes later he heard a crackling above him and knew the house was on fire. Crawling up the basement ladder, he lay flat on the ground and inched his way from the burning house. Slowly, painfully he dragged himself belly first over the rough ground, back to the trenches and safety.

"Look at the grub!" the men in the rifle pits yelled.

"It's sent us from our heavenly Father, just as the manna was sent to the children of Israel," another declared.

"We thought for sure they had you," another remarked. "Couldn't believe my eyes when you came crawlin' back to us."

"That boy risked his life to get it for us," another said, shaking his head in wonder. "He never would have returned had not God shielded him from the bursting shell."

The boy whom God shielded from the terror of that night was not really Franklin Thompson, as they all believed. In reality it was Sarah Emma Edmonds, who, disguised as a boy, served as field nurse, secret agent, and dispatch rider for the Michigan Infantry.

JOHN BROWN

Thou shalt have no other gods before me. Exodus 20:3.

Seven-year-old John Brown ran alone across the prairie. The warm wind that rippled the grass blew through his hair, making him feel as free as the golden eagle that soared above him. Suddenly John was no longer alone. An Indian boy appeared silently and ran beside him. It was his friend Leesolu, of the Seneca tribe.

The Indian boy sprinted ahead, leading John up a gentle slope that became a hill. At the top the two boys stopped and looked across the valley to where a party of Indians was moving.

"My people," Leesolu said. "We go far away to the west." He put his hand into a leather pouch that he wore around his waist and pulled out a small, shining yellow ball. "John," he said, placing the treasure in his friend's hand. Without another word Leesolu turned and raced toward the retreating figures.

John looked at the ball in his hand. It was a gift of friendship that he knew he would treasure always. He stayed on the hill, the yellow ball clasped in his hand, until the Indians moved across a rise of land and disappeared.

From then on the yellow ball went with John everywhere, secure in a leather pouch he made for it like the one Leesolu had worn. When he ran with it across the prairie it was almost as if his friend were with him again. He touched it often when he was working. When he was doing his lessons he placed it on the table where he could see it.

"That's a neat marble," other boys said. "What'll you trade for it?" John always shook his head. He would never trade his precious yellow ball. It meant too much to him.

"It's only a thing," his father said one day. "You should not love it. I see you looking at it with worship in your eyes. None but God Himself should receive the adoration you are giving that stone."

Then one day it was gone. He searched every possible place, but his precious treasure was lost. He ran to the hillside where he had received it, and cried. He knew that what his father had said was true, he had loved that stone too much. He would try never again to love anything more than God.

240

DAVID GLASGOW FARRAGUT

Remember how short my time is. Psalm 89:47.

David Glasgow Farragut, admiral in the United States Navy, lay stretched out on a table in his warship *Hartford*. His ship had just run the blockade at Mobile Bay and won a victory that would break the power of the Confederate fleet, but he was unaware of it. Captain Perkins and Dr. Palmer stared down at their unconscious commander.

The admiral groaned and opened his eyes. "What's going on? Where am I?"

"You're in the ship's galley, sir," Captain Perkins said. "You fainted. We thought for a moment you were dead."

"Sorry to disappoint you!" Farragut grinned and started to sit up.

"Lie still!" Dr. Palmer ordered, placing a restraining hand on the admiral's shoulder. "You're not going anywhere yet."

"But I've work to do," he protested weakly. "I'll be all right. I'm just tired."

Dr. Palmer cleared his throat. "Admiral Farragut, I don't believe in beating around the bush. I think you deserve to know the truth."

"Come on, Doc!" Farragut smiled. "Don't look so glum. The world's not coming to an end."

"For you it might be," Dr. Palmer curtly replied. "Admiral, you are a sick man. Time is running out. If you had only six months to live, what would you do with it? A wise man would make those last six months the richest days of his life."

"Are you telling me that I have only six months?"

"No. I can't rightly say how long you've got. It could be six days, six months, or six years, but time is running out. So, Admiral, plan your life from now on with that in mind."

"Well," the admiral sighed. "I'd want to serve my country to my last day. But at the same time, I'd want to spend all the time I could with my family. I don't know, Doc. That's a tough one."

If you knew you had only six days to live, what would you do with those days?

KIT CARSON

God . . . will with the temptation also make a way to escape, that ye may be able to bear it. 1 Corinthians 10:13.

Long before Kit Carson became a soldier in the Mexican War, he was a trapper in the wild, unsettled West.

"Our meat supply is almost gone," Kit announced to the group of mountain men gathered around their campfire near the Yellowstone River. "I'll leave you men to set the traps while I go shoot our supper!"

After tramping for several miles, he spotted an elk grazing in a secluded mountain meadow. Raising his rifle, he brought down the elk with his first shot.

"Good going!" he congratulated himself, then felt uneasy as though someone had heard him. Looking around, he saw two grizzly bears less than 15 yards from where he stood.

"I ain't takin' on you fellers!" Kit said, making a beeline for the nearest tree, a slender aspen. Dropping his rifle, he shinnied up the tree and lost a moccasin in the process.

The bears ambled over to the tree and ignored the moccasin and rifle. It was the man in the tree they wanted. One tried to climb the sapling, but it wasn't big enough for his claws to catch hold. The other bear decided shaking might do the trick. Kit wrapped his legs around the trunk and held on for dear life. He managed to break off one limb with which he hit one bear on the nose. The grizzly tossed his head and continued shaking the tree.

After half an hour the bears gave up and lumbered over to inspect the fallen elk. At last there was a way of escape! Kit slid down the tree, put on his moccasin, picked up his rifle, and quietly slipped away, leaving the elk for the grizzlies.

"Whew! That was a close one!" Kit said when he finally slowed down to wipe away the sweat.

Sometime you might get "treed" by the circumstances of your life. Like Kit Carson, you will feel that your end has come. In that moment of discouragement, wrap your legs around the "tree" and hang on. God will make a way of escape for you.

PHILIP HENRY SHERIDAN

Thou hast forsaken me, saith the Lord, thou art gone backward. Jeremiah 15:6.

The sun was not yet up on the morning of October 19, 1864, when a soldier dressed in a rumpled blue uniform rode up to the inn at Winchester, Virginia. Hastily he tied his horse and ran inside the inn. "Where's General Sheridan?" he asked. "I must see him at once."

Pushing open the door of the room where Sheridan lay asleep, the distraught soldier cried: "General Sheridan, wake up! Old Jube attacked our camp at dawn. Everything is in confusion."

"I can hear the artillery," Phil Sheridan responded as he jumped out of bed and began pulling on his trousers. "Where's your camp?"

"Cedar Creek."

"How far is that?"

"Fourteen as the crow flies . . . 20 by the road."

General Sheridan took the short cut, arriving to find his men in retreat. Jumping his horse over a rail fence, he rode to an elevation where all his men could see him. Waving his hat with his right hand, he steadied his prancing black stallion with his left and roared: "About-face, boys, about-face! We're going back. We're going to lick the socks off those scoundrels!"

"Hurrah! Sheridan is here!" the soldiers cheered, turning to face the enemy once more. Step by step they moved forward, retaking the ground they had lost. By late afternoon the Confederates were in retreat.

Nineteen hundred years ago a small band of 11 men were in retreat, hiding away in an upper room. They were going backward in their spiritual experience. They were ready to give up, when suddenly their resurrected Commander walked through the door. "About-face! You will be triumphant! Go forward!"

Are you advancing in your Christian experience, or have you turned around to go the other way? Do you feel whipped and beaten, discouraged and despondent? Listen to the voice of your General: "Turn around! You're going the wrong direction! Face the enemy! Victory can come only as you march forward!"

JOHN J. PERSHING

As a bird that wandereth from her nest, so is a man that wandereth from his place. Proverbs 27:8.

On October 6, 1918, Major Whittlesey's battalion was in a desperate situation. For four days it had been trapped in a deep ravine in northeastern France near the Belgian border. The men were surrounded by Germans on all sides. Their ammunition was nearly exhausted. Starvation was near.

"I've been trying to get through to headquarters for days," Major Whittlesey told his men. "Our signals are not reaching them. We've sent out several scouts, but none of them got through. All we have left are two carrier pigeons. I guess it wouldn't hurt to try them."

As one of his soldiers reached into the basket to take out the first pigeon the other one got loose and flew away without a message. Carefully, the major took out the remaining bird, named Cher Ami, and tied a message to his leg. The bird rose in a spiral, circled the area several times, then flew back into the ravine and perched on a tree.

"Get going!" the major yelled. "Scat!"

Soldiers threw sticks and stones at the pigeon, but he refused to budge. At last one of the men climbed the tree and shook the limb where he sat. "G'wan! Beat it!" he yelled.

This time Cher Ami took off on a tangent toward headquarters. He arrived there minus one eye and one leg and with a shattered breastbone.

For bravery Cher Ami received a French medal of honor. General John J. Pershing, commander of the American forces in Europe, went to the ship to see the pigeon off. He took her gently in his big hands and said, "I wish you a safe journey home to America. I hereby order you to have the best pigeon-cabin on board ship!"

When Cher Ami died, he was stuffed and given a place in the Smithsonian Institution, Washington, D.C.

Like Cher Ami, you and I have within us a homing instinct. God created us with a restlessness that is satisfied only when we come home to Him. Without Jesus, we are like a wandering carrier pigeon seeking its home.

ULYSSES S. GRANT

Call upon me in the day of trouble: I will deliver thee, and thou shalt glorify me. Psalm 50:15.

"Let's go fishing!" Ulysses called to his cousin Dan when school was out one spring afternoon. The two boys rode horseback to their usual fishing hole. They found the brook had been transformed by recent rains into a racing, wild river.

"Best not to fish here today," Dan cautioned.

"Aw, come on! You're just scared!" retorted Ulysses. Leaping off his horse, he took his fishing pole and headed for a log that jutted out into the water.

"Stay off that log," Dan warned. "You might fall in!"

Ignoring the warning, Ulysses began to crawl out on the log. He hadn't realized how fast the water was flowing. It made him dizzy just to look at it. He closed his eyes and edged his way forward. Suddenly the log shifted and began to roll.

"Help me, Dan!" Ulysses cried when he came up for air. The current swept him along like a piece of driftwood.

"Help, somebody, help!" Dan echoed, but there was nobody to help but himself. He ran along the bank, not knowing how to save his cousin.

"The bend!" Ulysses cried. "The willow tree."

At the bend a huge willow tree spread its branches across the stream. If Dan could reach it in time, he might be able to catch Ulysses as he went by. He slipped and slid in the wet grass along the bank. Somehow he had to reach that tree to save his cousin.

"O God, help me get there in time," Dan sobbed.

Dan hurled himself at the lowest branch of the tree and climbed out as far as he dared, hooking his legs around it. At that moment Ulysses came hurtling toward him. Dan reached down and managed to grab his shirt.

"Help it to hold," he prayed. It did. Ulysses reached up and seized the branch. He was safe.

When Ulysses grew up he became a Union general in the Civil War. In those dangerous times it gave him courage to remember how God had helped his cousin save him from drowning.

"WILD BILL" HICKOK

And knowledge shall be increased. Daniel 12:4.

The Sioux chiefs were preparing for the warpath. Hoping to persuade the Indians not to fight, General Phil Sheridan arranged a conference with the chiefs. He took "Wild Bill" Hickok with him to translate.

"Bill, tell these chiefs that it is not wise to fight the powerful White man, for he can do things they have never even dreamed possible," Sheridan began.

The Indians frowned and shook their heads.

"Tell them, Bill, that we have made great iron horses that run on wheels. Our trains can go three times as fast as their horses can run."

The chiefs scoffed at this statement.

"They don't believe you, General," Hickok said.

"Well, then, tell them how the White man has invented a boat that doesn't need paddles or sails. It runs on fire."

The Indians grunted their disbelief.

"All right, Bill, tell them about the telegraph. Tell them I have a little black box here and the Great White Father has a little black box in Washington. When I send signals from my box the Great White Father hears me, and when the Great White Father sends signals from his box I hear him."

Hickok was silent.

"Go on, man, translate it!" Sheridan ordered.

The old mountain man looked General Sheridan in the eye and said, "No, sir! Now *I* don't believe you!"

Can you imagine what those Indian chiefs and "Wild Bill" Hickok would say if they could see all of the inventions of the past 85 years? How could you describe to them radio, television, communication satellites, cars, airplanes, submarines, computers, and space shuttles? What would they think of elevators, escalators, washing machines, mixers, electric irons, and microwave ovens?

Did you know that there have been more inventions in the past 85 years than there were in all of history up until this century? This increase of knowledge is a sign that Jesus is coming soon.

ALEXANDER ARCHER VANDEGRIFT

As many as I love, I rebuke and chasten. Revelation 3:19.

Archer Vandegrift had just graduated from the Marine Basic School at Parris Island. He was on his first assignment in New Hampshire. His commanding officer was a stern-looking man with a handlebar mustache; his name was Theodore Porter Kane. Every other day Archer was the officer on duty.

One night when icy winds were blowing down from the North Pole, plunging temperatures to ten degrees below zero, the phone rang at Archer's station. It was 3:00 a.m.

"Marine headquaters, Vandegrift speaking," he answered.

"Colonel Kane here. I've a report of trouble in Kittery. Please round up some men and patrol the town. Take care of any disturbance and report back to me."

"Yes, sir!"

Getting his men was not so easy. "Give us a break, Vandegrift! We'll freeze our ears off in this weather!"

"Colonel's orders. Let's get moving."

The men dressed, pulled on their fleece-lined parkas, and set out on a march to the nearby town. The night was pitch black. The north wind stung their faces and made walking difficult. The village was as quiet as a graveyard. With no disturbance to quell, the men marched back to their barracks just as dawn was breaking.

Vandegrift found Colonel Kane sitting before a cozy fire. The half-frozen lieutenant gave his report. When he was finished, the colonel said, "Thank you, Mr. Vandegrift. You did an excellent job!"

Several months later he was talking with Mrs. Kane. "I'm sure your husband knew there was no disturbance," he told her. "He sent us out in that cold for nothing! Why?"

"Just remember, Mr. Vandegrift," she said, "Colonel Kane never gives such assignments to officers he doesn't like! It shows he considers you like one of his sons."

Do you sometimes wonder why God allows certain things to happen in your life? Perhaps God is teaching you as a father would teach his son. He tests only those He loves.

DOUGLAS MacARTHUR

A fool despiseth his father's instruction. Proverbs 15:5.

In the spring of 1898 18-year-old Douglas MacArthur took the entrance examination for West Point and passed. He was overjoyed until the day in June when his dad, Lieutenant Colonel Arthur MacArthur, got a new assignment.

"You have been appointed a brigadier general of volunteers to fight in the war against Spain. You are ordered to the Philippines at once to take charge," the letter from Washington said.

"Dad, that's wonderful!" Douglas burst out. "Aren't you excited about helping to give the Filipinos their freedom?"

"Yes, son, I'm proud to have a part in the action. They deserve their freedom, after nearly 400 years of colonial rule. Every man deserves to be free."

"I'm going with you," Douglas decided. "Who wants to study war from a book when there's a real one going on? I want to be part of the action, too. I'm going down right now to enlist!"

"Not so fast, young man," his father frowned. "Sit down and listen to what I have to say. This isn't the last war that will be fought. You can be sure there will be plenty in the coming years. There will be greater battles to be fought than the one to which I'm going now. Prepare yourself. Go to West Point."

"But, Dad . . . "

"Your father is right, Douglas," his mother agreed. "If you want to make the army your career, then you need to learn the discipline and strategy of West Point. When you are finished, you will be an officer, ready to help direct the action as your father is doing. You will do a much better job and enjoy it more if you are prepared."

"Oh, all right," Douglas said, conceding to their better judgment. "I'll go to West Point."

Near the end of his life he wrote in his biography, "At 18 one wonders how little parents understand; years later, the wonder is how wise they were!"

JAMES HAROLD DOOLITTLE

The pride of thine heart hath deceived thee. Obadiah 3.

Sixty years ago Jimmy Doolittle was a famous and daring airplane pilot. In September of 1922 Jimmy became a national celebrity when he flew from Florida to California in 21 hours and 19 minutes. He was also the first to fly "blind," using only his instruments to guide his takeoff and landing. He was a test pilot, making the girls scream with his full-power dives, loops, barrel rolls, spins, and turns.

"Jimmy Doolittle is just the man we need to send to Chile," an executive of the Curtiss Company said. "He can demonstrate our new P-1 fighter. He can prove that it is better than the planes made in Germany, Italy, and England."

Jimmy was delighted for another chance to show off his skill, and of course he was the center of attention from the moment he arrived in Santiago. A party was held in his honor the night before the air show.

"Are all American men as supple and acrobatic as Douglas Fairbanks?" someone asked, referring to a popular movie star of those days.

"Oh, sure!" Jimmy bragged. "We're all just like him!"

"Prove it!" someone challenged.

"Glad to oblige," he replied with a smile and a bow. Going to an open window, he climbed on the window ledge. "I'll do a handstand for you right here."

The window ledge crumbled under his weight, pitching him right out the window. He fell 20 feet, breaking both ankles. He was rushed to the hospital.

The next morning an ambulance delivered a much humbler Jimmy Doolittle to the airfield. His feet were in casts. He had to be lifted into the plane, and his feet were strapped to the rudder bars. After the air show, he spent six months in Walter Reed Hospital, waiting for his legs to heal properly.

Jimmy's pride had deceived him into thinking he could do anything. His pride caused him to throw caution to the winds. It made him feel that he was indestructible. Six months in the hospital taught him how deceptive pride is.

DWIGHT D. EISENHOWER

*And take . . . the sword of the Spirit, which is the word of God.
Ephesians 6:17.*

Dwight D. Eisenhower, one of the world's greatest generals, learned his first lesson in military tactics when he was 4 years old. It happened on his Uncle Luther's farm, north of Topeka, Kansas. Little Dwight saw a gander for the first time and went to investigate.

Suddenly the bird stretched out a long neck, opened its fierce-looking beak, and came hissing at the surprised boy. Terrified and sobbing, he turned and ran for the house. After that, whenever the gander saw Dwight, it charged.

"You've got to face up to Old Gander," Uncle Luther told him.

"I can't," Dwight cringed. "I'm scared he'll bite me."

"He won't if you do what I say," the older man said. "But first we have to get you a weapon." He produced an old broom from which he had cut off most of the straw. He showed Dwight how to hold it and swing it. "Now, I want you to go out there and show Old Gander who's boss of the barnyard."

Dwight took a deep breath and, broom in hand, walked cautiously toward the barn. Old Gander ruffled his feathers and waited. When Dwight was halfway to the barn, the goose charged.

"I'm the boss of the barnyard!" the pint-sized boy yelled, making his own charge with the broom high above his head. "Get out of my way, Old Gander!"

The bird turned to flee, but he received a thump on his back from Dwight's weapon.

"And that," General Dwight D. Eisenhower later said, "taught me never to negotiate with an enemy except from a position of strength."

Although you and I are not faced with Old Gander, we do face Old Dragon, the devil, every day. It's a frightening experience to be a teenager in 1988. The dragon is fiercer now than he has ever been at any time in history. Our only hope of defeating the dragon is to face him unafraid with God's Word, the Sword of the Spirit.

GEORGE S. PATTON, JR.

Wait on the Lord: be of good courage, and he shall strengthen thine heart: wait, I say, on the Lord. Psalm 27:14.

Probably you've had to wait many times in the doctor's office. After a while you get tired of looking at the magazines and wonder why he can't hurry up. You feel bored and wish that you could go play or at least watch TV. How would you like to spend 40 hours waiting for somebody? That's how long George Patton sat in the waiting room of General John J. Pershing.

It all started when a Mexican revolutionary general, named Pancho Villa, crossed over into New Mexico and destroyed the town of Columbus, killing some American soldiers. President Woodrow Wilson asked General Pershing to form a strike force to pursue Villa into Mexico. More than anything else, Patton wanted to be part of that strike force.

"Please, may I see General Pershing," George politely asked the receptionist at military headquarters.

"I'm sorry, but General Pershing is busy!"

"Then I'll wait."

Every time General Pershing opened the door, he saw that same second lieutenant sitting there in the corner. After 40 hours his curiosity got the better of him. "Who are you, and what do you want?"

"Lieutenant Patton, sir. I've been waiting for a chance to talk with you."

"Well, what about?"

"I want to go to Mexico as one of your aides, sir."

"I've already chosen my aides."

"Sir, if you take me, I can promise you'll never regret it. Surely you could use one more aide!"

General Pershing was so impressed that he did take Patton along as a special aide.

Sometimes we need the persistence of George Patton in our prayer life. God doesn't always immediately give us what we want. Sometimes we need to wait patiently on Him.

EDDIE RICKENBACKER

Then they cried unto the Lord in their trouble, and he saved them out of their distresses. Psalm 107:13.

The time was 1942. The United States had just entered World War II. Eddie Rickenbacker was flying with some other men from Hawaii to Australia; he carried a top-secret message for General Douglas MacArthur. On the way, he was to stop at Canton Island. Somehow he missed the island and circled for more than four hours trying to locate it. The plane's fuel ran out, and Rickenbacker was forced to make a crash landing in the ocean. The survivors had only three inflatable life rafts and four oranges.

On the seventh day the oranges were gone and the pain of hunger and thirst was intense. All the men wanted to talk about was food.

"Try not to even think of food," Rickenbacker cautioned. "It will only make you feel worse."

"Nothing could make me feel any worse!" Colonel Hans Adamson complained. His skin scorched by the tropical sun, had become swollen and blistered. The salt water made his flesh sting and crack. His mouth was covered with sores.

"Stop your bellyaching!" Captain Cherry ordered. "You're no worse than the rest of us!"

Although Eddie had warned the men not to drink salt water, Sergeant Alex had done it anyway. Now he lay unconscious in one of the rafts, babbling nonsense.

"It's time for prayers," Captain Cherry called.

"O God, deliver us or we die!" one of the men cried.

"Please send us food and water!" another begged.

The next day a miracle happened. A sea gull came out of nowhere and perched on Eddie's hat. Carefully he raised his arms and caught the bird. It was their first meal in more than a week! They used bits of the bird as bait and caught two fish for supper. That night rain came, and they had fresh water to quench their thirst. Day by day little miracles kept them alive until they were rescued after 24 days.

SAMUEL TAYLOR COLERIDGE

What time I am afraid, I will trust in thee. Psalm 56:3.

Samuel knelt beside his bed and prayed as usual:

> "Matthew, Mark, Luke, and John!
> God bless the bed that I lie on.
> Four angels round me spread,
> Two at my feet, and two at my head."

The small boy crawled under the warm comforter. His mother tucked the cover in so he wouldn't kick it off in the night. She then bent down to give him a kiss. "Good night, darling. Sleep tight!" she said and blew out the candle that lit his tiny room. She closed the door and left him alone in the dark.

Samuel stared at the shadows the moon made as it shone through the tree outside his window. A wind was blowing, and eerie shadows danced on his wall. One shadow resembled a long dragon. He could imagine fire shooting from its open mouth. He looked out the window to see if there was a real dragon coming into his room. He was sure he heard menacing footsteps on the roof. His heart beat faster. What awful monster would enter that window to carry him away?

"Mama!" He opened his mouth to scream, but the sound stuck somewhere in his throat.

Then he thought of the four angels in his prayer. He imagined two standing at the foot of his bed and another two standing near his pillows. He pictured them with shining swords in their hands, killing the army of monsters that came through his window. Suddenly Samuel wasn't scared anymore. He knew that God had sent His angels to watch over him in the night. They were stronger than any dragon he could imagine. He smiled and closed his eyes. Soon he was asleep.

Not long afterward, Samuel came down with a fever and had to stay in bed several days. He longed for company. "Mama," he said. "Why doesn't Lady Northcote come to see me?"

"She's afraid of catching the fever."

"Ah, Mama! The four angels around my bed aren't afraid of catching it!"

PERCY BYSSHE SHELLEY

He that hath mercy on the poor, happy is he. Proverbs 14:21.

One midsummer day Helen and her three sisters were sitting in the breakfast nook of the Shelley mansion when one of them said, "Who was that man who just passed by our window?"

The girls rushed to the window and peered out. They saw a poor farmer dressed in ragged clothing. He had a pitchfork over his shoulder. On the end of the pitchfork was a bundle of hay that must have come from their barn.

"Why, that dirty thief!" Helen exclaimed.

"Can you imagine him just walking in here like that in broad daylight?" another sister asked.

"Well, isn't somebody going to stop him?"

"Butler!" Helen cried, running to the big kitchen. "A thief just walked by the window with a pitchfork of hay. Please go stop him!"

"Very well, Miss Helen," the butler bowed. Hurrying to the front of the house, he called after the intruder. "I say there, who are you? And where are you going with that hay?"

The farmer stopped then and turned around. "Why, Master Bysshe," the butler exclaimed. "It's you!"

"Why are you dressed up in such a costume?" Helen laughed at the sight of her brother's sheepish look. "Where are you going with that hay?"

"I was going into Horsham to take this hay to a poor woman who has chilblains. She was advised to take hay tea, but she had no hay. She's too poor to buy any, so I thought I'd give her a little of ours. I thought it would look rather odd to see a country gentleman dressed in all his finery delivering hay to a poor woman, so I dressed like this, hoping I'd go unnoticed," 14-year-old Bysshe Shelley explained.

"Bysshe, Bysshe," Helen said, shaking her head. "You are too good to people. I do believe you'd give away half the estate if Father would let you. Why do you bother yourself with the poor?"

"I feel sorry for them," Shelley said. "Besides, it makes me happy to help people."

THOMAS PAINE

How shall we escape, if we neglect so great salvation? Hebrews 2:3.

Eight-year-old Tom sat quietly in a high-backed chair in his aunt's kitchen and listened as she read a sermon about God sending Jesus into the world to die for the sins of all mankind. As her voice droned on, Tom frowned and bit his lip to keep from speaking.

"Little boys are to be seen and not heard!" his mother had instructed him. He knew it wouldn't be polite to tell what he thought of the sermon.

"Jesus died on that cross for all the sinners in the world," his aunt said when she was finished. "He died for you, Tom. It's time we took you to church and got you confirmed."

"Can I go now, Auntie?" Tom said, jumping down from the chair.

"Yes, run along. I'll read you another sermon later."

"I don't want to hear any more sermons," Tom mumbled as soon as the kitchen door was shut behind him. "I'm not going to be confirmed, either. I don't believe what she told me about God killing His own Son. I think that's dumb!"

True to his word, Tom Paine refused to become a member of the church. For a while he was popular in the American colonies because of a pamphlet he wrote called *Common Sense*. It gave the reasons why Americans should be free of English rule. However, later in *The Age of Reason* he attacked religion; he told people they were foolish to believe what the ministers were telling them. He pooh-poohed the whole idea of Christianity and salvation.

Three days before his death someone asked Tom, "Do you wish now to believe that Jesus is the Son of God?"

"No," he replied. "I don't wish to believe."

Two pastors were called in to try to persuade him. "This may be your last opportunity to accept Jesus. Soon you will die, and unless you believe, you have no hope of eternity."

"Go away and leave me alone," the old man said, turning toward the wall. He then died an unbeliever, unhappy, alone, and without hope.

WASHINGTON IRVING

Thou, O Lord, art in the midst of us, and we are called by thy name. Jeremiah 14:9.

April 30, 1789, was a day of excitement in New York City. Cannon roared. Bells peeled. Trumpets blew. Drums beat. Fireworks lit the sky. The crowds cheered, "Long live George Washington, president of the United States!" Everyone strained to catch a glimpse of the one who had helped them get freedom.

Among that crowd was 5-year-old Washington Irving, who had been named for the commander-in-chief of the Revolutionary Army. As Washington rode along the street in a parade, the boy's nurse held him up in her arms. "Look, laddie," she said. "There goes General Washington, the man ye was named for!"

The boy saw the president sitting tall on a spirited horse. He looked distinguished in his brown homespun suit, his glittering sword at his side.

However, that brief look was not enough to satisfy young Irving's nurse. The day after the parade she was walking with the boy when she saw the president go inside a shop. Grabbing her little charge by the hand, she dashed across the street and into the store.

Confronting the president, she exclaimed in her Scottish brogue, "Please, your excellency, here's a bairn that's called after ye!"

"Well, now, is that so?" Washington responded. He looked down at the lad and smiled. "I'm glad to meet you, Washington. I hope you'll grow up to be a good boy. May God bless you," he said, laying one of his strong hands on the boy's head.

From that moment on George Washington was the hero of Washington Irving. Later in life, after he had become a writer, he wrote the *Life of George Washington.* He also wrote the biographies of Christopher Columbus, John Jacob Astor, Oliver Goldsmith, and Captain Bonneville. For some time he served his country as a diplomat in England and Spain. All his life he tried to live up to the proud name he had been given.

Because you love Jesus you are called a Christian. Are you trying your best to live up to the name you have been given?

ROBERT LOUIS STEVENSON

And the Lord God formed man of the dust of the ground, and breathed into his nostrils the breath of life; and man became a living soul. Genesis 2:7.

"Cummy," small Louis wheedled one afternoon, pulling at the skirts of his nurse. "I want to play outside."

"No, Louis," Miss Cunningham replied. "You've been really sick with that awful cold and cough. You're not well enough to go outside yet. Would you like nurse to read to you?"

"OK," Louis sighed. He sat on his bed with a quilt wrapped around him while she read exciting Bible stories.

"I've got some work to do now," Miss Cunningham said after a while. "Why don't you draw me a picture."

Obediently Louis got out his paper, pencils, and water colors. Lying on the rug in front of the fireplace, he was soon busy at work. Before he was finished, his mother came into his room to see how he was doing.

"Look, Mama!" he said, holding up his picture. "I have drawed a man. Shall I draw his soul now?"

"I like it just the way it is," Mama smiled. "Besides, you can't see a soul."

Was Mrs. Stevenson correct? Is the soul something you have but can't see? What shape is it? What does it look like? Is the soul an invisible part of you, something like a ghost, that floats off to heaven when you die? Many people think so.

However, a soul is not something you possess; it is what you are. Adam was created out of two ingredients: the dust of the ground and the breath of life. When God put those two things together, our verse says, he became a living soul. When we die, those two things separate. The dust goes back to the ground and the breath goes to God. Then there isn't a soul anymore until the resurrection.

Imagine making a wooden box. First you have a pile of boards and nails. You hammer the nails into the wood and build a box. That's like being born. Now tear the box apart. You again have just boards and nails. What happened to the box? It just doesn't exist anymore, not until someone puts it back together again. That's like death and the resurrection.

HANS CHRISTIAN ANDERSEN

For without me ye can do nothing. John 15:5.

It was a bright blue summer morning in Odense, Denmark. Eleven-year-old Hans Christian ran along the canal, feeling as free as the sea gulls that called above him. He was so happy, he wanted to sing.

Just then he passed an empty rowboat. "I wonder what it's like to stand and sing in a boat on the water?" he mused. "I think I'll find out." So he hopped aboard and began to sing. It was fun. Nobody was around, so he sat down and sang another song. A stork flew by, and he shouted, "Hi, stork! Listen to my song!" And he sang the stork a song.

Suddenly the boat came untied and started to drift away from shore. Hans lunged for the rope, but it had already splashed into the water. Slowly the boat began to drift downstream with the current. He looked for the oars, but there weren't any. He had no choice but to let the current take him where it would. What he didn't realize was that he was headed straight out of the canal into the river that would take him to the ocean.

"Oh, well, I might as well sing and enjoy my trip," he said to himself. He had a marvelous time until all of a sudden the boat hit a wooden bridge that spanned the canal. The sudden stop knocked Hans off his seat.

He scrambled up to find himself face-to-face with an old woman, who was holding his boat to the bank with the crook of her cane.

"My boy, whatever are you thinking of? In a moment your boat would have been out where no one could reach you!" the old woman scolded. "Come on, get out."

But Hans Christian was scared. He moved to the back of the boat and watched as a girl of about his age came running.

"I'll get it, Grandma," she said. Lying down on the bank, she reached for the rope and secured it around a stump. Hans Christian jumped ashore.

Many young people I know, like Hans Christian, are drifting on life's current, headed for certain destruction. They are powerless to change the direction of their lives. Without Christ they are like boats without oars.

HENRY DAVID THOREAU

Render to Caesar the things that are Caesar's, and to God the things that are God's. Mark 12:17.

Henry David Thoreau loved the outdoors when he was a boy, and he loved it when he became a man. In fact, he loved it so much that he built himself a little cabin by Walden Pond and spent many months there observing nature. He studied birds, plants, insects, and other wildlife. He wrote a book about his adventure called *Walden.*

One afternoon while Thoreau was still living at Walden Pond, he walked into town to get his shoe fixed at the cobbler shop. Outside the shop he met his neighbor Sam Staples, the friendly Concord jailkeeper.

"Hi there, Sam!" Thoreau greeted his friend, a big grin on his face. He saw people so seldom that it was fun to come to town.

Sam didn't smile. He cleared his throat and said, "Henry, I hate to do this, but I've got to arrest you."

"But whatever for?"

"It seems you haven't paid your poll tax. Now, I know you aren't making much money out there at Walden Pond. I'd be pleased to loan you a dollar so you can pay it."

"Thanks, Sam, but I've got the dollar to pay the tax. The problem is, I have no intention of giving a single penny to the government to be used in fighting the Mexican War. They're our neighbors, and we have done wrong in declaring war against them. I will have no part of such an aggressive act, even if it means that I must go to jail."

"I sure hate to do this, Henry," Sam said as he led the way to the county jail. Thoreau spent one night behind bars. The next morning one of his aunts paid his tax, and he was released.

If you had been in Thoreau's shoes, would you have paid the tax? Do you think you are responsible for the laws made by the men your tax dollars support?

Peter once faced a similar dilemma. His taxes were due, but he had no money. He wondered if he ought to give money to the cruel Romans, who were ruling his country unjustly. Jesus worked a miracle so he could pay his taxes.

HARRIET BEECHER STOWE

For the living know that they shall die: but the dead know not any thing. Ecclesiastes 9:5.

Five-year-old Hattie felt as if her heart would break. She had cried until her eyes were red and swollen, but still the awful lump would not leave her throat. She listened to the solemn tones of the minister talking about immortality and the resurrection, big words she couldn't understand.

Sobbing quietly, she followed the casket on the long walk to the burial ground. She hardly noticed the mourners around her, all dressed in black and crying, too.

She took the hand of her 3-year-old brother. Together they stood at the edge of the deep hole and watched the men lower the casket into the cold ground. Why were they putting her there? What did it mean to be dead? Where had Mama gone? Why would she never return?

"Mama has gone to heaven to be with Jesus," Daddy said, holding her close. "She's now walking the golden streets of the New Jerusalem, singing praises with the angels."

"That's strange," Hattie puzzled. "I always thought that heaven was up in the sky. Why did they put her in the ground?"

When they got back to the house, the mourners all sat around talking about the funeral and how dear Mrs. Beecher had gone to heaven. Three-year-old Henry listened for a while, then ran outside to the barn. He drug out an old shovel and started digging a hole in the garden.

"What are you doing, child?" his big sister Catherine cried. "You're getting your mourning suit all dirty! Daddy's not going to like it!"

"I'm going to heaven to find Mama," the small boy said.

Henry didn't know that even if he could have reached heaven he wouldn't have found his mother there. She was still in the casket, buried under six feet of earth. There she will sleep until Jesus comes. Until that moment when she hears His voice calling her forth, she will know nothing. Not until the resurrection day will she know that her daughter Harriet became famous for writing a book about slavery called *Uncle Tom's Cabin.*

JOSEPH PULITZER

Ye see then how that by works a man is justified, and not by faith only. James 2:24.

During the American Civil War Northerners often hired a substitute to take their place in battle. One of those hired was Joseph Pulitzer, from Hungary. When the war was over, he tried to find work in New York, but the job market was flooded with ex-soldiers. Someone suggested he go to St. Louis, and he started out walking there with only a few coins in his pocket.

Joseph arrived in East St. Louis in the middle of a snowstorm. Hungry, exhausted, and penniless, he approached the ferry entrance.

"Come on, kid, beat it!" the guard said. "You ain't getting on without a ticket!"

Joseph moved a little to one side and leaned against the fence. He had no place to go. His mind felt as numb as his body. He had to do something, but he couldn't think what. Then he heard the boatmen shouting to each other in German.

At the sound of this familiar language he gained sudden vitality and courage. He pressed close to the gate and screamed, "Hey! Please! Is there a job for me? Do you need any help on the boat? I've got to cross and I have no money."

"What ya want, kid?" One of the crew came over to the fence and peered at Joseph.

"I have no money for the ferry, and I'll freeze standing here. Haven't you got a job for me? I'll do anything."

"We need someone to shovel coal into the furnace that keeps the boiler going. We've got 12 more trips to make."

"I'll do it," Joseph said. "I must get across."

It seems to me that you and I are somewhat like Joseph Pulitzer standing outside the ferry gate. There is no way we can cross the river to heaven on our own. Jesus provides the ferry, but then two more things have to happen if we are to reach the other side. First, we have to be willing to get on the ferry; that's faith. Second, we need a ticket; that's works, the daily living of a godly life. God does expect something in return for the trip across. He asks for our love, our obedience, and our service.

MARK TWAIN

Watch and pray, that ye enter not into temptation. Matthew 26:41.

Mark Twain's real name was Samuel Langhorne Clemens. As a boy he had all sorts of adventures that gave him ideas for the books *Tom Sawyer* and *Huckleberry Finn.*

A measles epidemic hit Hannibal, Missouri, in 1845, the year Sam was 10. One by one his buddies caught the disease, and he was left with nobody to play with.

"Don't you dare leave this house!" his mother warned. "I don't want you catching measles."

But Sam wanted to catch the measles. To him it was unbearable that his buddies should experience something he hadn't. So he sneaked off to Will Bowen's house.

"You get right back home, Sam," Mrs. Bowen ordered.

Instead of going home, he sneaked in the back door and went upstairs to Will's room. After only 10 minutes Mrs. Bowen found him and sent him home.

"Guess I'll have to go at night," Sam decided. He waited until everyone was asleep at home, then climbed out a window and ran to the Bowens' house. He climbed up to Will's window and went inside. He climbed into bed with his friend. The two boys spent half the night talking and overslept the next morning. Sam was caught and marched home to his mother. Much to his satisfaction, the next day he was covered from head to toe with red spots.

"I ought to tan your hide!" his mother said. "But I reckon the fever will be punishment enough."

It was! For a week he burned with fever and his bones ached. For several days his family thought he was going to die.

Now, wasn't that a silly thing for Sam to do? He went running right into temptation, daring the measles to catch him. I can think of two people in the Bible who were warned to stay away from temptation but were just like Sam. They walked right into it and tempted the devil to catch them. Who were they? One was a woman, the other a man.

HORACE GREELEY

Ye are the salt of the earth. Matthew 5:13.

"You might as well know the truth, Horace," Mrs. Greeley told her 9-year-old son. "Your father has gone, and he won't be coming back."

"But why, Mama?"

"He had to," she replied. "They were going to arrest him because he can't pay his bills."

"Where's he gone?"

"Out West somewhere. As soon as he finds work, he'll send for us." Her tears were flowing freely now. "We've lost everything. They're coming tomorrow to take it away—the house, the barn, the livestock, the furniture."

"It's not fair!" Horace cried.

"I know, dear, but that's the way it is."

That night while his mother slept Horace took all of her dresses out of the closet and hid them in the woods. With them he put the seven precious books he owned. He was not going to let the government take everything!

The next morning he stood beside his mother and watched the sheriff and his men carry out their furniture. His mother stood quietly until they carted off her precious loom and spinning wheel. Then she broke down and cried.

Horace flung himself at the wheel and tried to get it away from the men. "Stop robbing my mother! It's not right!"

"Right or not, it's the law," the sheriff said, pulling him loose. "You can't fight the law, Horace."

When Horace grew up, he found a way to fight unjust laws. As the editor of the New York *Tribune,* he spoke out against what he felt was wrong, thus helping to make new laws.

Through his newspaper he became "salt" to his country. Just as a little salt spreads throughout the whole pot of stew, making everything taste better, so Horace's ideas spread throughout the nation, making it a better place to live.

Perhaps things are not the way you'd like them in your school or community? Why not be the salt that makes things better?

CHARLOTTE BRONTE

Be sure your sin will find you out. Numbers 32:23.

"Honk! Honk!" The geese's plaintive calls sounded above the howl of the wind and the crackle of the fire.

Charlotte listened to their cries as she took a steaming roast from the oven. She felt sorry for the two pet geese that shivered on the back doorstep.

"Adelaid and Victoria have come to call," Charlotte said.

"Eh, the poor beasts! I'll let 'em in for a spell by the warm fire." Tabby, the servant, started for the door.

She opened the door just wide enough for the geese to enter. They waddled over to the big black stove.

"I wish we didn't have to send them back to that open shed. The weather is frightful!" Charlotte said.

"They'd make a mess o' my kitchen floor," Tabby replied, frowning.

"What about the turf room?" Charlotte suggested. "The floor's such a disaster in there already."

The turf room was a little room to the left of the front door where turf was stored. Cut from the moors in autumn, the turf was used as fuel in the winter.

"Eh, that'll be fine," Tabby agreed, "but we must keep it a secret from your father."

That wasn't too hard. He never entered the turf room, and they were always careful to make sure his door was shut when they marched the geese down the hallway past his study.

Then one night as Charlotte escorted the geese down the hall, she heard her father's footsteps and the click of the study door opening. It was too late to turn back. Deep in thought, Mr. Bronte walked straight into the birds. "What have we here?" he asked.

"I'm sorry, Papa," Charlotte hastened to explain. "I was just taking the geese to the turf room."

"So I see," her father said, a twinkle in his eye. "How long has this been going on?"

If you've ever tried to hide something naughty you've done, you know exactly how Charlotte felt at that moment.

LOUISA MAY ALCOTT

Let him that stole steal no more. Ephesians 4:28.

"Let's play house," 8-year-old Louisa suggested to her new playmates. "I'll be the mama and you'll be my children."

She scurried around the barn and found some old jar lids to use for dishes. She filled these with hay and called, "Come and get it!"

The ragged, dirty children sat down before their "plates" of straw. Then one girl said, "I wish it were real food. I'm hungry. We didn't have much for breakfast."

"Oh, you poor things!" tenderhearted Louisa exclaimed. "I'll go right now and bring you something to eat."

Scrambling down the ladder of the hayloft, she ran into her aunt's kitchen. She went into the pantry, as she would at home, and helped herself to figs and cakes.

"These sure are good, Louisa," one of the boys said, licking his lips. "We never have stuff like this at home."

"I'll go get some more," Louisa replied. She skipped through the kitchen door and into the pantry. But when she came out with another plate of cakes, she was met by Aunt Fanny. The woman stood there with both hands on her hips, looking anything but pleased.

"And just where do you think you're going with those cakes, young lady?"

"To feed my friends in the barn," Louisa answered.

"You little thief!" her aunt scolded. "I can't believe this of Bronson's child. Go up to your room at once!"

The disgraced girl ran to her room and sat on a trunk crying. After a moment the door opened and a teenager in the family, Christopher, came in and sat beside her.

"Why is Aunt Fanny angry?" Louisa leaned against his shoulder and sobbed. "We always feed the poor at home."

"I know you meant to be kind, but, see, this isn't your home. It belongs to Aunt Fanny. It's not right to take things out of her pantry without asking her. That's stealing."

"I'm sorry," Louisa said. "I won't do it anymore."

When she grew up, Louisa used such experiences from her childhood to write the books *Little Women* and *Little Men.*

265

EMILY DICKINSON

As I live, saith the Lord God, I have no pleasure in the death of the wicked; but that the wicked turn from his way and live. Ezekiel 33:11.

Satan has discovered a clever way to make God look bad. It is the doctrine of an everlasting hell. One of those who believed this was Pastor Colton, who preached in the yellow brick church in Amherst, Massachusetts, where Emily Dickinson attended with her family.

One Sunday in 1845 when Emily was 15, Pastor Colton preached on the topic, "I love them that love Me."

"If you have been converted, God loves you. Oh, how He loves you, even as a father loves his child." Emily sat with rapt attention as he preached, drinking in every word.

"Now let's look at the sinner. Anger blazes from God's eyes as He condemns the transgressor to burn forever in the lake of fire. Oh, sinner, repent, or we will be hearing your cries of agony throughout eternity." Emily stiffened in her seat and lowered her head to hide a frown.

When she and her brother Austin were alone in the garden after dinner, Austin said, "I don't think you liked the sermon this morning. Am I correct?"

"How did you know?"

"You stiffened up like a ramrod when he began his hellfire-and-brimstone bit."

"I do wish Mr. Colton wouldn't talk about hell and everlasting punishment," Emily sighed. "I don't believe in a God like that. God wouldn't be that cruel. We are all His children, and I believe He loves us all, even when we're bad."

"I'm with you, sis," Austin said. "I'm not much interested in a God who tortures people."

I agree with Austin and Emily Dickinson. God is not cruel. He loves us all and wants us to be saved. He is sad when we choose death.

Yes, according to the Bible, sinners will be burned up, but it will not be an everlasting burning. They will burn up as trash is burned, leaving only the ashes. Read Malachi 4:1-3.

ADAM CLARKE

For a just man falleth seven times, and riseth up again.
Proverbs 24:16.

"One times 9 is 9. Two times 9 is 18. Three times 9 is 27 . . . "
The man walking along the road beside the country school-house smiled as he heard the chant of the multiplication tables. He turned his footsteps in at the gate.

"Seven times 9 is 63. Eight times 9 is 72. Nine times 9 is . . . "

"Excuse me," the stranger said. "Hearing the boys recite reminded me of my own struggle to learn the times tables. Would you mind if I sat in on the lessons for a spell?"

"Of course not," the teacher responded. He motioned toward a bench in the back of the room. "Make yourself at home."

Not much had changed since the visitor was a boy—the dusty blackboard, the water pot, the rows of desks, and a lad standing in the dunce's corner.

"What's wrong with the boy in the corner?" the visitor asked the teacher.

"Oh, that's Adam Clarke, the dumbest boy in school. He either cannot or will not learn his lessons."

Before leaving, the visitor went over and put his hand on Adam's shoulder. Looking into his eyes, the man read the hurt and shame the boy was feeling. "It cannot be true that you are no good at your lessons. Try again and try hard. Keep on trying, and I know you will succeed." With a squeeze of the boy's shoulder he was gone.

"That was the kindest thing anyone ever said to me," Adam revealed after he had become Dr. Adam Clarke, author of *Clarke's Commentary*. "Learning did not come to me easily. I was fonder of play than lessons, but every day I recalled the encouraging words of that visitor. I stuck to my task and succeeded."

What is difficult for you? It might be the times tables, memory verses, or metric measurement. It could be meeting strangers, speaking in public, or overcoming a bad habit. Whatever it is, keep trying and you will succeed.

TEMBER 16

WILLIAM COWPER

Jesus answered and said unto him, What I do thou knowest not now; but thou shalt know hereafter. John 13:7.

> "God moves in a mysterious way
> His wonders to perform;
> He plants His footsteps in the sea,
> And rides upon the storm."

God came to London one dark night in 1772, riding on the fog. It was one of those thick pea soup fogs that settle down sometimes in that city. Even with a light you could see but a few feet ahead.

The dark night matched the mood of the desperate man who paced the floor of a dismal apartment in the East End. Black circles under his eyes told of sleepless nights and fear-gripped days. Throwing himself onto a chair, he gazed at the dying embers of his fire.

I'm like those darkening coals, he thought. *Finished. Done. A failure. I would rather die than face the terrors of another night. The only way I can think to end my misery is to jump into the river.*

As though seized by a sudden madness, the man grabbed his coat and walked out into the night, locking the door behind him. He groped his way to the iron horse's head and the ring of the hitching post in front of his house. From there he followed the curbstone to the street corner, where a horse-drawn cab always waited.

"To the Thames, sir!" he said curtly.

They twisted and turned through the dark, foggy streets. After an hour and a half the driver admitted to being lost.

"Never mind," the passenger said, paying the fare. "I'll walk the rest of the way."

As he alighted he saw a familiar object. It was the iron horse's head in front of his own home. Certain then that God had been guiding in that fog, he climbed the stairs to his flat, where he knelt to ask forgiveness for what he had wanted to do. Out of that experience came the words of No. 107 in *The Seventh-day Adventist Hymnal,* with which we began our story.

In a time of my own dark despair I sang this song and found new hope and courage to go on.

ARTHUR GORDON

And this is the victory that overcometh the world, even our faith. 1 John 5:4.

A massive door swung open, revealing a spacious office with dark panelled walls and a huge polished desk. Behind it sat Thomas J. Watson, president of International Business Machines and one of the mightiest businessmen in America.

At the door stood Arthur Gordon, a young would-be writer who had experienced nothing but failure.

Mr. Watson rose and said, "Well, young man, it's nice of you to drop in. Sit down and tell me what I can do for you."

Arthur moved across the deep, rich carpet as though he were in a trance. He sat down in the leather chair the great man offered. "I've got an idea for a Spanish magazine that would include translations of the best articles from magazines published in this country. Since you're an authority on Latin America, I thought you might give me some pointers about how to get started."

"Not a bad idea at all," Mr. Watson said. He called in his secretary and told her, "These are the names of people I wish this young man to see. These are the things I want you to do for him."

"Now, young man," Mr. Watson continued when the secretary was gone. "I like your spunk. How would you like to work for IBM?"

"Thank you, sir," Arthur replied. "However, what I really want to do is write—but I seem to fail every time I try."

"Would you like me to give you a formula for success?" Watson asked. Arthur nodded, and Watson continued. "It's quite simple, really. Double your rate of failure!"

Arthur Gordon's mouth dropped open. "How can more rejection slips help me?"

"You're taking failure to be the enemy of success. It isn't. Rather, it is the best teacher. Every time you fail, sit down and figure out why. There must be a reason. Then don't repeat your mistake. That's how you learn."

Arthur Gordon followed Mr. Watson's advice. He doubled his failures and found success. He had learned how faith can turn defeat into victory.

ROBERT FROST

If two of you shall agree on earth as touching any thing that they shall ask, it shall be done for them. Matthew 18:19.

Robert Frost burst out of the house and slammed the door behind him. He sped down the board sidewalk toward the corner store. In his right hand he held a quarter.

"Go get me a pack of cigarettes," his dad had ordered. "And make it snappy!"

Robert pumped his arms as he'd seen athletes do, trying to make himself go faster. He wanted no excuse for his dad to be angry, because bad things happened when his dad was mad. Suddenly the quarter slipped from his sweaty hand and fell into a crack between the boards.

"Oh, no!" Robert cried. "I've got to find that quarter." Passersby helped him search, but it was no use. By this time he was frantic. Running ahead to the store, he begged, "Please give me a pack of cigarettes for my dad. He gave me a quarter, but I lost it."

"Tough luck, kid," the clerk said. "Nothin's free in this store." Robert could hear the men laughing as he left the store.

When he got home, he went first to his mother and told her what had happened. "I'm so scared to tell him, Ma," he said. "He'll beat me, I know. Will you go and tell him what happened?"

"No," Mrs. Frost said. "You must be man enough to face your father and tell the truth. But before you go, let's you and I kneel down and talk to Jesus about it. We'll ask Him to impress your dad to let you go unpunished."

Together they knelt then, mother and son, and agreed before Robert's heavenly Father what they wanted Him to do for his earthly father. After prayer Mrs. Frost gave Robert a little push. "Go on, Robert. Everything will be OK.".

His knees felt like water as he approached the desk where his father sat writing. He didn't bother to look up as Robert told his story of the lost quarter.

"Never mind," his dad said and continued his writing. Robert could hardly believe it!

NELLIE BLY

But made himself of no reputation, and took upon him the form of a servant, and was made in the likeness of men. Philippians 2:7.

What was it like to work in a factory 100 years ago? You can read about the inhumane conditions, but you will never really understand what it meant to come out of a dark room where you had to bend within inches of your task to see. You cannot know the torture to your eyes, back, and spirits, for you have not experienced what factory workers in those days went through.

Nellie Bly, the first woman reporter, understood, because she took a job in such a factory so she could write about it in the Pittsburgh *Dispatch.*

What were insane asylums like 100 years ago? You can never really understand because you have never been in one. You have never experienced the waiting in icy halls for rotten food you could barely swallow. You can never know the pain, humiliation, and fear of the inmates, for you were never there.

Nellie Bly pretended to be insane so she could get committed to Blackwell's Island, the worst asylum in New York City. What she wrote for the New York *World* brought about tremendous reforms in the treatment of the mentally ill. People believed what she wrote because she had experienced it.

What is it like to be unemployed and have to go to an agency to seek work? Nellie Bly got in line and applied for a job so she could find out.

What is it like to live in a rat-infested apartment in the slums, with no toilets or running water? Nellie Bly rented one and lived there for two weeks so she could write about it for her newspaper.

What is it like to be hungry, cold, and in pain? What is it like to be tempted? What is it like to see your loved ones sick with an incurable disease? What is it like to be alone in the world, with no one who cares? What is it like to struggle against prejudice in an unjust society? What is it like to die?

Jesus knows. He understands. He came into this world and lived as one of us so He could find out what it means to live in a world of sin.

271

HELEN KELLER

If ye keep my commandments, ye shall abide in my love.
John 15:10.

Obedience and love are two essential lessons of life that all of us must learn. However, 6-year-old Helen Keller had never learned them because she was blind and deaf as a result of a fever. Not knowing how to communicate with their little daughter, the Kellers had let her do whatever she wanted.

When Miss Anne Sullivan arrived to be her teacher, she found a girl that was more of an animal than a child. At mealtimes she ran around the room snatching food from people's plates. She shoved, kicked, and bit anyone that tried to prevent her from having her own way.

One morning when Helen stuck her hand in Miss Sullivan's porridge bowl, her teacher smacked her hand and put it back in her lap. Helen persisted in trying to eat her teacher's porridge instead of her own. Each time she got a slap.

"I can't stand to see you treat poor little Helen that way," Mrs. Keller cried.

"She doesn't understand that she's doing anything wrong," Mr. Keller said. "We have always let her do this. Please understand and be kind to her."

"I am being kind." Miss Sullivan held her ground. "Helen must learn to obey me before I can teach her anything else."

The Kellers were so upset they left the dining room, leaving Helen screaming and kicking on the floor. Miss Sullivan promptly locked the door and sat down to eat her cold porridge. Soon Helen was at her side, trying again to snatch some porridge. Again Miss Sullivan slapped her hand.

Helen ran to her mother's chair for sympathy but found it empty. She went to the door and found it locked. At last she sat down and began to eat her porridge. Miss Sullivan put a spoon in her hand that she threw to the floor. Her teacher persisted until Helen ate her porridge with a spoon.

About this episode Miss Sullivan wrote: "I suppose I shall have many such battles before she learns the only two essential things I can teach her, obedience and love."

JULES VERNE

Nor height, nor depth, nor any other creature, shall be able to separate us from the love of God. Romans 8:39.

God loves you so much that should you decide to run from Him, He will run after you. He will search for you as a shepherd looks for his lost sheep. He will seek you as a heartbroken father looks for his runaway boy. He will follow your trail until He finds you. He will do for you what Pierre Verne, of Chantenay, France, did for his son Jules.

The 11-year-old left home one day at the first streak of dawn. With his bundle of belongings he slipped out of the house. He hadn't gone far down the road before a neighbor woman called, "Jules, where are you going at this hour?"

"Sh!" he said, putting a finger to his lips.

"Why? What's up?"

"Never mind," he called over his shoulder and ran before she asked any more questions.

He was soon at a cafe near the docks, where he gave all his savings to a boy of about his age.

"Go with those men," the boy said, pointing to some seamen having breakfast at a nearby table.

Jules walked over to the table and announced, "I am the new cabin boy."

They nodded. "Follow us," they said.

Soon the ship set sail for the West Indies. However, Jules had no time to enjoy the trip, for he had work to do. He must wash dishes and carry meals to the captain and the crew. They kept him running up and down the steps from one deck to the other. Before their first stop Jules was wishing he had never left the comfort of his nice home.

When the ship docked at Paimboeuf, he was given some free time to go on deck. He found everyone excited about a steamboat coming down the river. He watched as the ship turned her bow into the docks beside his ship. As it came closer, he could hardly believe his eyes. There was his father at the rail. He waved and his dad waved back. He found himself actually happy his dad had found him. Life as a cabin boy was not as much fun as he'd expected.

CARL SANDBURG

The wages of sin is death; but the gift of God is eternal life through Jesus Christ our Lord. Romans 6:23.

"Hey, you guys! Be quiet!" a voice boomed out of the darkness. "I'm tryin' to sleep."

"It's a free country!" one of the roughest boys yelled. "We can make noise if we want to."

"You boys cut it out or I'll call the police!"

The boys stopped their game and sat down on the grass in the vacant lot.

"Do you reckon he means it?" one asked.

"Who cares?" the tough one sneered.

"I care," Carl Sandburg replied. "I don't want a patrol wagon ride to the police station."

The boys were quiet in their games for several nights, and then one night their shouting could be heard a block away. This time there was no booming voice out of the darkness. Instead, a patrol wagon pulled up to the vacant lot.

Frank Peterson, a big guy weighing 220 pounds, got out and approached the noisy boys, one of whom was Carl Sandburg. He smiled and spoke to them in a friendly manner. "Don't you boys know that people are trying to sleep?"

"Aw, we were just trying to have some fun."

"I know," Peterson said, "but can't you find some way to have your fun without disturbing the whole neighborhood?"

"We'll try," they all agreed.

"Good," said Officer Peterson. "Now that's a promise, and I expect you to keep it. If you don't, I'll have to arrest you 'cause it's against the law to disturb others."

Carl and his friends broke a city law. The consequences might have been a night in jail. However, Officer Peterson forgave the boys and gave them another chance.

You and I are guilty of breaking God's law. The penalty is death, eternal death. But in His great love, Jesus forgives us and lets us have another chance.

FRANCIS DAVID NICHOL

I will save thy children. Isaiah 49:25.

"Francis, Francis, you must be careful!" Mary Nichol cautioned her small son for the umpteenth time. "I can't keep my eye on you every minute. You've got to learn to watch out for yourself."

"Yes, Mama," the energetic boy answered.

"Now, promise me to look both ways before you cross a street. Do you want to get run down by a team of horses?"

"No, Mama," the wide-eyed boy said. "I promise to not run into the street without looking."

But little boys forget, and Francis Nichol was no exception. He dashed out into the street with not a glance to see what was coming.

"Look out!" a bystander screamed as he saw a team of horses galloping down the street, pulling a bouncing wagon.

Little Francis looked up to see the horses headed straight for him. He was too frightened to scream or run.

"Oh, no!" a woman screamed, covering her face. The little boy would surely be killed.

"Whoa! Whoa!" the driver yelled and pulled hard on the reins. When they stopped, the horses were so close that Francis could feel the warmth of their breath.

"You stupid idiot!" the driver bellowed. "What ya tryin' to do? Get yourself killed?"

Francis turned and ran all the way home to his mother.

"Thank You, Lord, for sending Your angels to watch over my boy," she prayed, and Francis determined not to make his angels work so hard again. However, it wasn't long before they had another chance to save him from death.

He was standing on the top rail of a neighbor's fence, feeding grass to their cow, when he lost his balance and went flying through the air, landing on one of the cow's horns. He was rushed to the hospital. The doctor said, "Francis is lucky to be alive. Another inch and he would have been killed."

"Thank You, Lord, for saving my boy," Mrs. Nichol prayed again. Her son grew up to serve the *Adventist Review* for 39 years as associate editor and editor.

NORMAN VINCENT PEALE

I heard the voice of the Lord, saying, Whom shall I send, and who will go for us? Then said I, Here am I; send me. Isaiah 6:8.

Try praying this prayer of Isaiah every day and see what God asks you to do. He will probably lead you to someone who needs help, just as He led Dr. Norman Vincent Peale, the man who wrote *The Power of Positive Thinking.*

While visiting the Morgans, Dr. Peale and his wife saw something that they liked. "Where could we get one like it?" Mrs. Peale asked.

The Morgans gave the name of the store. "When you go there, be sure to ask for Mr. Benton," Mr. Morgan said. "He is very kind and helpful."

Later they went to the store and asked for Mr. Benton.

"He's out right now for lunch," a clerk replied. "May I help you?"

"No, we'll come back later," Dr. Peale answered.

Later that afternoon they returned, only to find Mr. Benton had gone to the warehouse and wouldn't return that day.

"I'd be glad to help you," the clerk offered again.

"No," insisted Dr. Peale. "We'll be happy to come back. I really do want to see Mr. Benton."

"Honestly!" Mrs. Peale exclaimed when they were outside. "What difference does it make who waits on us?"

"I just feel I should, since he's a friend of the Morgans and they asked us to request him," Dr. Peale replied. "It won't hurt us to come back, and I feel I should see him for some reason."

"Well, count me out," Mrs. Peale said crossly. "I've wasted enough time!"

Two days later Dr. Peale returned to the store and found Mr. Benton in. "My name's Peale," he said, extending his hand. "At the Morgans' I saw something you sell. They sent me here."

"I know who you are, Dr. Peale," the young man said. "But the Morgans didn't send you here. God did. I planned to commit suicide a couple of days ago, but for some reason I decided to wait until today. I gave God one more chance to send me help. Here you are."

WILLIAM S. GILBERT

For there is one God, and one mediator between God and men, the man Christ Jesus; who gave himself a ransom for all. 1 Timothy 2:5, 6.

"Excuse me, ma'am." Thus spoke one of two well-dressed gentlemen who approached a nurse pushing a baby carriage in one of the parks of Naples.

"Should I know you?" she returned.

"No. We're friends of Mr. Gilbert. He asked us to find you and bring back Bab. Our car is just this way."

"Thank you for your message," the nurse said. But she was suspicious and so she picked up the baby and held him close. "I'll take him home myself. It's not far. I won't need your help."

"Oh, yes, you do, lady," the other man said, grabbing Bab.

"Help!" she screamed. "Those men have kidnapped my baby!" The men ran around the corner and disappeared. There was nothing to do but go home and break the news to the Gilberts.

"I'm sure they want to collect a ransom," Mr. Gilbert reasoned. "We'll inform the police and wait for their call."

"Oh, my poor darling!" Mrs. Gilbert cried. "If only I had kept you at home this would not have happened."

"There's no use crying over spilt milk." Her husband tried to console her. "Don't worry. We'll get him back."

But of course, Mrs. Gilbert did worry. What if the men hurt Bab? What if they hadn't taken the baby for a ransom but for sale to a childless couple? A thousand horrid prospects kept her awake all that night listening for a phone call.

The next morning there was a call asking for $125 to be left at a certain spot. The arrangements were made and the ransom delivered.

The little boy who was given back to his mother and father that day grew up to become Sir William S. Gilbert, the coauthor of the operetta *H.M.S. Pinafore* and a dozen other musical stage plays.

Why did Mr. Gilbert pay the ransom for his son? There can be no reason except that he loved him dearly. For that same reason, Jesus shed His blood on the cross of Calvary to pay your ransom. You are His child and He loves you dearly.

WINSTON CHURCHILL

Deliver me in thy righteousness, and cause me to escape.
Psalm 71:2.

A freight train rattled across the dry South African veld. Inside was an escaped prisoner of war, squeezed between bales of wool. He was a British journalist, Winston Churchill.

Earlier, the 25-year-old war correspondent had been on assignment from the London *Morning Post* when the troop train on which he was riding was stopped by a boulder on the tracks, placed there by a Boer ambuscade. Ignoring the rifle crossfire between English and Boers, Winston jumped from the train and began directing the removal of the boulder.

Soon the boulder was off the track and the train pulled away, leaving Winston standing there. Unarmed, he had no choice but to go with his Boer captors. He was taken to the Pretoria prison. He began at once to plan his escape. He carefully noted the time sentries exchanged their posts. In that brief second there was hope of jumping over the wall unnoticed.

One dark moonless night Winston waited in the shadows until the moment came when two guards faced each other and exchanged command. He sprinted across an open area and threw himself over a fence. He lay there for a moment listening for the sound of running footsteps. All was silent except for the measured tread of the sentry on duty. He got up and began the 200-mile walk to freedom. After several days he came upon a small settlement, where an Englishman helped smuggle him onto the freight train.

Most people remember Churchill as the fearless prime minister of England during World War II. However, at no time was he a greater man than the night he let a trainload of soldiers go free while he remained to be captured.

It seems to me that's what Jesus did for us. Satan laid an ambush for Planet Earth, but Jesus cleared the track and was captured by the enemy in order that we might go free. They put Him in a tomb with sentries on each side, but He walked out of that prison as the victor over death. Through His power we can escape any trap the devil lays for us today.

DOROTHY CLARKE WILSON

Many waters cannot quench love, neither can the floods drown it. Song of Solomon 8:7.

Nine-year-old Dorothy Clarke scraped frost from the dining room window and looked out onto a world dressed in white. Snow had fallen for several days, transforming the Maine countryside into a winter wonderland. Four feet of snow lay on the ground. Looking down the road, Dorothy saw several men trying to clear it.

She turned away from the window to warm herself by the wood stove. Something caused her to look up. What she saw made her gasp.

"Oh, Dad, look!" she screamed, pointing at the ceiling. Small flames played around the register that let hot air rise into the bedroom above.

Without a word, he ran to the kitchen for a fire extinguisher and put out the flames. Then he raced upstairs and found the furniture charred. The fire must have been smoldering for hours between the floor boards.

"Grab what you can and run to the neighbors!" Mr. Clarke called to his wife and daughter. "We've only a few minutes before the whole house goes."

Dorothy ran to the dining room sideboard and took out a red soap dish that held 45 pennies she'd been saving. Her mother rescued her doll, along with a few clothes. Then they fled to a neighbor's house and watched the destruction of their home.

The road crew cut across the field to help pass buckets of water up to her father on the roof of the outbuildings. When the fire had spent itself, leaving only two blackened chimneys, Mr. Clarke joined his family at the neighbor's.

He put his arms around his dear ones and held them close. "Let's pray," he said. "We must thank the Lord that we still have each other. The Lord is good."

The fire had destroyed the possessions of a lifetime, but it could not destroy their most important treasure—their love for each other.

JUPITER HAMMON

And thy word was unto me the joy and rejoicing of mine heart. Jeremiah 15:16.

The Black boy stood beside his master, Henry Lloyd, and looked at the ledger in which his birth was recorded. Carefully he scanned the long list of the names and birthdates of all the slaves on the farm. At last his finger came to his own name.

"I found it, master," Jupiter said.

"Let's hear you read it now," Mr. Lloyd encouraged his young slave. He had opened a school for all his slaves and was glad Jupiter had learned so quickly.

"Jupiter Hammon, born October 17, 1711."

"Excellent! Soon you'll be reading well enough to borrow some of my books."

As the years went by, Jupiter read many of Mr. Lloyd's books. The one he loved most of all was the Bible.

"Do you think I could earn money someway so that I could have my very own Bible?" the teenager asked his master one day.

"The neighbors have been asking for someone to do odd jobs. I don't mind if you go there in your spare time. You may keep the money you earn. Meanwhile, I'll order a Bible for you. Come to me when you have enough money."

Jupiter was 21 before he had saved the required amount. He walked proudly to Mr. Lloyd's study. "I have come to buy the Bible. Here are seven shillings and sixpence."

"Exactly right," his master said, placing the precious book in the youth's hands. "The Bible is yours."

"Mine!" Jupiter whispered, clutching it to his breast. "My very own Bible!"

Before long Jupiter was reading the Bible to the other slaves and preaching to them as well. One Christmas he sat down and wrote a poem about how much God's Word meant to him. Mr. Lloyd was so proud of it that he printed it to distribute to his friends. In 1761 Jupiter Hammon had become the first Black poet to have his work printed.

WILLIAM WELLS BROWN

I have been young, and now am old; yet have I not seen the righteous forsaken, nor his seed begging bread. Psalm 37:25.

William Brown, a fugitive slave, knew what it was to depend on the Lord for his next meal. Eventually he wrote the story of his flight to freedom in a book called *Narrative of William W. Brown: A Fugitive Slave.* He traveled in the United States and Europe to sell his book and speak at antislavery meetings.

Then in 1833 the day came when he was down to his last few coins. He wasn't too worried, because he had a speaking appointment on Tuesday, and this was Saturday. His only expense was to buy his ticket to Worcester, where the meeting was to be held. So he went to the train station to buy his ticket.

"How far is it to Worcester?" William asked. "I want to make sure I have enough money for a ticket."

"A little more than 100 miles," the stationmaster replied.

William walked away, knowing he didn't have enough to pay for it.

"I'll find someone to lend me the money," William decided. "I can pay them back from my book sales at Worcester."

But although he walked the streets all morning on Monday, he could find nobody willing to lend him his fare. It was nearly noon when he met a poor, hungry fugitive slave.

"Come with me," William said. "You and I are going to have us a nice hot bowl of soup." That took the last of his coins.

He walked the streets the rest of the day, searching for a person to loan him some money, but he went home that night without a cent.

"Lord, I don't know what more I can do," he prayed as he walked. "If You want me to go to that meeting, You'll have to send my fare."

He had been home but a few minutes when a man arrived with money for several books he had sold on William's behalf.

"Praise the Lord!" William said, going out to buy himself supper, as well as his ticket to Worcester.

ANNIE R. SMITH

When he, the Spirit of truth, is come, he will guide you into all truth. John 16:13.

The Holy Spirit guided Annie R. Smith in a remarkable way. It all started with her mother's request that she attend a meeting held by Elder Joseph Bates in Somerville, Massachusetts.

"I'll go, just to please my mother," Annie said.

That night she dreamed of arriving late at the meeting and taking a seat at the door. A man whom she had never seen was standing on the platform, pointing to a chart and saying, "Unto two thousand and three hundred days; then shall the sanctuary be cleansed."

On that same night Elder Bates dreamed of preaching in a meeting at which he changed his topic at the last minute. Then just as he began, the door opened and a strange woman entered, whom he took at once to be Sister Smith's daughter, Annie.

The next day Annie started out for the meeting with plenty of time to spare, but she lost her way and arrived late. She opened the door to find every seat filled except for one near the door. She sat down just as Elder Bates began to speak. He was pointing to a chart and saying, "Unto two thousand and three hundred days; then shall the sanctuary be cleansed."

I can't believe it! Annie thought. *It's exactly as I dreamed it would be! He is preaching the truth.*

Amazing! Elder Bates thought as he looked up to see the door open and the girl in his dream take a seat by the door. He had forgotten about his dream when he stood up to preach. He had another topic in mind, then for some reason, switched it to the message about the 2300 days and the sanctuary truth.

After the meeting Elder Bates shook Annie's hand and said, "You must be Sister Smith's daughter. I dreamed of you last night."

"And I dreamed of you and what you preached tonight," Annie exclaimed. "I believe it is the truth!"

Annie R. Smith became an editorial worker for the *Review and Herald.* She also wrote the words for three songs in *The Seventh-day Adventist Hymnal,* Nos. 439, 441, and 447.

HIPPOCRATES

I have set before you life and death, blessing and cursing: therefore choose life. Deuteronomy 30:19.

If you should decide to be a physician, you will need to enroll in a medical school. If you complete the courses, the day will come when you graduate. On that day you will take the Hippocratic Oath. In this oath you promise to always do your best to help people and to keep the secrets they share. These are words that Hippocrates, who lived 450 years before Christ, required of the doctors he taught.

Hippocrates grew up as boys do, playing games and enjoying life. Let's go back now 2,438 years to the time Hippocrates was 10 years old.

"Wait up," Hippocrates called to his friends, Philiseus and Herephon.

"Aristan is rounding up the guys for a game of ostracinda," Philiseus said. "We're meeting on the field behind his house."

The boys chose Aristan and Hippocrates as captains. Hippocrates drew a line on the ground with a stick. "Everybody on my team to the right. Aristan's team to the left," Hippocrates ordered. The boys stood in straight rows about a foot away from the line, facing Hippocrates, who stood in the middle.

In his hand Hippocrates held a piece of broken pot, white on one side and black on the other. "I choose black. Aristan has white. Are you ready?" The boys' muscles were taut as they waited for Hippocrates to throw the clay piece. He tossed it high into the air, shouting, "Night or day."

It landed white faceup. "Run, day, run!" yelled Aristan. The "day" team raced around the field, chased by the "night." Each person tagged was dragged off to prison. When all were caught the game started again.

Life on earth is something like a big ostracinda game. We are all on one side or the other. Either we're on the side of the powers of darkness or we're on the side of the powers of light. Each of us must choose the side on which we wish to play. I can tell you right now that "night" is going to lose. "Day" will win. Which side do you choose?

PHILIPPUS AUREOLUS THEOPHRASTUS BOMBAST VON HOHENHEIM

And I will write upon him my new name. Revelation 3:12.

Philippus Aureolus Theophrastus Bombast Von Hohenheim wanted a new name. Who wouldn't, with a name like that! It so happened that in European universities it was the custom for scholars to call themselves by Latin names. Philippus Aureolus Theophrastus Bombast Von Hohenheim decided he would be called simply Paracelsus. Celsus was a famous doctor who had written a book about medicine, which all medical students of the sixteenth century studied. Para meant beyond. By taking the name Paracelsus he was saying he planned to be a better doctor than Celsus.

Doctor Paracelsus experimented with new medicines and ways of treating the sick. He learned the importance of cleanliness and diet in the healing process.

When Froben, the famous printer in Basel, Switzerland, was about to lose his leg because of a sore that wouldn't heal, he sent to Strassburg to be attended by Dr. Paracelsus.

The servants led the doctor to a room where the velvet drapes had been pulled to shut out the light. The many candles in the room, as well as the body heat of all the people gathered to watch the man die, made the room stuffy.

"I have been bled and purged by the best doctors in Switzerland," the emaciated man whispered. "Now they say they must amputate my leg. To do so means certain death. You are my last hope, Dr. Paracelsus."

"Open the windows," Paracelsus ordered. "Let in the air and sun. Bring me hot water and towels. Prepare solid food. Everybody out and no visitors allowed."

Within three weeks the wound was completely healed. Dr. Paracelsus had lived up to his name.

The moment we accept Jesus we receive the name Christian. My new name is Dorothy May Eaton Watts Christian. What is yours? To receive His name means to receive His character, His love, His mind, and His way of doing things. Are you living up to your new name?

AMBROISE PARÉ

Ointment and perfume rejoice the heart: so doth the sweetness of a man's friend by hearty counsel. Proverbs 27:9.

If you cut your finger, how would you like for Mom to use boiling oil on it instead of a Band-Aid? Boiling oil was the standard treatment for wounds when Ambroise Paré became a doctor about 450 years ago.

In a makeshift army hospital in southern France, Dr. Paré worked all night under the smoking flames of torches, dressing wounds and amputating mangled arms and legs.

"I'm sorry I have to hurt you," the doctor said. "Be brave!"

There was no anesthetic. The soldier gripped the edge of the table as the surgeon sawed off his leg above the knee. Blood flowed freely until the doctor touched the man's blood vessels with a red hot iron. As if that weren't torture enough, the doctor poured a dipper of boiling oil on the raw stump.

All night that soldier screamed in pain along with the other patients in the field hospital. By morning all the patients were worse.

"I must give them another hot oil treatment," Dr. Paré decided. He motioned to his assistant.

"We have only enough for three patients, Doctor."

"Then I must think of something else!" The doctor scratched his head a moment. His eyes brightened as he thought of a possible solution. "Bring me all the eggs you can find," he ordered.

He beat the egg yolks with oil of roses and turpentine and poured the creamy mixture over the wounds of all but the three who received a second hot oil treatment. Only those three men screamed and got worse. The others slept peacefully and got better. For the remainder of his life Dr. Paré continued to experiment with ways to treat people without hurting them.

When someone you know is hurting inside, how do you treat him or her? Are your cruel, thoughtless words like boiling oil poured into an already bleeding heart? Or do you apply the soothing ointment of sweet, kind, caring words? Someone you meet today may need your healing touch. Will you give it?

MARCELLO MALPIGHI

The Lord hath need of him. Luke 19:31.

"A most interesting lecture you gave this morning," Giovanni Borelli, a mathematician, spoke to Marcello Malpighi, a teacher of anatomy at the University of Pisa. "What puzzles me is how the blood gets from the large arteries to the large veins that take the blood back to the heart."

"I'm also puzzled," Marcello replied. "Although I've spent many hours cutting up animals and sometimes even a human corpse, I cannot figure out how the blood flows through the tissues of the body between the two blood vessels. There must be something there we cannot see. If only we had a telescope that could see small things!"

"Ah, ha! But there is such a thing," his friend cried. "The spectacle makers in Holland have produced such an instrument. It's called a microscope. A Dutch sailor had one in Naples when I was a boy. I looked through it and saw the hairs on the leg of a flea."

"I must have one!" Marcello exclaimed. "Please order one for me at once."

It was several months before the precious microscope arrived. The two men could hardly contain themselves while they had the instrument put together. However, the connecting link between the veins and arteries eluded them.

Two years later Marcello used a stronger lens to look at the dried lung of a frog. There he saw tiny tubes branching out like many small fingers from the artery. These spread out, then came together again at the entrance of the vein.

"Each little tube is like a capillaris!" he said, using the Latin word for hair. "I will call them capillaries." We now know that these little blood vessels he discovered are like little pipelines taking oxygen and nutrients from the blood to all the cells of the body. They also collect carbon dioxide from the cells and send it back through the veins to the lungs.

Had you ever thought about being a "capillary" for Jesus? You can be a small channel through which God's love flows to your home and community. God needs you just as much as He needs teachers, preachers, and television ministers.

KARL LANDSTEINER

A man's heart deviseth his way: but the Lord directeth his steps. Proverbs 16:9.

Twelve-year-old Karl Landsteiner planned to be a musician when he finished school.

"You did exceptionally well today," his teacher had told him. "Soon you'll be ready for your first public recital."

As he walked along the tree-lined Vienna street, Karl pictured himself seated at a grand piano playing "The Blue Danube" for Emperor Franz Joseph. He could imagine the darkened theater crowded with applauding people. He swung his portfolio of music back and forth in time to the waltz he had just played.

He made his way through the crowded street, scarcely noticing where he was going. A jolt and a clatter brought him face to face with an elderly gentleman in a frock coat.

"Oh, p-pardon me, s-sir," Karl stammered. "I—I guess I was dreaming." He bent to pick up the old man's cane.

"I was also dreaming," the man's face crinkled into a smile. "Could you direct me to the Ringstrasse?"

"Keep going straight," Karl said. "You can't miss it."

That evening he sat at the table with his mother, reading the newspaper. A drawing of an old man with glasses caught his eye. He read: "Louis Pasteur predicts cholera will be conquered in the chemical laboratory."

"Mama! Look! I saw this man today. He asked me the way to the Ringstrasse." Excited, he read the report of the famous man's speech about microbes and parasites.

The next day Karl brought home an armload of books from the library. He read about Lister, Koch, Jenner, and Pasteur. For the first time the fascinating world of science opened before him. He knew now he must be a doctor. That chance encounter led him to the discovery of O, A, B, and AB blood types.

Like Karl you may have your plans for life, but who knows whom God might send to cross your pathway to turn your thoughts in a new direction. The people we meet in person or read about are often used by God to direct our steps.

FLORENCE NIGHTINGALE

Let us cleanse ourselves from all filthiness of the flesh and spirit. 2 Corinthians 7:1.

The toilets at Scutari Barrack Hospital had been plugged for weeks. Liquid filth floated over the floor and out into the hall. The men, sick with diarrhea, refused to wade through the mess, so large tubs were placed in each ward to be used as toilets. These were left standing unemptied for days at a time until the stench was unbearable.

Injured men lay on straw infested with fleas, lice, and cockroaches. Soldiers slept in the muddy, blood-soaked clothing that they had worn on the battlefield. Rats ran over their feverish bodies, nibbling on the rotting flesh of their wounds.

Florence Nightingale's heart ached for the men. How could human beings be allowed to live in such filth? Immediately she turned her crew of nurses into a cleaning brigade. They swept, scrubbed, and disinfected. They burned the dirty straw and made new mattresses for the men. They put tubs of water on to boil and washed all the bedding and clothing. New blankets, underwear, and shirts were bought.

When the day's chores of cleaning, washing, and cooking were done, the nurses went to bed, but not Florence Nightingale. She walked through the wards, a lamp in her hand, checking on her patients. She talked with them, listened to them, and held their hands when they were dying.

"Before she came there was nothing but cursing all day long," one soldier commented. "Now it's as holy as a church!"

"Am I in the right place?" a soldier who had just come in from the battlefield asked. He had heard about the filth of the hospital and was amazed to find it clean. "I think I must be in heaven!"

That soldier had the right idea. There will be nothing filthy allowed into heaven: no dirty books, no off-color jokes, no R-rated videos, no sewer language, no evil habits, and no unclean food. Do you need to clean out your closets and drawers and throw away some filth? Does your mouth need to be scrubbed by the Holy Spirit? Confess your uncleanness to Jesus and He will wash you white as snow!

WILLIAM HALSTED

In whom we have redemption through his blood, even the forgiveness of sins. Colossians 1:14.

It was past midnight when the train from New York arrived at Albany. Dr. William Halsted hired a horse-drawn cab and rushed to the hospital where his sister Minnie lay hemorraging after the birth of her first baby.

"We can't stop the bleeding," Sam, Minnie's husband, explained. "We know it will be a miracle if she lives. She has lost a tremendous amount of blood already."

Dr. Halsted could see that Minnie was desperately weak. He felt her pulse and found it only a slight flutter. She had only minutes to live unless the blood she had lost could be replaced. But this was 1881 and there was no blood bank.

"I have healthy blood," Dr. Halsted reasoned. "If I could get it into my sister's veins, it might help. However, there is a terrific risk. So little is known about the blood. Will my blood be accepted by her body? If she rejects it, she will die. But then, she's going to die anyway. I must take the risk!"

He stripped off his coat and rolled up his sleeves. "Tie this tourniquet around my upper arm, Sam," the doctor ordered. He pierced a vein in the crook of his arm and drew off a pint of rich, red blood. Carefully, he inserted the needle into his sister's vein and forced his blood inside. He repeated the operation, giving her a second pint of his own blood.

Each second seemed an eternity as Dr. Halsted sat by Minnie's side, his fingers on her pulse.

"It's working, Sam!" he whispered. "Come feel her pulse. The heartbeat is definitely stronger!"

"Look at her face!" Sam exclaimed. "Color is returning. The crisis is passed."

The Great Physician is standing by your side just now, taking your spiritual pulse. You need a transfusion of His blood if you're going to live. He shed that blood for you nearly 2,000 years ago on the cross of Calvary. He's waiting to see if you will accept or reject His offer of life. He will not force entry into your heart. The choice is yours.

ELIZABETH BLACKWELL

And who knoweth whether thou art come to the kingdom for such a time as this? Esther 4:14.

"I have decided to become a doctor," 24-year-old Elizabeth Blackwell announced to her family one day in 1845.

"If anyone can do it, you can," Harry said.

"You'll have a hard time," Sam noted. "There aren't any women doctors that I've heard of. Anyway, if that's what you want to do, we're behind you!"

"You'd make a terrible doctor!" Marian replied. "You're too impatient and unsympathetic."

"I can learn patience and sympathy just as I have to learn anatomy and chemistry," Elizabeth said.

"Think of all the blood. Yuck! I couldn't stand it." Ellen shivered.

"I wish your father were alive to see you show such courage!" Mrs. Blackwell said, smiling with pride.

Elizabeth knew it would take all the courage she had to become the first woman doctor. Prejudice against women in medicine was very strong. No women were studying in medical schools. In fact, it was doubtful that she would be admitted.

"It's a commendable idea," her friend, Harriet Beecher Stowe, agreed, "if you can do it. You have no idea of the hate you will generate if you decide to go on. I'm afraid the pressure will crush you."

To Dr. Abraham Cox she wrote for advice about how to apply for medical school. He gave her the information and a word of caution as well: "The idea is a good one, even valuable, but it won't work. No medical school will admit you. And even if they should, the expense is great. I don't see how you could accomplish your purpose."

Elizabeth sat on her bed and reread the letter from Dr. Cox. Should she proceed with her plan to become a doctor? Suddenly a memory verse she had learned as a child flashed into her mind: "Who knowest whether thou art come to the kingdom for such a time as this?"

"Dear God, I will do it!" Elizabeth vowed. "This is what You want me to do. I know You will see me through."

CLARA BARTON

Fear not, nor be dismayed, be strong and of good courage.
Joshua 10:25.

Clara Barton had none of these qualities on her first day of school. She was fearful, dismayed, weak, and of no courage whatsoever!

She rode to school that windy morning on the back of her big brother, Stephen. Everyone else seemed anxious to get to the little white schoolhouse.

At the door of the school Stephen set her down and took her hand as they entered the vestibule, which served as a cloak room. Clara was glad no one else was in the tiny room.

"I—I can't go in there," she whispered. Her heart hammered wildly in her chest. "I just can't. Take me home."

"What's wrong? Are you afraid?"

"Uh-huh," she said, her chin beginning to quiver.

"Everybody feels queer on their first day of school," Stephen said. "But you'll get used to it. Come on. It's almost time for school to start." He tugged at her hand.

"No, no!" she was crying in earnest now. "I'm scared!"

"Well, then you don't have any choice, do you? You've got to march into that room and sit down."

"But why? I don't want to."

"That's the reason you have to do it." Stephen said. Suddenly he seemed very old and very wise to the 4-year-old. "The thing you are scared of is the thing you must do!" He kissed her cheek then and wiped away her tears. She clung to him a moment and then he stood. "Come on. You've got to do it, Clara."

Somehow she found the courage in that moment to walk across the threshold into the schoolroom. Once she had faced it, school wasn't so bad after all.

Later, when she was a Civil War nurse, helping to start the American Red Cross, she had need to remember her brother's advice many times. "The thing you are scared of is the thing you must do!"

EPHRAIM McDOWELL

Now unto him that is able to do exceeding abundantly above all that we ask or think. Ephesians 3:20.

Dr. Ephraim McDowell traveled by horseback through the Kentucky wilderness of the early 1800s. It was in a backwoods cabin that he performed the first abdominal surgery in 1809, making medical history. Because he was considered the best surgeon west of the Allegheny Mountains, he was called to Nashville by Mr. Overton to operate on his wife, who had a tumor.

"But why have you called me all this way?" Dr. McDowell asked after the examination. "This surgery could have been done by a number of doctors right here in Nashville."

"I consider them all butchers!" Mr. Overton exclaimed. "I want none of them near her. They will bleed her to death."

"But I will need a medical assistant."

"I have asked my friend and neighbor, General Andrew Jackson, to assist you."

It was a difficult operation, but the untrained general did a fine job of following directions. When it was over he remarked, "I'd rather fight a passel of Indians in ambush than help with an operation!"

"What's your fee?" Mr. Overton asked as the doctor was packing to leave.

"Five hundred dollars."

"I'll mail it to you within a week."

Seven days later Dr. McDowell opened a letter from Mr. Overton and found a check for $1,500, three times what he had charged. He sent the check back, saying there was some mistake.

The check came back to him with a note: "There is no mistake. Even this amount cannot repay what you have done in restoring my wife."

Isn't God like that? His blessings always exceed our requests. His goodness and generosity are beyond our comprehension. The pity is that we ask so little! We cannot request anything of God that He cannot do much more than what we ask. We serve a big God, a wealthy God, who is able to do "exceeding abundantly above all that we ask or think."

BETHENIA OWENS-ADAIR

In the day when I cried thou answeredst me, and strengthenedst me with strength in my soul. Psalm 138:3.

"Please, Doctor, say you'll come," the frightened man begged. "My wife was nauseated for a while, then she got terrible stomach pains."

"Of course," Bethenia said, reaching for her black bag of surgical instruments. She rode with the man in his horse-drawn buggy the 10 miles into the wild Oregon country.

"We must operate at once in order to save your wife's life," Dr. Adair spoke crisply.

"No," the pale man said, shaking his head. "I didn't figure on having you operate."

"I've no choice," she said. "Build a good fire and put plenty of water on to boil."

He obeyed, stoking up the fire and hauling in a big wash boiler for the water. She prepared the kitchen table for the operation. She placed her instruments in a dishpan of boiling water and set them on a small table.

"I'm ready," she said. "Bring your wife in here and help her onto the table. You'll have to follow my directions and give the anesthetic."

Dr. Adair paused a moment to allow the anesthetic to take effect. Silently, she prayed, "Lord, I need You as I never have before. You know I've never done an appendectomy. I'm scared, but I believe You'll guide my hands and strengthen me. Please help this woman to live!"

She took a deep breath then, and reached for the knife. Swiftly but steadily she made the incision, found the appendix, and cut it out. Skillfully she sewed up the wound.

That night as she rode back to town, Dr. Adair looked up at the stars, thankful that God had been with her that night, helping her do the right thing. She knew the woman would live.

The next time you have something difficult to do for the first time, try to remember Dr. Bethenia Adair, the first woman doctor in the West. God can give you the skill and strength you need to do it.

JOHN MCLOUGHLIN

He that hath pity upon the poor lendeth unto the Lord; and that which he hath given will he pay him again. Proverbs 19:17.

The experience of Dr. John McLoughlin, chief factor of the Hudson's Bay Company for the whole Northwest, is an example of the truthfulness of this proverb.

He left the prosperous East in 1802 with nothing but the small amount of clothing and essentials that he could carry with him on a voyageur's canoe. When he retired in Oregon City 44 years later, he was the wealthiest man in the Oregon Territory. He built a lovely two-story white house and equipped it with the finest of rugs and furniture.

His house is now a museum. As you look at the crystal and the china you wonder how it was that he could have such a nice home when all his life he had given generously to the poor. When he was the chief factor, living at Fort Vancouver on the Columbia River, he was kind and generous to both Indians and White settlers.

One of the settlers who benefited from his kindness was William Beagle, who arrived at Fort Vancouver in 1843, nearly dead from typhus fever. Dr. McLoughlin kept the Beagles for two months. "I appreciate your kindness in letting us stay here," Mr. Beagle said when he had recovered. "How much do I owe you?"

"Tut, tut, tut! Take care of yourself, sir. That's all I ask," replied the white-haired doctor.

"But you've fed us and cared for us all these weeks!" the man exclaimed. "That's too much!"

"Then do what you can for some other man who is in trouble, and that will repay me," the kindly doctor replied. He sent them away with their canoes stocked with food.

Many who watched Dr. McLoughlin give so much away shook their heads and said, "Whatever will happen to his family?"

They need not have worried. God always returns to us what we give to the needy, but it comes back multiplied so that we have more to give again. When we divide what we have and subtract to give to others, God multiplies and adds and gives it back in our hands.

DOROTHEA LYNDE DIX

Thou shalt love thy neighbour. Matthew 5:43.

Are you supposed to love your neighbor if he's insane or a criminal? Dorothea Dix believed that we should. She spent most of her life trying to get better mental hospitals and prisons for those who would seem to be unlovely, unlovable people.

The worst case she ever saw was that of Mr. Simmons in the poorhouse at Little Compton, a village on Narragansett Bay. It was a bitterly cold, windy day in February when Dorothea followed the matron through a rutted yard, past broken-down barns, to a swampy field of frozen black mud.

She approached a tomblike stone structure. Going down some steps, she came to a door that was locked with a huge iron chain. The matron unlocked the padlock.

"Stand back!" the matron cautioned. "He's insane. Although he's chained, he could still kill you!"

Disregarding the warning, Dorothea entered a room so low that she had to bend her head. At first she couldn't see poor Simmons, but she heard his chain rattle. As her eyes became accustomed to the darkness she saw a bony man with white, mangled hair falling over his shoulders. Dressed in rags, he stood barefoot in the cold mud, a chain attached to his leg. He stared at her through sunken eyes as she reached out her arms and held him close.

She sobbed as she thought of the cruelty he had endured for three years in that dungeon. As she held him, he cried like a baby.

On April 10, 1844, an article she wrote was published in the newspaper. In it she said: "No doubt the people of Rhode Island profess to worship. Do they pray, I wonder, to the same God who looks down on poor Simmons?"

Moved by her pleas for mercy, people in that state rallied to build better homes for the mentally ill.

Now, I'm sure you don't know anyone as unlovely as poor Simmons. But there are people in your life whom it's hard to love because of the way they look or act. God expects you to love them, too. They also are your neighbors.

295

DANIEL HALE WILLIAMS

For I am poor and needy, and my heart is wounded within me. Psalm 109:22.

"Doctor Dan, come quickly! It's an emergency!"

Running to the emergency room of Chicago's Provident Hospital, the doctor found a young Black laborer lying on the operating table. Blood flowed from a one-inch wound on the left side of his chest.

"What happened?" Dr. Williams asked. Already his experienced fingers were exploring the wound.

"He was stabbed in a brawl at a nearby bar," an orderly replied. "We don't know how far it penetrated."

"It's hard to tell whether the heart is damaged," Dr. Williams said at last. "Keep a close check on his vital signs and call me if there's any change."

During the night, there were increased signs of shock. Bleeding persisted, and the patient complained of pain over his heart. Dr. Williams knew there must be injury to the heart and if it could not be repaired, the man would die.

"Prepare for surgery," he ordered. The doctor showed no signs of the turmoil in his mind. No open-heart surgery had ever been recorded. He knew he had to attempt the impossible. He had to try to save that man's life.

Opening the chest cavity, the doctor found the pericardium had been slit but there was little damage to the heart itself. With careful stitches he sewed up the pericardium and closed the wound.

Seven weeks later the man walked out of the hospital, healed. The wonder is that he survived, for this happened in 1893, before penicillin, when anesthesia was untested and there were very few surgical instruments.

Do you need heart surgery? I know a wonderful Heart Surgeon. He knows how to patch up broken and bleeding hearts that feel as if they can never love again. In an instant He can exchange a sin-hardened, cold heart for a pulsating, warm one. He can take away the pain caused by the arrows of unjust criticism. He can stop the flow of bitterness from a wounded heart. My Heart Surgeon can do wonders! Give Him a try!

SIR RONALD ROSS

A double minded man is unstable in all his ways. James 1:8.

Do you know any double-minded people? They really have no mind of their own, but follow whatever ideas are popular. If their friends like to sing gospel songs, then they are right in there singing and clapping their hands. But if their friends want to skip out of church and make fun of the preacher, then they skip out of church too. They take on the color of the group they are with.They are like Ronald Ross's chameleon, always changing to suit their environment.

Ronald Ross, who one day would discover the cause of malaria, was about 12 years old when he got his chameleon. His uncle, Dr. Charles Ross, brought it home to him from one of his sea voyages. The headmaster of Springhill School allowed Ronald to keep the chameleon in the school greenhouse, along with his pet snakes, lizards, and frogs.

"What? Another lizard?" the gardener laughed. "You're turning this greenhouse into a zoo."

"This is no ordinary lizard," Ronald explained. "This is a chameleon. Uncle says it will hide itself by changing color."

"Don't believe a word of it," the gardener grunted.

"Look!" Ronald gasped. "He's doing it now. You know he was brown when I took him out of the box. Now look at him; he's turning green because he's on that leaf."

"Sure enough," the old gardener agreed, nodding his head. "Never saw such a thing in my life!"

"It's grand!" his friends said as one by one they came to the greenhouse to see his magic lizard. Once they saw it turn blue when it was placed on the blue sweater of a boy's arm.

"Look how its eyes move separately," Ronald often pointed out to his friends. "The eye on the right can watch us while the eye on the left watches a fly."

Isn't that just how a "Chameleon Christian" looks at life? With one eye he's watching how his Christian friends behave, while he uses the other to keep an eye on the world. He wants somehow to enjoy both lifestyles, depending on where he is and whom he's with.

297

EMILY DUNNING BARRINGER

"Woe unto you, . . . hypocrites! for ye devour widows' houses, and for a pretence make long prayer. Matthew 23:14.

In Christ's day there were people who made a pretense of being holy, who in reality were sinners. They're around today, too. These are the phonies, the pretenders, the actors. Sometimes they're really pretty good, like Beckie.

Emily Dunning, the first woman ambulance surgeon, was on call at Gouverneur Hospital in New York City. The phone rang. It was a policeman: "We've got a woman dyin' here on the street corner. Send an ambulance at once!"

Dr. Dunning jumped into the ambulance, the driver cracked his whip, and the horses set off at top speed. Emily held on with both hands and prayed all the way there that the woman wouldn't die before she arrived. She needn't have worried.

The policeman was doing his best to keep back the crowd of curious onlookers. The woman was making plenty of noise.

Emily knelt beside her. It was obvious by the way she clutched her stomach that the pain was there. Probing the woman's stomach, Dr. Dunning felt a large, hard mass, like a tumor.

"Do somethin' for me quick, Doctor," the poor woman cried. "I can't stand this pain much longer."

"Bring the stretcher," she ordered the driver.

"Everything's going to be OK," Emily soothed the trembling woman. "I'm taking you to the hospital."

At the hospital Emily gave the woman a sedative, then did a more thorough examination. She was puzzled. Things were not quite right for a proper diagnosis, so she called in the senior surgeon for a second opinion.

"So! You're back with us again, Beckie!" the doctor joked. Turning to Emily, he explained, "Beckie is notorious. She lives on the street, and whenever she gets too hungry or wants a good bed, she fakes an illness or a tumor and gets brought in. I'm not surprised you fell for it. She's really pretty good, isn't she?"

Are you a phonie like Beckie, faking interest in eternal things? You can really get pretty good at the game. However, you'll never fool God. There'll be no phonies in heaven.

ALICE HAMILTON

For God shall bring every work into judgment, with every secret thing, whether it be good, or whether it be evil. Ecclesiastes 12:14.

Dr. Alice Hamilton was a pioneer in the field of industrial medicine. It was her job to inspect factories and mines to find out whether the workers were being poisoned by carbon monoxide, lead, mercury, or other dangerous substances.

On one occasion she was invited to inspect a smelter in Missouri. She began her inspection with a tour of Smelter Hill, where the workers lived in unpainted, dilapidated wooden shacks.

"You're that woman from Washington, aren't you?" one woman asked. "You've come to inspect the smelter."

"Yes, I'm Dr. Hamilton. How did you know?"

" 'Cause they've been cleaning up a storm ever since they heard you was comin'. A doctor came out and checked all the men for lead. Forty of them have to stay home tomorrow."

"That's interesting," Dr. Hamilton replied. "What else have they done?"

"In the room where my husband works, they tore out the whole ceiling because the lead showed," the woman replied.

The next day Dr. Hamilton inspected the smelter in silence.

"Well, what do you think of our smelter?" the owners asked. "Did you find everything in order?"

"I really can't say," Dr. Hamilton began. "What I saw was not the way things really are, but the way you want me to see them. I spent the day in Smelter Hill yesterday and learned about your efforts to cover up your cases of lead poisoning. I'm really puzzled as to how to report this to Washington."

"Guess we can't fool you!" one man said sheepishly. "You may have the doctor's reports. We'll do whatever you say."

A cover-up is an attempt to fool ourselves that things are better than they are. This is dangerous because it prevents us from making needed changes. The Divine Inspector sees things as they really are. His report in the judgment will reveal all.

MOTHER BICKERDYKE

Whereby are given unto us exceeding great and precious promises. 2 Peter 1:4.

Mother Bickerdyke volunteered as a nurse during the American Civil War and worked mainly with the armies of Grant and Sheridan. Generals and medical directors alike soon learned not to interfere with Mother Bickerdyke's care for her wounded soldiers.

On one occasion a new medical director came to her hospital for inspection. Everything was in perfect order, except he noticed six eggs under a sick man's pillow.

"Nurse! Come here," he said. "Remove those eggs to the kitchen. I'll have no hen's nests in the wards."

"Please don't take my eggs," the soldier begged. "Mother Bickerdyke gave them to me."

"I don't care who gave them to you. They've got to go!"

The nurse gathered up the eggs, leaving the sick soldier weeping in his pillow. She found Mother Bickerdyke in the kitchen and told her what the doctor had ordered.

Mother Bickerdyke picked up a whole pail of eggs and marched into the ward, her blue eyes blazing. "Doctor, you listen to me!" she scolded, pointing a finger at him. "What harm is it to humor a sick man with a few eggs? He can't eat and longs for the day he can have a hard-boiled egg. Those eggs under his pillow were his promise of better things to come. They represented his hope."

"Here, John," she said, placing the whole pail under his bed. "I brought you a whole pailful of eggs, and you may keep them there until they hatch, if you want to!"

Mother Bickerdyke strode out of the ward. The doctor thought it wise to say no more about John's eggs.

All of us need a nest of eggs for those times when the going is tough. Each egg in our private nest is a promise of better days to come.

Here are six eggs in my nest of promises: Psalm 34:7; Proverbs 3:5, 6; Isaiah 41:10; Matthew 11:28; Philippians 4:13; and Philippians 4:19. Look them up to see if you like them. If not, make up your own nest of promises.

CHARLES HORACE MAYO

The everlasting God, the Lord, the Creator of the ends of the earth, fainteth not, neither is weary. Isaiah 40:28.

Teenager Charlie Mayo stood in the doorway and watched as his father prepared a patient for surgery. The operating table was the living-room sofa. At the patient's head stood the anesthetist. Next to him stood Charlie's older brother, William, whose job it was to keep the instruments in order and pass them to his father.

"We're ready to begin," Dr. Mayo announced.

The assisting doctor poured chloroform drop by drop onto a pad of gauze that lay over the woman's nose.

"I'm going to make the incision now," Dr. Mayo said. "Whenever you see the patient begin to move, pour on a few more drops of chloroform."

Carefully Dr. Mayo made a long cut across the woman's abdomen. Swiftly he clamped off the blood vessels around a large tumor and began to cut it away. It was more than the assisting doctor could take; he fell to the floor, unconscious.

"Charlie, come take over for him."

Stepping over the prostrate form of the anesthetist, Charlie took his place at the head of the sofa. At the slightest movement, he poured on a few more drops of chloroform.

The anesthetist awoke as Dr. Mayo was closing the incision. "I'm sorry, Dr. Mayo," he apologized.

"You're not the first person to faint at the sight of blood," Dr. Mayo replied.

"But I'm a doctor. I'm ashamed that I didn't do as well as your teenage son." That son grew up to be Dr. Charles Mayo, who operated on hundreds in his clinic in Rochester, Minnesota.

If you had been there, would you have fainted? Blood is only one thing that makes people faint. Some shrink from pain. Others from the fear of a new situation. Some faint from heat and others from hunger. Still others collapse from sudden fright. However, there is no situation bad enough to cause God to faint. Even when you feel weak and wobbly kneed, He doesn't. The whole world isn't going to fall apart just because you feel that way. You can count on the everlasting God.

301

WILLIAM JAMES MAYO

Be not afraid, only believe. Mark 5:36.

Would you be afraid to cut open a dead man? Will Mayo, the older brother of Charlie, wasn't a bit afraid. He'd been doing it since he was so small he had to stand on a chair and hold on to the dead man's hair so he wouldn't fall. Of course, his father, the county coroner, was always there.

One stormy night Will went with his dad to an abandoned hotel where the dead man they were to examine had lived alone as its caretaker. As they walked to the lonely spot where the old hotel stood the kerosene lantern Will carried cast weird shadows on the ghostly trees.

The door creaked as they opened it. Cautiously they walked through the dark, musty hallway to the room where the dead man lay on the floor. Will set the lantern on a chair so it wouldn't make shadows on the corpse.

When his father was finished with the examination, he said, "I've got to call on a patient. I'm going to leave you to close the incision and pack up the pieces of tissue I've removed for study. When you've finished, return home."

Will hurried to complete the task. He didn't like to be alone with a corpse. There was something sinister about the way the empty building sighed and moaned. He felt as though a million evil things lurked in the darkness, ready to grab him. He shivered as he finished wrapping the pieces of tissue. Stuffing them into his jacket pocket, he picked up the lantern to face the threatening darkness.

Somehow he made it through the hallway and out the front door. Overhead, the weather-beaten hotel sign creaked eerily as it swung in the wind. That was all he needed to make him run all the way home.

If you're in a group, share stories about when you have felt like Will did in the old hotel. If you're alone, then simply think about a time you felt that way.

What should you do the next time you're in a scary situation? Our verse today tells us to believe and not be afraid. Make a list of things you believe that would help you not to be scared.

SISTER ELIZABETH KENNY

I will lift up mine eyes unto the hills, from whence cometh my help. My help cometh from the Lord. Psalm 121:1, 2.

Twenty-three-year-old Elizabeth Kenny galloped across the lonesome Australian bush, racing the sun. At last she came to a bark-roofed slab hut beneath the boughs of a towering eucalyptus.

"Thank God, you've come!" Mr. MacNeil said as he helped her down from the saddle.

"What's wrong?"

"It's Amy. She can't move and she's in awful pain."

Entering the low hut, Elizabeth found the 2-year-old lying motionless on a cot. She tried straightening the child's leg, which was drawn up toward her chin. Amy screamed in pain. Baffled, Elizabeth knelt beside the girl's bed and prayed. "God, help me. I don't know what to do."

She thought then of Dr. McDonnell. She rode to the nearest town, where she sent a telegram and waited for the reply. It said: "Infantile paralysis. No known treatment. Do the best you can."

Elizabeth walked from the telegraph office to where Thunderbolt waited. If the doctor didn't know what to do, then how could she, an untrained nurse, know how to help? With one hand on the horse's neck, she looked up to the star-studded sky and repeated a verse she had learned as a child, "I will lift up mine eyes unto the hills, from whence cometh my help."

Back in the hut she reexamined the child. It looked to her as if the muscles were tightened. Heat should relax them. First she tried a dry salt poultice, but still the girl cried. Next she tried a linseed poultice, with no better results.

"Maybe moist heat is what I need," she said, grabbing a woolen blanket and tearing it into strips. These she dipped in hot water. After she wrung out the hot water, she wrapped the painful limbs. Amy's crying stopped. She slept. For several days Elizabeth continued her hot-water treatments. After the muscles relaxed and the pain was gone, she taught Amy how to use her muscles again.

For the first time a person with polio was not left a cripple. Sister Kenny's hot-water treatment was soon used in hospitals around the world.

CHARLES RICHARD DREW

He that trusteth in riches shall fall. Proverbs 11:28.

Eight-year-old Charles Drew crawled carefully along the limb of an oak tree that hung low over an open-air stage. Below him Bert Williams and his troupe of minstrels sang to a large audience.

"You'd better come back!" whispered his friend Eddie from the fork of the tree. "You're going to fall!"

"No, I'm not!" Charles boasted, inching his way along the limb. A shower of bark fell on one of the banjo players, and he paused a moment to brush it off his nose.

Just then the boy's legs slipped, and he grabbed for the limb with both hands. He dangled there for a moment, trying to hook one leg over the limb so he could pull himself back up to safety. His short brown legs kicked frantically, but he couldn't swing them high enough to get over the limb.

His acrobatics caught the attention of the audience. Thinking it was part of the act, they began to laugh. The musicians looked up to see what was happening and stopped playing. Charles lost his grip and plummeted to the stage right in front of Bert Williams.

"Well, now, I've heard tell o' folks that'd do pretty near anything to get into vaudeville, but ain't this goin' a bit too far, sonny boy?"

The crowd roared. Charles picked himself up and began to run, the stage manager right behind him shouting, "Grab that kid!" Charles outran the stage manager and disappeared into the darkness.

When Charles grew up, he discovered the use of blood plasma for transfusions. He learned how to preserve plasma for long periods of time. His blood bank helped save the lives of thousands of soldiers in World War II.

We all get ourselves out on a limb at times. Because of our real or imagined popularity, wealth, intelligence, or superior strength we take chances we shouldn't. We venture farther and farther over Satan's territory, thinking a little bit of fun won't hurt. We think we can stop and pull back whenever we've séen enough. Sooner or later we'll experience our fall, just like Charles Drew.

EDITH CAVELL

Love your enemies. Matthew 5:44.

Edith Cavell was an English nurse who helped hundreds of Allied soldiers escape from Belgium into Holland during World War I. When captured and tried, rather than tell a lie she admitted what she had done. She was sentenced to be shot on October 12, 1915.

On the day before her execution she asked to see Chaplain H.S.T. Gahan, who had recently been freed from a concentration camp. He was allowed to visit her in her prison cell.

"I'm so sorry to hear about your sentence," Pastor Gahan said, groping for words of comfort. "I don't know what I can say to make it easier for you."

"I don't fear death," Edith said quietly. "God has given me these weeks of quiet in prison to prepare me for the end. There is but one thing that concerns me now."

"Yes? Go on."

"In this hour when I stand in view of God and eternity I realize that patriotism is not enough. I must have no hatred or bitterness toward anyone. I must love my enemies. Please pray for me." She rose then and knelt beside her metal cot, and the minister joined her.

Together, on their knees, the two celebrated Communion service. The pastor read some verses and prayed. The next day Chaplain Gahan was allowed to be with her during the execution.

She was tied to a post before an officer and a firing squad of eight soldiers.

"Attention!" the officer commanded.

At that moment one of the soldiers broke rank and laid down his gun. "I cannot in conscience fire upon a woman. I'm sorry, sir."

The other men hesitated.

"Mutinous swine!" the officer snarled. He pulled out his pistol and shot the soldier.

Forgetting she was tied to the post, Edith reached out in mercy and compassion toward the soldier. "Patriotism is not enough," she said. In that moment Pastor Gahan knew she had found love for her enemy.

FERDINAND SAUERBRUCH

For we trust we have a good conscience, in all things willing to live honestly. Hebrews 13:18.

Twenty-year-old Ferdinand Sauerbruch sat in the examination hall in Cologne, Germany, and stared at the blank sheet of paper in front of him. The examiner read a long passage from Greek, which the students were supposed to write down and translate into German. The problem was that Ferdinand didn't know how to write Greek; he had only learned to read it.

Ferdinand had come prepared with the translations of probable questions in his pocket. All he needed to do was to copy the right one. Now his plans were fouled up because the teacher had asked him to take dictation, which he could not do.

Ferdinand cupped his hand to his ear as though he were deaf, and yelled, "What did you say?"

The examiner shouted, "Are you hard of hearing?"

"Yes, very."

"I can't stand here shouting the text," the teacher said. "It would disturb the others. I'll have to make an exception and give you the written text to translate."

As soon as the teacher's back was turned, Ferdinand dug out his notes and found the translation that matched the Greek text he had been given. Quickly he copied it.

When the results were announced, the examiner gave out all the grades except Ferdinand's. When the others were gone, he said, "You've translated the whole passage without mistake. Truly I would have said you were a genius, except for the fact that you translated the next two sentences, which I did not have written down. I do not believe you are deaf. You have copied and deserve to fail. I'm ashamed to see what you have done."

Ferdinand was ashamed, too. He hated telling his mother that he was a cheat and a liar. He decided it was much wiser to live honestly. He later became a famous surgeon.

Why do you think it was important that Ferdinand learned the lesson of honesty? Why is it wrong to cheat? Whom are you hurting when you copy someone else's work?

LINDA RICHARDS

Be ye all of one mind, having compassion one of another, love as brethren, be pitiful, be courteous. 1 Peter 3:8.

"Stop it, I tell you!" a nurse spoke crossly to the mute young man on the hospital bed. "Let go of my arm!"

"What's going on here?" white-haired Linda Richards, the nursing supervisor, asked.

"Jimmy grabs my hand every time I pass his bed," the nurse complained. "He annoys me!"

Miss Richards sat down beside poor Jimmy. She put one arm around his shoulder and stroked his arm with the other. At last she spoke softly, "Do you like your nurse very much?"

Jimmy nodded.

"You've been trying to talk to your nurse, haven't you, Jimmy? You've been trying to tell her that you feel lonesome and need somebody to love you. Right?"

Once more the patient nodded. Tears ran down his cheeks as she continued to talk to him and stroke his arm.

Later in her office Miss Richards explained to the young nurse, "All he wanted was a little tender loving care. We all understand that people who are hurting physically need that kind of attention. You would hurry to help someone in pain from an accident, wouldn't you?"

"Of course, but—but—Jimmy is crazy. That makes it different somehow."

"But it shouldn't," Miss Richards continued. "The mentally ill have feelings, too. They are here because they feel unwanted, unloved. They hurt terribly inside."

"Then Jimmy wasn't trying to harm me?"

"Of course not. He just wanted to know that you cared about him as a human being."

Now, before you condemn that young nurse for her lack of compassion, think about the times you ignore people who act strangely, seem retarded, or are handicapped in some way. What a difference your love and compassion could make!

GEORGE SAVA

For the Son of man is not come to destroy men's lives, but to save them. Luke 9:56.

George was a soldier in the Russian Revolution when he decided to follow the example of Jesus. He was fighting beside his best friend, Serge, when Serge was hit with an enemy bullet. George couldn't stop at that moment, but he went back later to carry his friend out of the line of fire. Then he went in search of a doctor. There was none in sight. At last he found two nurses. They undid Serge's shirt and stared at the blood trickling from his chest.

"Don't just sit there! Do something!" George cried.

"There's nothing we can do," one nurse said. "He needs a surgeon. That bullet must be removed or he'll die."

"Then do it!" George ordered.

"We can't," the other nurse wailed. "We've never done it before. Besides, we have no knife."

"Then I'll do it myself," George said, pulling out his pocketknife. "I won't let my friend die!"

"Don't use that knife!" the first nurse warned. "It's dirty and we have no disinfectant. If he doesn't die when you remove the bullet, he'll die afterward from infection!"

Running to a nearby fire, George thrust the knife into the flame. When it was white hot, he withdrew it and returned to his dying friend. "Now tell me what to do," he commanded.

Carefully he followed their instructions, cutting through the flesh to the bullet and lifting it out. Through the long hours of the night George sat beside his friend as he slept peacefully.

"I can save thousands!" George exulted. "I'll never kill again!" George left the army and went back to school to become a doctor.

Can you imagine Jesus as a soldier mowing down the enemy with a machine gun? Would you carry a gun in time of war, or would you become a medic to help save people's lives? Can you imagine Jesus even playing with a toy gun when He was a child? Should you pretend to kill in a game of cops and robbers if you would not do it in real life?

ALICE FITZGERALD

Jesus saith unto him, I am the way, the truth, and the life: no man cometh unto the Father, but by me. John 14:6.

Alice Fitzgerald sat in the cab of the old army truck, her head stuck out the open window. The driver had his head poked out the other side, trying to see the road in the pitch-black darkness of the French countryside. It was World War I, and they were on their way to the front-line hospital.

"Nurse, we're lost," the soldier admitted at last, stopping the truck. In the stillness they could hear gunfire. "We're near the trenches, and I don't know if that fire is from the enemy or the Allies."

"Well, why don't we go on and find out?"

"Want to get killed?" the driver laughed. "They wouldn't know who we were in the darkness. They'd shoot first and check later."

"Then we must go back and find the road we missed," Alice decided. "There was a farmhouse back a few miles."

In no time they were at the house, banging on the door. It was a long time before an old man opened the door and said something in rapid French. "I don't understand him. Do you?" the driver asked Alice. She nodded.

"We're lost," Alice spoke to the farmer in perfect French. "Tell us how to reach the London Casualty Clearing Station." He gave her the directions she wanted.

On the way to the truck, she told the soldier, "We need to go back another mile and turn left. That road will take us directly to the station. We must have missed it somehow in the darkness."

There are many young people who are just as lost as Alice Fitzgerald and her driver were that dark night of long ago. Unsure of the way to eternal life and happiness, they follow along the broad highway where most people travel. Suddenly they realize that they're headed for trouble! The smart thing to do then is to turn around and find the right road. It is not the way of worldly pleasure. It is not the way of money and fame. It is not even the way of church membership. It is the way of the cross. Are you on the right road?

CONNIE GUION

Whosoever hateth his brother is a murderer. 1 John 3:15.

"M-m-m! Do those muffins ever smell delicious!" Elsie Frank said, smiling at her friend. The two girls got up every morning at 5:00 a.m. to prepare breakfast for the 60 girls who attended the boarding academy.

"The proof of the pudding is in the eating!" Connie joked as she opened the oven and took out a pan of the fluffy, golden-brown muffins. She broke one open and gave half to Elsie.

Connie took a bite and spit it out. "Yuck! That's horrid! What's wrong with it?"

"Tastes salty to me," said Elsie.

"Oh, no!" Connie groaned, running to the sugar crock. She stuck in her finger and licked it. "Salt! Somebody has replaced the sugar with salt. I wonder who?"

"Rhoda Baker, of course. Who else would be so mean?"

"Yeah, it sounds like her."

"First she throws dishwater in your face! Now this!"

"Come on! Let's forget about Rhoda. We've got to make another batch of muffins before breakfast is served in twenty minutes!"

"We can't do it!"

"Of course we can. Now stir up the fire and dump these muffins while I make another batch with sugar."

Twenty minutes later the girls were served fresh, steaming muffins. Rhoda refused to take her share.

"No, thank you," she sneered. "I'd rather eat dirt than your crummy muffins. We need a new cook!"

"Why didn't you slap her mouth good?" Elsie asked. "She deserved it after all she's done to you."

"She can't help the way she is. To tell you the truth, I feel sorry for her. Anyway, I've no time to hate. Why should I make myself miserable just because she is?"

Connie, who later became a remarkable physician, knew that hate was a killer of happiness and friendship. It can even eat away inside a person and make that person physically sick. When you hate, it activates forces that destroy you, and leads you to wish the destruction of others. It makes you a murderer.

BENJAMIN SPOCK

Canst thou make him afraid as a grasshopper? Job 39:20.

Have you ever walked through a field in midsummer and seen the grasshoppers jump up ahead of you? They don't know that you mean them no harm. To them you are a giant, seeking their destruction. In fear they flee from an imaginary disaster.

Eight-year-old Benjamin Spock was like a frightened grasshopper jumping from hideout to hideout to escape make-believe enemies. He refused to go near the Horner house because he was convinced a dinosaur lived at the bottom of the cellar stairs. He gave the thicket at his house a wide berth because he was sure lions waited there to pounce upon him. He even hid from fire engines!

His greatest fear, however, was that he'd be kidnapped by the Italian immigrant women who lived in his town. This was a fear he shared with more than one boy his age.

"There comes one of those Italian women now," his friend Mansfield said, dodging behind a tree. "See those big bags they wear around their waists?"

"Y-Yes!" Already Benny's heart was pounding in his chest. He peeped around the tree and saw the bags the women used to gather dandelion greens. He could picture himself smothering inside of one of the dark bags. "Let's hide!" he said, taking off down the street, Mansfield close behind him. They didn't stop until they were inside Benny's house. Behind the safety of a locked door, they watched the women through the window.

"I wonder what they do with the children they put in those bags?" Benny shivered at the terrible thought.

"What nonsense!" Mrs. Spock said when Benny told her his fears. "They're only going to the fields to gather greens."

Benny remained unconvinced. Just to make sure, he'd keep a good long distance between him and those brown bags. When he grew up, he wrote a book to help parents understand the needs and fears of their children. Ask your parents if they have it.

Do you sometimes feel as jumpy as a grasshopper? It might be helpful to share your fears with someone older to find out if they are real or imaginary.

DAVID HARTMAN

My grace is sufficient for thee: for my strength is made perfect in weakness. 2 Corinthians 12:9.

Paul, author of today's verse, and David Hartman had something in common. They both prayed earnestly for God to heal them, but the answer was, "No. Instead I will give you strength to overcome your handicap."

The retinas of both David's eyes disintegrated, leaving him totally blind by the time he was 9 years old.

"I knew someone who lost his sight and prayed every day to get it back," one of his teachers told him. "One morning he woke up and could see a little. Each day it got better, until he was completely healed. It all happened through prayer."

There was nothing David wanted more than his sight. Every night he read his braille Bible and knelt to plead with God for a miracle. The next morning his world was just as dark, but he kept up his prayer for several years, expecting every morning that he'd be able to see.

One day another teacher mentioned something David would be required to do the next year at the school for the blind. "I won't be here next year," David spoke with confidence.

"Why not?"

"I'm getting my sight back."

"That is not going to happen," his teacher said firmly.

"Oh, yes it is! I know it!"

That night he told his mom about the incident. "She won't believe me, but I will be able to see next year, won't I?"

"No," his mother spoke gently. "You will always be blind. You will never see again."

And it was true. God never did answer David's prayer the way he wanted. Instead He gave him strength to rise above his handicap. He gave him courage to enter medical school. He helped him learn through his fingers, ears, and nose. He gave him a wife who cared. He gave him the ability to live a normal life in spite of his blindness. He helped him become a doctor.

"I realize now that God has given me a greater miracle," David said later. "He has enabled me to succeed in spite of my blindness."

FREDERICUS JOHANNINE PRITHAM

Then they cry unto the Lord in their trouble, and he saveth them out of their distresses. Psalm 107:19.

Fred J. Pritham, a country doctor in backwoods Maine, saw some unusual cases in his time. One was a woman who had fallen down a flight of stairs, scraping off a four-inch hunk of scalp in the process. Neighbors did their best to stop the bleeding.

"I always use flour," one neighbor said, pouring a cup of white flour onto the open wound. Soon the flour was a sticky red mess, and the bleeding continued.

"I'll bet molasses will do the trick," suggested another friend. She tipped a whole jug of thick syrup onto the patient's head, but the bleeding did not stop.

"I've got an idea!" an old farmer said. Going to the fireplace, he scooped up a shovelful of hot ashes and placed it on top of the other applications. The pain was so great that the poor woman passed out.

"I think we'd best call Doc Pritham," said the wisest neighbor of all.

When the doctor arrived, he found a thick layer of hardened molasses candy mixed with matted hair, flour, blood, and ashes. It took him nearly an hour to clean up the mess.

"Next time," he said with a twinkle in his eyes, "call me first! It would sure make things a whole lot easier."

Why is it that we humans so often wait until we've got ourselves into a sticky, painful mess before we call upon the Great Physician? There seems to be something about us that makes us want to try our own remedies first.

What Bible character got himself into one slimy mess in a fish's belly before he remembered to ask God for help?

Who ended up in jail with both eyes put out before he remembered to depend on God instead of himself?

Which disciple of Jesus was forever getting himself into sticky situations because he wanted to try his own way of doing things? One time he nearly drowned, and another time he made things worse by cutting off a man's ear.

THOMAS JEFFERSON

Though he was rich, yet for your sakes he became poor, that ye through his poverty might be rich. 2 Corinthians 8:9.

It's not very often that you hear of a rich man who voluntarily becomes poor. Thomas Jefferson was such a man. He left the luxury of his beautiful mansion, Monticello, to live in a drafty house in Washington, D.C. He laid aside the silks and velvets of a country gentleman to wear the common clothing of an ordinary farmer.

On one occasion a man from Connecticut was out riding in Washington when he spotted a man in an ordinary brown suit riding a thoroughbred horse. He pulled alongside and said, "I say there! What would you take for your horse?"

"It's not for sale. Why do you ask?"

"I'm looking for a good horse to get me out of town fast. I can't stand that man Jefferson!"

"Is that so? Have you ever seen him?"

"No, but I'd know him anywhere. He wears fancy clothes, two gold watches, and rings on every finger! The hypocrite! He talks about equality, but lives like a king!"

"I think someone has misinformed you," his new acquaintance said. "He dresses no better than I. In fact, I have business at the White House tomorrow. Be there at ten and I'll arrange an introduction."

The man in the brown riding suit was waiting near the entrance of the White House the next morning at ten when the Connecticut visitor arrived. He was about ready to welcome his guest when a servant arrived with a letter.

"Mr. President!" The servant said, handing him a letter. Embarrassed, the man from Connecticut turned and ran down the White House steps without greeting his riding companion, President Thomas Jefferson.

What Thomas Jefferson gave up for eight years was nothing compared to what Jesus, the king of glory, gave up for 33 years. He risked heaven that we might gain eternity. He became a pauper that we might become princes. He exchanged His crown for a cross of shame that we might exchange our crosses for crowns of joy.

JAMES MADISON

Love not the world, neither the things that are in the world.
1 John 2:15.

The White House table was set for dinner. While she waited, Mrs. Madison sat at a desk near a window, writing to her sister. She could hear the roar of cannon across the Potomac River and see the rockets bursting against the blue August sky.

"Shall I serve Madame her dinner now?" a servant asked.

"No, thank you. I'll wait for President Madison and our guests. They should be coming any minute now, with news of victory." She waved him out of the dining room, then drew back the curtains to see if her husband was coming.

What she saw was an army in retreat. People were rushing through the streets of Washington, looking for an escape route from the city. At that moment Mr. Carroll, a friend of the family, burst into the White House dining room.

"Mrs. Madison, you must leave at once. The British are on their way to burn the city. You will surely be captured if you remain. Come! There is no time to lose!"

Hurrying to her husband's office, she grabbed up a file of important government papers. Next she ran to the large Gilbert Stuart portrait of George Washington. The frame was screwed tightly to the wall and she had no screwdriver. Breaking the frame, she took out the portrait, gathered up the government papers, and fled through the streets toward Georgetown.

Four days later the Madisons returned to Washington to find the White House a charred ruin. How do you think they felt as they rooted around in the ashes for familiar treasures?

Adam, Eve, Jacob, Moses, and Lot's family all had to flee their homes. Try to imagine what they might have taken with them as they fled. Were there some intangible things they took that were more important than the material things they may have carried?

If you had to flee your home and you could take only one small suitcase, what would you put in it? How much do you love your possessions?

JOHN QUINCY ADAMS

*But that which ye have already hold fast till I come.
Revelation 2:25.*

John Adams, minister to the Netherlands, stood on the deck of the frigate *Alfred,* anchored near the white cliffs of Dover. Next to him was his brother, Thomas, who would serve as his secretary. Nearby was Tilly, their valet. Together they scanned the luggage as it was brought up from the hold.

"Ah! There are our trunks!" Tom said.

Within minutes the Americans were seated in a horse-drawn carriage with their two trunks strapped to the front.

"Keep your eyes on that trunk," John warned his brother. "It contains dispatches from our government to Chief Justice John Jay, who is in London to negotiate a treaty."

"I'll wager the British ministry would pay a spy well for those instructions!"

"The French Directory would also like to get their hands on them, I'm sure. We must not let that happen."

They covered the miles between Dover and London by nightfall. Traffic was heavy as they approached London Bridge. Suddenly, in spite of the noise, John heard two thumps.

"Stop!" he yelled to the driver.

Thomas was already out of the carriage, waving his arms for the coach behind them to halt. He rescued one of the trunks while John got the other.

"Those ropes were cut!" the driver said. "Somebody wanted your luggage!"

"We'll keep the trunks inside for the rest of the journey," John decided. "I will not let these papers out of my hands until I deliver them to Chief Justice Jay this very night."

Evidently you also have something valuable that an enemy government wants. What is it that Jesus asks you to hold on to until He comes? What is in your "trunk" that Satan would snatch away if he could? Might it be your good character? Could it be your church membership? Do you suppose it is your faith?

ANDREW JACKSON

Can a woman forget her sucking child, that she should not have compassion on the son of her womb? yea, they may forget, yet will I not forget thee. Isaiah 49:15.

Andrew Jackson might not have lived to be the seventh president of the United States had it not been for his mother's love. At 13 he and his 16-year-old brother, Robert, joined the American Revolutionary Army to fight the British. When Andrew was 14, they were both prisoners of war.

The prison stockade at Camden, South Carolina, was crowded with sick and dying men. There was no medicine, and nothing to eat but stale bread. But then, Andrew didn't feel much like eating, for he had smallpox. His body ached from the fever. Next to him on the filthy straw, his brother tossed and moaned.

"Cheer up, lad," whispered one of the older soldiers, moving close to Andrew so he'd not be overheard. "Nathanael Greene and his men are camped nearby. They've come to rescue us!"

"Oh, for some of my mom's chicken dumplings!" Andrew cried. He felt better already. That night he cut a hole in the board covering the window in his room so he could watch the action. He was horrified to see the American soldiers leisurely eating their breakfast and cleaning their guns. The next thing he saw was the smoke of musket fire. Soon the Americans were in retreat.

"It's no use," Andrew told Robert. "We'll die before they get us out of here."

But they didn't die. Their mother had not forgotten them. She rode the 40 miles to Camden, worked her way past the sentries, and got an interview with the British commander.

"Please, sir," she begged, "I have heard there's going to be an exchange of prisoners. My two boys are in your prison, and they're all I've got since my husband died. I need them to help work the farm. Have mercy on a poor widow woman and give me my boys!"

"Well, I don't suppose it matters much who I let go," the commander said. "Take your boys, Mrs. Jackson, and go home."

Mothers are pretty neat people. They love you when no one else does. They remember when all the world forgets. Yet Jesus loves you more than a mother. He will never forsake you.

JAMES KNOX POLK

He that believeth and is baptized shall be saved. Mark 16:16.

"It's time we had the baby baptized," Jane Polk said as she sat in a rocker by the fire, nursing her firstborn son.

"Can't say I like the idea of Parson Wallis doin' the baptizin'," Sam Polk remarked as he leaned one arm on the mantelpiece and stared at the fire.

"Oh, Sam!" Mrs. Polk sighed. "He's a good preacher."

"I don't need him tellin' me what to do in matters of politics. As long as he's the parson you'll not find my name on the church books."

"Can't you forget your quarrel with Parson Wallis long enough to have your son baptized? Please, Sam."

"If that's what you want, go ahead. I'll not hinder you."

"Thank you, Sam. Let's plan on it for this Sunday."

On the following Sunday, Sam took Jane and tiny James to the Presbyterian meeting house seven miles away in Providence, North Carolina.

"We've brought the baby for you to baptize," Mrs. Polk greeted Parson Wallis.

"And what about you, Mr. Polk? Are you ready to join the church?" the minister asked.

"I can't see what that's got to do with it! Just leave me out of this and go ahead with the baptizin'."

"No, I refuse to baptize your son unless you will profess your faith and obedience to the will of God."

"Then he can do without the baptizin'!" Sam replied. "Come on, Jane, we're goin' home."

James Knox Polk, eleventh president of the United States, was not baptized until 54 years later. By then he understood Bible teaching and decided the matter for himself.

Actually, the Bible nowhere suggests infant baptism. That is something that came into the Christian church hundreds of years after the Bible was written. Rather, it teaches that you must be old enough to accept Jesus as your Lord and Saviour. If you have made that decision, it's time to talk to your parents and your pastor about being baptized.

318

ABRAHAM LINCOLN

Who hath saved us, and called us . . . according to his own purpose. 2 Timothy 1:9.

"I'll race you to the Nice Stone," Abe challenged his friend Austin Gollaher.

"OK!" Austin agreed. "Ready, set, go!" And the boys were off through the greening forest toward Knob Creek, where a large flat rock jutted out from a tall cliff. They reached the stone at the same time, laughing and panting. From it they could survey the countryside for miles around.

"Look down there," Abe said, pointing to the sparkling water of Knob Creek. "It's a black bass and it's trapped in the shallows."

"I'll bet we could catch it with our bare hands!"

The boys climbed down the cliff and crept up to the pool where the fish floundered. In a few minutes they had the big bass on the grassy bank.

At that moment there was a deafening crash above the boys' heads, and they were showered with small pieces of stone and clods of dirt. Looking up, they saw that a huge boulder from the cliff above had fallen directly on the spot where the two boys had stood minutes before.

"Whew! That was a close one!" Austin said. "If you were still standing there, you'd be as flat as a pancake!"

"I don't reckon we'd better play up there anymore," Abe decided. "I see two more rocks that look like they're getting ready to drop."

Why do you think Abe saw that black bass and decided to move just when he did?

Austin Gollaher had an answer. When he was an old man he used to say, "God watched over Abe Lincoln. He didn't want him killed, because there were no others like him. And He wanted to use Abe for a big purpose."

God is watching over you, too. He has a purpose for your life. He has a place for you that no one else can fill. His plan for you is greater than anything you can now imagine. Trust in Him, seek His guidance, and He will lead you to the work He wants you to do for Him.

JEFFERSON DAVIS

Though he were a Son, yet learned he obedience by the things which he suffered. Hebrews 5:8.

Have you ever wondered why God sometimes lets us have our own way when He knows disaster will be the outcome? Often that's the only way we'll learn the lessons He wants us to learn. Experience is sometimes the best teacher there is.

Take, for instance, 10-year-old Jeff Davis, who one day was to become President Jefferson Davis of the Confederacy. One day he arrived home from school before noon and sought out his father, who was picking cotton.

"Why are you home so early?" Mr. Davis inquired. He set down his sack of cotton and wiped his neck with his handkerchief.

"I've quit school, Father. I had a quarrel with the headmaster and I don't want to go back."

"I see," Mr. Davis said calmly. " I respect your decision. However, no one on this plantation remains idle. Since you have chosen not to work with your mind, then you must work with your hands. Go get a sack and begin to work."

"This is fun!" Jeff said. "I like it a whole lot better than school."

However, by nightfall his enthusiasm had waned considerably. His back ached and his fingers were sore. Exhausted, he flopped onto his bed and was soon asleep.

The next morning his father called him while it was still dark. "Get up, Jeff. We've got to be in the fields by dawn."

Jeff rubbed his eyes and made himself get up and dress by candlelight. He dragged himself down to the kitchen for breakfast. Wearily he trudged out to the field and began picking just as the sun peeped over the hill.

"Go rest a spell under the shade of that tree," Mr. Davis told Jeff at noon. "You look like you're going to faint."

"No, I'll keep going," Jeff replied. "But tomorrow I'm going back to school."

Dropping his sack of cotton, Mr. Davis ran to his son and embraced him. "Good for you, Jeff! You've learned the lesson I intended. I hope you never forget it."

JAMES ABRAM GARFIELD

Agree with thine adversary quickly, whiles thou art in the way with him; lest at any time the adversary deliver thee to the judge. Matthew 5:25.

It was the end of James Garfield's first day of working for Captain Letcher as a driver for the canalboat *Evening Star*. He had spent the day driving the two mules that pulled the boat through the water. It was dark as they approached the locks at Akron, Ohio. The bowman ran ahead to prepare the first lock.

"Don't turn this lock!" the bowman from another boat shouted. "I got here first!"

"No, you didn't," the *Evening Star* bowman protested. "I was here first, and we're going through!"

"Let's fight it out!" the crew on the other boat yelled.

"What do you say, Captain Letcher?" his men asked. "Shall we take them up on their offer?"

"I don't think we ought to fight," James said.

"Chicken."

"Scaredy-cat."

"Go on back home to your mama if you're afraid."

"I'm not afraid. It just doesn't make good sense to me," James replied.

"Why not?" asked Captain Letcher.

"Because what would be gained? Even if we won the fight we would have lost more time than if we let them go first."

"You know, kid, you make good sense," the captain said. Then to the bowman he shouted, "Let them go. We'll take our turn."

Long before James A. Garfield became the twentieth president of the United States, he had learned an important lesson. Most things are just not worth fighting over. Sometimes it's better to yield to your opponent.

Is your place in line really worth fighting over? Is one point in a baseball game worth wasting a whole recess in a shouting match? Is having your own way really as important as getting on with the game? Is proving your point worth all the money and time it might cost you to take it to court? Usually giving in and taking turns is the better way.

ZACHARY TAYLOR

Ye do err, not knowing the scriptures. Matthew 22:29.

"Good morning, General!" the Baton Rouge postmaster greeted the town's most distinguished resident, General Zachary Taylor, hero of the Mexican War.

"Good morning!" the general replied. "I sure hope you've no more letters for me."

"You certainly have a lot of fans!" the postmaster said from behind an armload of mail for the general. "The American people sure do like you, General."

"I wish they liked me well enough to pay the postage themselves," General Taylor complained. "Soon I'll be broke just paying all the postage due."

"Most of this pile is marked postage due. Do you want to accept it?"

"No! I've had enough. You can dump it as far as I'm concerned."

"But I'm not allowed to destroy mail. I'll have to send it to the dead letter office in Washington."

"Then send it. I refuse to pay any more postage."

A few days later the general was lunching with a friend. "Have you received word from Philadelphia yet?"

"No. What are you talking about?"

"There was a very important letter sent to you sometime ago. You should have had it by now."

"Oh, no! I'll bet it was in that batch I sent to the dead letter office."

On his next trip into Baton Rouge he asked the postmaster to recall his postage-due letters. When they came he found the important letter. It was an invitation from the Whig party to be their candidate for president of the United States. By ignoring his letters he almost lost the chance of a lifetime.

The Bible is a collection of important letters to you from God. Have you ignored them? They are the same as dead letters until you open them and read. Somewhere inside the covers of your Bible there are messages for you. You are making a big mistake by not reading them. To leave them unopened is to miss the chance of eternity.

THEODORE ROOSEVELT

Lord, I pray thee, open his eyes, that he may see. 2 Kings 6:17.

Thirteen-year-old Theodore Roosevelt pointed his gun at the woods and pulled the trigger.

"You missed it by a mile!" Cousin John scoffed.

"Stupid! Don't you know how to hit a target?" Theodore's brother Elliott was plainly disgusted.

"What target?" Theodore demanded.

"That one! Right over there!"

"I guess I know a target when I see one. There's no target at all."

"Oh, come on, Theodore, of course there's one. Can't you see that white board down there with the colored rings?"

"No, of course I can't see what's not there!"

"OK," said John, taking Theodore by the shoulders. "Forward march! I'll prove it to you!"

Five feet away from the target Theodore saw a white blur. Then suddenly there it was, as plain as day.

"I'll bet your father doesn't know you can't see," John exclaimed. "He'd never have given you a gun if he'd known."

"Please don't tell him," Theodore begged.

"He's got to know you can't see!" insisted Elliott.

"But I can see!" Theodore objected. "I just can't see faraway things."

When Mr. Roosevelt found out, he took Theodore to the eye doctor and got him a pair of steel-rimmed glasses with thick lenses. A whole new world opened up to him.

Elisha's servant had a similar problem. He couldn't see what Elisha saw, so Elisha prayed for God to open his eyes so that he could see the angels fighting for them against the Syrian army. What an exciting new world opened before him when his spiritual eyesight was corrected.

Are you spiritually nearsighted? Do you have a hard time seeing God at work in your life? Do you find it difficult to read the signs of the times that show Christ's coming is near? Don't scoff at what others see just because you can't see it. Instead, ask God to open your eyes. The glasses of faith will work wonders!

BENITO JUÁREZ

If the Son therefore shall make you free, ye shall be free indeed. John 8:36.

A soft mountain breeze rippled the waters of the lake and tugged at Benito's ragged straw hat. He pulled his poncho closer around his thin brown body and stared at his uncle's sheep as they fed on the green hillside. His dark eyes swept the bushes for any movement that would indicate trouble for the sheep. As long as there were snakes and mountain lions, the sheep could not be free.

Not far away the 20 adobe huts of Guelatao village reflected the golden warmth of the afternoon sun. The proud people who lived in that village and toiled on the hillsides were his relatives and friends, all Zapotec Indians. At night they sat around their fires and told stories of the long-ago days before the Spaniards came. As long as there were foreign soldiers in the land, his people would not be free.

Freedom! That was what young Benito dreamed about as he stared at his sheep and the village beyond. He must do something to make life better for himself and his people.

"You can't do anything unless you get an education," his uncle told him. "You must go to the big city and work for the foreigners. You must learn their language and go to their schools."

So one day Benito set out to walk the 70 miles from his mountain village to the big city of Oaxaca, with its many churches and strange people. He learned Spanish and studied law, and when the opportunity came to lead his people to freedom, Benito was ready. The little shepherd boy grew up to become president of Mexico and a national hero.

But still in the land of Mexico as in every other country on earth there are people in bondage, slaves to their own passions and desires. Alcohol has many in chains. Drugs keep others enslaved. Thousands are shackled by evil habits.

In every country God needs brave young people, like Benito Juárez, who will go forth in the name of Jesus to set people free from sin and the power of Satan. Are you willing to be that kind of freedom fighter?

JAN CHRISTIAAN SMUTS

O God, thou knowest my foolishness; and my sins are not hid from thee. Psalm 69:5.

What do mothers, teachers, and God have in common? They share that uncanny ability of sniffing out trouble and discovering the very thing you are trying to hide. Sixteen-year-old Jan Christiaan Smuts learned this during his fourth year at a boarding school in South Africa.

When he became sick from the strain of preparing for his final examinations, the Stofbergs took him into their home and nursed him back to health.

"The boy must have complete bed rest," the doctor ordered. "He must eat plenty of nourishing food and sleep as much as possible. He is to do absolutely no reading.

"Oh, no!" Jan groaned. "How will I ever survive without books to read?" He tried, but after a few days of sleep he was so bored he was ready to break the rules.

Looking around for an accomplice in his "crime," he decided on Hennie, the Stofbergs' 3-year-old son. When they were alone one day, Jan called the boy to his bed and whispered, "Hennie, do you like cherry suckers?"

"Uh-huh."

"I'll give you one cherry sucker for every book you bring to me. You must be very careful not to let Mama and Papa see you. If they do, they'll take away the book, and you won't get your sucker."

In a few minutes the toddler was back with a book. Jan put a piece of red candy into his hand. "Good for you, Hennie."

Before long Jan had quite a collection of books stashed away under his pillow and blankets.

"What do we have here?" Mrs. Stofberg asked as she pulled the blanket away from Jan's secret library. "How do you expect to get well if you won't follow doctor's orders?"

Have you ever tried hiding something from your mom? I once smuggled three puppies up two flights of stairs to my bed, only to get caught when my mom came to tuck me in.

Hiding things from God is even harder. It's impossible.

WOODROW WILSON

*Their tongue is as an arrow shot out; it speaketh deceit.
Jeremiah 9:8.*

If you had lived in Augusta, Georgia, 120 years ago you might have been lucky enough to belong to the Lightfoot Club. Members of this group included Tommy Wilson, Pleasant Stovall, Will Fleming, and Joseph Lamar.

One day the club met in Tommy's backyard to plan their fun for the day. "Who wants to play Civil War?" Will asked.

"Naw! We've played that all week. I'm tired of it," Joseph said.

"Me too!" agreed Pleasant.

"I know!" said Tommy. "Let's dress up as Indians and go hunting in the forest. We can make bows and arrows out of willow limbs."

"Hurrah!" the boys all shouted. "That's going to be great fun!"

Soon the boys were whooping through the woods with their bows and arrows, shooting at imaginary game. "I wish we had some real animals to shoot," Joseph said.

"I know," suggested Will. "Let's get Tommy's cousin Jessie. She can be a deer or a squirrel."

Before long the boys were chasing "squirrel" Jessie up a tree. Tommy, the fearless brave, drew his bow and let an arrow fly. It hit her on the back, knocking her out of the tree.

Gathering the unconscious girl in his arms, Tommy took her home to his aunt Marion, sobbing all the way. "I did it. I'm the murderer. I killed her with my arrow."

"She's not dead," Aunt Marion said as she hurried to get cold water to wash Jessie's face. "But I think it's time to stop playing with those bows and arrows."

Tommy grew up to become President Woodrow Wilson. During his eight years in office he was hit plenty of times by the sharp arrows of censure and criticism.

Can you think of a time when sharp words pierced you like an arrow? Can you remember a time when your unkind, cruel words brought pain to a friend? Don't you think it's time we stopped playing Indian hunters with our tongues?

HERBERT HOOVER

He healeth the broken in heart, and bindeth up their wounds. Psalm 147:3.

There was no television a hundred years ago when Bertie Hoover was your age. However, he didn't miss it at all, because he had his father's blacksmith shop. He could stand there by the hour watching his father hammer out horseshoes and nails. There was something exciting about the ring of the anvil and the smell of tar.

One day young Bertie ran barefooted into the shop. Coming in out of the sunshine, his eyes not yet being adjusted to the dimmer light, he didn't notice the scrap of red-hot metal on the floor.

"Ow-eeee!" he screamed as one bare foot landed on top of the hot metal. It sizzled into his tender flesh, shooting pain all the way up his leg.

Realizing what had happened, his father picked him up and plunged him feet first into a barrel of cold water. After a while the pain was gone, and he carried the boy to the house. Mother Hoover carefully wrapped Bertie's foot in clean strips of cloth.

For days Bertie hobbled around, unable to put pressure on his sore foot. At last the day came when his bandage was removed and he could wear shoes again. The wound was healed, but a scar remained for the rest of his life.

When he was president, Mr. Hoover used to joke about the "brand of Iowa" that he carried on the sole of his foot.

It seems to me that sin is like a piece of red-hot metal. It can hurt really bad and make a mess of our lives. In our pain and desperation we cry out to God for help. He comes to us then with the healing balm of Gilead. He forgives us and binds up our wounds. Eventually the pain goes away, but we are never quite the same again. In His love He heals us, but a scar remains.

Brain cells destroyed by drug use are gone forever. A lung lost through smoking cannot be restored. A heart seared by angry words can never be as it was before. A broken relationship can be mended, but a scar remains. Impure thoughts can be forgiven, but they leave behind their mark.

ADOLF HITLER

For the king of Babylon stood at the parting of the way, at the head of the two ways. Ezekiel 21:21.

Sooner or later we all stand where the king of Babylon stood, at the parting of the ways, at the crossroads of life. We cannot go back; we must choose one way or the other. On that decision hangs our eternal destiny.

Adolf Hitler reached that point when he was 16. It was nearly midnight as he and his friend, Gustl Kubizek, stepped out of the opera house in Linz, an Austrian city on the Danube River. They had just watched the performance of Richard Wagner's *Rienzi,* the fairy-tale story of a poor boy of ancient Rome who became the ruler of a vast empire.

The two young men walked silently through the cobbled streets until they reached the country. As if propelled by an invisible force, Hitler led the way up a steep hill called the Feinberg. At the top they looked down on the Danube River shimmering in the moonlight.

Hitler turned and took the hands of his friend. "Something important has happened to me tonight, Gustl. As I watched the story of *Rienzi* unfold I seemed to be seeing my future. I too am a poor boy like Rienzi. I too will rise to become the ruler of a great empire. You will hear much about me in the future, my friend."

The two youths then walked down the hill, but that night they had stood at the crossroads. Hitler chose the way that led him to become the mad dictator of World War II, bringing death to millions. Gustl's way led him to become the conductor of a symphony orchestra, bringing joy to thousands.

Hitler and his friend met again 30 years later. "Remember that moonlit night on the Feinberg?" Adolf asked.

Gustl nodded.

"In that hour it began," Hitler said. And what a difference that hour made in the course of history! As James Russell Lowell wrote:

> Once to every man and nation
> Comes the moment to decide,
> In the strife of Truth with Falsehood,
> For the good or evil side.

FRANKLIN DELANO ROOSEVELT

Whosoever will, let him take the water of life freely. Revelation 22:17.

It was plain that something was bothering Franklin. He moped around the house and picked at his food. Finally Mrs. Roosevelt called him to her room. "Sit down, Franklin," she said. "I want to talk to you."

Franklin sighed as he dropped onto a chair.

"What's wrong with you, Franklin? Are you unhappy?"

"Yes, ma'am."

"But why? Your father and I have given you everything a boy could desire. What more do you want?"

"My freedom," Franklin responded. "I've no time to play or do anything I want to do. From the time I get up until I go to bed, I have to do what somebody tells me to do."

"I see," said his mother. "So you want freedom to do just what you'd like without interference?"

"Right!"

"I'll talk it over with your father. You may go now."

The next morning at breakfast his father announced, "Today there are no rules. You are free to do as you please."

"Yippee!" Franklin grabbed his jacket and dashed out the door. He didn't stop running until he reached the bottom of the hill at the Hudson River. All day he roamed the woods, looking for birds. He didn't even bother to go home for lunch. It was dusk before he showed up, tired and hungry. Nobody asked where he'd been or what he'd done. Supper was over, and he want to the kitchen to help himself to whatever he could find. He was filthy, but no one told him to take a bath. He decided to do it anyway. Then he fell onto his bed exhausted.

The next morning he climbed the stairs to his schoolroom and sat down opposite his teacher. School wasn't so bad now that he was there by his own free choice.

I think God was very wise when He made us with the freedom to choose, don't you? He really wants us to be saved, but we don't have to be if we don't want to be.

WINSTON CHURCHILL

Keep back thy servant also from presumptuous sins. Psalm 19:13.

"Let's play deer and hounds," 18-year-old Winston Churchill suggested.

"How do you play?" asked Jack, his 12-year-old brother.

"I'll be the deer," Winston explained, with the leadership one would expect of a future British prime minister. "You and Cousin will be the hounds. Count to one hundred; then try to catch me."

"Okay! We're counting! One, two, three. . . ." The two boys closed their eyes. "Ninety-eight, ninety-nine, one hundred! Ready or not, you shall be caught!" The two "hounds" were off at top speed in the direction Winston had gone.

"Let's split up," Jack said at last. "You follow his trail. I'll circle around and try to head him off!"

Within a short time the "hounds" had their "deer" trapped in the center of a bridge that spanned a deep ravine. "We've got you!" they yelled.

"Not yet, you don't!" Winston shouted, eyeing the tops of the pine trees that were growing out of the ravine. *Surely I can jump to the top of one of them and tumble through the branches to the bottom,* he reasoned. He jumped, missed the tree, and fell onto the rocks 30 feet below. Winston remained unconscious for three days and had to stay in bed for three months.

Of course you haven't done anything so foolhardy! You have never been so presumptuous! Or have you? To be presumptuous is to be overconfident. The presumptuous person takes unwarranted risks. He takes the goodness of God for granted.

Did you ever ride a bike down a steep hill, without holding the handlebar, praying all the time, "Dear God, please don't let me crash!"

Did you ever break the Sabbath, steal, lie, or swear, and think, *Aw, it doesn't really matter. God is good. He wouldn't keep me out of heaven for something so small as that!*

Did you ever eat junk food, stay up late at night, or play outside without proper clothing, then ask God to keep you well?

HARRY S. TRUMAN

That ... prayers ... be made for all men; for kings, and for all that are in authority. 1 Timothy 2:1, 2.

Vice President Truman dashed out of the meeting room and sped the length of the Capitol basement and the tunnel leading to the Senate Office Building. His heart was racing as he ordered his chauffeur to bring his car.

"To the White House, Pennsylvania Avenue entrance," he ordered. Within minutes he was in Mrs. Roosevelt's second-floor study.

"Harry," she said, "the president is dead."

"Oh, no!" Tears flowed down Truman's cheeks. "Is there anything I can do for you?"

"I would like to go to Warm Springs to bring his body home," she said. "Would it be all right if I used a government plane?"

He stared at her a moment, wondering why she was asking him. Then it dawned on him. He was now the president. "Of course, Mrs. Roosevelt. We'll do anything we can to help."

In a daze he called Chief Justice Harlan Stone to come to the White House to swear him in. Then he called his wife and asked her to join him for the ceremony.

It was all so unreal—so unexpected. Harry S. Truman had been vice president less than three months and felt unprepared for the awesome responsibility that was now thrust upon him.

He told reporters the next day, "Boys, if you ever pray, pray for me now. I don't know whether you fellows ever had a load of hay fall on you, but when they told me yesterday what had happened, I felt like the moon, the stars, and all the planets had fallen on me."

I don't envy the responsibility of presidents and prime ministers. The happiness and wellbeing of millions of people rests in their hands. Jobs for the unemployed, homes for the homeless, care for the aged and sick, and food for the hungry are deep concerns of theirs. Nuclear war, strikes, terrorism, and human rights are problems they go to sleep with at night. Don't forget to pray for them today; they need your prayers.

JOMO KENYATTA

Look unto me, and be ye saved, all the ends of the earth: for I am God, and there is none else. Isaiah 45:22.

Oh, how the chiggers itched! The tiny insects had bored their way into Kamau's feet as he walked through the tall grass. He soaked his feet and rubbed them but it did no good. Then after the itching came fever. He lay on a straw mat in his mother's hut and grew steadily weaker.

"My son is going to die! My son is going to die!" his mother wailed. "The spirits are angry, Ngengi."

So Kamau's father visited the witch doctor's hovel with a gift of a sheep and begged him to heal his son.

"You have offended your ancestral spirits," the old man declared. "You must now give a large beer-drinking party. Let there be much feasting and dancing, and then the spirits will be happy."

But in spite of the sheep and the party, Kamau became worse.

"I've heard that the White man has strong magic medicine," Kamau's mother suggested when all else had failed and the boy was near death. "It can do no harm to take him to the Christian mission."

Ngengi didn't want to go, but the child's mother gave him no peace until they made the journey to Fort Hall, near Nairobi. There Kamau lay on a bed with white sheets while the doctors examined him. At his father's insistence he swallowed the strange medicine they offered. In a short time Kamau was well.

"The White man's God is stronger than the witch doctor," Kamau spoke with awe. "He is stronger than the evil spirits. I want to stay and learn the White man's magic."

Kamau's parents finally agreed. By the time he finished mission school, Kamau had learned to love Jesus. But although he accepted the White man's God, he did not accept the White man's government. When he was older Kamau changed his name to Jomo Kenyatta and led the struggle for Kenya's independence.

You may not sympathize with Jomo Kenyatta's dreams nor agree with the methods he used to achieve them, but I am sure you agree that the wisest decision he ever made was to follow Jesus. Have you made that decision?

KWAME NKRUMAH

Lest any root of bitterness springing up trouble you. Hebrews 12:15.

On June 12, 1949, a crowd of 60,000 had gathered in Accra, Ghana, to hear Kwame Nkrumah speak on behalf of independence. There was a deafening cheer as he rose to speak.

"In all political struggles there come rare moments, hard to distinguish but fatal to let slip," the handsome Black man said. "This is one of those moments. What do you want me to do? Shall I pack my things and leave this dear Ghana of ours?"

"No! No! No!" the crowd chanted.

"Should I remain here and keep my mouth shut?"

"No! No! Stay with us. Open your mouth. Speak."

"Shall I throw in my lot with the people of this country for full self-government now?"

"Yes! Yes! Yes!" The crowd roared its approval.

"I will lead you to victory!" Nkrumah promised.

A few months later frightened government officers had the revolutionary leader thrown in jail, expecting that that would be the end of his new party. But it wasn't; others took up the leadership and continued the campaign for independence.

Meanwhile, conditions in the prison were appalling. Eleven men were crowded into one tiny cell. There was nothing to eat but tasteless cornmeal porridge three times a day. They could have no books and no paper.

This presented a problem to Nkrumah, because it was important that he get messages out of the jail to the leaders of the independence movement. He was able to scrounge a small pencil stub. For paper he used the few sheets of toilet tissue he was allowed. When that wasn't enough, he traded his daily food ration with hungry prisoners for their toilet paper ration. In this way he kept the independence movement alive.

After Nkrumah became the first prime minister of Ghana, he declared, "I came out of jail into the assembly without the slightest feeling of bitterness toward Britain."

In this experience Kwame Nkrumah gave an example to all who face unjust treatment. With God's help such an attitude is possible.

JOHN FITZGERALD KENNEDY

Now then we are ambassadors for Christ. 2 Corinthians 5:20.

Jack Kennedy spent the summer of 1939 in England with his father, the American ambassador. Joining Jack on a tour of Europe were his roommate, Torby MacDonald, and a friend, Byron White. Their trip took them through Berlin to Munich, where they visited the tomb of Nazi agitator Horst Wessel. They parked the car near the tomb and went inside to see the perpetual flame.

When they emerged, they were greeted with a shower of rocks from a gang of German toughs.

"Hey, cut it out!" Torby yelled.

"Come on," Byron, an all-American halfback, motioned to the others. "Let's show these German bullies a thing or two!"

"Hold it!" Jack ordered. "No fights! We're going to get into our car and beat it as fast as we can!"

The other two followed his lead, sprinting to the car. Safely inside, Jack revved up the engine and left their tormentors standing in a cloud of dust.

"Why didn't you let us fight?" Byron asked.

"Yeah!" Torby agreed. "We could have given them a licking!"

"They mistook us for English tourists," Jack explained. "Anyway, it wouldn't do for the son of the United States ambassador to Britain to be arrested for brawling with a gang of German hoodlums. Can you imagine what that would look like in the papers tomorrow?"

"'American Ambassador's Son Mauls Helpless German Youth!' I guess that wouldn't sound so good," Torby agreed.

"To say nothing of all the diplomatic red tape my dad would have to go through to get us out of jail," Jack added.

You and I are also ambassadors. We represent the King of kings wherever we go. People will judge all Christians by the way we act. How do these headlines sound?

"Christian Ambassador Arrested for Dope Peddling"

"Representative of the King of Kings Cheats on Exam"

"Angry Christian Ambassador Beats Up Non-Christian"

CHOU EN-LAI

Behold, now is the accepted time; behold, now is the day of salvation. 2 Corinthians 6:2.

On April 11, 1927, a messenger ran on soft-soled shoes through the narrow streets of Shanghai to the house where Chou En-lai slept. He whispered something to a guard at the door and disappeared as silently as he had come.

"Sir, wake up!" the guard spoke softly. "The general has betrayed you. You must escape!"

Chou slipped out into the night and began to run. Keeping to the shadows, he worked his way toward the city's edge, hoping to hide in the countryside. Before dawn he was captured.

Although Chou gave a false name, he felt sure the commander recognized him, for Chou had taught the commander's brother at Whampoa Academy. There was a hint of recognition in the commander's eyes, but he said nothing.

That night rough hands shook Chou awake. His heart pounded as he tried to see the man who had come for him. It was too dark. "Who are you?" he asked.

"Never mind. Come with me. Quickly," the voice whispered.

Outside in the pale moonlight Chou recognized his former student, brother of the commander who had questioned him. They moved quickly to a side entrance of the prison, where the two guards conveniently looked the other way as the fugitives passed through the gate. Chou gripped his friend's hand to express his thanks.

"You must get out of the city tonight, for there are posters everywhere offering a reward for your capture," his ex-student warned. "Travel only at night and do not use your own name. Go now! There is no time to lose."

Although we may not agree with many choices Chou En-lai made, we can certainly agree that, had he ignored the warning, Chou would never have become the premier of China. Our verse for today has a warning that is even more important. Jesus offers you a way of escape. Your eternal destiny is at stake. To delay is dangerous. Tomorrow may be too late.

LYNDON BAINES JOHNSON

Rejoice not against me, O mine enemy: when I fall, I shall arise. Micah 7:8.

Have you ever tried to do something difficult, only to fall flat on your face in the attempt? Then you can understand how Lyndon felt the day he tried to ride a Mexican burro.

"Want to ride my new burro?" Milt asked Lyndon.

The little burrow shook his head angrily and flipped his long ears. He pawed the ground and rolled his big brown eyes at the boys. "Hee-haw! Hee-haw!" he brayed. "I dare you to come and try!"

"Sure!" said Lyndon. "I've ridden lots of horses, so I know I can ride that little burro. Hold his head for me."

The animal stood perfectly still while Lyndon mounted. As soon as Milt let loose of his head, the burro exploded into a flurry of activity. He jumped, kicked, and bucked Lyndon right off his back. The surprised boy slid along the ground, ripping his overalls on a tree root and cutting a deep gash in his leg. Blood poured from the cut, and Lyndon felt faint. Tying up the cut with a handkerchief, he ran home.

"I'm never going to ride that burro again!" Lyndon told his grandfather Johnson the next day. "Look what he did to me!"

"Just because you got thrown once is no reason not to try again," the old man said. "With your wits and long legs you ought to be able to ride him."

"How?" Lyndon wasn't sure he liked the idea.

"Don't sit so tight. Try to relax. Then if he tries to throw you, catch yourself with your outside foot and shove yourself back on him again. If he succeeds in tossing you off, then don't let him win. Just pick yourself up and try again. If you stick to it, you'll succeed."

The next day Lyndon tried his grandfather's advice, and it worked. Oh, sure, he got thrown a few times, but he didn't give up. Each time he got right back on, and before long the burro gave up and walked peacefully with Lyndon astride.

The next time life throws you for a loop and you fall flat on your face, remember Lyndon Johnson and the burro. Get up and try again. Keep at it until you succeed.

INDIRA GANDHI

Take no thought how or what ye shall speak: for it shall be given you in that same hour what ye shall speak. Matthew 10:19.

It was early morning as the train in which future Prime Minister Indira Gandhi was traveling pulled into a station in northern India.

"Chai! Chai!" the tea vendor stopped at her window. "Hot tea for madame?"

Beyond him she could see hundreds of angry men shouting and shaking their fists. "What's going on?" she asked.

"It's a Muslim. He wants to get on the train, and the Hindus are trying to stop him."

She could hear their voices clearly. "Murder to Muslims!"

"Rajiv, listen to me." She knelt beside her 3-year-old. "Mommy has got to go and stop those men. You must be a big boy and take care of baby Sanjay until I return."

Hurriedly wrapping her sari around her waist, she ran to the door of the train. Spotting the ringleaders, she pushed her way through the crowd and grabbed their arms.

"Stop!" she demanded, her dark eyes flashing authority. "I will not let you kill that man!"

"Go away, woman!" The men tried to shake her off.

"No! I insist that you stop this riot immediately. Muslims have the same rights as Hindus. Let the man go!"

"Please, madame, you don't understand . . . "

"I understand perfectly what you want to do. It cannot be done, I tell you! It must not be done!"

While Mrs. Gandhi argued with the Hindus, the Muslim slipped away and boarded the train.

"All aboard!" the conductor called. The warning bell clanged, and Mrs. Gandhi jumped on as the train began to move.

"I never thought about what I was going to do or say," Mrs. Gandhi said later. "It was just one of those things that had to be done, and I did it."

Who knows when you might be called upon to act with such courage. No need to worry. God will give you the words to say and the strength to do what must be done.

JULIUS KAMBARAGE NYERERE

When I was a child, I spake as a child . . . : but when I became a man, I put away childish things. 1 Corinthians 13:11.

Ten-year-old Kambarage raced through the dusty East African village of Butiama. He didn't stop until he reached the mud-and-grass hut of his friend Abdulla. He circled the house, hoping his friend would be in the garden. He was.

"Abdulla!" the chief's son called as he nimbly hopped over rows of beans and corn. "I've got a wonderful idea!"

"What is it?" Abdulla dropped his hoe and waited for the news, his black eyes sparkling with excitement.

"Tonight the men are leaving for a hunting trip. Let's go with them."

"They'd never let us."

"We won't ask their permission; we'll just follow along. When they see how well we can shoot they won't send us back!"

"OK," Abdulla whispered. "I'll be ready."

That night as the first stars began to show, the hunting party quietly slipped into the jungle, with Abdulla and Kambarage not far behind. It was several hours before the hunters reached their camping place beside a stream.

Before dawn the boys edged their way to the waterhole and hid themselves in some bushes. Suddenly they saw a gazelle moving gracefully through the trees toward the water. They took aim and let their arrows fly. The gazelle leaped into the air, then dropped to the ground. The two boys burst from their hideout shouting, "We did it! We did it!"

From that moment the men included the boys in their hunting trip. One of those who proved his manhood that day was Julius Kambarage Nyerere, the first president of what is now Tanzania.

Do you wish your parents would treat you more like an adult? The secret is to prove that you can behave as one, accepting the responsibilities of an adult. Too many teenagers want the privileges of adulthood without accepting the responsibilities that go along with it.

CHARLES DE GAULLE

For Satan himself is transformed into an angel of light.
2 Corinthians 11:14.

During World War I Charles de Gaulle, who later became president of France, was captured by the Germans and put in a prisoner-of-war camp.

"It's our duty to escape," De Gaulle told fellow prisoners. "We've got to find a way to get out of here."

"It's hopeless," the prisoners moaned. "Everyone who tries gets caught and put in solitary confinement."

"I've got to try!" De Gaulle declared.

At last he figured out the perfect way to escape undetected. He'd dress up as a German soldier and simply walk out the gate. Getting the uniform was not easy, but at last he got one somehow. The problem was that it was several sizes too small for his six-foot-five frame. He pulled up his socks to try to make them meet the pant legs but they didn't quite make it.

"You look ridiculous!" the men of his barracks teased.

Charles adjusted his cap, straightened his shoulders, and walked out of the barracks. He made it through the compound unnoticed. At the gate he saluted the sleepy guard, walked nonchalantly down the road, and soon disappeared from view around a bend.

The German sentry frowned as it began to dawn on him that there had been something strange about the soldier who had just walked out the gate. He was very tall. And the way his clothes fit was really strange, as though the uniform had shrunk. He reported his suspicions to the commander. The barracks were checked and Charles de Gaulle was found missing. Within a short time he was caught and placed in solitary confinement.

Inspiration tells us that we can expect Satan to appear as an "angel of light" impersonating the second coming of Jesus. Many will be deceived (read Matthew 24:24). He will be dressed in Christlike clothing and do Christlike things. Miracles and wonders will be performed. You'll have to be really sharp to realize that things don't quite fit. If you know your Bible, you'll not get taken in by the devil's disguise.

GOLDA MEIR

Let no man despise thy youth. 1 Timothy 4:12.

Eighty years ago schools did not provide textbooks. Each student had to buy his own, but for some, this was impossible.

"It's not fair!" cried 10-year-old Golda Meir when she saw her friends struggling without books. "Why should children be discriminated against just because they're poor?"

"I agree," said her best friend, Regina Hamburger. "If I had the money, I'd buy books for all the kids who need them."

Golda's eyes lit up. "I've got an idea!" she said. "Why don't we form a club to collect money for needy children?"

"That's a marvelous idea!" exclaimed Regina.

"We'll ask all our friends from school," Golda continued. "We can call it American Young Sister Society."

"Excellent! I can't wait to get started."

The club members decided to hold a "ball" in Milwaukee's Packen Hall. They chipped in their allowances and collected from their neighbors until they had enough money to print announcements and rent the hall. The girls planned a program of speeches followed by refreshments.

On the day of the "ball" the auditorium was packed. The girls recited poems and gave passionate speeches explaining the needs of poor children for books.

"Please dig deep into your pockets and help the needy children of our city!" Golda cried, her chestnut braids swinging. "These kids have good brains. They deserve an equal chance to get an education. Don't let us down! We are counting on you!"

A newspaper reporter and photographer were there. The next day Golda Meir and her American Young Sister Society made the front page. "We must thank 10-year-old Golda Meir for jogging us adults into an awareness of the injustice being done to the city's poor children," the newspaper said.

Thanks to Golda, the poor children of Milwaukee got their textbooks. Many years later she continued to help people when she became prime minsiter of Israel. Golda proved that young people can make a difference. You don't have to wait until you're an adult to do something worthwhile for others.

RICHARD NIXON

So then every one of us shall give account of himself to God.
Romans 14:12.

All was dark in the White House except for the Lincoln Sitting Room, where Richard Nixon sat alone. Dark circles under his eyes told of the tremendous strain he had been under for two years. Outrage over the Watergate incident had grown into a cry for his impeachment. Rather than put his country through a lengthy trial, the president had decided to resign. He looked at his watch. It was 2:00 a.m. on August 8, 1974.

He yawned and laid aside his resignation speech. Slipping to his knees, he prayed silently for the strength to go through with his decision.

Rising then, he gathered up his notes and turned out the light. He walked to his own room and prepared for bed. On his pillow he found a note from his daughter Julie. "I love you, Daddy," it said. "I am very proud of you." She begged him to wait a week or 10 days before making his decision.

"If anything could have changed my mind at this point, this would have done it," Nixon said later. "But my mind was made up."

The next day Rose Mary Woods, the president's secretary, told him, "Your wife and daughters want to be in the Oval Office when you deliver your resignation speech. They want the world to know they are with you."

"It's simply out of the question," he replied.

"Then could they be in the next room?"

"No. Please explain to them that this is something I will have to do alone. The decision is mine alone and I need to face the cameras alone."

It's going to be like that when you face the judgment bar of God. In that hour you, like President Nixon, must stand alone to give an account for what you have done.

Your dad, as much as he would like to, cannot answer for your actions. Your mother, as much as she loves you, cannot change the record you make for yourself. From the time you are able to understand the difference between right and wrong—from that moment, you must be accountable to God for what you do.

JIMMY CARTER

Will a man rob God? Yet ye have robbed me. But ye say, Wherein have we robbed thee? In tithes and offerings. Malachi 3:8.

Jimmy sat on the edge of his seat and waited for the collection plate to come his way. He reached his right hand into the pocket of his Sunday pants and felt the penny his father had given him for the offering.

I don't want to give away my nice shiny penny, Jimmy thought. *I could buy lots of things with a penny.*

"Then keep your penny," a little voice seemed to say. "Just pretend to put it in the collection plate. No one will know the difference."

A sly smile turned up the corners of Jimmy's mouth. What a good idea!

"Better still, while your hand is in the plate pretending, why not take another penny out? Then you'll have two pennies and you can buy twice as much stuff," the tempter continued.

Jimmy reached for the collection plate with his left hand. His right hand came out of his pocket and into the plate. When it came out of the plate, there was a second penny hidden inside.

He was quite pleased with himself until he got home. He took the two pennies out of his pocket and laid them on the dresser while he changed into his play clothes. Just then his father came into the room.

"Where did these two pennies come from?" he asked.

"Er—uh—um."

"Jimmy, look at me. Did you take a penny out of the offering?"

Frightened, the boy nodded his head.

"I'm going to have to whip you, Jimmy," Mr. Carter said sadly. "You must understand the wrong of what you did. It's bad enough to steal from anyone, but today you have robbed God. You have stolen the money that belonged to Him."

The peachtree switching he got was painful enough that Jimmy still remembered it 50 years later when he was president of the United States. He said, "That was the last time I ever thought about stealing."

ANWAR EL-SADAT

Evening, and morning, and at noon, will I pray. Psalm 55:17.

"God is greatest!" Four times the muezzin repeated the call to worship from atop the minaret of the al-Aqsa Mosque in Jerusalem.

Inside the mosque that January day in 1977 was Anwar el-Sadat, president of Egypt. He knelt with hundreds of other Muslims, facing Mecca.

"I confess that there is no God but Allah!" His voice blended with the others as he bent forward, touching his forehead to the ground.

That historic visit occurred during his trip to Israel, where he went seeking a way to stop the hostilities between his country and that land. It was the beginning of communications that led to the signing of the Egyptian-Israeli peace treaty two years later at Camp David in the United States.

While Sadat was at Camp David, his host, Jimmy Carter, faced an unusual problem in scheduling conferences. President Sadat could not be interrupted during the five times a day when Muslims are required to pray. No matter where President Sadat went, he kept up his daily prayer schedule.

"To me, God is everything that I cherish," Sadat said once. "I believe that everything comes from God and God is everything. I wouldn't think of missing my appointments with Him."

Five times a day for nearly 60 years Mr. Sadat had prostrated himself in prayer. More than 100,000 times he had touched his forehead to the floor. As a result there was a dark callus in the center of his forehead.

And so President Carter and Prime Minister Begin waited while President Sadat prayed.

Are you that much in earnest about keeping your appointments with God? Do you remember to pray when you are staying overnight with a friend? Or are you ashamed to let it be known that you pray before you go to bed? Are you embarrassed to bow your head and ask the blessing when you are eating out in a restaurant? How much does God mean to you?

JOHN ELIOT

He that giveth unto the poor shall not lack. Proverbs 28:27.

"Here's your salary, Pastor," the church treasurer said, handing over a bundle of money tied in a large handkerchief. "It's all there, nearly 10 pounds!"

"You certainly have tied it up well," Pastor Eliot said. He smiled as he saw the number of knots the treasurer had made.

"That's to keep you from giving it all away before you get home," the treasurer answered. "You are really much too generous, Pastor."

"Ah, but I can't help giving to those in need," Pastor Eliot replied, placing the bundle of money into his coat pocket. "Besides, do I look like I'm starving?"

"Well . . . no, sir," the treasurer admitted, for John Eliot was a portly gentleman with full, rounded cheeks and a double chin.

Instead of going directly home, John Eliot turned down a side street of Roxbury, Massachusetts to where a poor family lived on the edge of town.

"How are things going?" Pastor Eliot asked, but his practiced eye noticed the sunken cheeks of the children, the furrowed brow of the mother, and the barrenness of the table.

"The Lord wants me to share something with you," he said as he drew out the handkerchief and laid it on the table. The children gathered around as he tried to undo the knots. It seemed the more he pulled, the tighter they became.

"Never mind," he said, handing the handkerchief with his whole month's salary wrapped inside to the needy mother. "The Lord must have meant it all for you."

There wasn't a happier man in all Roxbury than John Eliot as he walked home emptyhanded. He had no doubt that the Lord would return all he had given away.

Besides being the pastor of a church in Roxbury, John Eliot traveled by horseback to visit surrounding Indian villages. He won more than a thousand of the Indians to Christ and trained 24 Indian pastors. In addition, he translated the Bible into Algonquian for his Indian converts.

344

DAVID BRAINERD

Who maketh . . . his ministers a flame of fire. Hebrews 1:7.

Two hundred forty-four years ago the land of New Jersey and Pennsylvania was wild country inhabited by Indians, wolves, bear, and deer. At the forks of the Delaware River, near present-day Easton, Pennsylvania, there was a small clearing where stood a settler's log cabin.

Inside the bare room, a pot of cornmeal mush bubbled over an open fire, while at the rough table sat a thin young man writing by the light of a tallow candle. The man paused a moment to stare into the fire, then he dipped his quill in ink and wrote, "Oh, that I could be 'a flame of fire' in the service of my God!" The writer was David Brainerd, missionary to the Indians.

Was he lonely? Yes. Whole months went by without his seeing another English person.

Was he strong? No. He became weak from constant exposure, inadequate food, and the hardships of pioneer life. He died of tuberculosis before he was 30.

Were the Indians responsive? No, not at first. At times he became so discouraged that he spent a whole day without food, on his knees in the forest, crying to God to send His Spirit to change the hearts of the savages.

"Oh, God," he cried out with tears streaming down his cheeks, "I am willing to die if only I can be used to promote Thy kingdom!"

Did God answer his prayer? Yes. On August 8, 1745, after more than two years of labor and tears, he was preaching to a large group of Indians on the story of the prodigal son. Then suddenly it seemed as if the power of God came like a mighty wind, pushing the Indians to their knees.

"They were universally praying and crying for mercy in every part of the house," he wrote afterwards. Drunkards were changed, a witch doctor was saved, and the whole assembly converted by the power of God.

When I consider how God used David Brainerd, my heart cries out, "Oh, God, make me 'a flame of fire' to bring Your warmth and love to a cold world."

345

HANS EGEDE

Who delivered us from so great a death. 2 Corinthians 1:10.

The captain of the Danish ship *Hope* shivered in spite of the fur-lined parka he wore. An icy wind whipped the rigging of his ship and threw sheets of rain in his face. Above the roar of the storm he could hear the crashing of ice against ice. Shielding his eyes with his hands, he saw a solid wall of ice surrounding his frail ship. Like a giant frost-covered vise the walls of ice were moving in. Within minutes his ship would be smashed to splinters.

Fighting against the wind and the slippery deck, he made his way to the ladder that led to the cabin below where Hans Egede and his family were on their knees praying.

"We're going to crash! Prepare to die!" he shouted, then went back to his post.

Gertrude and the children began to sob quietly. The oldest boy, Paul, opened frightened eyes to see his father still kneeling calmly in prayer, his face raised toward heaven.

"O God, save us!" Hans cried. "You made a way in the Red Sea, and I know You are able to make a way now in this wall of ice. Your arm is not shortened that it cannot save. We trust in You now for deliverance, for You have called us to this land to do Your work."

Suddenly the wall of ice parted as though split by a mighty wedge. The amazed captain steered his ship through the channel into open sea.

"You can stop praying now, Pastor," the captain shouted down the ladder. "A way opened in the wall of ice. We are sailing now in open sea!"

"Praise the Lord!" Hans said. "He has delivered us from certain death." The next moment Hans, Gertrude, Paul, and the other three children were in each other's arms, laughing and crying and praising God for what He had done.

Later that day, July 3, 1721, the *Hope* anchored in a safe harbor. Hans Egede and his family set foot on land for the first time in two months, excited to be the first missionaries to Greenland.

WILLIAM CAREY

Go ye into all the world, and preach the gospel to every creature. Mark 16:15.

"Is there any other business to place before this convention?" Chairman Ryland asked.

In the back of the room 25-year-old William Carey jumped up. "I'm wondering if the Lord's command to the apostles to teach all nations is required of us today."

"Sit down, young man!" Dr. Ryland ordered. "When God wants to convert the heathen, He can do it without your help!"

Obediently Mr. Carey sat down, but he didn't stop thinking about what he had said. He went home to study his Bible and read all he could find about other nations. He made a large map of the world, which he tacked to the wall of his cobbler's shop. On it he jotted down the facts of the people who lived in each country. The more he studied, the more certain he became that the time was ripe to take the gospel into all the world.

In 1792 William was asked to preach at the Baptist Association meeting. He chose as his text Isaiah 54:2, "Enlarge the place of thy tent."

"The Lord is calling us to take the good news of His saving grace to the heathen who sit in darkness," Carey thundered. "We must look beyond our narrow circle to the farthest corners of earth, where millions have never even heard the name of Christ. We must not only expect great things from God, but we must attempt great things for Him!"

Here and there men nodded in agreement, but the meeting was dismissed with no action taken. Carey could stand it no longer. He grabbed Pastor Andrew Fuller and exclaimed, "Aren't we going to do anything about it?"

As a result of that meeting a missionary society was formed, and William Carey was sent to India. He stayed there 40 years and translated the Bible into 40 different languages. In spite of all he and hundreds of other missionaries have done in the past 200 years, there are still thousands of villages in India where the name of Christ is not known. Millions don't know that Jesus loves them. Will you go and teach them?

347

SAMUEL MILLS

The field is the world. Matthew 13:38.

A marble globe sitting atop a large granite shaft near Williams College, Williamstown, Massachusetts, is the only monument in the world that is dedicated to a haystack. On it are chiseled the words of today's text and the words "The Birthplace of Foreign Missions, 1806."

Five young men were headed for some willows near the college to have a prayer meeting when rain began to fall. The nearest shelter was a haystack. The rain kept up for some time, and the students discussed their favorite topic, foreign missions.

"I think it's time we in America sent missionaries to foreign fields," declared Samuel Mills, the leader of the group.

"I agree with you," said James Richards. "Wouldn't it be neat to send someone to India to work like William Carey?"

"I don't think now is the time," disagreed Harvey Loomis. "Conditions will be better at a later date."

"While we wait, millions are going into Christless graves," Samuel replied emphasizing his point. "We must send someone immediately!"

"But how?" wondered Byron Green.

"We don't have much money. We aren't even prepared to go yet. We need to finish our schooling first," said Francis Robbins.

"What you say is true," Samuel reasoned, "but we can do all we can to stimulate interest in foreign missions in our school as well as others. We can talk to the experienced pastors and convince them of our idea. We can do it if we will! I know we can!"

"We're with you," the others agreed. "We can do it if we will, so let's do it!"

Soon a missionary society was formed, with the backing of several churches. Adoniram Judson and five other missionaries were sent to India, and others followed.

The field is still the world. The harvest is ripe, but the reapers are few. Thousands of young people like Samuel Mills are needed who will pray . . . and work for a lost world.

ADONIRAM JUDSON

But God said unto him, Thou fool, this night thy soul shall be required of thee. Luke 12:20.

"I'm tired of all this talk about religion!" 20-year-old Adoniram told his father, a Congregational minister. "I don't believe in God anymore, so I see no reason why I shouldn't live the way I want. I'm going to New York to become an actor."

"We're sorry you feel that way," his dad said, "but you're old enough to make your own decisions. Meanwhile, Mother and I will continue to pray for you every day."

Adoniram had a great time in New York City. It was fun to be an actor, traveling from town to town putting on plays. One night the troop was booked into a small country hotel. The owner called Adoniram aside.

"I thought I should tell you that there's a young man dying in the room next to yours," he whispered. "The doctor says he will be gone before morning. I do hope this will not disturb you. The walls are quite thick, and I don't anticipate any trouble."

"Oh, that's dreadful." Adoniram shuddered as he thought of someone dying so close to his bed. "Anyway, I expect I'll sleep well after our long trip. I'm beat!"

The next morning he asked the owner, "Well, did the young man die, as the doctor predicted?"

"Yes," the landlord said.

"What was his name?"

When the owner spoke his name, Adoniram turned pale. He felt sick and hurried from the room lest he faint. Back in his own room, he sat on his bed with his head in his hands and wept. The dead man had been his best friend in college. He was the very one who had influenced Adoniram to give up his faith in God.

"He's gone into eternity," Judson moaned. "He died without God and without hope. That could have been me!"

In that moment Adoniram knew that there was a God and that he too must someday face his Maker. He resigned the theater group and returned to school to study for the ministry.

ROBERT MOFFAT

I shall give thee the heathen for thine inheritance. Psalm 2:8.

"It's raining! It's raining!" Laughing and shouting, the Bechuana natives scurried to their huts near the Kuruman River.

"Where is Hela Ka Rare?" someone wondered. "What did he do to bring the rain?"

"I'll go find out," one man offered. He dashed through the welcome shower to the hut of the witch doctor, only to find him asleep, unaware that the rain had come.

"What did you do to bring the rain?" the visitor asked.

"Uh . . . uh . . . well . . ." The witch doctor looked around his hut, trying to think of a suitable answer. Then he saw his wife over in a corner, shaking a milk sack to make butter. He pointed a bony finger at her and said, "There! My wife is churning rain as fast as she can!"

The man ran back to the waiting villagers to spread the news, "The witch doctor has churned the rain out of a milk sack! What a powerful man! He can do anything!"

But Hela Ka Rare couldn't do quite everything; he couldn't get rid of Robert Moffat.

During one severe drought Hela Ka Rare sat in front of his hut and stared at the sky. A crowd gathered to see him make rain come out of the clouds. He moved his hands in circles and chanted his prayers to the cloud spirits, but nothing happened.

"It's because the missionaries are here!" he proclaimed. "The cloud spirits are angry with us for allowing them to stay. We must get rid of them."

However, Robert Moffatt wasn't about to leave. Even when faced by a chief whose spear was poised to kill, he refused to leave. Instead, he stepped bravely forward and bared his chest. "Go ahead. Kill me," he said. "I am ready to die." Awed by Moffatt's bravery, the villagers let him stay.

Soon thousands were attending his meetings and confessing Jesus as their Saviour. Even Hela Ka Rare gave his heart to the Lord and forsook his evil practices. After 50 years in Africa, the Moffats went home to England, satisfied that the Lord had kept His promise.

ROBERT MORRISON

Not by might, nor by power, but by my spirit, saith the Lord of hosts. Zechariah 4:6.

"I want to work for You, Lord," 25-year-old Robert Morrison prayed. "Please send me to the field where the difficulties are the greatest."

He thought that place surely must be somewhere in the jungles of Africa. Instead, the call came for China. There he would have to deal not with primitive tribesmen but with sophisticated people who boasted a civilization established thousands of years before Christ.

The first obstacle Morrison faced was getting there. When he tried to book passage on an East India Company ship, the captain said, "Sorry! It's against company policy to take missionaries to China!"

Undaunted, Robert took a ship to New York, where he arranged passage on an American trading ship.

"We're going to Macao, a Portuguese trading post near Canton, China," the American captain said. "Is that OK?"

"That's close enough!"

Though happy to sell the missionary passage, the captain was dubious about the results. "Do you really expect to make an impression on the idolatry of the mighty Chinese empire?"

"No, sir," Morrison quietly replied, "but I expect God will!"

Once he was in China, it seemed to Robert that God wasn't in nearly the hurry he was. Progress was painfully slow. It was almost impossible to get a tutor, as the Chinese had been forbidden to teach their language to the foreigners. In spite of this difficulty, Robert mastered the language in two years and began to translate the Bible into Chinese. Because of the death penalty for any who would change religion, it took seven years before the first person accepted Christ.

Although Christian missionaries are no longer welcome in China, there are thousands of faithful Christians in the country who are witnessing for Him. Before Jesus comes the land of China will experience a mighty outpouring of God's Spirit. Pray that it will be soon!

JOSEPH WOLFF

The Lord is good, a strong hold in the day of trouble; and he knoweth them that trust in him. Nahum 1:7.

The year was 1844. In the Muslim city of Bukhara the English missionary Joseph Wolff sat in his prison cell reading his Bible. There was a click of a key in the door and his friend, an old Muslim teacher, entered the room.

"Abdul Samat Khan is determined to kill you," the old man whispered. "There is only one way your life can be saved."

"Become a Muslim? No, thank you."

"You must do it to save your life," the old teacher insisted. "Only say once, 'God is great and Mohammed is His prophet.' Once safely in England, you can continue to be a Christian."

"I cannot deny my Saviour," Joseph replied.

The old man rose then and shook his head in sorrow. He embraced the missionary and said, "I'm afraid I'll never see you alive again. With your attitude, only death can result."

"So be it," the courageous missionary answered. "I will not stop trusting Jesus, even to save my neck."

Wolff knew now that he would be executed. He didn't mind dying, but he dreaded the torture that often preceded death. In his pocket he carried a powerful drug that he could swallow to take away the pain. But as his execution hour approached he threw away the drug, deciding to trust only in Jesus.

Kneeling at the barred window, he prayed, "Thank You, Lord, for being with me in this cell. Please take care of my family. Give me the strength to endure torture and death for Your sake."

Arising, he went to the low table beside his bed and picked up his Bible. On one of the flyleaves he wrote, "My dearest Georgiana. I have loved you unto death. Bukhara, 1844."

He heard then the sound of marching guards. The cell door opened and he was taken before the ruler of Bukhara.

"Today I have received a letter from the shah of Persia demanding your release. Here are clothes and a man who will travel with you. Go. You are a free man!"

"Thank You, Lord" was all Joseph could say.

MARCUS WHITMAN

And unto him that smiteth thee on the one cheek offer also the other. Luke 6:29.

The crowd of angry Indians crowded closer around Dr. Marcus Whitman, shaking their fists. From the door of the mission house his wife, Narcissa, watched as Tilkanaik stepped forward and hit her husband on the chest.

"Oh, God, help Marcus not to get angry," she prayed.

Marcus did not strike back. This seemed to anger the Indians even more. Tilkanaik's face was distorted in rage as he reached out and seized the doctor's left ear, giving it a twist. The braves all stood tense, waiting for the missionary to strike back so the fight could begin.

Marcus gritted his teeth and said nothing. As soon as the Indian released his hold, Marcus calmly turned his head, offering his right ear. Furious now, the enraged chief twisted both ears. Still Marcus did nothing.

Determined to get Whitman to retaliate, Tilkanaik snatched off the doctor's straw hat and threw it in a mud puddle.

"Please pick it up for me," Dr. Whitman calmly asked one of the Indians, who did as asked. Without another word Dr. Whitman put the hat back on his head, mud and all.

Twice more the angry chief tore the hat off Whitman's head and threw it in the mud. Twice more Whitman put it back on.

"It's impossible to make the White man fight," one Indian mumbled.

"See how bravely he stands there," noticed another.

Finally old Tilkanaik gave up and retreated with his warriors.

Narcissa ran to her husband then, her eyes shining. "Marcus Whitman, you are a man and a Christian to be proud of!"

The next time a bully tries to pick a fight with you, stop a moment and consider your three choices: fight, flight, or focus on Christ's method of silent confrontation. Which do you think takes the most courage? Which is the most effective method? Why?

HUDSON TAYLOR

Open thy mouth wide, and I will fill it. Psalm 81:10.

"Whatever are we going to do?" Mrs. Jones wailed. "We have no food in the house, and company is coming for supper."

"All I have is one Chinese cash," her husband sighed. "We'll just have to keep trusting the Lord to supply our need."

"But can't you do something?"

"My dear, Hudson and I have been doing something. We've been praying about it all morning."

"Perhaps there's something in the house we could sell," suggested Hudson Taylor, who boarded with the Joneses.

After searching the house, they decided on a wall clock. Mr. Jones and Mr. Taylor took it to a clock merchant, who said, "I'll keep it for a week. If it works at the end of the week, I'll pay you the money."

"Oh, no!" Mr. Taylor said, retrieving the clock. "We need the money today."

Returning home, they looked for something else to sell, and chose the iron stove. Perhaps they could sell it at the foundry across the river. They put it in a wheelbarrow and took it to the river, where they looked for a boat.

"That will cost you two cash," the boatman said.

"But we have only one cash!" exclaimed Mr. Jones.

There was nothing to do but wheel the stove back home. By now it was lunchtime, but there was nothing to eat. They searched the empty cupboards and finally discovered a tin containing a little cocoa. They mixed it with hot water, and that was lunch.

"Only four hours until our company comes," said Mr. Taylor. "There is nothing left to do but pray. God knows our needs. He has told us to ask and we will receive."

The three missionaries got on their knees again and began to plead with God to keep His promise found in today's text. While they were still praying, there was a knock on the door. It was the mailman with several letters. Among them was a letter from London mailed two months before. It contained a bank draft, or check. The two men cashed it, then hurried to the market to buy the groceries needed to prepare supper.

MARY SLESSOR

To another the gifts of healing by the same Spirit. 1 Corinthians 12:9.

One hundred years ago an intrepid little Scotswoman, Mary Slessor, was famous along the Calabar River of Nigeria for her gifts of healing. With knowledge gained from reading medical books and with courage and faith in the Great Physician, she worked miracles and saved hundreds of lives.

One day the chief of a fierce tribe living in Okuri became seriously ill. His slaves and wives were already chained in anticipation of his death, ready to be slaughtered the moment he ceased to breathe.

"Send for the white Ma of Ekenge," one of his wives begged the headman. "She has powerful medicine."

"I will go with you in the morning," Mary promised the messenger when he explained the situation.

"No," Edem, the Ekenge chief, advised. "It is an eight-hour journey. The rivers are in flood, and deep mud covers all the paths you must take. If he dies, you will be killed."

"Regardless, I must go," Mary said, and made her preparations.

Heavy rain was falling the next morning as Mary set out at dawn. Her shoes soon fell apart in the water and mud, and she walked on barefooted. Drenched and mud-spattered, she arrived that evening in Okuri to examine the chief.

"All my bones feel as if they are on fire and a devil is pounding in my head," he groaned. His temperature was 104°F. and his dark skin had a yellowish tinge.

Mary had no idea what was wrong with him. She breathed a quick prayer for guidance as she looked through her medical bag. She treated him then with a mixture of aspirin and quinine, followed by a dose of bromide. She sat up with him all that night and the next day. Toward the next evening his fever subsided.

"God has heard our prayers," Mary told the waiting natives. "Your chief will live." After three days she went back home, happy that once again she had been able to bring healing and the message of God's love to someone in need.

JAMES CHALMERS

Save me, O God; for the waters are come in unto my soul.
Psalm 69:1.

"Come see my boat!" James called to his friends. "The caulking is dry and she's ready to go!"

"Oh, it's only an old herring box," one of the boys said when he saw it. "That's no boat."

"Yes, it is," James insisted. "See how I've sealed it with tar I got from Ol' Pete, the fisherman."

"I'll bet it won't float," scoffed another friend.

"Of course it will," said James. "We'll take turns riding in it. I'll go first and show you how it works. You guys take the rope so I don't get carried away by the current."

James pushed his boat into the water and jumped in. The box floated, and his friends ran along the shore pulling James and his boat through the water.

"This is fun!" James called. "Who wants to be next?"

"Me! Me! Me!" they all shouted at once. Then the line snapped. The boys watched, horrified, as the current gripped the herring box and carried it far away from shore.

"Help! Help!" James screamed.

Further down the shore a Scottish fisherman looked up from mending his net to see John being swept toward the Firth of Clyde. He pushed his boat into the water and began rowing with all his strength toward the tiny dot in the middle of the stream.

"Hurry!" James cried. "My boat is sinking!" The waves were tossing the small box around like a cork, filling it with water.

Soon the fisherman's boat was beside his box. Strong arms reached down and picked him out of the water just as the box disappeared beneath the waves. The boy the fisherman rescued that day was James Chalmers, who grew up to be a pioneer missionary in New Guinea.

Do you have an awful feeling of panic when you look at your life? Are the waves of sin and guilt about to sink your boat? You cannot save yourself. Cry out to God; help is only a prayer away.

ALEXANDER MACKAY

Then said Jesus unto him, Go, and do thou likewise. Luke 10:37.

"Come into my office a minute," the managing director of a Berlin locomotive plant called to his engineer.

"I hope nothing is wrong," Alec said.

"On the contrary, I'm very pleased with your work. In fact, we're planning to build a plant in Russia and it's my idea to put you in charge of that operation. Are you interested?"

"Wow! What an opportunity!" Alec exclaimed.

"I thought you'd see it that way. When would you be ready to leave?"

"I'm sorry, sir, but I can't accept your offer, as exciting as it sounds."

"But why not? Is it the salary? The distance?"

"No, none of those. You see . . . " Alec hesitated. "I have already pledged myself to work of a different nature."

"I don't understand. Has another firm offered you more money?"

"No, sir. It's a promise I made to God. I've decided to go as a missionary to Africa."

"Whatever for?" the manager asked.

"Ever since I read about the sacrifice David Livingstone made to take the gospel of Christ to the people of Africa, I have felt God calling me to work for Him there. I want to help finish the work Livingstone began."

"I must say I consider it a total waste of your talents, Mackay." The businessman then got up and ushered Alec to the door.

That night Alec opened his diary and read the words he had written on May 3, 1874: "This day, last year, David Livingstone died—a Scotsman and a Christian, loving God and his neighbor. He gave his life for Africa. 'Go, and do thou likewise.' "

Alexander Mackay quit his job shortly after that to follow in the footsteps of his hero. When he died after 12 years in Africa, someone said, "Africa has lost the best missionary she has had since David Livingstone."

Could God be calling you to a similar sacrifice?

WILFRED GRENFELL

A friend loveth at all times. Proverbs 17:17.

At the age of 14 Wilfred Grenfell left home to attend the famous public school Marlborough College. Within days he had been nicknamed The Beast, partly because of his large, untidy mop of hair and partly because he was such a good wrestler.

Wilfred's best friend was called Mad G because he thought of nothing, it seemed, but science. His hands were always stained from work in the laboratory, and he could talk for hours about his dream inventions. He cared nothing for his personal appearance and refused to become interested in sports.

The two boys were opposites in many ways. Wilfred was strong, robust, and athletic, while Mad G was frail, sensitive, and bookish. Wilfred found school easy and spent little time on his lessons while Mad G seemed to always have his nose in a book. While Wilfred was popular, Mad G was either ignored by others or picked on by the bullies.

One day on the way out of class someone hit Mad G with a lump of coal. Wilfred was at his side in a moment. "Your head is bleeding badly," he said. "We've got to get you to the hospital."

"Don't tell anyone how I got hurt," Mad G begged. "If the headmaster finds out, then the other boys will hate me even more than they do."

"OK," agreed Wilfred. "But I'm going to make sure something like this doesn't happen again. I'll sit with you in all our classes and if I catch anybody picking on you I'm going to give him what he deserves!"

Wilfred never had to carry out his threat. Nobody wanted to tangle with The Beast.

Wilfred Grenfell became a physician who gave his life to work in the wild, desolate mass of ice, snow, and rocks called Labrador. There he was a friend to fishermen and Eskimos, as he had been to Mad G at Marlborough College.

A friend is someone who lets you in when the whole world shuts you out. A friend accepts you, "warts and all." A friend is what Wilfred was to Mad G.

ALEXANDER DUFF

Oh that men would praise the Lord for his goodness, and for his wonderful works to the children of men! Psalm 107:8.

Anne clung to her husband, Alexander Duff, as their small lifeboat tossed about on the troubled sea like a fishing cork. In the half light of a stormy dawn they saw that the ship on which they had come from Scotland had gone down.

All night they and a few others had drifted aimlessly on the angry sea somewhere off the Cape of Good Hope. Mr. and Mrs. Duff were bound for India, but they had no idea how they'd get there.

Suddenly someone shouted, "Land!"

Straining their eyes against the wind, Alexander and Anne saw the form of a small island rising out of the water. The men in the boat began to row with increased vigor, and soon all were safely on what appeared to be an uninhabited island.

"Hey! Look what I found!" someone yelled. The man was waving a water-soaked Bible. Opening it, he read the name Alexander Duff.

"I can't believe it!" Alexander exclaimed. "The last time I saw my Bible it was lying on my bed in the cabin where I had been praying when the call came to abandon ship. It has followed me all these miles of ocean to this island. God is so good!"

"Let's have a prayer meeting," someone suggested. "Mr. Duff will read to us from his Bible that can swim!"

There on that windswept beach, with sea gulls crying and waves thundering, the bedraggled passengers gathered around as Alexander read Psalm 107, called the traveler's psalm. Read the whole psalm right now. Notice especially verses 23-31, which talk about those who "go down to the sea in ships."

"Those verses pretty well tell our experience," Duff said, and the others nodded their heads in agreement. They knelt then on the muddy shore and praised the Lord for His goodness to them in saving their lives, and especially Duff's precious Bible.

It wasn't long before two islanders found them and gave them penguin eggs to eat. The same men rowed 40 miles to the Cape of Good Hope to get help for the shipwrecked people.

SUNDAR SINGH

Christ died for our sins according to the scriptures.
1 Corinthians 15:3.

Fifteen-year-old Sundar Singh laughed as he watched flames destroy the Bible he had thrown into the fire. His Hindu friends stood with him joking as the book burned.

That night when his friends had gone home and the fire had gone out, the boy kicked the charred remains and felt suddenly sick inside.

"What have I done?" he moaned as he tossed on his bed. "I have destroyed a holy book. I shouldn't have done it, even though I don't agree with what it says."

For three nights Sundar Singh couldn't sleep. On the third night he opened his eyes for the hundredth time and noticed the clock said 4:30. Then, lifting his eyes toward the ceiling, he noticed a strange globe of light.

He got up and opened the door to see if there was something outside causing the light. There was nothing. He lay back down and stared at it. Out of the light appeared the form of Christ. He spoke in Hindustani, "Why do you persecute Me? See, I have died on the cross for you and for the whole world."

Sundar Singh quickly bowed before the Lord, his face to the ground. Later he wrote in his book *With and Without Christ:* "My heart was filled with inexpressible joy and peace, and my whole life was entirely changed. To all eternity I shall never forget His glorious and loving face, nor the few words which He spoke."

The next day he told his friends, "I am a Christian now. These hands that burned in scorn the Word of God are now redeemed by Christ's love. My only ground of pardon and forgiveness is in the cross of Jesus, my Lord."

Determined to change his son's mind, Mr. Singh sent him to visit a wealthy uncle. The uncle showed Sundar a large safe full of money and jewels. "These are yours," he said, "if you will renounce Christianity. Please don't disgrace your family by being a Christian."

"If you offered me the whole world I could not turn my back on Jesus, who died for me," Sundar said.

JOHN HYDE

Pray without ceasing. 1 Thessalonians 5:17.

If there was ever anyone who prayed without ceasing it was John Hyde, missionary to India. Once he prayed for 36 hours, kneeling on the floor with his Bible open before him. On another occasion he prayed for 10 days without any food or sleep. He was known to go for a whole month with very little food or rest so that he could pray. He often prayed all night, then went the next day to witness about God's love. "Praying Hyde," the people called him — "the man who never sleeps."

Why did he pray so much? His answer was "We must keep near Jesus. It is He who draws souls to Himself through us." When he wasn't praying, John Hyde was working to bring men and women and young people to Jesus.

Often "Praying Hyde" would confront people he met on the train. Sometimes he rode past his station because he wanted to continue talking to someone about Jesus. One of these was a teenager who had been a Christian but decided he was missing a lot of fun.

"I'm tired of hearing about God," the boy told Mr. Hyde, who happened to be on the same train with him. "I'm going home to Lahore to have a good time. No more of those stupid rules for me. I'm going to do what I want."

"Please don't turn from the Saviour." The missionary spoke earnestly as tears ran down his cheeks. "Why are you leaving Him who loves you so much?"

"Come on, man, get off my back," the youth demanded. "I told you I don't want to hear any more about religion!"

"I'll be praying for you," the missionary said as the young man turned away.

The next morning the conductor noticed the same young man was back on the train, going in the opposite direction. "That was a mighty short visit," he commented.

"I'm going back to see Missionary Hyde," the boy admitted. "I couldn't sleep last night. All I could see was him and his tears. I want to tell him I've decided to be a Christian after all."

FERDINAND A. STAHL

*Ah Lord God! . . . there is nothing too hard for thee."
Jeremiah 32:17.*

Missionary Stahl emerged from a small stone house in a remote mountain village were he had gone to treat the sick. Walking over to the corral where he had left his horse, he found the animal missing.

"Someone has stolen my horse!" he shouted. Soon he was surrounded by friendly Indians who promised to help him find the thief. They fanned out in all directions, leaving Mr. Stahl to walk the main road.

Not a mile down the road Stahl saw a man on horseback coming his direction, and sure enough, he was riding the stolen horse. The missionary tried to act as if he didn't notice, hoping he could get close enough to grab the bridle. He was within 50 feet of the horse when the rider suddenly wheeled and sped off in the opposite direction.

Mr. Stahl's shoulders sagged as he walked back to the village. He was particularly worried because the horse was borrowed from Chief Comacho.

As he walked he prayed, "Dear Lord, I read in my Bible that once You helped a young man find a borrowed axhead that was lost, so I know You are willing to help those who lose borrowed things. You know I've borrowed that horse from Chief Comacho. Please help me get it back. I know nothing is too hard for You."

Going back to his host in the village, the missionary reported, "I saw a man riding the stolen horse, but I couldn't catch him."

"Your horse is here," the Indian replied. "Just a few minutes ago a little boy came leading the horse. He said a man had asked him to deliver it to my house."

Missionary Stahl mounted the horse and continued his journey to help those in need. For 30 years he and his wife served God in South America, first in the Andes Mountains of Peru and later along the Amazon River of Brazil. Time and again God worked miracles in their lives, proving that He can indeed do anything!

ABRAM LA RUE

I the Lord have called thee in righteousness, and will hold thine hand, and will keep thee. Isaiah 42:6.

An old man sat in the door of his shepherd's hut in California and wrote a letter to the General Conference of Seventh-day Adventists, Battle Creek, Michigan. It went something like this: "Dear Brothers in the Lord,

"I have recently received the Advent message and regret that I have wasted the past 60 years. However, I've been passing out truth-filled literature. Already I've prepared a good group of interested believers in Tehama County, and young W. M. Healy is working with them.

"However, I sense a distinct call of God to take this message to the people of China. I'm familiar with that part of the world, as I visited many ports there as a seaman.

"Sincerely yours,

"Abram La Rue"

The General Conference brethren smiled as they read his request. Of course they couldn't send someone so old to China. He had no useful training and would never learn the language. They wrote back something like this:

"We do not think it advisable to send someone of your age into such a difficult field. We suggest that you confine your witnessing to the islands of the Pacific. Of course, we have no funds available and you would need to do so at your own expense.

"Sincerely yours,

"General Conference Committee"

"I know just the place!" Brother La Rue said, clapping his hands. "Hong Kong is an island, and it's only a mile from mainland China. I'm sure God has called me and will be with me even if the church doesn't think so!"

Working his way across the Pacific, he landed at last in Hong Kong. There he began a literature ministry among the foreign sailors. He also printed some tracts in Chinese. By the time the first official Adventist missionaries arrived 13 years later, La Rue had seven people ready for baptism.

ASA T. ROBINSON

Ask, and it shall be given you. Matthew 7:7.

A. T. Robinson sat in the spacious office of Cecil Rhodes, premier of Cape Colony, and watched him write a letter of introduction to Dr. Jameson in Bulawayo, where Adventists were hoping to open a mission station.

Mr. Rhodes smiled as he finished the letter. Folding it carefully, he placed it in an envelope and addressed it before handing it over to Elder Robinson.

"Give this to Dr. Jameson when you get to Bulawayo," he said. "He will cooperate with you."

Elder Robinson entrusted the letter to Peter Wessels and A. Druillard. Traveling by oxcart, the two men took six weeks to make the journey to Bulawayo.

After reading the letter from Premier Rhodes, Dr. Jameson asked, "Gentlemen, how much land do you people want?"

Peter scratched his head a moment. He wasn't sure what he should say. After all, they didn't know the price of the land and they had only $2,500 to spend on the project.

If he has any brains he'll ask for 6,000 acres, Brother Druillard thought, but he kept quiet as they had agreed that Wessels was to be the spokesman.

"Well, sir, to tell you the truth, we need 12,000 acres, but it will depend on the terms upon which we can get it," Peter said at last.

"Terms?" laughed Dr. Jameson. "Rhodes commands me to give you all the land you need. Do you want better terms than that?"

The 12,000 acres they chose was 35 miles west of Bulawayo. It had a wooded area for the mission buildings, and much good farm land. They named it Solusi Mission, after the chief of the largest village on their property.

I would love to have heard Wessels and Druillard talk that night around their campfire. I'm sure Mr. Druillard was glad he was not the spokesman, for they would have had only 6,000 acres. I'm sure Mr. Wessels was wishing he had asked for 20,000 acres! It is one of the rules of life that we don't reach higher than the goals we set; we don't receive more than what we ask.

MERRITT C. WARREN

For it is written, He shall give his angels charge over thee, to keep thee. Luke 4:10.

Seventy-five years ago it was dangerous to travel after dark in the mountains of Szechwan Province, China. Robber bands lurked in the shadows, waiting for lonely travelers. Pastor Warren had sent his carriers on ahead, and now he walked through the mountains alone and without a light.

Crossing over a bridge, he began climbing his second mountain when he noticed a large house built about 150 feet from the bridge, to the right of the path. Warm rays of light shone from its windows. As Pastor Warren came even with the house, the large double doors opened, and two tall men stepped out onto the veranda.

"May I borrow a light?" the missionary asked. "My lantern has gone out."

"Certainly," one of the men answered. He went back inside and returned with a piece of flaming bamboo, which he used to light the candle in Pastor Warren's paper lantern. "Where are you going?" he inquired.

"To Chintaipu."

"I am going that way myself. May I travel with you?"

"I'd be glad for the company," Elder Warren said, though he wasn't sure he really was. Maybe this was one of the robbers. He determined to keep his eyes open.

As if reading his thoughts, the man said, "There are many robbers on this road. Every night they work this section of the trail. I'm glad I can travel with you."

After some time they came to a fork in the path. "This is where I must leave you," his companion said.

"Aren't you going to Chintaipu?"

"No, I'm turning here. It isn't far now to the city. You will be safe. Thank you for letting me walk with you."

The next time Pastor Warren traveled that road he came through in daylight. He recognized the bridge he had crossed. However, there was no house on the side of the mountain, nor any level place where a house could have been. Suddenly he understood that an angel had walked with him that night.

ANDREW G. STEWART

Blessed are the peacemakers. Matthew 5:9.

Into the Sabbath stillness of the island of Atchin a shot rang out and native drums began to beat.

"Our neighbors are quarreling," Pastor Stewart told his wife. "I'll go see if there's anything I can do." At the chief's compound he found scores of painted, armed men sitting around their leader.

"I come as your friend," he said. "Can't we do something to settle the matter without fighting?"

"It is the fault of the other village," one warrior declared. "They started the fight."

"I will talk to the other chief," the missionary said. "Perhaps we can make peace."

At the other village he found another council of war. "I come as your friend," he said. "Why are you preparing for war?"

"One of their men has tried to steal one of our women," Chief Maltek Mare growled. "We went to the chief of his village with our complaint and he fired his gun at us. Now we will have war. It is his fault."

"Isn't there some way we can stop the quarrel before blood is shed?" Pastor Stewart asked. "Come to the mission compound tomorrow and I will listen to you talk."

"We will come, but the guns must be left at home," Chief Maltek Mare proposed.

The missionary carried the news to the other village; then he went home to wait. All night the threatening drums beat the sounds of war. Just as dawn was breaking the rhythm changed.

"We have decided not to have war," the chiefs sent word. "We will come to the mission to talk."

After everybody had spoken, an old man suggested they follow an ancient ceremony to seal their agreement. They dug a hole, and all the warriors of both sides spit into it. Then in the hole they planted a young tree, living symbol of their pledge of peace.

I don't know about the spitting part, but I like the idea of planting something to symbolize the peace of two people. What a neat way to landscape our schools, churches, and homes!

HARRY WILLIS MILLER

And it shall come to pass, as soon as the soles of the feet of the priests . . . shall rest in the waters . . . that the waters of Jordan shall be cut off. Joshua 3:13.

Harry Miller, medical student, was afraid of dead bodies. The thought of a corpse sent shivers down his spine and made his knees weak. As a boy he had run into the cornfield to hide from passing funerals. At the hospital he gave the morgue a wide berth. He avoided all contact with corpses until his friend Stoops got a job helping with postmortems.

"Come to the morgue tonight and help me," Stoops offered.

"No, thanks." Harry tried to sound nonchalant. "I really couldn't spare the time from my study."

"How better to study anatomy than in the morgue with a real body to poke into?" Stoops teased.

"Some other time, maybe," Harry replied. "I've got to go now." He had to get away before Stoops saw his goose bumps.

A couple of nights later, Stoops renewed his invitation. "An old lady fell down the hospital steps and we're going to do a postmortem tonight. It will really be interesting!"

"I really don't have the time . . ."

"I do believe you're scared, Harry Miller!"

Harry knew that if word got out that he was afraid of corpses, the other students would tease the life out of him. There was nothing to do but go. "OK, I'll be there," he said.

He went that night, trembling all the way. What if he should faint? Yet somehow he had to get hold of himself and go into that room with the dead body. He prayed, took a deep breath, and pushed the door of the morgue open. The moment he stepped into the room his fear left. Shortly after, Harry Miller applied for a job in the morgue!

Fear sometimes comes rushing toward us like a mighty river in flood. We stand before it trembling, unable to see a way through. Like the priests at the river Jordan, like Harry Miller at the door of the morgue, we need to step forward into our fear. As we do, it will roll back like the waters of the Jordan, and we can cross over to confidence and joy.

LILLIAN FORD

I will say of the Lord, He is my refuge and my fortress: my God; in him will I trust. Psalm 91:2.

Lillian Ford was sitting in her home outside of Cajababa, Ecuador, visiting with Mrs. Schwerin, a guest from Quito, when blood-curdling yells and the sound of gunfire brought them to their feet. They watched as poncho-clad Indians raced down the hills waving knives and clubs, only to be mowed down by soldiers in the valley.

"What's going on?" Mrs. Schwerin cried.

"The Indians have been celebrating the Feast of the Three Wise Men and have been drinking too much liquor," Lillian answered. "Also, we've heard rumors that they were planning an uprising against the White people. That's why the soldiers are there."

"I wish our husbands were home now," Mrs. Schwerin said.

Lillian saw some Indians who had been to their clinic running past her. "Stop!" she shouted. "The soldiers will kill you if you go on!" But the angry Indians paid no heed.

Meanwhile, the husbands of the two women were trying to reach home to protect their wives and property, but the road was blocked by hostile Indians who pelted them with stones. Fleeing White settlers told them tales of horror and urged them not to go on. At last there was nothing to do but go back to town and pray for the safety of the women at the mission.

The next day the battle was over and the men were able to reach home. "Praise God! You're safe!" Pastor Ford said, taking Lillian in his arms.

Later, Lillian asked some friendly Indians why they had not attacked the mission.

"The men were afraid when they saw your house guarded by armed soldiers," he replied.

Mrs. Ford's eyes opened wide. There had been no Ecuadorian soldiers in the mission compound that day. A warm glow of thankfulness came over her as she realized angels had guarded her and her friend.

LEO B. HALLIWELL

They shall bear thee up in their hands, lest thou dash thy foot against a stone. Psalm 91:12.

Leo Halliwell steered the *Luziero* up a desolate stretch of river where the jungle closed in deep and green on both sides. Suddenly he noticed three well-dressed men in a canoe waving to him.

"Can you give us a tow upstream?" one man called.

Although Leo had a rule of "no hitchhikers," something impressed him to stop. "Throw them a line, Jack," he called to his 15-year-old son.

Two men climbed aboard, while the third stayed in the canoe. They stood beside Leo at the wheel, and one of them said, "Which side of the rocks are you going on?"

"What rocks?" the missionary asked.

The man grabbed the wheel out of Leo's hand and turned it completely around. The boat shot away from the bank out into the middle of the river.

Leo looked back and saw, not 20 feet away from where they had been heading, the jagged points of hundreds of rocks beneath the surface of the water. One more second and the mission boat would have been ripped to shreds on the rocks.

"Oh, thank you!" Leo exclaimed. "You saved our boat and likely our lives!"

The man smiled and said nothing. In a few minutes they had passed the dangerous section of river, and the hitchhiker gave the wheel back to Leo. "Sir, thank you for the ride," he said. "If you don't mind stopping, we'll get out."

Leo thought it strange, since there were still no signs of habitation along the riverbank. He stopped, and the two men climbed back into the canoe and pushed off into the current.

"Watch where they go," Leo called to Jack. "I didn't see a boat landing."

"Dad, they've disappeared!" Jack called.

Leo turned from the wheel. The river was empty. There was no bend in the river, no sign of struggle, no cry for help. The three men and their boat were gone. As Leo turned back to the wheel the words of today's text came to his mind.

PAUL BRAND

And that thou bring the poor that are cast out to thy house?
Isaiah 58:7.

Sadogopan was an outcast, rejected, shunned, ignored, despised. He was a beggar and lived with others like himself in a miserable hutment outside of town. He was a leper.

Born in a respectable, educated family, his future looked bright until that awful day as a teenager when the doctor shook his head and said, "It's leprosy. There's nothing I can do."

So Sadogopan left home to live the life of a leper. Ugly sores developed on his toes. His hands became paralyzed, the fingers curled tightly against the palms. His face was deformed.

Then one day another beggar came limping into his hut with good news. "There is a doctor in Vellore . . . an Englishman. . . . He can make lepers well again!"

With hope in his heart Sadogopan set out for Vellore. When he tried to get on a bus, he was ordered off. Never mind, he would walk. Eventually he arrived, his feet bleeding, his clothes in rags.

"Where is the leprosy doctor?" he inquired.

"You must mean Dr. Paul Brand. Just follow that road, and you'll come to his house."

Sadogopan hobbled the last few yards to the Brand home, where he was met by a smiling English woman.

"I'm so sorry," she said. "Dr. Brand is out of town."

Sadogopan turned to go, the disappointment almost too much to bear. Mrs. Brand quickly read in his bleeding feet and drooping shoulders the story of his long journey.

"Don't go away," she called after him. "Come and stay in our home until the doctor returns. We would be honored to have you." For the first time since he contracted leprosy, he felt wanted, loved, and important as a human being.

I doubt if you have any lepers calling at your door, but there are kids in every school who are treated as though they were lepers. Other kids don't want to sit with them or play with them. They are the outcasts whom Jesus expects you to befriend today. Will you?

IDA SCUDDER

I will send a famine in the land, not a famine of bread, . . .
but of hearing the words of the Lord. Amos 8:11.

Seven-year-old Ida Scudder closed her eyes against the glare of the noontime sun as she emerged from the coolness of the stone church. Beyond the church compound the parched, brown countryside testified of months without rain.

"Mama, may I ride home with you and Mary Ayah in the bullock cart?" Ida asked.

"You don't want to walk with your brothers?"

"Not today. It's too hot."

"Very well, up you go." Her mother gave her a boost to the straw-covered bed of the wooden cart, then climbed up herself. Mary Ayah, who had cared for Ida since she was a baby, joined them. She pulled her red sari over her head for protection against the sun as the cart rattled down the dirt road in a cloud of dust.

"Ayoh! Look at those poor children!" exclaimed Mary Ayah.

Ida craned her neck to see. "Where, Ayah? You mean those two lying beside the road? What happened?"

"They're dead," the servant replied. "Starved, no doubt."

The sun was still shining, but Ida felt suddenly cold from the top of her head to the tips of her toes. Her stomach felt sick and she wanted to cry, but no tears would come. The bullock cart moved on toward home and the lines of hungry children Ida knew would be there waiting to be fed. She and her brothers would help pass out rice, milk, and bread to hundreds of outstretched hands. It was a daily chore.

Ida Scudder was living through the Great Famine of 1877, when 60 million people in southern India were hungry. That year more than 5 million died. As long as she lived, Ida would never forget the endless sea of outstretched hands.

Today there is another kind of famine in the world, a famine for the Word of God. Millions are dying for want of spiritual nourishment. They are starving for what you get every day in worship, at school, in church. They stretch out their hands for a knowledge of God. You have plenty; won't you share so that others may live?

ALBERT SCHWEITZER

Thou shalt not kill. Deuteronomy 5:17.

"Let's climb.the hill behind the church and shoot birds," Henry Brasch called to 8-year-old Albert Schweitzer."

Albert's homemade slingshot dangled from his hand as he climbed the hill with his friend. He didn't really want to shoot birds, but neither did he want to be called a sissy.

It was springtime in the Alsatian Valley. There was a sweetness in the air, the smell of rain, earth, and growing things. Birds flitted through the orchards that covered the hillsides. Blackbirds, robins, bullfinches, and doves joined in a glorious chorus in praise of spring.

"Come on, Albert," Henry said, placing a smooth stone in the leather pouch of his sling, "let's see who can hit that blackbird over there!"

Just then the church bells began to ring. It was as though they were playing the accompaniment for the bird choir on the hillside. It was more than tenderhearted Albert could take. He threw his slingshot to the ground and, waving his arms, ran toward the tree where the blackbird sat.

"Shoo! Shoo, blackbird!" he yelled. "Fly away so you'll be safe!"

The blackbird obeyed.

"Hey, stupid! What did you do that for?" Albert's friend came running toward him.

"I didn't want the bird to be hurt," Albert admitted. "They have feelings too, just like you and me."

"Spoil sport!" Henry grumbled as they walked back down the hill, their game over.

But Albert didn't mind. He had done what he had to do, and he knew he'd never kill another creature if he could help it. It seemed to him the evening chimes seemed to be saying "Thou shalt not kill!"

This was the beginning of Albert Schweitzer's "reverence for life" that he wrote about when he was older. He grew up to be one of the outstanding men of the twentieth century: preacher, teacher, philosopher, musician, writer, physician, and missionary to Africa.

OVID ELBERT DAVIS

I was not disobedient unto the heavenly vision. Acts 26:19.

In a jungle clearing at the foot of Mount Roraima in Guiana, a group of naked Indians squatted in a circle around the chief's hut as he told them of his strange dream.

"A man in shining clothes came to me with a message for our people," he began. "He told me how God made the world in seven days and rested on the seventh. When He made the world it was perfect, but the people He put here were bad. Because they would not listen they had to die, and all their children must die. All the people in this tribe must die."

"Ayoh! Too bad! Too bad!" the Indians moaned.

"But listen to me," the chief continued. "That is not all. This God who made the world is coming back for all His children. He is going to take them to a beautiful, new country where no one is ever sick and no one ever dies."

"Good! Good!" the Indians nodded their heads.

"But that is not yet all," the chief went on. "He wants us to get ready for His coming. We must stop eating the pig and drinking beer. We must stop killing. We must have only one wife. We must keep our houses clean."

"Ayoh! These are hard sayings," the people sighed.

"The man in shining clothes told me that He will send someone to teach us how to live. It will be a White man who comes from a far country. He will carry a black book. We must follow what the black book says."

"Good! Good! We will follow it," the people agreed. But though they waited for many years, no one came. The old chief died, but still they looked for the White man from a far country with a black book.

One day in 1910 a cry went out to the Akawaio villages, "He has come. The White man from a far country with the black book has come!"

The man was Ovid Elbert Davis, president of the Guiana Mission. The next summer he returned and organized a permanent mission for the Akawaio Indians. While there he died of blackwater fever and was buried at the foot of Mount Roraima.

MOTHER TERESA

Beloved, let us love one another: for love is of God. 1 John 4:7.

Twelve-year-old Agnes Bojaxhiu, of Skopje, Yugoslavia, loved God with all her heart and vowed she would share that love with others. That decision led her to become a missionary to Calcutta, India, where she is known as Mother Teresa.

One day while she was riding on a train, God spoke to her. He said, "Teresa, I want you to leave the convent and live in the slums with the poorest of the poor. There you will show My love to the sick and dying, the orphans and lepers."

Obedient to her call, Teresa began roaming the dirty streets, looking for people she could love.

First she found children who needed an education. She gathered them into a mud hut. With no furniture, no books, no blackboard, and no paper or pencils, she began to teach them. She wrote their lessons in the dirt on the floor of the hut.

Next, Mother Teresa found dying people to love. She found them lying on the streets, with cockroaches and rats crawling over them. She fed them, treated them, clothed them, and made them feel loved and wanted again.

After that, she decided to open a home for abandoned children. She went about the city picking up babies thrown away onto piles of garbage. She nursed them and loved them and found parents for them so they could grow up to be happy and healthy human beings.

Her next project was a home for lepers, the outcasts of Indian society.

Then she tackled the problem of caring for retarded people whom nobody else wanted.

In 1979 Mother Teresa won the Nobel Peace Prize. When she accepted it she said, "I receive it in the name of the hungry, of the homeless, of the crippled, for all those people who feel unwanted and unloved—the throwaways of society."

"I am just a little pencil in God's hand," she said once. "God is writing His love letter to the world in this way, through works of love."

Will you be a little pencil for God today?

SCRIPTURE INDEX

GENESIS

2:7........................Sept. 5

EXODUS

20:3........................Aug. 19
20:10 ....Mar. 9
20:12 ....Aug. 5
20:13 ....May 3
20:16 ....July 5
23:2 ....May 4

LEVITICUS

19:30 ....Apr. 23
23:19 ....July 13
32:23 ....Sept. 12

DEUTERONOMY

5:17 ....Dec. 29
30:19 ....Oct. 1

JOSHUA

1:5............................Feb. 6
3:13 ....Dec. 24
10:25 ....Oct. 9
24:15 ....Jan. 3

1 SAMUEL

1:11 ....June 4
16:7 ....Feb. 27

1 KINGS

6:9 ....May 27

2 KINGS

6:17 ....Nov. 10

ESTHER

4:14........................Oct. 8

JOB

12:7 ....Feb. 29
39:20 ....Oct. 29

PSALMS

1:1 ....July 10
2:8 ....Dec. 7
5:3 ....Apr. 14

8:5..........................July 26
16:8........................Jan. 19
18:2........................Jan. 27
19:1........................July 8
19:13 ....Nov. 17
23:4........................June 19
26:11 ....Aug. 3
27:1........................Mar. 4
27:14......................Aug. 30
32:1........................June 25
34:6 ....Aug. 15
34:7........................June 26
37:5........................Feb. 7
37:24......................Jan. 23
37:25......................Sept. 29
40:1........................May 12
40:8........................Apr. 1
42:8........................Apr. 9
42:11 ....Apr. 5
50:15......................Aug. 24
55:17......................Nov. 30
56:3........................Sept. 1
62:8........................July 12
60:4........................Jan. 9
69:1........................Dec. 13
69:5........................Nov. 12
69:14 ....Feb. 10
71:2........................Sept. 26
81:10......................Dec. 11
84:2........................Apr. 17
89:34......................Aug. 16
89:47......................Aug. 20
89:48......................June 10
91:2........................Dec. 25
91:5........................Aug. 18
91:11 ....June 16
91:12......................Dec. 26
92:12......................May 11
107:8......................Dec. 16
107:13 ....Aug. 31
107:19 ....Oct. 31
109:5......................Feb. 9
109:22....................Oct. 14
111:7......................Jan. 1
119:9......................July 19
119:11....................Aug. 9
119:30....................July 7
119:127..................Mar. 14
119:130..................Feb. 2
119:160..................Mar. 2
119:165..................Jan. 12
121:1, 2................Oct. 21
138:3....................Oct. 11

139:7 ....June 20
141:3 ....Aug. 2
147:3......................Nov. 14

PROVERBS

1:10........................July 6
3:5..........................June 12
3:6..........................Apr. 18
3:12........................May 8
4:7..........................May 10
6:6..........................July 31
6:27........................July 24
11:28......................Oct. 22
12:22......................Jan. 6
14:8........................June 21
14:12......................Jan. 24
14:21......................Sept. 2
15:1........................June 23
15:5 ....Aug. 27
15:23 ....Feb. 20
15:33 ....Mar. 12
16:9........................Oct. 5
16:18......................Mar. 10
17:5........................Apr. 6
17:17......................Dec. 15
18:8........................July 21
19:17......................Oct. 12
22:1........................May 22
22:29......................Feb. 5
23:7........................Feb. 28
24:16......................Sept. 15
27:8 ....Aug. 23
27:9........................Oct. 3
28:13......................Feb. 26
28:27......................Dec. 1
31:27......................Mar. 25

ECCLESIASTES

3:1..........................Apr. 19
3:3..........................Mar. 8
4:9 ....Mar. 28
5:5..........................Apr. 29
7:9..........................Apr. 11
7:19........................July 9
9:5..........................Sept. 8
9:10........................Apr. 25
9:11........................Feb. 15
12:14......................Oct. 17

SONG OF SOLOMON

8:7......................Sept. 27

ISAIAH

6:8......................Sept. 24
30:21....................Apr. 26
40:28......................Oct. 19
41:10......................May 6
42:6........................Dec. 20
43:19......................Apr. 28
45:22......................Nov. 19
49:15......................Nov. 4
49:25......................Sept. 23
58:7........................Dec. 27
59:1........................Mar. 22
59:2........................Jan. 2
65:24......................Feb. 24

JEREMIAH

9:8........................Nov. 13
14:9......................Sept. 4
15:6......................Aug. 22
15:16....................Sept. 28
32:17......................Dec. 19

EZEKIEL

18:4......................Apr. 16
20:12......................Jan. 4
21:21......................Nov. 15
33:11......................Sept. 14
34:27......................Aug. 1

DANIEL

12:4......................Aug. 25

JOEL

2:28......................June 13

AMOS

4:12......................Aug. 6
8:11......................Dec. 28

OBADIAH

3............................Aug. 28

MICAH

6:8........................Apr. 30
7:8........................Nov. 23
7:19......................July 15

NAHUM

1:7........................Dec. 9

ZECHARIAH

4:6........................Dec. 8

MALACHI

3:2........................Feb. 14
3:8........................Nov. 29
3:17......................Jan. 21

MATTHEW

5:3........................June 2
5:7........................Mar. 17
5:9........................Dec. 23
5:13......................Sept. 11
5:25......................Nov. 8
5:39......................Jan. 15
5:43......................Oct. 13
5:44......................Oct. 23
6:13......................May 29
6:33......................May 2
6:34......................May 21
7:1........................Mar. 29
7:7........................Dec. 21
7:12......................Feb. 23
7:14......................May 18
8:19......................July 28
10:8......................July 27
10:19....................Nov. 24
10:23....................July 4
11:28....................Feb. 22
13:38....................Dec. 5
13:45....................Mar. 7
18:19....................Sept. 18
19:26....................Mar. 20
21:28....................June 30
21:42....................Apr. 20
22:29....................Nov. 9
23:8......................Jan. 16
23:14....................Oct. 16
24:36....................July 2
25:40....................May 23
26:41....................Sept. 10
26:52....................Jan. 14
26:73....................Mar. 15
28:20....................Feb. 12

MARK

1:11......................Mar. 16
5:36......................Oct. 20
7:37......................June 11
8:36......................Mar. 3

[LUKE intro column]

9:23......................Feb. 17
11:25....................Aug. 4
12:17....................Sept. 7
13:13....................July 3
13:36....................Aug. 7
16:15....................Dec. 4
16:16....................Nov. 5

LUKE

4:10......................Dec. 22
5:27......................May 5
6:29......................Dec. 10
9:56......................Oct. 26
9:62......................Jan. 8
10:37....................Dec. 14
11:9......................July 23
12:20....................Dec. 6
14:33....................May 14
15:6......................July 1
15:24....................Aug. 11
18:1......................Apr. 27
19:10....................Jan. 25
19:31....................Oct. 4
22:42....................Feb. 21

JOHN

2:5........................May 17
3:7........................June 8
6:37......................Apr. 3
8:36......................Nov. 11
13:7......................Sept. 16
13:35....................Jan. 5
14:2......................Mar. 24
14:3......................June 14
14:6......................Oct. 27
14:13....................June 24
14:15....................June 17
15:5......................Sept. 6
15:10....................Sept. 20
16:13....................Sept. 30
17:4......................Jan. 31

ACTS

4:12......................July 17
5:29......................Feb. 8
10:28....................June 27
17:11....................Apr. 24
26:19....................Dec. 30

ROMANS

1:17......................June 5
2:1........................May 30
3:23......................May 9
5:8........................Jan. 30

5:12 ....July 16
6:23 ....Sept. 22
8:26 ....Apr. 13
8:28 ....June 6
8:39 ....Sept. 21
10:14 ....Jan. 26
12:18 ....Mar. 6
13:7 ....July 18
13:8 ....May 13
13:14 ....June 1
14:10 ....Mar. 26
14:12 ....Nov. 28

1 CORINTHIANS

2:10 ....Feb. 4
4:10 ....Mar. 18
7:7 ....July 11
9:24 ....May 25
9:27 ....May 31
10:13 ....Jan. 29
10:13 ....Aug. 21
10:31 ....Apr. 12
11:26 ....Aug. 13
12:9 ....Dec. 12
12:22 ....Apr. 15
13:8 ....June 22
13:11 ....Nov. 25
15:3 ....Dec. 17
15:52 ....Mar. 31
15:57 ....May 24

2 CORINTHIANS

1:10 ....Dec. 3
3:18 ....July 20
5:17 ....June 28
5:20 ....Nov. 21
6:2 ....Nov. 22
6:14 ....Mar. 27
6:17 ....May 7
7:1 ....Oct. 6
8:9 ....Nov. 1
8:12 ....Apr. 7
11:14 ....Nov. 26
12:9 ....Oct. 30
13:7 ....Feb. 11
13:7 ....Apr. 21
13:8 ....June 3

GALATIANS

2:20 ....July 22
4:4, 5 ....May 1
6:2 ....Aug. 8

EPHESIANS

2:14 ....Mar. 5
3:20 ....Oct. 10
4:28 ....Sept. 13
4:31 ....June 29
4:32 ....Apr. 4
6:1 ....Feb. 25
6:13 ....Aug. 12
6:17 ....Aug. 29

PHILIPPIANS

2:7 ....Sept. 19
2:13 ....Feb. 16
4:13 ....Jan. 11
4:19 ....June 18

COLOSSIANS

1:14 ....Oct. 7
1:27 ....Jan. 7
4:5 ....Apr. 8

1 THESSALONIANS

5:8 ....Mar. 19
5:17 ....Dec. 18
5:22 ....May 16

1 TIMOTHY

2:1, 2 ....Nov. 18
2:5, 6 ....Sept. 25
4:7 ....May 28
4:12 ....Nov. 27
4:14 ....Apr. 2
6:10 ....Jan. 13

2 TIMOTHY

1:9 ....Nov. 6
2:24 ....Aug. 17

HEBREWS

1:7 ....Dec. 2
2:3 ....Sept. 3
4:16 ....May 15
5:8 ....Nov. 7
9:27 ....June 7
10:22 ....June 9
11:1 ....Feb. 3
11:26 ....Feb. 18
12:1 ....May 26
12:2 ....Jan. 22

12:15 ....Nov. 20
13:18 ....Oct. 24

JAMES

1:8 ....Oct. 15
1:25 ....Mar. 21
2:24 ....Sept. 9
3:5 ....Jan. 10
3:8 ....Feb. 19
4:7 ....July 30
5:16 ....May 19

1 PETER

1:18, 19 ....Apr. 22
1:25 ....Mar. 1
2:17 ....July 25
2:21 ....Apr. 10
3:8 ....Oct. 25
5:8 ....Jan. 18

2 PETER

1:4 ....Oct. 18
1:21 ....Jan. 17
3:9 ....June 15
3:18 ....Mar. 30

1 JOHN

1:9 ....Mar. 23
2:15 ....Nov. 2
3:15 ....Oct. 28
4:7 ....Dec. 31
4:18 ....July 29
5:4 ....Sept. 17

3 JOHN

2 ....Jan. 20

REVELATION

1:3 ....Feb. 1
1:7 ....Feb. 13
1:18 ....Mar. 13
2:25 ....Nov. 3
3:11 ....May 20
3:12 ....Oct. 2
3:17 ....July 14
3:19 ....Aug. 26
3:20 ....Mar. 11
4:11 ....Aug. 10
5:9 ....Aug. 14
21:4 ....Jan. 28
22:17 ....Nov. 16

PEOPLE INDEX

Adams, John Quincy ....November 3
Alcott, Louisa May ....September 13
Alexander the Great ....March 4
Alfred the Great ....March 11
Allen, Ethan ....August 7
Amundsen, Roald ....January 30
Andersen, Hans Christian ....September 6
Anderson, Marian ....April 28
Arc, Joan of ....August 4
Archimedes ....July 1
Asoka ....March 6
Augustine ....June 1
Augustus, Caesar ....March 8

Bach, Johann Sebastian ....April 1
Baffin, William ....January 24
Balboa, Vasco Nunez de ....January 10
Barringer, Emily Dunning ....October 16
Barton, Clara ....October 9
Bates, Joseph ....June 18
Beach, Walter Raymond ....June 30
Beethoven, Ludwig van ....April 5
Bell, Alexander Graham ....February 20
Bering, Vitus ....January 19
Bessemer, Henry ....February 14
Bethune, Mary McLeod ....June 24
Bickerdyke, Mother ....October 18
Bjorkland, Garry ....May 26
Blackwell, Antoinette Brown ....June 13
Blackwell, Elizabeth ....October 8
Bliss, Philip ....April 26
Bly, Nellie ....September 19
Bolívar, Simón ....August 10
Bonaparte, Napoleon ....March 28
Bonneville, Benjamin ....August 15
Bowie, James ....August 14
Boyle, Robert ....July 7
Brahe, Tycho ....July 3
Brahms, Johannes ....April 14
Braille, Louis ....February 25
Brainerd, David ....December 2
Brand, Paul ....December 27
Bronte, Charlotte ....September 12
Brown, John ....August 19
Brown, William Wells ....September 29
Bruce, Robert ....March 18
Bunche, Ralph ....June 29

Cabeza de Vaca ....January 16
Cabot, John and Sebastian ....January 9
Campanella, Roy ....May 6
Canute ....March 12
Carey, William ....December 4
Carson, Kit ....August 21
Carter, Jimmy ....November 29
Cartier, Jacques ....January 12
Cartwright, Edmund ....February 9
Carvajal, Felix ....May 29
Carver, George Washington ....July 25

Cavell, Edith..October 23
Chalmers, James ....December 13
Charlemagne ....March 10
Chopin, Frédéric...April 8
Churchill, Sir Winston ....September 26, November 17
Clarke, Adam..September 15
Clark, William ....January 28
Cleopatra ....March 7
Cobb, Ty ....May 2
Coleridge, Samuel Taylor ....September 1
Columbus, Christopher ....January 5
Constantine the Great...March 9
Cook, James ....January 20
Copernicus..July 2
Copland, Aaron..April 27
Cortes, Hernando ....January 13
Costa, Michael..April 15
Cowper, William..September 16
Crockett, Davy...August 11
Croesus..March 3
Cunningham, Glenn...May 30
Curie, Marie and Pierre...July 24

Da Gama, Vasco...January 8
Daimler, Gottlieb..February 16
Dalton, John...July 14
Da Vinci, Leonardo ....February 2
Davis, John...January 22
Davis, Jefferson...November 7
Davis, Ovid Elbert..December 30
Davy, Sir Humphry...July 20
Debussy, Claude..April 22
De Gaulle, Charles...November 26
Delker, Del..April 30
De Pavie, Aymery...August 3
De Soto, Hernando ....January 17
Diaz, Bartholomew...January 7
Dickinson, Emily..September 14
Didrikson, Babe...May 27
DiMaggio, Joe...May 5
Dischinger, Terry...May 12
Dix, Dorothea Lynde...October 13
Doolittle, James Harold...August 28
Drake, Francis..January 18
Drew, Charles Richard ....October 22
Drysdale, Don ....May 8
Duff, Alexander..December 16
Dvorak, Antonin ....April 17

Eastman, George...February 26
Edison, Thomas Alva...February 21
Edmonds, Sarah Emma...August 18
Edward III..March 16
Egede, Hans..December 3
Einstein, Albert...July 26
Eisenhower, Dwight D...August 29
El-Sadat, Anwar ....November 30
Elgar, Edward...April 21
Eliot, John..December 1
Elizabeth I ....March 21
En-Lai, Chou..November 22

Ericson, Leif..January 3
Eric the Red..January 2

Faraday, Michael...February 8
Farragut, David Glasgow...August 20
Felix, Ray..May 11
Fermi, Enrico ....July 27
Fitzgerald, Alice..October 27
Fleming, Alexander ....July 23
Ford, Henry..February 23
Ford, Lillian...December 25
Foster, Stephen Collins...April 13
Francis of Assisi, Saint..June 2
Franklin, Benjamin ....February 5
Franklin, John..January 25
Friesell, Red...May 19
Frobisher, Martin...January 21
Frost, Robert..September 18
Fulton, Robert..February 10

Galilei, Galileo...February 3
Gallaudet, Thomas...June 11
Gandhi, Indira...November 24
Gandhi, Mohandas ....June 25
Garfield, James Abram...November 8
Gehrig, Lou..May 3
Gilbert, William S..September 25
Goddard, Robert H. ....February 28
Goodyear, Charles..February 17
Gordon, Arthur..September 17
Gorgas, William Crawford..July 22
Graham, Billy...June 28
Grant, Ulysses S. ....August 24
Greeley, Horace ....September 11
Greene, Nathanael...August 8
Grenfell, Wilfred..December 15
Grieg, Edvard...April 18
Guion, Connie..October 28
Gutenberg, Johannes...February 1

Halliwell, Leo B. ....December 26
Halsted, William..October 7
Hamilton, Alice..October 17
Hammon, Jupiter..September 28
Hammurabi..March 1
Handel, George Frideric ....April 2
Hartman, David..October 30
Harvey, William...July 5
Hayden, Franz Joseph ....April 3
Henry V. ....March 19
Herjulfson, Bjarne..January 1
Hickok, "Wild Bill"...August 25
Hippocrates..October 1
Hitler, Adolf...November 15
Hohenheim, Phillipus Aureolus Theophrastus B. V. ....October 2
Hoover, Herbert ....November 14
Houston, Sam...August 13
Howe, Elias ....February 13
Howe, Gordie...May 15
Hudson, Henry...January 23
Huss, John...June 4

Huygens, Christian ....July 8
Hyde, John ....December 18

Ikhnaton ....March 2
Irving, Washington ....September 4
Isabella of Spain ....March 20
Ivan the Terrible ....March 23

Jackson, Andrew ....November 4
Jackson, Mahalia ....April 29
Jackson, Stonewall ....August 16
Jefferson, Thomas ....November 1
Jenner, Edward ....July 12
Johnson, Lyndon Baines ....November 23
Johnson, Rafer ....May 22
Joliet, Louis ....January 26
Josephine ....March 29
Juarez, Benito ....November 11
Judson, Adoniram ....December 6

Keller, Helen ....September 20
Kelvin, Lord ....July 15
Kennedy, John Fitzgerald ....November 21
Kenny, Sister Elizabeth ....October 21
Kenyatta, Jomo ....November 19
Kepler, Johannes ....July 4
Khan, Genghis ....August 1
King, Martin Luther, Jr. ....June 27
Koch, Robert ....July 16
Kosciuszko, Thaddeus ....August 9

Landsteiner, Karl ....October 5
La Rue, Abram ....December 20
La Salle, Sieur de ....January 27
Lavoisier, Antoine-Laurent ....July 10
Lee, Robert E. ....August 17
Leeuwenhoek, Anton Van ....February 4
Lewis, Meriwether ....January 28
Lincoln, Abraham ....November 6
Lind, Jenny ....April 12
Linnaeus, Carolus ....July 11
Lister, Joseph ....July 19
Liszt, Franz ....April 10
Livingstone, David ....January 31
Loues, Spiridon ....May 25
Louis XIV ....March 24
Luther, Martin ....June 5
Lyon, Mary ....June 12

MacArthur, Douglas ....August 27
MacDowell, Edward ....April 20
Mackay, Alexander ....December 14
Madison, James ....November 2
Magellan, Ferdinand ....January 11
Malpighi, Marcello ....October 4
Mann, Horace ....June 10
Marconi, Guglielmo ....February 24
Margaret ....March 14
Maria Theresa ....March 25
Marie Antoinette ....March 26
Marshall, Jim ....May 18
Marshall, Peter ....June 26

Mather, Cotton...June 7
Mathias, Bob ....May 21
Mayo, Charles Horace...October 19
Mayo, William James...October 20
McCormick, Cyrus..February 12
McDowell, Ephraim..October 10
McLoughlin, John..October 12
McNeil, John..June 19
Meineke, Don...May 10
Meir, Golda ....November 27
Meitner, Lise ....July 28
Mendel, Gregor Johann ....July 18
Mendelssohn, Felix..April 7
Mikita, Stan..May 14
Miller, William..June 14
Miller, Harry ....December 24
Mills, Samuel ....December 5
Moffat, Robert..December 7
Moody, Dwight L...June 20
Morrison, Robert ....December 8
Morse, Samuel Finley Breese...February 15
Mozart, Wolfgang Amadeus..April 4
Muir, John..July 30

Newton, Isaac..July 9
Nichol, Francis David..September 23
Nightingale, Florence..October 6
Nixon, Richard..November 28
Nkrumah, Kwame...November 20
Noyon, Chepe ....August 2
Nurmi, Paavo ....May 31
Nyerere, Julius Kambarage ....November 25

Owens, Jesse..May 23
Owens-Adair, Bethenia..October 11

Paderewski, Ignace Jan ....April 23
Paine, Thomas ....September 3
Pare, Ambroise...October 3
Pasteur, Louis..July 17
Patton, George S. ....August 30
Peale, Norman Vincent ....September 24
Peary, Robert Edwin ....January 29
Pershing, John J. ....August 23
Peter the Great..March 27
Pheidippides ....May 24
Philippa ....March 17
Pizarro, Francisco ....January 14
Polk, James Knox ....November 5
Polo, Marco ....January 4
Pritham, Fredericus Johannine...October 31
Pulitzer, Joseph...September 9

Rachmaninoff, Sergei Vassilievitch...April 25
Randolph, Virginia ....June 23
Reaumur, Rene Antoine Ferchault de...February 29
Reed, Walter..July 21
Revere, Paul ....August 6
Richard, Maurice..May 13
Richards, Linda ....October 25
Richard the Lionhearted..March 15
Rickenbacker, Eddie...August 31

Robinson, Asa T. ....December 21
Robinson, Jackie ....May 4
Rockne, Knute ....May 17
Roentgen, Wilhelm Konrad ....February 27
Roosevelt, Franklin Delano ....November 16
Roosevelt, Theodore ....November 10
Ross, Ronald ....October 15
Rote, Kyle ....May 16
Rudolph, Wilma ....May 28
Ruth, Babe ....May 1

Salk, Jonas E. ....July 29
Sandburg, Carl ....September 22
Sauerbruch, Ferdinand ....October 24
Sava, George ....October 26
Schubert, Franz ....April 6
Schumann, Robert ....April 9
Schweitzer, Albert ....December 29
Scudder, Ida ....December 28
Selvy, Frank ....May 9
Shelley, Percy Bysshe ....September 2
Sheridan, Philip Henry ....August 22
Shih Huang Ti ....March 5
Sholes, Christopher L. ....February 18
Sibelius, Jean ....April 24
Singh, Sundar ....December 17
Slessor, Mary ....December 12
Smith, Annie R. ....September 30
Smuts, Jan Christiaan ....November 12
Sousa, John Philip ....April 19
Spallanzani, Lazzaro ....July 13
Spock, Benjamin ....October 29
Stahl, Ferdinand A. ....December 19
Stevenson, Robert Louis ....September 5
Stewart, Andrew G. ....December 23
Stowe, Harriet Beecher ....September 8
Sullivan, Anne ....June 22

Tasman, Abel ....January 15
Taylor, Zachary ....November 9
Taylor, Hudson ....December 11
Tchaikovsky, Peter Ilich ....April 16
Teresa, Mother ....December 31
Thoreau, Henry David ....September 7
Thorp, Jim ....May 20
Torricelli, Evangelista ....July 6
Travis, William Barret ....August 12
Truman, Harry S. ....November 18
Turner, Charles Henry ....July 31
Twain, Mark ....September 10

Vandegrift, Alexander Archer ....August 26
Verdi, Guiseppe ....April 11
Verne, Jules ....September 21
Vespucci, Amerigo ....January 6
Victoria ....March 30
Volta, Alessandro ....February 6

Warren, Merritt C. ....December 22
Washington, Booker T. ....June 21
Washington, George ....August 5
Watt, James ....February 7

383

Wesley, John ....June 9
Westinghouse, George...February 19
Wheeler, Frederick...June 17
White, Ellen ....June 15
White, James ....June 16
Whitefield, George...June 8
Whitman, Marcus..December 10
Whitney, Eli ....February 11
Wilhelmina...March 31
William the Conqueror...March 13
William the Silent ....March 22
Williams, Daniel Hale ....October 14
Williams, Ted...May 7
Wilson, Dorothy Clarke...September 27
Wilson, Woodrow..November 13
Wolff, Joseph..December 9
Wright, Wilbur and Orville...February 22
Wycliffe, John ....June 3

Zwingli, Ulrich ....June 6